# STAY IN A PUB

# STAY IN A PUB

Edited by
## Dave Cromack

*Published by*
**Troubador Publishing**
9 De Montfort Mews
Leicester LE1 7FW, UK
Tel: (+44) 116 255 9311
Email: books@troubador.co.uk
Web: www.troubador.co.uk

ISBN 1 899293 23 X

The publishers and editors have made every effort to ensure the accuracy of
information presented in this guide; however, they can accept no responsibility
for any loss, injury or inconvenience sustained by any traveller as a result of
information contained in this guide.

Typesetting: Troubador Publishing Ltd, Leicester, UK
Printed and bound by Cromwell Press Ltd, Trowbridge, Wilts

t² is an imprint of Troubador Publishing Ltd

# CONTENTS

# PREFACE

"Why is it every time I advertise my Pub accommodation in a tourist guide, they stick me in the guesthouse section". I was having a bit of a moan, "I keep telling them I'm a Pub but they never listen, they just ignore me, and every year they just stick me back in the guesthouse section." I could see my wife was getting fed up listening to me, but I chuntered on regardless: "What we need" I continued "Is an accommodation guide especially for Pubs". My wife gave me one of her, stop moaning looks – I stopped moaning. "Look she explained, as if talking to a child, "If you're so worried about it why don't you start your own guide?" I looked at her: "OK, I will" I said. "How difficult can it be?" My wife quietly left the room and gently patted me on the head.

An old saying springs to mind: "Act in haste, repent at leisure". Although an undertaking such as this shouldn't be taken quite so unprofessionally, I must admit I haven't repented – in fact, I have thoroughly enjoyed compiling this first edition of *Stay in a Pub*. This book accompanies the popular web site www.stayinapub.com, which includes regular updates to many of the entries contained here.

*Stay in a Pub* is a truly national Pub accommodation guide that includes all types of Pubs / Inns in every area of the country. There are Pub guides, of course, but these tend to be specialist publications covering particular types of Inns or specific areas of the country. Travellers would need to carry a whole shelf full of books around if they wanted to stay in Pub accommodation throughout the length and breadth of the British Isles.

Pubs with accommodation are actually quite rare. It is estimated that only about 8% of all pubs offer any sort accommodation. If they were spread evenly over the whole country, there would be just one pub for every 20 square miles. It is not surprising that many people who would love to stay in a Pub often have trouble finding one, and eventually give up looking.

There is nothing quite like the British Pub. Many people throughout the world have tried to copy it – they give bars names like "The Royal Oak" or "The Winston Churchill", but they never seem to be the same as the pubs we have at home. I believe the British pub is a unique combination of the British country, the British people, the British weather and the quirky British liquor laws – you need all these ingredients to produce the genuine British Pub!

We have listed over 2200 pubs in this guide. I have visited quite a few, but I haven't judged or rated any of them. The reason is that no matter what I think about a Pub, every Pub is always someone's favourite. All types of Pubs, Inns or Taverns have been included, so it doesn't matter whether you enjoy eating a gourmet meal in sumptuous surroundings, or prefer egg and chips in the public bar, you are bound to find a Pub that's right for you – so dive in, enjoy yourself and the best of British luck!

**Dave Cromack**
March 2004

# LEGENDS

**Average price**

| | | |
|---|---|---|
| **£** | = | £55.00 pppn or below |
| **££** | = | below £80.00 pppn |
| **£££** | = | above £80.00 pppn |

**Facilities available**

| | | |
|---|---|---|
| **BG** | = | Beer Garden |
| **BM** | = | Bar Meals |
| **C** | = | Children welcome in some or all areas |
| **P** | = | Parking |
| **PW** | = | Pets Welcome |
| **R** | = | Restaurant |

# WHAT IS A PUB?

It was the sort of day you didn't want to work. The sun was shining and the office was hot. Sitting at my desk I could see across the street to the open door of New Inn Public house. I began thinking of the pints of Old Frothy I would soon be enjoying when all of a sudden, BANG! The office door crashed open and in stomped Hilda. "So you think you know what a pub is then, do you?" she cackled. "Ok then clever dick, what's the difference between Pubs, Taverns, Inns, and Hostelries?" Just as abruptly she left. Hilda is a very strange woman – she likes to see everyone happy except me.

Her question had never occurred to me before; I'm not even sure why she asked me. I have never cared what a pub is called; all that matters is that it sells good beer. But curiosity got the better of me, and to show Hilda how useful and resourceful I could be. I decided to investigate.

I reasoned the best place to find out the definition of these ancient words would be to look in the old trusty office dictionary. This is what I found:

**Pub** (pub) *n.* (colloq) public-house *n.* inn, or tavern for sale of alcoholic liquors for consumption on premises

**Inn** (in) *n.* a house that provides lodging accommodation for travellers; a hotel.

**Tavern** (tav'-ern) *n.* licensed house for sale of liquor; inn; hostelry [L. *taberna, booth*].

**Hostelry** (hos'telry) *n.* an inn derived from [L. *hospes, a host or guest*]

Ok, so what did the dictionary tell me?

A **pub** is an inn or tavern that sells liquor to the public
An **inn** is a hotel that provides accommodation,
A **tavern** sells booze and is an inn or hostelry
And a **hostelry** is an inn!

Well that seems quite straightforward to a twisted mind

The only trouble is, it's wrong! Most pubs are called Inns, Taverns and Hotels, yet most don't offer accommodation. In fact only about 8% of all Public Houses in Britain have any sort of accommodation. This means there are 92% who will be less than helpful when the tired traveller comes along looking for shelter.

To be fair, the confusion is caused by tradition. Inns and Taverns did originally offer lodgings, but as times changed most publicans concentrated on their drink trade, and accommodation was largely forgotten. The names of the pubs, however, often stayed the same.

Nowadays the only really sure way of knowing if an Inn offers accommodation is to ask. Unfortunately, contacting 70,000 Pubs scattered across the whole of Great Britain can be a very time consuming business.

But now, thanks to pub passionate people like Hilda things are a lot easier. The traveller no longer has to contact hundreds of pubs or worry whether a pub is called an inn, a tavern or an anything else, because Hilda will do it all for them.

Hilda spends all day phoning and contacting pubs, chatting to customers, questioning bar staff, harassing managers and finding out as much as she can about Inns, Taverns, Hostelries and Pubs. If Hilda has entered a pub onto the *stayinapub.com* web site, and then it makes its way into this, book you can bet your life she has talked to someone at the pub and it will (or did at the time) offer accommodation. And why does Hilda do all this? She says it gives her a warm glow just to know she has helped a tired traveller to bide awhile, relax and rest his or her weary head....

If only she could feel the same about me when I feel the need for a quiet moment.

# PUB GAMES

One evening on my way home, I nipped into my local for a couple of pints of best bitter. I noticed George, who is the captain of the pub's dart team, looking a bit concerned.

"What's up George?" I said casually, although I could guess what the problem might be.

"Mike can't make the match tonight" he replied glumly. "The team is going to be one person short. You don't fancy a game tonight do you Dave?"

Normally I would have jumped at the chance to spend a night in the pub playing darts, but tonight I had to decline. "Sorry" I said. "I've already arranged to go to the pictures with my wife," but I added, "Why don't you ask that chap over there?" George looked down the bar towards the man sitting alone at the end of the bar. "Do you know him?" he asked. "No" I said. "I've never seen him in here before, but you never know he might help you out, he can only say No!"

It turned out the chap's name was Ron. He was working locally and had booked into the pub for a couple of nights. He agreed to play that night and saved the team from forfeiting any league points. Ron is now quite a regular in the bar; every time he is working in this area he stays at the pub, and has come to know the locals and has made many friends.

This may seem an unusual occurrence, but in fact this sort of thing happens all the time. Pub games are one of the best ways of breaking the ice and meeting new people. For those of you who wouldn't know your Dartboard from your Pool cue, but who nevertheless would like to join in, I have listed some of the games that are played in the pubs today. I have also included some of the more common rules. Be careful with the rules however, as these do tend to change from area to area!

## DARTS

This is played on a numbered dartboard with a double score outer ring and a treble score inner ring. It also has an outer bulls eye (score 25) and an inner bulls eye, which is worth double 25 (50).

The most common game of darts is called 501, the object of which is to score exactly 501 points. Players take it in turns to throw their (3) darts. A player must finish on a double score to win. For example, if a player scores 499 throughout the game, he/she is left with just 2 more points to score. The only way to do this and win the game would be to score Double 1. Another example would be if a player has scored 401 through the game – he/she could win the game by scoring treble 20 (60) and then double 20 (40) to achieve the final 100. You do not need to throw all your darts on the final throw.

The line you throw from is usually about 7 feet 9 inches from the dartboard. This line is called The Oche, pronounced Okee (The O is soft as in Office).

## POOL

Most of the pubs in Britain play 8-ball pool. This game consists of the cue ball and 15 object balls. The 15 balls usually consist of 7 red balls, 7 yellow balls and a black 8 ball. The idea of the game is to legally pot one set of balls and finally the black ball to win the game.

Be very careful and familiarise yourself with the local rules, as every area of the country seems to have a different interpretation of this game.

## CRIB

Crib is a fairly complicated card game. Players record their scores on a pegboard, the first player to go round the pegboard twice wins.

There are 2 ways of gaining points:

1.      A player may gain points when playing his cards. This is called pegging. For example if an opposing player lays down a 4 of clubs and you lay down a 4 of any other suit you would gain 2 points, if, however, your opponent then laid another 4 of any suit he/she would be awarded 6 points. A fourth consecutive card of a kind would gain 12 points. There are many other ways of scoring (pegging) including runs, last card and causing the laid cards to add up to 15. For example, your opponent lays down a 9 if you then laid a 6 you would gain 2 points.

2.      The second way of scoring is to add up the points in your hand. This is fairly similar to pegging. The points are scored by pairs, 3 or 4 of a kind, runs, counting the number of times you can make 15, etc.

If you have never played crib before and someone approaches you in the bar and asks "would you like to make up a team for crib", my advice is to develop a sudden case of Bombay Belly and rush to the toilet. I have known people who have been learning crib for months and are still not be very good at it. If, however, you were asked to join in a friendly and casual game, have a go – it's fun!

## DOMINOES

There are many dominoes league in the country, but mainly dominoes is played for fun (and minimal stakes) in the bar. There can't be many people who haven't played dominoes at some time. Even if the game is as alien to you as a Martian pasty, it doesn't take long to pick up.

A popular version of dominoes is "Fives and Threes". The players in this game have to lay their dominoes in turn so that the end numbers are divisible by five or three. For example, if the two end numbers were a 4 and a 2, a player would have to lay down a domino (dom) which would keep the end two doms divisible by 5 and 3. On the end with the 2 a player could lay a 2/5 or a 2/1, but not a 2/4.

Dominoes is fun but beware – the beer seems to flow pretty quickly whilst playing!

## SKITTLES

This is an old traditional game that requires an alley. Because of this, comparatively few pubs are able to entertain skittle matches. In my part of the world, Dorset, there are plenty of alleys, and the sport is a very popular.

The game is rather like 10 pin bowling, except there are nine wooden pins (skittles) and a smaller wooden ball. The skittles are placed so that the ball may pass between them without hitting anything – very frustrating. The game is not automatic, so the skittles have to be put up by hand. The posh teams sometimes hire a bloke to do this! He is called a "Stickerupera."

Skittles is a team game. The object of the game is to knock down more skittles than the opposition. That's about it really.

Skittle nights are noisy, rowdy and fun. If you ever have the chance of playing in a skittles match don't hesitate, do it.

## QUIZZES

Quizzes are an increasingly popular pub past time. Pubs hold open quiz nights and there are also leagues for team matches. OK if you like that sort of thing.

My favourite is the music quiz – this can sometimes get out of hand and end up as a sing along!

Pub games are a very important part of pub life. In fact in some areas, pubs would not survive the winter without their teams. Whenever possible, make an effort and get involved in the pub activities. I am sure with a little effort you will be surprised how friendly people are and how they will try to make to feel at home.

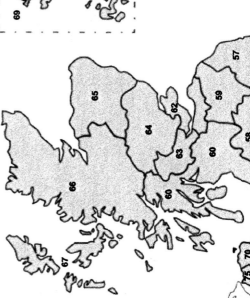

## Scotland

58) Dumphries and Galloway
59) Borders
60) Strathclyde
61) Lothian
62) Fife
63) Central
64) Tayside
65) Grampian
66) Highlands
67) Western Isles
68) Orkney Islands
69) Shetland Islands

## Northern England

44) Cheshire
45) Merseyside
46) Greater Manchester
47) South Yorkshire
48) West Yorkshire
49) Humberside /
East Riding of Yorkshire
50) North Yorkshire
51) Lancashire
52) Isle of Man
53) Cumbria
54) Durham
55) Cleveland
56) Tyne and Wear
57) Northumberland

## Central England

31) Hereford and Worcester
32) Warwickshire
33) Northamptonshire
34) Cambridgeshire
35) Suffolk
36) Norfolk
37) Lincolnshire
38) Leicestershire
39) Nottinghamshire
40) Derbyshire
41) Staffordshire
42) West Midlands
43) Shropshire

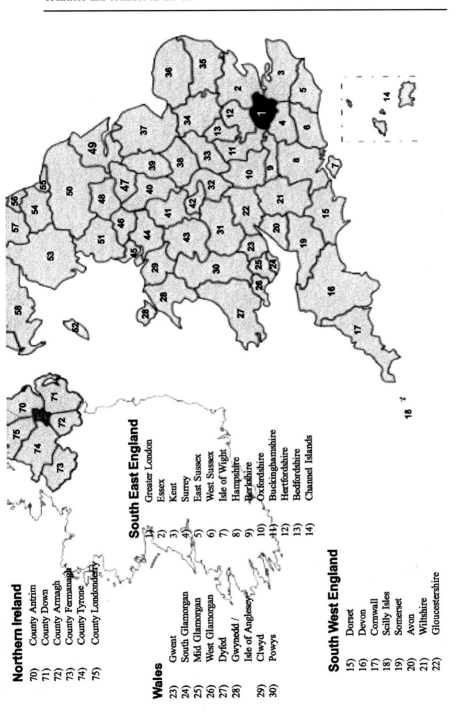

## Northern Ireland

70)  County Antrim
71)  County Down
72)  County Armagh
73)  County Fermanagh
74)  County Tyrone
75)  County Londonderry

## Wales

23)  Gwent
24)  South Glamorgan
25)  Mid Glamorgan
26)  West Glamorgan
27)  Dyfed
28)  Gwynedd /
     Isle of Anglesey
29)  Clwyd
30)  Powys

## South East England

1)  Greater London
2)  Essex
3)  Kent
4)  Surrey
5)  East Sussex
6)  West Sussex
7)  Isle of Wight
8)  Hampshire
9)  Berkshire
10)  Oxfordshire
11)  Buckinghamshire
12)  Hertfordshire
13)  Bedfordshire
14)  Channel Islands

## South West England

15)  Dorset
16)  Devon
17)  Cornwall
18)  Scilly Isles
19)  Somerset
20)  Avon
21)  Wiltshire
22)  Gloucestershire

## DISTANCE (BY ROAD) FROM LONDON IN MILES AND KILOMETRES

| Town / City | Miles | | | Kilometres |
|---|---|---|---|---|
| Aberdeen ... | ... | 521.5 | ... | ... | 839.3 |
| Aberystwyth | ... | 204.9 | ... | ... | 329.8 |
| Antrim | ... | 471.3 | ... | ... | 758.5 |
| Armagh | ... | 413.1 | ... | ... | 664.8 |
| Ayr | ... | 399.0 | ... | ... | 642.1 |
| Berwick-upon-Tweed ... | 342.9 | ... | ... | 551.8 |
| Birmingham | ... | 118.6 | ... | ... | 190.9 |
| Blackpool | ... | 235.9 | ... | ... | 379.6 |
| Bournemouth | ... | 105.7 | ... | ... | 170.1 |
| Braemar | ... | 489.6 | ... | ... | 787.9 |
| Brighton | ... | 50.2 | ... | ... | 80.8 |
| Bristol | ... | 117.2 | ... | ... | 188.6 |
| Cambridge | ... | 58.4 | ... | ... | 94.0 |
| Cardiff | ... | 150.1 | ... | ... | 241.6 |
| Carlisle | ... | 307.2 | ... | ... | 494.4 |
| Doncaster | ... | 170.6 | ... | ... | 274.6 |
| Dover | ... | 74.8 | ... | ... | 120.4 |
| Dundee | ... | 456.9 | ... | ... | 735.3 |
| Dungiven | ... | 505.5 | ... | ... | 813.5 |
| Edinburgh | ... | 398.9 | ... | ... | 642.0 |
| Enniskillen | ... | 433.9 | ... | ... | 698.3 |
| Exeter | ... | 194.8 | ... | ... | 313.5 |
| Fishguard | ... | 245.1 | ... | ... | 394.5 |
| Fort William | ... | 503.8 | ... | ... | 810.8 |
| Glasgow | ... | 401.5 | ... | ... | 646.2 |
| Gloucester | ... | 105.0 | ... | ... | 169.0 |
| Great Yarmouth | ... | 132.3 | ... | ... | 212.9 |
| Harwich | ... | 77.1 | ... | ... | 124.0 |
| Holyhead | ... | 262.9 | ... | ... | 423.1 |
| Inverness | ... | 558.7 | ... | ... | 899.1 |
| John O' Groats | ... | 674.6 | ... | ... | 1085.7 |
| Kingston-upon-Hull | ... | 179.3 | ... | ... | 288.6 |
| Kyle of Lochalsh | ... | 576.5 | ... | ... | 927.8 |
| Land's End | ... | 307.0 | ... | ... | 494.1 |
| Leeds | ... | 194.7 | ... | ... | 313.3 |
| Leicester | ... | 101.8 | ... | ... | 163.8 |
| Lincoln | ... | 134.5 | ... | ... | 216.5 |
| Liverpool | ... | 211.8 | ... | ... | 340.9 |
| Manchester | ... | 199.0 | ... | ... | 320.3 |
| Newcaslte-upon-Tyne ... | 281.1 | ... | ... | 452.4 |
| Norwich | ... | 112.7 | ... | ... | 181.4 |
| Nottingham | ... | 127.5 | ... | ... | 205.2 |
| Oban | ... | 492.2 | ... | ... | 792.1 |
| Omagh | ... | 524.0 | ... | ... | 843.3 |
| Oxford | ... | 58.8 | ... | ... | 94.6 |
| Plymouth | ... | 235.9 | ... | ... | 379.6 |
| Portsmouth | ... | 78.1 | ... | ... | 125.7 |

| Town / City | | Miles | | | Kilometres |
|---|---|---|---|---|---|
| Sheffield | ... | 160.6 | ... | ... | 258.5 |
| Shrewsbury | ... | 159.8 | ... | ... | 257.2 |
| Southampton | ... | 80.9 | ... | ... | 130.2 |
| Strangford | ... | 500.9 | ... | ... | 806.1 |
| Stranraer | ... | 408.6 | ... | ... | 657.6 |
| Swansea | ... | 187.2 | ... | ... | 301.3 |
| York | ... | 206.5 | ... | ... | 332.3 |

# North England

## CHESHIRE

**ALPRAHAM**
**Tollemache Arms**
Chester Road, Alpraham, Cheshire CW6 9JE
Tel: 01829 260030    **££ - P - 4 rooms**
Country Pub 5 miles from Nantwich

**BOLLINGTON, MACCLESFIELD**
**Church House Inn**
Church Street, Bollington, Macclesfield,
Cheshire SK10 5PY
Tel: 01625 574014    **£ - P - 5 rooms**
Friendly town local 10 minutes drive to
Macclesfield

**BRERETON GREEN, SANDBATCH**
**Bears Head**
Newcastle Road South, Brereton Green,
Sandbatch, Cheshire CW11 7RS
Tel: 01477 544732    **£ - P - 24 rooms**
Vintage Inn / Pub with Motel, 3 miles from
Sandbatch

**BROXTON, nr CHESTER**
**Egerton Arms Hotel**
Whitchurch Road, Broxton, nr Chester,
Cheshire CH3 0JW
Tel: 01829 782241    **P - 7 rooms**
Country Inn on the main A41

**CHESTER**
**Chester Bells**
21 Grosvenor Street, Chester,
Cheshire CH1 2DD
Tel: 01244 324022    **£ - P - 7 rooms**
Town centre location

**Pied Bull**
57 Northgate Street, Chester,
Cheshire CH1 2HQ
Tel: 01244 325829    **£**
Town centre Pub

**Ye Olde Coach and Horses**
North Gate Street, Chester, Cheshire
Tel: 01244 325533    **£ - 7 rooms**
Traditional town centre Pub, next to the Town
Hall

**CHOLMONDELEY**
**The Cholmondeley Arms**
Cholmondeley, Cheshire SY14 8BT
Tel: 01829 720300    **££ - P - 6 rooms**
Email: guy@thecholmondeleyarms.co.uk
Country Inn 6 miles from Whitchurch

**CONGLETON**
**The Kings Arms**
56 Earle Street, Congleton, Cheshire
Tel: 01270 584134    **£ - P - 3 rooms**
Local town Pub, 2 minute walk to the town
centre

**COTEBROOK, TARPORLEY**
**The Alvanley Arms**
See main entry on page 2

**CREWE**
**Brunel Arms**
156 West Street, Crewe, Cheshire CW1 3HG
Tel: 01270 215260    **£ - 3 rooms**
Community Pub specialising in workers
accommodation

# The Alvanley Arms

Cotebrook, Tarporley,
Cheshire CW6 9DS

££ - P - 6 rooms

Tel: 01829 760200
Fax: 01829 760696
Web: www.alvanleyarms.co.uk

The Alvanley Arms is a 400-year-old family run Inn that has a theme, throughout, related to Shire Horses. The Rosettes, pictures, photographs, harnesses and horseshoes that adorn the walls identify the Inn with the adjacent Cotebrook Shire Horse Stud.

The Inn has seven, *en suite*, individually designed bedrooms, each with a character and charm of It's own, with wonderful views over the Cheshire countryside.

The Oak beamed bar offers a wide range of hand pulled cask ales; a large selection of wines and malt whiskies and a welcoming log fire. There is an extensive traditional menu and an imaginative specials menu. All meals are freshly prepared to order with all ingredients sourced from local suppliers.

Please telephone Alistair or Janet on **01829 760200** to discuss your individual needs.

---

## EATON, CONGLETON
**Plough Inn Hotel**
Macclesfield Road, Eaton, Congleton,
Cheshire
Tel: 01260 280207     **££ - P - 8 rooms**
Email: trev@plough76.fsnet.co.uk
Country Inn approximately 2 miles from Congleton

## FARNDON
**The Farndon Arms**
High Street, Farndon, Cheshire
Tel: 01829 270570     **£ - P - 7 rooms**
Email: info@farndonarms.com
Web: www.farndonarms.com
Rural Inn 5 miles from Chester

## HALE, nr MANCHESTER
**Corbans**
Hele Road, Hale, nr Manchester, Cheshire
Tel: 01619 804347     **££ - P - 5 rooms**
Country Inn and Restaurant 10 miles from Altringham

## HIGHER BURWARDSLEY, TATTENHALL
**The Pheasant Inn**
See main entry on page 3

## KNUTSFORD
**The Angel**
98 King Street, Knutsford, Cheshire WA16 6HQ
Tel: 01565 750245     **£ - P - 8 rooms**
Located in the centre of Knutsford

## MILLBROOK, STALYBRIDGE
**Church Inn**
422 Huddersfield Road, Millbrook, Stalybridge, Cheshire SK14 3JL
Tel: 01613 382813     **£ - P - 7 rooms**
Village Inn 2 miles from Stalybridge

## NANTWICH
**The Red Cow**
Nantwich, Cheshire CW5 5NF
Tel: 01270 628581     **P - PW - letting rooms**
4 miles west of Crewe

# The Pheasant Inn

*Higher Burwardsley, Tattenhall,*
*Cheshire CH3 9PF*

**££ - P - R - BM - BG - PW - C - 10 rooms**

Tel: 01829 770434   Fax: 01829 771097

Email: reception@thepheasant-burwardsley.com

Web: thepheasant-burwardsley.com

The Pheasant enjoys a beautiful rural setting with extensive views across the Cheshire plain to the Welsh hills. Here you can get far away from it all... but remain astonishingly close to the city. Chester is a mere 15 minutes away by car. Our stone-flagged conservatory blends traditional charm with the best of contemporary style. Here cuisine becomes theatre – with our expert chefs the stars of the show. Our discreet service and imaginative presentation make every meal an occasion.

Housed in delightful old Cheshire sandstone buildings, our *en suite* rooms combine style and comfort with every modern facility right through to digital satellite channels. Whether you come to drink, dine or unwind for a few days in one of our ten charming rooms, this atmospheric location will quickly have you under its spell.

---

## OVER PEOVER, KNUTSFORD
**The Dog Inn**
Well Bank Lane, Over Peover, Knutsford,
Cheshire WA16 8UP
Tel: 01625 861421   **££**
Village Inn with Excellant rooms

## PLUMLEY, KNUTSFORD
**Golden Pheasant Hotel**
Plumley Moor Road, Plumley, Knutsford,
Cheshire WA16 9RX
Tel: 01565 722261   **£ - P - 8 rooms**
Email: helenageorge@care4free.net
Country Pub 10 minute drive to Northwich

## SUTTON
**Sutton Hall**
Bullocks Lane, Sutton, Cheshire SK11 0HE
Tel: 01260 253211   **£££ - P - 10 rooms**
Country village Inn / Restaurant 2 miles from Macclesfield

## TARPORLEY
**Foresters Arms**
92 High Street, Tarporley, Cheshire CW6 0AX
Tel: 01829 733151   **£ - P - 4 rooms**
Country Inn on the outskirts of Tarporley

## WARMINGHAM
**The Bears Paw Hotel**
School Lane, Warmingham, Cheshire CW11 9QN
Tel: 01270 526317   **££ - P - 6 rooms**
Village Inn 3 miles from Crewe

## WARRINGTON
**Kings Head Inn**
40 Winwick Street, Warrington,
Cheshire WA2 7TU
Tel: 01925 639060   **£ - P - 11 rooms**
Town Pub 2 minute walk to the town centre

## WILMSLOW
**Kings Arms**
Alderley Road, Wilmslow, Cheshire SK9 1PZ
Tel: 01625 522187   **£ - P - 6 rooms**
Web: www.kingsarms.com
Near the centre of Wimslow, features an island bar and Thai restaurant

## WETTENHALL, WINSFORD
**Boot and Slipper**
Longling, Wettenhall, Winsford,
Cheshire CW7 4DN
Tel: 01270 528238   **£ - P - 4 rooms**
Country Pub 4 miles from Winsford

# CLEVELAND

## GUISBOROUGH
**Fox and Hounds**
Slape Wath, Guisborough, Cleveland
TS14 6PX
Tel: 01287 632964 **££ - P - 15 rooms**
Country Inn situed 2 miles from Guisborough

## LOFTUS, NR SALTBURN-BY-THE-SEA
**White Horse Inn**
73 High Street, Loftus , nr Saltburn-by-the-
Sea, Cleveland TS13 4HG
Tel: 01287 640758 **£ - P - 3 rooms**
Village Inn 12 miles from Whitby

## LOFTUS, SALTBURN-BY-THE-SEA
**Station Hotel**
Station Road, Loftus, Saltburn-by-the-Sea,
Cleveland TS13 4QB
Tel: 01287 640373 **£ - P - 5 rooms**
Email: stationloftus@aol.com
Pub and hotel in the centre of Loftus

## REDCAR
**The Claredon Hotel**
See main entry below

**O'Grady's**
20 Queen Street, Redcar, Cleveland TS10 1AE
Tel: 01642 477624 **£ - Letting rooms**
Irish theme bar in central Redcar, 5 minutes
from the beach

## SALTBURN-BY-THE-SEA
**The Grapes**
Scaling Dam, Saltburn-by-the-Sea, Cleveland
Tel: 01287 640461 **£ - P - 5 rooms**
Country Inn 10 miles from Whitby

**The Wharton Arms**
133 High Street, Skelton,Saltburn-by-the-Sea,
Cleveland TS12 2DY
Tel: 01287 650618 **£ - P - 5 rooms**
Village Inn 2 miles from Saltburn

---

# The Claredon Hotel

*High Street, Redcar, Cleveland TS10 3DU*

**£ - P 10 rooms**

Tel: 01642 484301   Fax: 01642 775819
Email: fitzyone44618340@aol.com

A friendly hotel serving a good selection of beer, lager and fine wines. Our restaurant has a
high standard of delicious wholesome food. Look for the daily blackboard specials and traditional Sunday roasts. We serve a delicious full English breakfast. En suite bedrooms are tastefully
decorated and furnished with colour TV, tea/coffee and refreshments.

STOCKTON-ON-TEES
**Lambton Castle**
High Street, Stockton-on-Tees, Cleveland
TS18 1UB
Tel: 01642 643188    **£ - 3 rooms**
Located in the centre of Stockton

**O'Caseys**
27 / 31 Bridge Road, Stockton-on-Tees,
Cleveland TS18 3AE
Tel: 01642 670880    **£ - P - 7 rooms**
Irish theme Pub situated on the edge of the
town

# CUMBRIA

AINSTABLE
**New Crown Inn**
Ainstable, Cumbria
Tel: 01768 896273    **£ - P - 2 rooms**
Village Inn 13 miles from Carlisle

ALLONBY
**Ship Inn**
Main Street, Allonby, Cumbria CA15 6PD
Tel: 01900 881017    **££ - P - 7 rooms**
17th century coaching Inn located close to the
Lake District

ALSTON
**Angel Inn**
Front Street, Alston, Cumbria CA9 3HU
Tel: 01434 381363    **£ - P - 3 rooms**
17th century Inn in situated this large village

**George and Dragon Inn**
Garrigill, Alston, Cumbria CA9 3DS
Tel: 01434 381293    **£ - P - 4 rooms**
Web: thegeorgeanddragon@btopenworld.com
Village Inn 4 miles from Alston

ALVERSTON
**Piel Castle**
37 Market Street, Alverston,
Cumbria LA12 7LR
Tel: 01229 582374    **£ - Letting rooms**
A locals' town centre pub with pool table,
games, etc

AMBLESIDE
**Old Dungeon Ghyll Hotel**
Great Langdale, Ambleside,
Cumbria LA22 9JY
Tel: 01539 437272    **££ - P - Letting rooms**
Ideal for walkers, 7 miles from Ambleside

**Tower Banks Arms**
nr Sawrey, Ambleside, Cumbria LA22 0LF
Tel: 01539 436334    **££ - P - 3 rooms**
Located in Beatrice Potter country

ARMTHWAITE
**Dukes Head**
Front Street, Armthwaite, Cumbria CA4 9PB
Tel: 01697 472226    **£ - P - 5 rooms**
Village Inn 11 miles from Carlisle

ASKHAM
**The Punchbowl Inn**
Askham, Cumbria CA1 02P
Tel: 01931 712443    **££ - P - 6 rooms**
Village Inn 4 miles from Penrith

## ASKHAM, PENRITH
**Queens Head Inn**
Askham, Penrith, Cumbria CA10 2PF
Tel: 01931 712225    **££ - Letting rooms**
Country Inn 6 miles from Penrith

## BAMPTON GRANGE, BAMPTON
**Crown and Mitre Hotel**
Bampton Grange, Bampton, Penrith, Cumbria
CA10 2QR
Tel: 01931 713225    **£ - P - 5 rooms**
Country Inn in the lake district 10 miles from
Penrith

## BARBON, VIA CARNFORTH
**Barbon Inn**
Barbon, via Carnforth, Cumbria LA6 2LJ
Tel: 01524 276233    **££ - P - 10 rooms**
Village Inn 3 miles from Kirby Lonsdale

## BARROW-IN-FURNESS
**Cross Keys Hotel**
Preston Street, Barrow-in-Furness, Cumbria,
Tel: 01229 828447    **£ - P - 5 rooms**
Town centre Pub

**Peacock Inn**
145–147 Cavendish Street, Barrow-in-Furness,
Cumbria LA14 1DJ
Tel: 01229 823807    **£ - Letting rooms**
Town centre local

## BASSENTHWAITE LAKE
**Pheasant Inn**
Bassenthwaite Lake, Cumbria CA13 9YE
Tel: 01768 772219    **£££ - P - 20 rooms**
Coaching Inn. Restaurant specialises in local
fare

## BEETHAM
**The Wheatsheaf Hotel**
Beetham, Cumbria LA7 7AL
Tel: 01539 562123    **££ - P - 6 rooms**
16th century country Inn 15 minutes drive to
Kendal

## BOOT, ESKDALE
**Woolpack Inn**
Boot, Eskdale, Cumbria CA19 1TH
Tel: 01946 723230    **£ - P - Bunkhouse**
16th century traditional Lake District Inn

## BLAWITH
**The White Hart Inn**
Blawith, Cumbria LA12 8JB
Tel: 01229 861229    **££ - P - 6 rooms**
Country Inn 7 miles from the town of
Ulverston

## BRAITHWAITE, NR KESWICK
**Coledale Inn**
Braithwaite, nr Keswick, Cumbria CA12 5NT
Tel: 01768 778272    **££ - P - PW - 12 rooms**
Georgian Inn with beautiful views. Pets are
welcome

## BRAMPTON
**Blacksmiths Arms Hotel**
Talkin Village, Brampton, Cumbria CA8 1LE
Tel: 01697 73452    **£ - P - 5 rooms**
Ideal for walkers and fishermen, 2 miles from
Talkin Tarn

## BROUGH
**Castle Hotel**
Main Street, Brough, Cumbria CA17 4AX
Tel: 01768 341252    **£ - P - 14 rooms**
Small village hotel with a public bar

## CARK AND CARTMEL
**Engine Inn**
Station Road, Cark and Cartmel, Cumbria
LA11 7NZ
Tel: 01539 558341    **£ - P - 5 rooms**
Village Pub 7 miles from Kendal

## CARLISLE
**Drove Inn**
See main entry on page 7

## CARTMEL FELL
**The Cavendish**
Cartmel Fell, Cumbria LA11 6QA
Tel: 01539 536240    **££ - P - 10 rooms**
Village Inn 12 miles from Kendal

## CARTMEL FELL
**Masons Arms**
Strawberry Bank, Cartmel Fell,
Cumbria LA11 6NW    **£ - P - 3 flats**
Tel: 01539 568486    **+ 1 cottage**
Country Pub situated 8 miles from
Windermere

# Drove Inn

*Roweltown, Carlisle, Cumbria CA6 6LB*

*£ - P - R - BM - BG - C - Pets - 3 star - 4 rooms*

Tel: 01697 748202    Fax: 01697 748054

Email: droveinn@hotmail.com

Enjoy the peacefulness of our beautiful North Cumbria countryside in our well-appointed rooms or as self-catering guests in our adjoining cottage. The Cottage sleeps up to 9 and includes its own kitchen and lounge, and has its own washing and drying facilities. The Drove Inn is a traditional family run Pub just a stone's throw from Scotland and Gretna and 1 hour from the Lake District. Carlisle is just 16 miles away and Brampton / Longham 9 miles. The Pub has its own farm so you can roam the fields amongst our Swalesdale sheep or even fish the river Lyne.

Room Tariff from: Single £25.00 – Double £40.00 – Family £50.00
Cottage (up to 9 people) £350 per week

## COCKERMOUTH
**Wordsworth**
43 Main Street, Cockermouth, Cumbria CA13 9JS
Tel: 01900 822757    **£ - 17 rooms**
Recently refurbished town centre Pub / hotel

## CONISTON
**Black Bull Inn**
1 Yewdale Road, Coniston,
Cumbria LA21 8DU
Tel: 01539 441335    **££ - P - 15 rooms**
Village Inn 8 miles from Ambleside

**Church House Inn**
Torver, Coniston, Cumbria LA21 8AZ
Tel: 01539 441282    **£ - P - 5 rooms**
Email: info@churchhouseinn.com
Web: www.churchhouseinn.com
Village Inn 3 miles from Coniston

## CROSTHWAITE, KENDAL
**The Punch Bowl Inn**
Crosthwaite, Kendal, Cumbria LA8 8HR
Tel: 01539 568237    **££ - P - 3 rooms**
Email: enquiries@punchbowl.fsnet.co.uk
Web: www.punchbowl.fsnet.co.uk
Coaching Inn 5 miles from Kendal

## CULGAITH
**The Black Swan**
See main entry on page 8

## DALTON-IN-FURNESS
**The Black Dog Inn**
Holmes Green, Broughton Road, Dalton-in-Furness, Cumbria LA15 8JP
Tel: 01229 462561    **£ - P - 2 rooms**
Email: jack@blackdoginn.freeserve.co.uk
Old Coaching Inn
**CAMRA PUB OF THE YEAR 1998 / 99**

## DENT, SEDBURGH
**The Sun Inn**
Main Street, Dent, Sedburgh,
Cumbria LA10 5QL
Tel: 01539 625208    **£ - P - 4 rooms**
Web: www.dentbrewery.co.uk
Home of the Dent Brewery. 5 miles from Sedburgh

## ELTERWATER
**The Britannia Inn**
Elterwater, Cumbria LA22 9HP
Tel: 01539 437210    **££ - P - 9 rooms**
Country village Inn 3 miles from Ambleside

## ENNERDALE BRIDGE
**Shepherds Arms**
Ennerdale Bridge, Cumbria
Tel: 01946 861249    **££ - P - 8 rooms**
Email: enquiries@shepherdarmshotel.co.uk
Village Inn 7 miles from Whitehaven

# The Black Swan

Culgaith, Nr Penrith, Cumbria CA10 1QW

**££ - P - 7 rooms**

Email: info@blackswanculgaith.co.uk
Web: www.blackswanculgaith.co.uk

The Black Swan is a traditional 17th century Cumbrian Inn with oak beams, an open fire in winter and a picturesque beer garden for summer. The Inn is situated in the Eden Valley, midway between Appleby and Penrith and close to the river Eden. The Settle to Carlisle railway runs through the village.

At the Inn you will find the finest quality in food, real ale and accommodation. Shooting, fishing, golf, swimming and walking are all to hand.

From Junction 40 on the M6 the Culgaith turn off is 6 miles east on the A66 (on the left hand side, B6412) and is immediately after crossing Eden Bridge. The Black Swan Inn is a mile off the A66 and is well sign-posted

## ESKDALE GREEN
**Bower House Inn**
Eskdale Green, Cumbria CA19 1DE
Tel: 01946 723244    **£ - P - 25 rooms**
Country Inn situated 40 miles from
Whitehaven

## ESKDALE GREEN
**King George IV Inn**
Eskdale Green, Cumbria CA19 1TS
Tel: 01946 723262    **£ - P - 4 rooms**
Country Inn 5 miles from Gosforth

## GRANGE-OVER-SANDS
**Pig and Whistle**
Cartmel, Grange-over-Sands,
Cumbria LA11 6PL
Tel: 01539 536482    **£ - Letting rooms**
Country Inn 8 miles from Windermere

**Hare and Hounds Inn**
Bowland Bridge, Grange-over-Sands,
Cumbria
Tel: 01539 568777    **£ - P - 14 rooms**
Email: innthelakes@supanet.com
Web: www.bowlandbridge.co.uk
Former 17th century coaching Inn located in
the Carmen Fells

## GRASMERE
**The Travellers Rest Inn**
Keswick Road, Grasmere, Cumbria LA22 9RR
Tel: 01539 435604    **££ - P - 8 rooms**
Village Pub 15 minutes walk to Grasmere

## GREAT CORBY
**The Corby Bridge Inn**
Great Corby, Cumbria
Tel: 01228 560221    **£ - P - 3 rooms**
Village Inn 5 miles from Carlisle

## GREAT LANGDALE
**The New Dungeon Ghyll Hotel**
Great Langdale, Cumbria, LA22 9JY
Tel: 01539 437213    **£ - P - 20 rooms**
Country Inn / hotel 20 minutes drive to
Ambleside

## GRIZEBECK
**The Greyhound Inn**
Grizebeck, Cumbria LA17 7XJ
Tel: 01229 889224    **£ - P - 5 rooms**
Village Inn 6 miles from Ulverston

## HALE
**The Kings Arms**
See main entry on page 9

HAWKSHEAD
**Kings Arms Hotel**
The Square, Hawkshead, Cumbria
Tel: 01539 436372 **££ - P - 10 rooms**
Email: info@kingsarmshawkshead.co.uk
Web: www.kingsarmshawkshead.co.uk
More a small hotel with a public bar used by
the locals. Located in the centre of the village

**Queens Head Hotel**
Main Street, Hawkshead, Cumbria LA22 0NS
Tel: 01539 436271 **£ - P - 15 rooms**
Village Inn 3 miles from Ambleside

**Sun Inn**
Main Street, Hawkshead, Cumbria LA22 0NT
Tel: 01539 436236 **££ - P - 8 rooms**
16th century coaching Inn in the village centre

HEVERSHAM
**The Blue Bell Hotel**
Princes Way, Heversham, nr Kendal,
Cumbria LA7 7EE
Tel: 01539 562018 **££ - P - 21 rooms**
Former vicarage, loads of character

HOLMROOK
**The Burnmoor Inn**
Boot, Holmrook, Cumbria CA19 1TG
Tel: 01946 723224 **££ - P - Rooms**

Email: stay@burnmoor.co.uk
Web: www.burnmoor.co.uk
16th century country Inn located at the base
of Sca Fell Pike

KENDAL
**Cock and Dolphin**
2 Milenthorpe, Kendal, Cumbria LA9 5AS
Tel: 01539 728268 **£ - P - 4 rooms**
Community Pub on the outskirts of Kendal

**New Inn**
98 Highgate, Kendal, Cumbria LA9 4HE
Tel: 01539 722484 **£ - P**
Letting rooms in the centre of Kendal

**Union Tavern**
159 Sticklandgate, Kendal, Cumbria LA9 4RF
Tel: 01539 724004 **£ - P - 10 rooms**
Email: uniontavern@edirectory.co.uk
Web: www.edirectory.co.uk/uniontavern
On the outskirts of Kendal, with a good food
trade

KESWICK
**Pack Horse Inn**
Pack Horse Yard, Keswick, Cumbria
Tel: 01768 771389 **£ - Letting rooms**
A busy town centre Pub, serving good
Jennings ales

KESWICK
**Bank Tavern**
47 Main Street, Keswick, Cumbria CA12 5DA
Tel: 01768 772663    **£ - 5 rooms**
Busy town Pub

**Swinside Inn**
Newlands, Keswick, Cumbria CA12 5UE
Tel: 01768 778253    **£ - P - 6 rooms**
Email: theswinsideinn@btinternet.com
Web: www.kesnet.co.uk
Traditional 500-year-old Inn, oak beams and
log fires

KIRBY LONSDALE
**Pheasant Inn**
Casterton, Kirby Lonsdale, Cumbria LA6 2RY
Tel: 01524 271230    **£ - P - 11 rooms**
Near the lakes and dales, beautiful location

LONGTOWN, CARLISLE
**Graham Arms Hotel**
Longtown, nr Carlisle, Cumbria CA6 5SE
Tel: 01228 791213    **£ - P - 15 rooms**
Email: office@grahamarms.com

Web: www.grahamarms.com
Old coaching Inn on the A7, 7 miles from
Carlisle and 4 miles from Gretna Green

MILNTHORPE
**Bulls Head Hotel**
5 Beetham, Milnthorpe, Cumbria LA7 7QL
Tel: 01539 562133    **£ - P - 5 rooms**
Village Pub 8 miles from Kendal

**Cross Keys Hotel**
1 Park Road, Milnthorpe, Cumbria LA7 7AD
Tel: 01539 562115    **££ - P - 8 rooms**
On the A6, small town hotel / Pub with
restaurant

NETHER WASDALE
**The Screes Inn**
See main entry below

NEWBY BRIDGE
**Newby Bridge Hotel**
Newby Bridge, nr Alveston,
Cumbria LA12 8NA
Tel: 01539 531222    **£££ - P - 35 rooms**
Large country house hotel with a public bar

# The Screes Inn

*Nether Wasdale, Cumbria CA20 1ET*

Tel or Fax: 019467 26262
Email: info@thescreesinnwasdale.com
Web: www.thescreesinnwasdale.com

Nestling in the heart of the Wasdale valley, The Screes Inn is a family run establishment with beautiful views of the surrounding fells, situated only a short walk away from Wastwater. Nether Wasdale is not only an ideal base to explore the high fells but also offers numerous low-land walks. Bridleways offer an excellent opportunity for mountain biking, and Wastwater, England's deepest lake, offers a magnificent opportunity to practice your diving, swimming, paddling or simply having a picnic on the shore.

The Screes Inn has a large, comfortable bar area with a roaring log fire. We serve a good choice of real ales, fine wines and a large selection of malt whiskies. Also served is a wide range of traditional and vegetarian meals, all produced on the premises using fresh local produce.
For accommodation we currently have five letting bedrooms, all rooms are comfortable and with *en suite* facilities. We aim to have nine *en suite* bedrooms, two of which will be fully wheelchair friendly by 2003/2004 and The Screes itself, will have full wheelchair access and facilities. [Please check before visiting].

OXENHOLME
**Station Inn**
Oxenholme, Kendal, Cumbria LA9 7RF
Tel: 01539 724094    **££ - P - 7 rooms**
Country Inn 2 miles from Kendal

PENRITH
**Boot and Shoe Inn**
Greystoke, Penrith, Cumbria, CA11 0TP
Tel: 01768 483343    **£ - P - 4 rooms**
16th century village Inn just 5 miles from
Penrith

**The Queens Head**
Tirril, Penrith, Cumbria CA10 2JF
Tel: 01768 863219    **££ - P - 7 rooms**
Email: bookings@queensheadinn.co.uk
Web: www.queensheadinn.co.uk
Village Inn 3 miles from Penrith

POOLEY BRIDGE
**Pooley Bridge Inn**
Pooley Bridge, Lake Ulswater,
Cumbria CA10 2NN
Tel: 01768 486215    **££ - Letting rooms**
Village Inn 7 miles from Penrith

RAVENSTONEDALE
**The Fat Lamb**
Crossbank Ravenstonedale, Kirkby Stephen,
Cumbria CA17 4LL
Tel: 01539 623242    **££ - P - 12 rooms**
Traditional Pub between the Lake District and
the Yorkshire Dales

SEDBERGH
**The Bull Hotel**
Main Street, Sedburgh, Cumbria LA10 5BL
Tel: 01539 620264    **££ - P - 15 rooms**
Email: bullhotel@btinternet.com
Web: www.bullatsedburgh.co.uk
Town centre hotel and Pub

**Dalesman Country Inn**
Main Street, Sedbergh, Cumbria LA10 5BN
Tel: 01539 621183    **£ - P - 7 rooms**
Web: www.thedalesman
Recently refurbished pub with a very
traditional feel

STAVERLEY
**The Watermill Inn**
Ings, Staverley, Kendal, Cumbria LA8 9PY
Tel: 01539 821309    **£ - P - 7 rooms**
Email: all@watermill-inn.demon.co.uk
Web: www.watermill-inn.demon.co.uk
Good ale CAMRA listed 2 miles from
Windermere

TORVER
**Wilson Arms**
Torver, nr Coniston, Cumbria LA21 8BB
Tel: 01539 441237    **£ - P - 8 rooms**
Located 3 miles from Coniston with spectacu-
lar views

TROUTBECK
**The Troutbeck Inn**
Troutbeck, Penrith, Cumbria CA11 0SJ
Tel: 01768 483635    **£ - P - 7 rooms**
Email: enquiries@troutbeck_inn.com
Web: www.troutbeck_inn.com
Country Inn 9 miles from Penrith

ULVERSTON
**The Stan Laurel Inn**
The Ellers, Ulverston, Cumbria
Tel: 01229 582814    **£ - P - 3 rooms**
Located 5 minutes stroll to the town centre

WASDALE
**Bridge Inn**
Santon Bridge, Wasdale, Cumbria CA19 1UX
Tel: 01946 726221    **££ - P - 18 rooms**
Village Inn 12 miles from Egremont

WINTON
**Bay Horse Inn**
Winton, nr Kirkby Stephen,
Cumbria CA17 4HS
Tel: 01768 371451    **£ - P - 2 rooms**
Village Inn 2 miles from Kirkby Stephens

# COUNTY DURHAM

## BARNARD CASTLE
**Fox and Hounds**
Gotherstone, Barnard Castle, Co Durham
DL12 9PF
Tel: 01833 650241     **££ - P - 3 rooms**
Email: mcarlisle@foxcothe.freenetname.com
Web: www.foxcotherstone.co.uk
Country Inn 4 miles from Barnard Castle

**High Force Hotel and Micro Brewery**
Forest in Teesdale, Barnard Castle,
Co Durham DL12 0XH
Tel: 01833 622222     **£ - P - 6 rooms**
Country Inn opposite 'High Force', England's
highest waterfall

**Moorcock Inn**
Hill Top, Gordon Bank, Eggleston, Barnard
Castle, Co Durham DL12 0AU
Tel: 01833 650395     **£ - P - 7 rooms**
Email: zach1@talk21.com
Web: www.moorcock-inn.co.uk
Country Inn within beautiful walking country

**The George and Dragon Inn**
Boldron, Barnard Castle, Co Durham DL12 9RF
Tel: 01833 638215     **£ - P - 2 rooms**
Village Inn 2 miles from Barnard Castle

**The Old Well Inn**
21 The Bank, Barnard Castle,
Co Durham DL12 8PH
Tel: 01833 690130     **££ - 10 rooms**
Email: reservations@oldwellinn.co.uk
Web: www.oldwellinn.co.uk
Old Coaching Inn located in this historic town

## BROOMPARK
**The Loves**
17 Front Street, Broompark,
Co Durham DH7 7QT
Tel: 01913 849283     **£ - P - 2 rooms**
Email: karen.paul@tinyonline.co.uk
19thC Inn 5 minutes walk from the centre

## CHESTER-LE-STREET
**Butchers Arms**
Middle Chare, Chester-le-Street, Co Durham
Tel: 01913 883605     **£ - 4 rooms**
Local town Pub just off the main street

## CONSETT
**Castlside Inn**
The Grove, Consett, Co Durham DH8 8EB
Tel: 01207 581443     **£ - P - 9 rooms**
Local Pub 1 mile from Consett town centre

## CROOK
**Bar 56**
56 Hope Street, Crook, Co Durham DL15 8DG
Tel: 01388 762432     **£ - P - 14 rooms**
Traditional Inn 7 miles from Durham City

## CROXDALE
**Croxdale Inn**
Front Street, Croxdale, Co Durham DH6 5HX
Tel: 01388 815727     **£ - P - 12 rooms**
Email: croxdale@talk21.com
Country Inn 4 miles from Durham

**The Daleside Arms**
Croxdale, Co Durham
Tel: 01388 814165     **£ - P - 4 rooms**
Village Inn 4 miles from Durham

## DARLINGTON
**The Devonport**
Middle One Row, Darlington,
Co Durham DL2 1AS
Tel: 01325 332255     **££ - P - 16 rooms**
Email: thedevonport@easynet.co.uk
Located at the edge of the village overlooking
the River Tees, 2 miles from Darlington

## DARLINGTON
**The Boot and Shoe**
Church Row, Darlington, Co Durham DL1 5QD
Tel: 01325 287501     **£ - 9 rooms**
Located near the centre of Darlington

## DURHAM
**Bay Horse Inn**
Brandon Village, Durham, Co Durham DH7 8ST
Tel: 01913 780498     **£ - P - 10 rooms**
Accommodation consists of 10 purpose-built
chalets, 3 miles from Durham centre

**O'Neills Inn**
91a Claypath, Durham, Co Durham DH1 1RG
Tel: 01913 836951     **£ - 8 rooms**
City centre Irish Pub with accommodation

**The Three Horse Shoes Inn**
Running Waters, Sherburn House, Durham,
Co Durham DH1 2HR
Tel: 01913 720286     **£ - P - 6 rooms**
Web: www.smoothhounds.co.uk/
Country Inn About 5 minute drive to Durham

**Victoria**
86 Hallgarth Street, Durham, Co Durham
Tel: 01913 865269     **Rooms**
Traditional Pub with excellent *en suite* accommodation

**Ye Old Elm Tree**
12 Crossgate, Durham, Co Durham DH1 4PS
Tel: 01913 864621     **£ - P - 2 rooms**
City Centre Pub

## FERRYHILL
**Badgers Sett**
Market Street, Ferryhill, Co Durham EL17 8JH
Tel: 01740 654322     **£ - P - 8 rooms**
Email: manorhousehotel@barbox.net
Family run small hotel with public bar 6 miles
from Durham City

## HIGH SHINCLIFFE
**The Avenue Inn**
Avenue Street, High Shincliffe,
Co Durham DH1 2PT
Tel: 01913 865954     **£ - P - 8 rooms**
Email: wenmah@aol.com
Village Inn 2 miles from Durham

## MIDDLETON-IN-TEESDALE
**Teesdale Hotel**
Middleton-in-Teesdale, nr Barnard Castle,
Co Durham DL12 0QG
Tel: 01833 640264     **££ - 10 rooms**
Town centre old coaching Inn

## NEWFIELD
**Newfield Inn**
New Field Road, Newfield, Chester-le-Street,
Co Durham DH2 2SP
Tel: 01913 700565     **£ - P - 3 rooms**
Village Inn 3 miles from Chester-le-Street

## PITY ME
**Lambton Hounds Inn**
62 Front Street, Pity Me, Durham,
Co Durham DH1 5DE
Tel: 01913 864742     **£ - P - 8 rooms**
Email: lambtonhounds@aol.com
Country Inn 5 miles from Durham City

## RAMSHORE
**The Bridge Inn**
1 Gordon Lane, Ramshaw, Bishop Auckland,
Co Durham DL14 0NS
Tel: 01388 832509     **£ - P - 7 rooms**
Email: bridgeinnramshaw@barbox.com
Village Inn 4 miles from Bishops Auckland

## ROMALDIRK
**The Rose and Crown**
Romaldirk, Co Durham DL12 9EB
Tel: 01833 650213     **£££ - P - 12 rooms**
Email: hotel@rose-and-crown.co.uk
Web: www.rose-and-crown.co.uk
Village hotel / Inn situated 6 miles from
Barnard Castle

## SEDGEFIELD
**Dun Cow Inn**
43 Front Street, Sedgefield, Stockton-on-Tees,
Co Durham TS21 3AT
Tel: 01740 620894     **££ - P - 6 rooms**
Village Inn 10 minute drive to Stockton

## SHINCLIFFE
**Seven Stars Inn**
Shincliffe, Co Durham DH1 2NU
Tel: 01913 848454     **£ - 8 rooms**
Country Inn 2 miles from Durham City

## STANHOPE
**Pack Horse Inn**
8 Market Place, Stanhope, Bishop Auckland,
Co Durham DL13 2UJ
Tel: 01388 528407    **£ - P - Rooms**
Town Pub right in the Market Place

**Queens Head**
89 Front Street, Stanhope,
Co Durham DL13 2UB
Tel: 01388 528160    **£ - P - 4 rooms**
Family run Village Inn in Weardale

## STANLEY
**The Beamish Mary Inn**
No Place, Beamish, Stanley,
Co Durham DH9 0QH
Tel: 01913 700237    **£ - P - 4 rooms**
Village Inn 2 miles from Stanley

**The Oak Tree In**
Tantobie, Stanley, Co Durham DH9 9RF
Tel: 01207 235445    **£ - P - 6 rooms**
Village Inn about 20 minutes drive to Durham

**Punch Bowl**
Craghead, Stanley, Co Durham DH9 6HF
Tel: 01207 232917    **£ - Rooms**
Village Inn 6 miles from Craghead

# GREATER MANCHESTER

**BOOTHSTON**
**Queens Arms**
184 Chaddock Lane, Boothston, Greater
Manchester M28 2DN
Tel: 01617 903455    **Rooms**
Semi rural location on the outskirts of
Boothston

**CHORLTON-CUM-HARDY**
**Spread Eagle**
526–528 Wilbraham Road,
Chorlton-Cum-Hardy, Greater
Manchester M21 9LD
Tel: 01618 610385    **Rooms**
Owned by local brewer Joseph Holt

**DIGGLE**
**Diggle Hotel**
Station Houses, Diggle, Greater
Manchester OL3 5JZ
Tel: 01457 872741    **£ - P - 3 rooms**
Email: digglehotel@freeserve.co.uk
Village / country Inn 20 minute drive to
Oldham

**ASHTON-IN-MAKERFIELD**
**Caledonia Hotel**
13 Warrington Street, Ashton-in-Makerfield,
Greater Manchester OL6 6AS
Tel: 01613 397177    **££ - P - 3 rooms**
Located in the centre of Ashton-in-Makerfield,
leave M6 at J24

GRASSCROFT
**Farrars Arms**
56 Oldham Road, Grasscroft, Oldham, Greater
Manchester OL4 4HL
Tel: 01457 872124     **£ - P - 3 rooms**
Village Inn 3 miles from Oldham

GREENFIELD
**The Railway**
11 Shaw Hall Bank Road, Greenfield,
Greater Manchester OL3 7JZ
Tel: 01457 872307     **£ - P - 4 rooms**
Village Inn just 20 minutes by train to
Manchester city centre

LOWTON
**Red Lion**
324 Newton Road, Lowton (Lane Head),
Greater Manchester
Tel: 01942 671429     **£ - P - 4 rooms**
Semi rural location, with own bowling green,
5 minute drive from J22 M6

LYDGATE
**White Hart**
51 Stockport Road, Lydgate,
Greater Manchester OL4 4JJ
Tel: 01457 872566     **£££ - P - 12 rooms**
Email: charles@whitehart.co.uk
Country / village Inn 7 miles from Burnley

MANCHESTER
**Burton Arms**
31 Swan Street, Greater Manchester M4 5JZ
Tel: 01618 343455     **£ - 10 rooms**
Five minutes walk from the town centre

**Smithfield Hotel and Bar**
37 Swan Street, Manchester, Greater
Manchester M4 5JZ
Tel: 01618 394424     **£ - 9 rooms**
Family run Inn 2 minutes walk from
Manchester town centre

PRESTWICH
**The Church Inn**
Church Lane, Prestwich,
Greater Manchester M25 1AJ
Tel: 01617 986727     **£ - P - 5 rooms**
Email: tom.gribben@virgin.net
Located on the outskirts of Manchester

ROCHDALE
**Brittannia Inn**
4 Lomax Street, Rochdale, Greater
Manchester
Tel: 01706 646391     **£ - 3 rooms**
Local Pub 5 minutes walk to the town centre

**The Reed Hotel**
Reed Hill, Rochdale,
Greater Manchester OL16 1DF
Tel: 01706 646696     **£ - P - 5 rooms**
Town centre Inn and restaurant. Good beer
guide listed

STOCKPORT
**Armoury Inn**
31 / 33 Greek Street, Stockport,
Greater Manchester SK3 8BD
Tel: 01614 805055     **£ - 1 Room**
Town Pub

WEST TIMPERLRY
**Pelican Lodge**
Manchester Road, West Timperley,
Greater Manchester WA14 5NH
Tel: 01619 627414     **£ - P rooms**
Large S and N Premier Lodge, just refurbished

WIGAN
**Swan and Railway**
80 Wallgate, Wigan, Greater Manchester
Tel: 01942 495032     **Rooms**
Traditional Pub, good food and a warm wel-
come

WORTHINGTON
**Crown Inn**
Platt Lane, Worthington, Greater Manchester
Tel: 01257 421354     **£ - P - 10 rooms**
Village Inn 7 miles from Wigan

# HUMBERSIDE / EAST RIDING OF YORKSHIRE

## BEVERLEY
**Cross Keys Hotel**
8 Lair Gate, Beverley, East Riding
Tel: 01482 882573    **£ - P - 14 rooms**
Town centre Pub

## BRIDLINGTON
**Pack Horse Inn**
7 Market Place, Bridlington, East Riding
Tel: 01262 675701    **P - Rooms**
Olde Worlde Pub in the old part of town

## DRIFFIELD
**The Bell**
46 Market Place, Driffield,
East Riding YO25 6AN
Tel: 01377 256661    **£££ - P - 19 rooms**
Large town centre hotel with bar

**Manor House Inn and Restaurant**
Fridaythorpe, Driffield, East Riding YO25 9RT
Tel: 01377 288221    **£ - P - 7 rooms**
Village Inn 10 miles from Driffield

**Ship Inn**
Scarborough Road, Langtoft, Driffield, East
Riding YO25 3TH
Tel: 01377 267243    **£ - P - 5 rooms**
Country Pub 5 miles from Driffield

**St Quintin Arms Inn**
Harpham, Driffield, East Riding YO25 4QY
Tel: 01262 490329    **£ - P - 4 rooms**
Village Inn 4 miles from Driffield

**Triton Inn**
Sledmere, Driffield, East Riding YO25 3XQ
Tel: 01377 236644    **£ - P - 5 rooms**
Email: thetritoninn@sledmerefsbusiness.co.uk
18thC Inn between York and the east coast

## FOSTER-ON-THE-WOLD
**Plough Inn**
Foston-on-the-Wold, nr Driffield,
East Riding YO25 8BJ
Tel: 01262 488303    **£ - P - rooms**
Pub with a caravan site 6 miles from Driffield

## HOLME-UPON-SPALDING MOOR
**Ye Olde Red Lion Hotel**
Old Road, Holme-upon-Spalding Moor, East
Riding YO4 4AD
Tel: 01430 860220    **££ - P - 8 rooms**
17thC coaching Inn 25 minutes drive to York

## HUGGATE
**The Wolds Inn**
Huggate, East Riding YO42 1YH
Tel: 01377 288217    **£ - P - 3 rooms**
Village Inn 9 miles from Driffield

## HUTTON CRANSWICK
**White Horse Inn**
Main Street, Hutton Cranswick,
Humberside YO25 4QR
Tel: 01377 270383    **£ - P - 8 rooms**
Email: ctomlinson@amserve.net
Village Inn 2 miles from Beverley

## NORTH DALTON
**The Star Inn**
Warter Road, North Dalton,
East Riding YO25 9UX
Tel: 01377 217688    **P - PW - 6 rooms**
Web: www.innonthepond.com
18th century coaching Inn, pets welcome

PATRINGTON
**Hildyard Arms**
1 Market Place, Patrington, Hull,
East Riding HU12 0RA
Tel: 01964 630234 **£ - P - 3 rooms**
Village Inn 15 miles from Hull

RUDSTON
**Bosville Arms**
High Street, Rudston, Driffield,
East Riding YO25 4UB
Tel: 01262 420259 **£ - P - 6 rooms**
Email: hogan@bosville.freeserve.co.uk
Web: www.bosville.freeserve.co.uk
Country motel, village Inn and restaurant

SOUTH BOLTON
**Pipe and Glass Inn**
West End, South Bolton, nr Beverley,
East Riding HU1 7BN
Tel: 01430 810246 **£ - Rooms**
Country Inn 6 miles from Beverley

WELTON
**Green Dragon Hotel**
Cowgate, Welton, Hull, East Riding HU15 1NB
Tel: 01482 666700 **£ - P - 11 rooms**
Village Inn 10 miles from Hull

WHITBY
**Duke of Wellington Inn**
Danby, Whitby, East Riding YO21 2LY
Tel: 01287 660351 **££ - P - 7 rooms**
Email: llord@dukeofwellington.freeserve.co.uk
Web: www.danby-dukeofwellington.co.uk
18th Century Inn in the heart of the North
Moors

WILBERFOSS
**The Steer Inn**
Hull Road, Wilberfoss, York,
East Riding YO41 5PE
Tel: 01759 380600 **£ - P - 14 rooms**
Email: kevin@steerinn.co.uk
Country Inn with its own caravan site

# ISLE OF MAN

DOUGLAS
**Glen Helen Lodge Hotel**
Glen Helen, St Johns, Douglas,
Isle of Man IM4 3NP
Tel: 01624 801294 **£ - P - 14 rooms**
Country Inn 14 miles from Douglas

PEEL
**The Creek Inn**
Station Place, Peel, Isle of Man PM5 1AT
Tel: 01624 842216 **£ - P - 4 apartments**
Harbour-side Inn with outside seating area

SULBY
**Sulby Glen Hotel**
Sulby Cross Road, Sulby, Isle of Man IN7 2HL
Tel: 01624 897240 **£ - P - 11 rooms**
Email: sulbyglenhotel@manx.net
Located 4 miles from Ramsey

# LANCASHIRE

ASHLEY
**Ross's Arms**
130 Higher Green Lane, Ashley,
Lancs M29 7JB
Tel: 01942 874405     **£ - P - 6 rooms**
Village Inn 10 miles from Manchester

BACUP
**The Irwell Inn**
71 Burnley Road, Bacup, Lancs OL13 8DB
Tel: 01706 873346     **£ - 7 rooms**
Email: kevin@irwellinn.com
Web: www.irwellinn.com
Town centre Pub

ADLINGTON
**White Bear Inn**
5a Market Street, Adlington,Chorley,
Lancs PR7 4HE
Tel: 01257 482357     **P - 4 rooms**
200 year old Inn with traditional food and ales

ARKHOLME, CARNFORTH
**The Redwell Inn**
See main entry below

BELMONT VILLAGE
**Black Dog Inn**
2 Church Street, Belmont Village,
Lancs BL7 8AB
Tel: 01204 811218     **£ - P - 3 rooms**
Village Inn 10 minute drive to Bolton

BLACKO
**Moorcock Inn**
Gisburn Road, Blacko, Lancs BB9 6NF

# The Redwell Inn

*Kirkby Lonsdale Road, Arkholme, Carnforth,*
*Lancashire LA6 1BQ*

**££ - P - 6 rooms**

Tel: 015242 21240     Fax: 015242 21107
Email: julie@redwellinn.co.uk     Web: www.redwellinn.co.uk

The Redwell Inn accommodation comprises of 6 bedrooms, all ensuite with beautiful views and cosy guest lounge to relax and unwind in.

There is a tastefully decorated restaurant with an extensive menu and wine list and a cosy bar to relax in after your hearty meal. In winter snuggle up in front of our log fires, or in summer retreat to the lovely beer garden and sample the stunning scenery.
There is ample off road parking. All major credit cards are accepted.

Tel: 01282 614186 **£ - P - 3 rooms**
Pub and restaurant with beautiful views over
the Admergill Valley

**BLACKPOOL**
**Ramsden Arms Hotel**
204 Talbot Road, Blackpool, Lancs FY1 3AZ
Tel: 01253 623215 **£ - P - 4 rooms**
Town Pub 5 minutes walk to the sea

**Cherry Blossom Inn**
2 Warley Road, corner North Promenade,
Blackpool, Lancs FY1 2JU
Tel: 01253 355533 **£ - P - 15 rooms**
Blackpool seaside Pub / hotel

**BARNOLDSWICK**
**White Lion Hotel**
Riley Street, Earby, Barnoldswick,
Lancs BB18 6NX
Tel: 01282 842377 **£ - P - 3 rooms**
Village Inn between Burnley and Skipton

**BURNLEY**
**Coach and Horses Inn**
48 Church Street, Burnley, Lancashire, BB11
2DL
Tel: 01282 423478 **£ - 3 rooms**
Located near Burnley town centre

**BURNLEY**
**The Pendle Inn**
Barley, Burnley, Lancs BB12 9JX
Tel: 01282 614808 **££ - P - 9 rooms**
Email: john@pendleinn.freeserve.co.uk
Web: www.pendleinn.freeserve.co.uk
Country Pub 3 miles from Nelson

**BURSCOUGH**
**Martin Inn**
Mescar Lane, Burscough, Lancs L40 0RT
Tel: 01704 892302 **P - rooms**
Village Inn 2 miles from Omskirk

**CANAL SIDE**
**Owd Nell's Canal Side Tavern**
Guys Thatched Hamlet, Canal Side,
Garstaring, Lancs PR3 0RS
Tel: 01995 640010 **££ - P - 53 rooms**
Lovely thatched Pub next to the Lancashire
Canal

**CLITHEROE**
**Copy Nook Hotel**
Bolton, by Bowland, Clitheroe, Lancs BB7 4NL
Tel: 01200 447205 **££ - P - 6 rooms**
Food orientated Inn 5 miles from Clitheroe

**The Moorcock Inn**
Waddington, Clitheroe, Lancs BB7 3AA
Tel: 01200 422333 **££ - P - 11 rooms**
Family-run pub overlooking the Ribble Valley

**White Lion Hotel**
11 Market Place, Clitheroe, Lancs BB7 2BZ
Tel: 01200 426955 **£ - P - 7 rooms**
Town centre Pub

**FOULRIDGE**
**The Hare and Hounds**
Old Skipton Road, Foulridge, Colne,
Lancs BB8 7PD
Tel: 01282 864235 **£ - P - 5 rooms**
Email: hareandhounds1@hotmail.com
Web: www.hareandhounds.com
Village Inn 1 mile from Colne

**GALGATE**
**New Inn**
59 Main Street, Galgate, Lancs
Tel: 01524 751643 **£ - P - 3 rooms**
Village Inn 5 miles from Lancaster

**The Stork Hotel**
Conder Green, Galgate, Lancs LA2 0AN
Tel: 01524 751234 **£ - P - 10 rooms**
Country Inn 4 miles from Lancaster

**GARSTANG**
**Eagle and Child**
3 The High Street, Garstang, Preston,
Lancs PR3 1EA
Tel: 01995 602139 **P - 4 rooms**
Village Inn 10 miles from Preston

**GOOSNARGH**
**Ye Horns Inn**
Horns Lane, Goosnargh, Preston,
Lancs PR3 2FJ
Tel: 01772 865230 **££ - P - rooms**
Email: enquiries@yehornsinn.co.uk
Web: www.yehornsinn.co.uk
18thC country Inn (signed from) Goosnargh

## GREAT HARWOOD
**Royal Hotel**
2 Station Road, Great Harwood, nr Blackburn,
Lancs BD6 7BA
Tel: 01254 883541     **£ - 4 rooms**
Email: janice@rocknroyal.co.uk
Live music, real ales. Half a mile from the
town centre

## HASLINGDEN
**Odywers**
2 Blackburn Road, Haslingden, Rothendale
Valley, Lancs BB4 5QQ
Tel: 01706 211996     **£ - P - Rooms**
Village Inn 5 miles from Accrington

## HAWKSHAW
**Red Lion**
81 Ramsbottom Road, Hawkshaw, nr Bury,
Lancs
Tel: 01204 856600     **Letting rooms**
A former coaching Inn of great character

## HEATH
**Bay Horse Hotel**
Babylon Lane, Heath, Charnock, nr Chorley,
Lancs PR6 9ER
Tel: 01257 480309     **£ - P - 6 rooms**
Country Inn/restaurant 3 miles from Chorley

## HESKIN GREEN
**Farmers Arms**
85 Wood Lane, Heskin Green, Lancs PR7 5NP
Tel: 01257 451276     **£ - Letting rooms**
Email: andy@farmersarms.co.uk
Web: www.farmersarms.co.uk
Country Inn between the M6 and Eccleston

## HODDLESDON
**Old Rosins Inn**
Treacle Row, Pickup Bank, Hoddlesdon,
Darwin, Lancs BB3 3QD
Tel: 01254 771264     **Letting rooms**
Old country Inn and restaurant in heart of the
Lancashire Moors

## LANCASTER
**Farmhouse Tavern**
Morcombe Road, Lancaster, Lancs LA1 5JB
Tel: 01524 69255     **£ - P - 5 rooms**
Country Inn 1 mile from Lancaster

**Farmers Arms Hotel**
Penny Street, Lancaster, Lancs LA1 1XT
Tel: 01524 36368     **£ - P - 15 rooms**
Local town pub 2 minutes from the centre

## LANESHAWBRIDGE
**The Emmot Arms**
Keighley Road, Laneshawbridge,
Lancs BB8 7HX
Tel: 01282 863386     **£ - 3 rooms**
This village Pub started life as an 18thC
farmhouse

**The Hargreaves Arms**
Keighley Road, Laneshawbridge, Colne,
Lancs BB8 7EJ
Tel: 01282 863470     **Letting rooms**
Old fashioned country pub. Real traditional
ales and home cooked food

## LITTLE ECCLESTON
**The Cartford Hotel**
See main entry on page 21

## LONGRIDGE
**The Corporation Arms**
Lower Road, Longridge, nr Preston, Lancs
Tel: 01772 782644     **Letting rooms**
An archetypal English Pub set in the Ribble
Valley

## LOWER BENTHAM
**Punch Bowl Hotel**
Lower Bentham, nr Lancaster, Lancs LA2 7DD
Tel: 01524 261344     **£ - Letting rooms**
Country Inn approximately 12 miles from
Lancaster

## NORDEN
**Brown Cow**
832 Edenfield Road, Norden, Rochdale,
Lancs OL12 7RB
Tel: 01706 649467     **£ - P - 1 room**
Village community Pub 3 miles from Rochdale

## ROCHDALE
**Flying Horse Hotel**
37 Packer Street, Town Hall Square, Rochdale,
Lancs OL16 1NJ
Tel: 01706 646412     **£ - P - 11 rooms**
Town centre Pub right in the middle of town

# The Cartford Hotel

*Cartford Lane, Little Eccleston, Lancs PR3 0YP*

### P - Letting rooms

Tel: 01995 670166

The Cartford Hotel is a country riverside free house with easy access to Blackpool and the Lake District and renowned for its special and home made ales. It is English Tourist Board 3 Diamond rated and a local Camra Pub of the Year Winner.

It is one of very few pubs to have its own "Hart" brewery attached, and is a must for real ale fans.

SALFORD
**Bee Hive Inn**
74 Holland Street, Salford, Lancs M6 6FE
Tel: 01617 457623    **£ - 5 rooms**
Local Pub 2 minutes walk to the town centre

SHARPLES, BOULTON
**Cheetham Arms**
987 Blackburn Road, Sharples, Bolton,
Lancs BL1 7LG
Tel: 01204 301372    **£ - P - 4 rooms**
Old coaching Inn on the main road 3 miles
from Bolton

TODMORDEN
**Bergh of Brandstatter**
Cross Stone Road, Todmorden,
Lancs OL14 8RQ
Tel: 01706 812966    **£ - P - 6 rooms**
Austrian style hotel and bar 4 miles from
Hebdon Bridge

TOWNEND SLAIDBURN, CLITHEROE
**Hark to the Bounty Inn**
Townend Slaidburn, Clitheroe, Lancs BB7 3EP
Tel: 01200 446246    **£ - Letting rooms**
Email: roomsisobel@hark-to-bounty.co.uk
Web: www.hark-to-bounty.co.uk
13th century Inn, from A59 take the B6478

TRAWDEN
**The Rock Hotel**
Church Street, Trawden, Lancs BB8 8RU
Tel: 01282 863005    **£ - P - 3 rooms**
Traditional Inn, beer garden and children's
play area

WHALLEY, CLITHEROE
**The Bayley Arms**
Avenue Road, Hurst Green, Whalley,
Clitheroe, Lancs BB7 9QB
Tel: 01254 826478    **£ - P - 8 rooms**
Village Inn / hotel and restaurant 10 minutes
drive to Clitheroe

WHITEWELL, CLITHEROE
**The Inn at Whitewell**
Forest of Bowland, Whitewell, Clitheroe,
Lancs BB7 3AT
Tel: 01200 448222    **££ - P - 17 rooms**
On the river Hodder, guests may fish from the
Inn's own grounds

WHITTINGTON
**Dragons Head**
Main Street, Whittington, Lancs LA6 2NY
Tel: 01524 272383    **£ - P - 3 rooms**
Village Pub 12 miles from Morcambe

WORTHINGTON
**The Crown Inn**
Platt Lane, Worthington, nr Wigan,
Lancs WN1 2XF
Tel: 01204 888300    **£ - P - 10 rooms**
Semi rural village Inn with restaurant 3 miles
from Wigan

WREA GREEN
**The Villa**
Moss Side Lane, Wrea Green, nr Preston,
Lancs
Tel: 01772 684347    **Letting rooms**
Set in its own grounds, stunning dining room

# MERSEYSIDE

## BROMBOROUGH, WIRRAL
**The Dibbinsdale Inn**
Dibbinsdale Road, Bromborough, Wirral,
Merseyside CH63 0HJ
Tel: 01513 345171     **£ - P - 13 rooms**
Local Inn 6 miles from Birkenhead town
centre

## ECCLESTON, ST HELENS
**Griffin Inn**
Church Lane, Eccleston, St Helens,
Merseyside WA10 5AD
Tel: 01744 27907     **£ - P - 11 rooms**
Email: reservations@griffininn.fsbusiness.co.uk
Local village Pub 10 minutes from St Helens

## HESWALL
**The Jug and Bottle Hotel**
Mount Avenue, Heswall,
Merseyside CH60 4RH
Tel: 01513 425535     **£ - P - 5 rooms**
Village Inn located in the centre of Heswall

## LIVERPOOL
**The Feathers Inn**
1 Paul Street, Vauxhall Road, Liverpool,
Merseyside L3 6DX
Tel: 01512 361203     **£ - P - 7 rooms**
Located 10 minutes walk from city centre

## LOWER HESWALL
**The Black Horse**
School Hill, Lower Heswall,
Merseyside CH60 0DP
Tel: 01513 422254     **£ - P - 9 rooms**
Village Inn 500 yards from the centre of
Heswall

## PORT SUNLIGHT, WIRRAL
**Bridge Inn Hotel**
Bolton Road, Port Sunlight, Bebington, Wirral,
Merseyside CH62 4UQ
Tel: 01516 458441     **££ - P - 19 rooms**
Village Inn 2 miles from Birkenhead

## RAINFORD, ST HELENS
**The Wheatsheaf Hotel**
Ormskirk Road, Rainford, St Helens,
Merseyside WA11 7TA
Tel: 01744 884346     **£ - P - 2 rooms**
Country Pub 2 miles from St Helens

## SOUTHPORT
**The Berkeley Arms**
19 Queens Road, Southport,
Merseyside PR9 9HN
Tel: 01704 500811     **£ - P - 11 rooms**
Email: info@berkeley-arms.com
Web: www.berkeley-arms.com
Friendly local Pub 10 minutes walk to
Southport town centre

## WILLASTON
**The Nags Head**
Hooton Road, Willaston, Merseyside
CH64 1SJ
Tel: 01513 272439     **£ - P - 4 rooms**
Village Inn 20 minute drive to Birkenhead

# NORTHUMBERLAND

Berwick-Upon-Tweed

Alnwick

Rochester

Ashington

Hexham

## ALLENHEADS
**Kings Head Hotel**
Market Place, Allenheads, Northumberland
NE47 9BD
Tel: 01434 683681     **£ - 3 rooms**
Located in the centre of Allendale

**The Allenheads Inn**
Allenheads, Northumberland NE47 9HJ
Tel: 01434 685200     **£ - P - 8 rooms**
Village Inn 20 miles from Hexham

## ALNMOUTH
**Saddle Hotel**
24–25, Northumberland Street, Alnmouth,
Northumberland NE66 2RA
Tel: 01665 830476     **££ - 8 - rooms**
Family friendly village Inn 3 miles from
Alnwick

## ALNWICK
**Blue Bell Inn**
Embleton, Alnwick,
Northumberland NE66 3UP
Tel: 01665 576639     **£ - P - 3 rooms**
Country Inn 7 miles from Alnwick

**The Oaks**
South Road, Alnwick, Northumberland
Tel: 01665 510014     **Rooms**
On the outskirts of Alnwick. Fine ales

## BAMBURGH
**Victoria Hotel**
Front Street, Bamburgh,
Northumberland NE69 7BP
Tel: 01668 214431     **£££ - P - 29 rooms**
Town centre hotel with a public bar, family
friendly

## BELLINGHAM
**Rose and Crown**
West View, Bellingham,
Northumberland NE48 2AS
Tel: 01434 220202     **£ - P - 3 rooms**
Traditional village Inn located 17 miles from
Hexham

## BERWICK-UPON-TWEED
**Pilot Inn**
31 Low Greens, Berwick-upon-Tweed,
Northumberland TD15 1LZ
Tel: 01289 304214     **P - 3 rooms**
Traditional old fashioned town Pub

## BLANCHLAND
**Lord Crewe Arms**
Blanchland, Northumberland DH8 9SP
Tel: 01434 675251     **£££ - P - 19 rooms**
Village Inn located 10 miles from Hexham

## BRAMPTON
**Kirkstyle Inn**
Slaggyford, Brampton,
Northumberland CA6 7PB
Tel: 01434 381559     **£ - P - 3 rooms**
Traditional country Inn located 5 miles from
Alston

## CARTERWAY HEADS
**Manor House Inn**
Shotley Bridge, Carterway Heads, Consett,
Northumberland DH8 9LX
Tel: 01207 255268     **£ - P - 4 rooms**
Web: www.scoot.co.uk/manor.house/
Traditional country Inn located 9 miles from
Corbridge

CHATHILL
**The Pack Horse Inn**
Ellingham, Chathill,
Northumberland NE67 5HA
Tel: 01665 589292     **£ - P - 5 rooms**
Email: grahem.simpson@farmline.com
Web: www.thepackhorseinn.co.uk
Village Inn 11 miles  from Alnwick

CHATTON
**The Percy Arms Hotel**
Main Road, Chatton,
Northumberland NE66 5PS
Tel: 01668 215244     **££ - P - 8 rooms**
Country Inn 15 miles from Alnwick

CHESWICK, BERWICK-UPON-
TWEED
**Cat Inn**
Great North Road, Cheswick, Berwick-upon-
Tweed, Northumberland TD15 2RL
Tel: 01289 387251     **£ - P - 7 rooms**
Country Inn 5 miles from Berwick

CHOPPINGTON
**Half Moon Inn**
Half Moon Street, Choppington,
Northumberland NE62 5TT
Tel: 01670 853528     **£ - P - 4 rooms**
Email: t.forster@ukonline.co.uk
Traditional Village Inn 2 miles from Morpeth

CORBRIDGE
**The Angel Inn**
Main Street, Corbridge,
Northumberland NE45 5LA
Tel: 01434 632119     **££ - P - 5 rooms**
Country Inn 20 minutes drive to Newcastle

**Dyvels Hotel**
Station Road, Corbridge,
Northumberland NE45 5AY
Tel: 01434 633633     **£ - P - 6 rooms**
Village Inn 1.5 miles from Hexham

CRASTER, ALNWICK
**The Cottage Inn**
Dunstan Village, Craster, Alnwick,
Northumberland NE66 3SZ
Tel: 01665 576658     **££ - P - 10 rooms**
Village Inn 7 miles from Alnwick

FALSTONE, HEXHAM
**The Pheasnt Inn**
by Kielder Water, Stannersburn, Falstone,
Hexham, Northumberland NE48 1DD
Tel: 01434 240382     **£ - P - 8 rooms**
Email:thepheasantinn@kielderwater.demon.co.uk
16th century Inn with stone walls, oak beams
and log fires

FELTON
**Cook and Barker Inn**
Newton-on-the-Moor, Felton,
Northumberland NE65 9JY
Tel: 01665 575234     **££ - Rooms**
17th century Inn located half a mile from the
A1 south of Alnwick

GUIDE POST, CHOPPINGHAM
**Anglers Arms Inn**
Sheepwash Bank, Guide Post, Choppington,
Northumberland NE62 5NB
Tel: 01670 822300     **£ - P - 5 rooms**
3 star Inn on the outskirts of Choppington

HALTWHISTLE
**Grey Bull**
Main Street, Haltwhistle,
Northumberland NE49 0DL
Tel: 01434 321991     **£ - P - 7 rooms**
Email: pamgreyb@aol.com
18th century coaching Inn

HAYDON BRIDGE
**Anchor Hotel**
John Martin Street, Haydon Bridge, nr
Hexham, Northumberland NE47 6AB
Tel: 01434 684227     **££ - P - 10 rooms**
Village Pub 7 miles from Hexham

HEXHAM
**Barrasford Arms**
Barrasford, Hexham,
Northumberland NE48 4AA
Tel: 01434 681237     **£ - P - 5 rooms**
Country Inn 9 miles from Hexham

**Bay Horse Inn**
West Woodburn, Hexham,
Northumberland NE48 2RX
Tel: 01434 270218     **£ - P - 5 rooms**
Country Inn 21 miles from Hexham

**The Blackcock Inn**
Falstone, Hexham, Northumberland NE48 1AA
Tel: 01434 240200    **£ - P - 4 rooms**
Email: blackcock@falstone.fsbusiness.co.uk
Web: www.smoothhound.co.uk/hotels/black.html
Country Inn 26 miles from Hexham

**Coach and Horses**
Priestpopple, Hexham, Northumberland
Tel: 01434 600492    **£ - P - 6 rooms**
Town centre Pub

**The Hollybush Inn**
Greenhaugh, Hexham,
Northumberland NE48 1PW
Tel: 01434 240391    **£ - 3 rooms**
Village Inn 25 miles from Hexham

HOLY ISLAND,
BERWICK-UPON-TWEED
**The Ship**
Marygate, Holy Island, Berwick-upon-Tweed,
Northumberland TD15 2SJ
Tel: 01289 389311    **££ - P - 3 rooms**
Email: theship@holyisland7.freeserve.co.uk

Web: www.lindisfarneaccommodate.com
Recently refurbished, a craft shop is attached

LONGFRAMLINGTON
**Granby Inn**
Front Street, Longframlington,
Northumberland NE65 8DP
Tel: 01665 570228    **££ - P - 5 rooms**
Village Inn 11 miles from Morpeth

LONGFRAMLINGTON, MORPETH
**The Anglers Arms**
Weldon Bridge, Longframlington, Morpeth,
Northumberland NE65 8AX
Tel: 01665 570655    **£ - P - 5 rooms**
Web: www.anglersarms.com
Listed riverside Inn and Pullman restaurant

LOWICK, BERWICK-UPON-TWEED
**Black Bull Inn**
Main Street, Lowick, Berwick-upon-Tweed,
Northumberland TD15 2UA
Tel: 01289 388228    **£ - P - 3 rooms**
Email: tom@blackbullowick.freeserve.co.uk
Village Inn 9 miles from Berwick

# Redesdale Arms Hotel

*Rochester, Nr Otterburn,*
*Northumberland NE19 1TA*

**££ - P - 10 rooms**

Tel: 01830 520668    Fax: 01830 520063
Email: redesdalehotel@hotmail.com
Web: www.redesdale-hotel.co.uk

The Redesdale Arms Hotel is located 12 miles from the England–Scotland border on the A68 in the beautiful Rede Valley, which itself is part of the Northumberland National Park.
We offer bed and breakfast or full hotel accommodation in comfortable rooms all with Northumberland country hospitality at its very best, and is personally run by its proprietors, Hilda and Johnny Wright.

The bar area has pillars of stone reminiscent of days gone by, while the lounge has comfortable chairs and tables with an open fire and beautiful country pictures adorning the walls.
The restaurant serves local Northumberland produce, succulent local organic beef / lamb, fresh seafood from our nearby coastal waters and vegetables locally grown to give you tastes that may only be a distant memory, and recipes that change daily that our chef is proud of.
Please take the time to view our site; we do look forward to hearing from you.

## MORPETH
**Hermitage Inn**
Warkworth, Morpeth,
Northumberland NE65 0UL
Tel: 01665 711258     **£ - 5 rooms**
Traditional village Inn 10 miles from Morpeth

## PONTELAND
**Diamond Inn**
Main Street, Ponteland,
Northumberland NE20 9BB
Tel: 01661 872898     **££ - P - 12 rooms**
Village Inn 8 miles from Newcastle

## PENNINGTON, ALNWICK
**Masons Arms**
Stamford, Pennington, Alnwick,
Northumberland NE66 3RX
Tel: 01665 577275     **£ - P - Rooms**
Email: masonsarms@lineone.net
Web: www.masonsarms.net
18th century country Inn on the B1340

## ROCHESTER, NR OTTERBURN
**Redesdale Arms Hotel**
See main entry on page 25

## SEAHOUSES
**Bamburgh Castle Hotel**
Seahouses, Northumberland NE68 7SQ
Tel: 01665 720283     **£££ - P - 20 rooms**
Village hotel and Pub 12 miles from Alnwick

**The Olde Ship Hotel**
9 Main Street, Seahouses,
Northumberland NE68 7RD
Tel: 01665 720200     **£££ - P - 18 rooms**
Village Inn 15 miles from Alnwick

## SLALEY, HEXHAM
**Rose and Crown Inn**
Main Street, Slaley, Hexham,
Northumberland NE47 0AA
Tel: 01434 673263     **£ - P - 3 rooms**
Email: rosecrowninn@supanet.com
Web: www.smoothound.co.uk/hotels/
Olde country Inn with a cosy public bar

## TWEEDMOUTH, BERWICK-UPON-TWEED
**The Rob Roy**
Dock Road, Tweedmouth, Berwick-upon-
Tweed, Northumberland TD15 2BQ
Tel: 01289 306428     **£ - 2 rooms**
Email: therobroy@btinternet.com
Web: www.therobroy.co.uk
Riverside Pub 1 mile from Berwick-upon-
Tweed

## WOOLER
**Anchor Inn**
2 Cheviot Street, Wooler,
Northumberland NE71 6LN
Tel: 01668 281412     **£ - 2 rooms**
Town Pub 2 minutes walk from town centre

# NORTH YORKSHIRE

## ACASTER MALBIS
**The Ship Inn**
Moor End, Acaster Malbis, North Yorkshire
Tel: 01904 703888    **£ - P - 8 rooms**
Riverside country Inn 3 miles from York

## ALDBOROUGH
**The Ship Inn**
Low Road, Aldborough, nr Boroughbridge,
North Yorkshire YO51 9ER
Tel: 01423 322749    **£ - P - 3 rooms**
Village Inn 1 mile from Boroughbridge

## AMPLEFORTH
**White Horse Inn**
West End, Ampleforth,
North Yorkshire YO62 4OC
Tel: 01439 788378    **£ - P - 2 rooms**
Family run traditional Inn. Children welcome

## AINTHORPE, nr DANBY, WHITBY
**The Fox and Hounds Inn**
Ainthorpe, nr Danby, Whitby,
North Yorkshire YO21 2LD
Tel: 01287 660218    **££ - P - 7 rooms**
Email: ajbfox@global.net
Country Inn and restaurant 15 miles from
Whitby

## AYSGARTH
**George and Dragon Inn**
Aysgarth, North Yorkshire DL8 3AD
Tel: 01969 663358    **££ - P - 7 rooms**
Country Inn 15 miles from Richmond

## BAINBRIDGE
**Rose and Crown Hotel**
Bainbridge, North Yorkshire DL8 3EE
Tel: 01969 650225    **£ - P - 12 rooms**
Email: stay@rose-and-crown.freeserve.co.uk
13th century coaching Inn 7 miles to Leyburn.
Pets welcome

## BEDALE
**Green Dragon Inn**
Exelby, Bedale, North Yorkshire DL8 2HA
Tel: 01677 422233    **£ - P - 3 rooms**
Traditional village Inn 2 miles from Bedale

**Greyhound Country Inn**
Hackforth, Bedale, North Yorkshire DL8 1PD
Tel: 01748 811415    **£ - P - 4 rooms**
Traditional village Inn 4 miles from Bedale

**The Castle Arms Inn**
Snape, Bedale, North Yorkshire DL8 2TB
Tel: 01677 470270    **££ - P - 9 rooms**
Email: castlearms@aol.com
Beautifully refurbished 14th century Inn

## BOROUGHBRIDGE
**Black Bull**
6 St James Square, Boroughbridge,
North Yorkshire YO5 9AR
Tel: 01423 322413    **£ - P - 6 rooms**
Located in the centre of a small country town

## BROMTON-ON-SWALE,
RICHMOND
**Farmers Arms Inn**
Catterbridge, Bromton-on-Swale, Richmond,
North Yorkshire DL10 7HZ
Tel: 01748 818062    **£ - P - 3 rooms**
Country Inn with rooms and a caravan site 4
miles from Richmond

## BUCKDEN
**The Buck Inn**
Buckden, North Yorkshire BD23 5JA
Tel: 01756 760228    **££ - P - 14 rooms**
Email: info@thebuckinn.com

Within the Yorkshire Dales, 20 miles approximately from Skipton

## CASTLETON
**The Downe Arms Inn**
High Street, Castleton,
North Yorkshire YO21 2EE
Tel: 01287 660223     **P - 6 rooms**
Village country Inn 10 miles from Guisborough

**Moorlands Hotel**
High Street, Castleton, nr Whitby, North
Yorkshire YO21 2DB
Tel: 01287 660206     **££ - P - 11 rooms**
Located in the centre of Castleton

## CLAPHAM
**New Inn**
Clapham, North Yorkshire LA2 8HH
Tel: 01524 251203     **£ - P - 19 rooms**
Village Inn 6 miles from Settle

## CLOUGHTON, SCARBOROUGH
**Blacksmiths Arms Inn**
High Street, Cloughton, Scarborough,
North Yorkshire
Tel: 01723 870244     **£ - P - 11 rooms**
Country Inn 6 miles from Scarborough

## COXWOLD
**Fauconberg Arms**
Main Street, Coxwold, North Yorkshire YO6 4AD
Tel: 01347 868214     **££ - P - 4 rooms**
Country Inn with restaurant 6 miles from Thirsk

## CRACOE, nr SKIPTON
**The Devonshire Arms**
Cracoe, nr Skipton, North Yorkshire BD23 6LA
Tel: 01756 730237     **Rooms**
Classic traditional Yorkshire Dales Inn

## CROPTON, NR PICKERING
**The New Inn**
See main entry below

## DARLTON-ON-TEES, DARLINGTON
**Chequers Inn**
Dalton-on-Tees, Darlington,
North Yorkshire DL2 2NT
Tel: 01325 721213     **£ - P - 5 rooms**
Overlooks the village green, Darlington 3 miles

## EAST HESLERTON, NR MALTON
**The Snooty Fox Lodge**
East Heslerton, nr Malton,
North Yorkshire YO17 8EN
Tel: 01944 710554     **£ - P - Rooms**

---

# The New Inn

*Cropton, nr Pickering,  North Yorkshire YO18 8HH*

**££ - P - R - BM - PW - C - 9 rooms**

Tel: 01751 417330
Fax: 01751 417310
Email: newinn@cropton.fsbusiness.co.uk
Web: www.croptonbrewery.co.uk

Set close to the wild moors featured so prominently in the popular *Herriot* and *Heartbeat* TV series, the New Inn at Cropton is the perfect weekend hideaway whatever the season.

Guests are accommodated in 9 attractively furnished double or twin bedded rooms, each with *en suite* bathroom, full central heating and tea / coffee making facilities.

The village Bar with its beamed ceiling and cosy fire is the focal point of the village and an ideal place to relax with the locals after a day's outing and a fine meal. There is never a shortage of good conversation, which is perhaps one reason why many of our guests return time and time again. Some are even in our winter darts team.

# The Ganton Greyhound

*Ganton, Nr Scarborough, North Yorkshire YO12 4NX*

**P - All rooms *en suite***

Tel: 01944 710116    Fax: 01944 712705
Email: stay@gantongreyhound.com
Web: www.gantongreyhound.com

The Ganton Greyhound, set beside the Ganton Championship Golf Course, has all e-suite rooms tastefully furnished and with tea / coffee making facilities, TVs, computer ports, hair dryers and direct dial telephones.

There are four coastal resorts, and their attractions, nearby. The pub is also close to the beautiful North Yorkshire Moors and *Heartbeat* country.

Email: snootyfox@tinyworld.co.uk
Web: www.thesnootyfox.co.uk
Very comfortable, caters for special needs

## ESCRICK
**Black Bull Inn**
Main Street, Escrick, North Yorkshire Y19 6JP
Tel: 01904 728245    **££ - 10 rooms**
Village Inn 15 minute drive to York

## FYLINGTHORPE, WHITBY
**Fylingdales Inn**
Thorpe Lane, Fylingthorpe, Whitby,
North Yorkshire YO22 4TH
Tel: 01947 880433    **£ - P - 3 rooms**
Country Inn 5 miles from Whitby

## GANTON, NR SCARBOROUGH
**The Ganton Greyhound**
See main entry above

## GARGRAVRE, SKIPTON
**Old Swan Inn**
20 High Street, Gargrarve, Skipton, North
Yorkshire BD23 3RB
Tel: 01756 749232    **£ - P - Rooms**
Roadside Inn on the main A65 to the lakes

## GRASSINGTON, SKIPTON
**The Foresters Arms**
20 Main Street, Grassington, Skipton, North
Yorkshire BD23 5AA

Tel: 01756 752349    **£ - P - 7 rooms**
Email: theforesters@totalise.co.uk
Old coaching Inn near the village centre

## HARDRAW, HAWES
**The Green Dragon Inn**
See main entry on page 30

## HARROGATE
**Bay Horse Inn**
Burnt Yates, Harrogate,
North Yorkshire HG3 3EJ
Tel: 01423 770230    **££ - P - 16 rooms**
Country Inn 5 miles from Harrowgate

**Cuttlers On the Stray**
19 West Park, Harrogate,
North Yorkshire HG1 1BL
Tel: 01423 524471    **£££ - P - 19 rooms**
Bar and restaurant in the centre of
Harrowgate

**The New Inn**
Burnt Yates, Harrogate,
North Yorkshire HG3 3EG
Tel: 01423 771070    **££ - P - 8 rooms**
Email: newinn@chrisgnaylor.force9.co.uk
Web: www.chrisgnaylor.force9.co.uk
Village Inn 15 minutes drive to Harrogate

**Royal Oak Inn**
Oak Lane, Dacre Banks, Harrogate, North

# The Green Dragon Inn

*Hardraw, Hawes, North Yorkshire DL8 3LZ*

Tel: 01969 667392
Email: info@greendragonhardraw.com
Web: www.greendragonhardraw.com

This famous Wensleydale Inn with origins going back at least to the 13th century sits astride the Penine Way in the sleepy hamlet of Hardraw near Hawes. It has 16 *en suite* bedrooms, 7 self-catering apartments, a large function room and camping facilities. Features live music every Saturday, and music festivals in the summer months.

Follow the footsteps of J M W Turner, William Wordsworth and in recent times Kevin Costner (during the filming of *Robin Hood Prince of Thieves)* and visit our waterfall 'Hardraw Force' the highest single drop fall in England – access is only gained through the Inn.

May: sword dancing / beer festival, July: Upper Wensleydale gathering, folk and crafts, September: world famous Hardraw Scaur Brass Band contest.
Average room price Single = £23.00 / Double = £46.00 / Family = £69.00 Parking, a great beer garden, pets and children welcome

---

Yorkshire HG3 4EN
Tel: 01423 780200      **£ - P - 3 rooms**
Email: royaloakdacre@aol.com
Web: www.theroyaloak.co.uk
Traditional listed village Inn 11 miles from Harrogate

**Queens Head Inn**
Kettlesing, Harrogate,
North Yorkshire HG3 2LB
Tel: 01423 770263      **P - 7 rooms**
Country Inn located just 5 miles from Harrowgate

## HAWES
**White Hart Inn**
Main Street, Hawes, North Yorkshire DL8 3QL
Tel: 01969 667259      **£ - P - 7 rooms**
Email: whitehart@wensleydale.org
Web: www.wensleydale.org
17th century coaching Inn close to the Yorkshire Dales

## HELMSLEY
**The Feversham Arms Hotel**
1 High Street, Helmsley,
North Yorkshire YO62 5AG
Tel: 01439 770766      **£££ - P - 17 rooms**
Located in the centre of Helmsley on the market square

## HEWORTH, YORK
**The Nags Head**
56 Heworth Road, Heworth,York,
North Yorkshire YO3 0AD
Tel: 01904 422989      **£ - P - 5 rooms**
Suburban community Pub, 15 minutes walk from York centre

## HINDERWELL
**Brown Cow Inn**
55 High Street, Hinderwell,
North Yorkshire TS18 5AT
Tel: 01947 840694      **£ - P - 2 rooms**
Village Inn 8 miles from Whitby

**Ship Inn**
Port Mulgrave, Hinderwell, nr Whitby,
North Yorkshire TS13 5JZ
Tel: 01947 840303    **£ - P - PW - 4 rooms**
Email: kayhartley@lineone.net
Set in a seaside hamlet, pets welcome

## HOVINGHAM
**The Worsley Arms Hotel**
Main Street, Hovingham,
North Yorkshire YO62 4LA
Tel: 01653 628234    **£££ - P - 19 rooms**
Country hotel with public bar, Malton 8 miles

## HUBBERHOLME
**The George Inn**
Hubberholme, North Yorkshire BD23 5JE
Tel: 01756 760223    **£ - P - 6 rooms**
Very rural traditional country Inn 20 miles from
Skipton

## INGLETON, CARNFORTH
**The Station Inn**
Ribblehead, Ingleton, Carnforth,
North Yorkshire LA6 3AS
Tel: 01524 241274    **£ - P - 5 rooms**
Rural Pub close to railway station 12 miles
from Settle

**The Wheatsheaf**
22 High Street, Ingleton, Carnforth,
North Yorkshire LA6 3AD
Tel: 01524 241275    **£ - P - 9 rooms**
Web: smoothhound.co.uk/stayatthewheatsheaf
Country Pub 18 miles from Kendal

## KILNSEY
**Tennant Arms**
Kilnsey, nr Grassington,
North Yorkshire BD23 5PS
Tel: 01756 752301    **£ - P - 10 rooms**
Email: fred.bedford@btopenworld.com
Village Inn 12 miles from Skipton

## KIRKMOORSIDE
**Lion Inn**
Blakey Ridge, Kirkmoorside,
North Yorkshire YO62 7LQ
Tel: 01751 417320    **£ - P - 9 rooms**
Web: www.lionblakey.co.uk
Family run Inn with open fire

## KNARESBOROUGH
**The General Tarleton Inn**
Boroughbridge Road, Knaresborough,
North Yorkshire HG5 0QB
Tel: 01423 340284    **££ - P - 14 rooms**
Village Inn 3 miles from Knaresborough

## LEYBURN
**Sandpiper Inn**
Market Place, Leyburn,
North Yorkshire DL8 5AT
Tel: 01969 622206    **££ - P - 2 rooms**
Email: hsandpiper99@aol.com
17th century Inn located in the centre of
Leyburn

## LONG PRESTON, SKIPTON
**Maypole Inn**
Maypole Green, Main Street, Long Preston,
Skipton, North Yorkshire BD23 4PH
Tel: 01729 840219    **£ - P - 6 rooms**
Email: landlord@maypole.co.uk
Web: www.maypole.co.uk
17th century Inn located right on the village
green

## MALTON
**Suddaby's Crown Hotel**
See main entry on page 32

**Wentworth Arms Hotel**
111 Town Street, Old Malton, Malton,
North Yorkshire YO17 0HD
Tel: 01653 692618    **££ - P - 5 rooms**
Email: wentwortharms@btinternet.com
18th century Inn close to the North Yorkshire
moors

## MASHAM
**Bruce Arms Public House**
3 Little Market Place, Masham, nr Rippon,
North Yorkshire HG4 4DY
Tel: 01765 689372    **£ - 2 rooms**
Community local 10 miles from Rippon

## MIDDLEHAM
**Black Swan Hotel**
Market Place, Middleham,
North Yorkshire DL8 4NP
Tel: 01969 622221    **£ - 7 rooms**
Located in the centre of this market town

# Suddaby's Crown Hotel

*12 Wheelgate, Malton, North Yorkshire YO17 7HP*

**P - 9 rooms**

Tel: 01653 692038
Email: suddaby@crownhotel.plus.com
Web: www.suddabyscrown.co.uk

Suddaby's Crown Hotel is a Georgian Inn at the centre of the Market Town Wheelgate Malton twixt York and the Moors / Coast, and has it's own brewery at the rear of the premises. There are nine comfortable bedrooms including two *en suite* rooms in the annexe, these are open all year round, except for Christmas.

---

### MIDDLEHAM, LEYBURN
**Black Bull Inn**
Market Place, Middleham, Leyburn,
North Yorkshire DL8 4NX
Tel: 01969 623669    **£ - 3 rooms**
Email:  blackbull@tinyworld.co.uk
Country Inn in the centre of this market town

### NESBOROUGH
**Board Inn**
3 High Street, Nesborough,
North Yorkshire HG5 0ET
Tel: 01423 863314    **£ - P - 5 rooms**
Located in the centre of this historic market
town 14 miles from York

### NORTHALLERTON
**The Blue Bell Inn**
Ingleby Cross, Northallerton,
North Yorkshire DL6 3NF
Tel: 01609 882272    **£ - P - 5 rooms**
Email: david.kinsella@tesco.net
Close to teesside and the North Yorkshire
moors, ideal for walkers

### NORTHALLERTON
**The Wishing Well Inn**
Great Langton, Northallerton,
North Yorkshire DL7 0TE
Tel: 01609 748233    **£ - P - 4 rooms**
Email: liz.boynton@ukonline.co.uk
Village Inn 7 miles from Northallerton

**White Swan Inn**
Danby Wiske, Northallerton,
North Yorkshire DL7 0NQ
Tel: 01609 770122    **£ - P - 4 rooms**
Web: www.coast2coast.co.uk\whiteswaninn
Village Inn 4 miles from North Alington

### OLDSTEAD, NR HELMSLEY
**The Black Swan Inn**
See main entry on page 33

### PATELEY BRIDGE
**The Sportsmans Arms Hotel**
Wath-in-Nidderdale, Pateley Bridge, North
Yorkshire, HG3 5PP
Tel: 01423 711306    **££ - P - 11 rooms**
Village Inn with hotel located 14 miles from
Harrogate

### PICKERING
**The Black Swan**
18 Birdgate, Pickering, North Yorkshire
YO18 7AL
Tel: 01751 472286    **£ - P - 9 rooms**
Town centre hotel with a public bar

**Fox and Hounds Country Inn**
Sinnington, Pickering, North Yorkshire
Tel: 01751 431577    **££ - P - 10 rooms**
Email: roomsfoxhoundsinn@easynet.co.uk
Provides catering for all the family, AA 2 star
rated

# The Black Swan Inn

*Oldstead, nr Helmsley,
North Yorkshire YO61 4BL*

**££ - P - R - BM - BG - PW - C - 6 rooms**

Tel / Fax: 01347 868387
Email: blackswan@oldstead.fsworld.co.uk
Web: www.theblackswaninn.com

The Black Swan Inn overlooks rolling meadows and woodland and with its own beer garden, within easy reach of many of Yorkshire's best loved attractions.

The Drovers Bar, with its open fires, stone flagged floor and beamed ceiling, was once a stopping place for early travellers. Traditional ales are served from the Robert 'Mousey' Thompson built wooden bar, which features the famous Thomson mouse.

The comprehensive menu comprises a blend of traditional homemade Yorkshire fare and a variety of more international dishes. Pets are welcome in all our rooms and bar area. The area around the Black Swan makes for an ideal dog-walking environment for the whole family. Room tariff starts at Single £35.00 and Double £59.00

PICKERING
**The Horseshoe Inn**
Levisham, Pickering,
North Yorkshire YO18 7NL
Tel: 01751 460240     **£ - P - 6 rooms**
Village Inn 8 miles from Pickering

**The New Inn**
Thornton-le-Dale, Pickering,
North Yorkshire YO18 7LF
Tel: 01751 474226     **£ - P - Rooms**
Traditional Inn with open fires, weekend packages available

PICKHILL
**Nags Head Country Inn**
Pickhill, North Yorkshire YO7 4JG
Tel: 01845 567391     **££ - P - 17 rooms**
Country Pub off the A1 7 miles from Thirsk

POTTO, NORTHALLERTON
**Dog and Gun Inn**
2 Cooper Lane, Potto, Northallerton,
North Yorkshire DL6 3HQ
Tel: 01642 700232     **£ - P - 5 rooms**
Country Inn 5 miles From Stokesley

RICHMOND
**Bay Horse Inn**
Ravensworth, Richmond,
North Yorkshire DL11 7ET
Tel: 01325 718328     **£ - P - 1 room**
Country Inn 10 miles from Darlington

**Black Lion Hotel**
12 Finkle Street, Richmond,
North Yorkshire DL10 4QB
Tel: 01748 823121     **£ - P - 13 rooms**
Town centre Pub

**The Buck Inn**
27 - 29 Newbiggin, Richmond,
North Yorkshire DL10 4DX
Tel: 01748 822259     **£ - P - 6 rooms**
Olde world Pub near the town centre

**The Buck Hotel**
Reeth, Richmond,
North Yorkshire DL11 6SW
Tel: 01748 884210     **££ - 10 rooms**
Email: enquiries@buckhotel.co.uk
Web: www.buckhotel.co.uk
Village Inn 12 miles from Richmond

# The Shoulder of Mutton Inn

*Kirby Hill, Richmond, North Yorkshire DL11 7JH*

Tel: 01748 822772
Email: info@shoulderofmutton.net
Web: www.shoulderofmutton.net

A 200 old traditional inn, The Shoulder Of Mutton stands on the edge of the tiny, picturesque village of Kirby Hill and enjoys magnificent views of Holmedale. It is an ideal base from which to explore the magnificent North Yorkshire Dales National Park, the North York Moors National Park, the North Pennine Valleys and the East Yorkshire coastline.

Open log fires burn in the bar area, where guests may enjoy drinks (including hand-pulled cask ales, a large selection of malt whiskies and a comprehensive wine list) and bar meals in a relaxing atmosphere.

Our comfortable accommodation comprises four double rooms and one family room, all with *en suite* facilities, colour televisions and tea/coffee trays.

**Charles Bathurst Inn**
Arkengarthdaly, Richmond,
North Yorkshire DL11 6EN
Tel: 01748 884567      **££ - P - 18 rooms**
Email: info@cbinn.co.uk
Web: www.cbinn.co.uk
Country Inn 15 miles from Richmond

**Dalesway Lodge**
Scotch Corner, Richmond,
North Yorkshire DL10 6NT
Tel: 01748 822833      **£ - P - 6 rooms**
Family run hotel and bar 3 miles from
Richmond

**The Shoulder of Mutton Inn**
See main entry above

RIPON
**The Bull Inn**
Church Street, Ripon,
North Yorkshire HG4 6JQ
Tel: 01677 470678      **££ - P - 5 rooms**
Village Inn 4 miles from Ripon

**White Horse**
61 North Street, Ripon,
North Yorkshire HG4 1EN
Tel: 01765 603622      **£ - 8 rooms**
Town Pub 150 yards from the centre

ROSEDALE ABBEY
**The Milburn Arms Hotel**
Rosedale Abbey, North Yorkshire YO18 8RA
Tel: 01751 417312      **££ - P - 11 rooms**
Email: info@milburnarms.co.uk
Web: www.milburnarms.co.uk
Large village Inn/hotel 10 miles from Pickering

SCARBOROUGH
**Cellars**
35–37 Valley Road, Scarborough,
North Yorkshire YO11 2LX
Tel: 01723 367158      **£ - P - 11 apartments**
Town centre Pub 5 minutes from the beach

**Falcon Inn**
Whitby Road, Cloughton, Scarborough,
North Yorkshire YO13 0DY
Tel: 01723 870717      **£ - P - 6 rooms**
Country Pub 7 miles from Scarborough

SETTLE
**Golden Lion Hotel**
Duke Street, Settle,
North Yorkshire BD24 9DU
Tel: 01729 822203      **Rooms**
Email: bookings@goldenlion.yorks.net
Web: www.yorkshirenet.co.uk/stayat/goldenlion
17th century town centre hotel and bar

**The Talbot Arms**
High Street, Settle, North Yorkshire BD24 9EX
Tel: 01729 824452    **3 rooms**
Email: carmeltassie@aol.com
Family run town Pub

SHAROW, RIPON
**Half Moon Inn**
Sharow Lane, Sharow, Ripon,
North Yorkshire HG4 5BP
Tel: 01765 600291    **£ - P - 3 rooms**
Email: halfmoon@bronco.co.uk
Web: www.ripon.org/Webads/halfmoon
Village Inn 2 minutes drive to Ripon

SKIPTON
**Blue Bell Inn**
Kettlewell, Skipton,
North Yorkshire BD23 5QX
Tel: 01756 760230    **P - Rooms**
Email: info@bluebellinn.co.uk
Web: www.bluebellinn.co.uk
17th century coaching Inn. Home-cooked
meals. Traditional ale

**Craven Heifer Inn**
Grassington Road, Skipton,
North Yorkshire BD23 3LA
Tel: 01756 792521    **£ - P - 20 rooms**
Email  philandlyn@cravenheifer.co.uk
Web: www.cravenheifer.co.uk
Traditional Inn with views over the Dales

**Dog and Partridge**
Tosside, Skipton, North Yorkshire BD23 4SQ
Tel: 01729 840668    **£ - P - 4 rooms**
Coaching Inn 7 miles from Settle

**The Red Lion Hotel**
See main entry below

**The Tempest Arms**
Elslack, Skipton,
North Yorkshire BD23 3AY
Tel: 01282 842450    **P - Rooms**
A traditional rural Yorkshire Inn

SCAGGLETHORPE NR MALTON
**The Ham and Cheese Inn**
See main entry on page 36

SOUTH END, OSMOTHERELY
**Three Tuns Inn**
South End, Osmotherley,
North Yorkshire DL6 3BN
Tel: 01609 883301    **££ - P - 7 rooms**
Inn with restaurant 8 miles from Nth Allerton

STOKESLEY
**The Buck Inn**
Chopgate, Stokesley, Middlesborough,
North Yorkshire TS9 7JL
Tel: 01642 778334    **£ - P - 5 rooms**
Email: buckinn@aol.com
Village Inn located just 5 miles from Stokesley

---

# The Red Lion Hotel

*By the Bridge at Burnsall, Skipton,*
*North Yorkshire BD23 6BU*

**P - Rooms**

Tel: 01756 720204
Email: redlion@daelnet.co.uk

The Red Lion Hotel is a 16th Century Ferryman's Inn set on the banks of the River Wharfe in the loveliest of Yorkshire Dales villages.

This welcoming hostelry offers a traditional Oak panelled bar serving real ales and excellent wines – an AA rosette restaurant and superb bar / brassiere menu featuring locally reared meat and game. Characteristic accommodation, antiques, log fires, beamed ceilings, fantastic walking and fishing. Civil Wedding licence and up-to-date conference facilities.

# The Ham and Cheese Inn

Scagglethorpe Nr Malton, North Yorkshire YO17 8DY

**£ - P - Rooms**

Tel: 01944 758249

Whether it's the coast or the countryside you prefer, the Ham and Cheese Inn is a perfect spot to enjoy a warm and relaxing time. Situated halfway between York and Scarborough near to the A64. Our rooms are *en suite* and tastefully decorated.

After enjoying a traditional English meal prepared and served by our professional catering team. You can sample our first class ales and wines whilst relaxing around the large log fire.
Prices from £24.50 per person B&B

### THIRSK
**Lord Nelson Inn**
40–41 St James Green, Thirsk,
North Yorkshire YO7 1AQ
Tel: 01845 522845    **£ - P - 4 rooms**
Email: cot@supanet.com
Market town Inn just 2 minutes walk to the centre

**Whitestonecliffe Inn**
Sutton-under-Whitestonecliffe, Thirsk,
North Yorkshire YO7 2PR
Tel: 01845 597271    **££ - P - 6 rooms**
Web: www.whitestonecliffe.co.uk
Village Inn 4 miles from Thirsk

**Ye Jolly Farmers of Olden Times**
Dalton, Thirsk, North Yorkshire YO7 3HY
Tel: 01845 577359    **£ - P - 4 rooms**
Traditional village Inn located 4 miles from Thirsk

### THORGANBY
**Jefferson Arms**
Thorganby, North Yorkshire YO4 6DB
Tel: 01904 448316    **££ - P - 5 rooms**
Village Inn 8 miles from York

### THORNTON WATLASS
**The Buck Inn**
Thornton Watlass, North Yorkshire HG4 4AH
Tel: 01677 422461    **££ - P - 7 rooms**
Country Inn 3 miles from Bedale

### THRESHFIELD
**The Old Hall Inn**
Threshfield, North Yorkshire BD23 5HB
Tel: 01756 752441    **P - 4 rooms**
                            **+ 1 cottage**
Local village Inn located just 9 miles from Skipton

### UPPER POPPLETON
**Red Lion Motel and Country Inn**
Boroughbridge Road, Upper Poppleton, York,
North Yorkshire YO26 6PR
Tel: 01904 781141    **£ - P - 17 rooms**
Email: reservations@redlionhotel.com
Web: www.redlionhotel.com
Country Inn 3 miles from York

### WASS
**Wombwell Arms**
Wass, North Yorkshire YO6 4BE
Tel: 01347 868280    **££ - P - 3 rooms**
A country village Inn located 9 miles from Thirsk

### WEAVERTHORPE, MALTON
**The Star Inn**
See main entry on page 37

**The Bluebell Inn**
Main Street, Weaverthorpe, Malton,
North Yorkshire YO17 8EX
Tel: 01944 738204    **£ - P - 7 rooms**
Village Inn 10 miles from Driffield

# The Star Inn

*Weaverthorpe, Malton, North Yorkshire YO17 8EY*

**£ - P - Rooms**

Tel: 01944 738273    Fax: 01944 738273
Email: info@starinn.net    Web: www.starinn.net

The Star Inn is in the midst of the Yorkshire Wolds. This well renowned award winning village inn offers quality accommodation, an excellent reputation for fine food and traditional real ales.

Listed in the *CAMRA Good Beer Guide* continuously for 16 years, also in the AA Top 500 and English Tourist Board 3 Diamond quality assurance rated. Ideally located for York, East Coast and North York Moors National Park.

# The Wensleydaye Heifer Inn

*West Witton, Wensleydale, North Yorkshire DL8 4LS*

**P**

Tel: 01969 622322    Fax: 01969 624183
Email: info@wensleydaleheifer.co.uk

This beautifully restored 17th century coaching inn has welcomed visitors to the Dales for over 370 years. The Wensleydale Heifer Inn nestles in the picturesque village of West Witton in the heart of Wensleydale and The Yorkshire Dales National Park, making it the perfect base from which to enjoy the green dales and brooding moors. Beautifully restored, The Wensleydale Heifer celebrates the traditions of a coaching inn – roaring open fires, cosy snugs, fine food and luxurious bedrooms.

Each of the hotel's nine *en suite* bedrooms are individually and richly decorated using local landmarks as themes. Three of the rooms have four-poster beds. Exposed stonework and beams, and crackling log fires create the atmosphere in the Heifer's award-winning restaurant, bistro and pub dining areas.

WEST AYTON
**Ye Olde Forge Valley Inn**
5 Pickington Road, West Ayton, nr
Scarborough, North Yorkshire YO13 9JE
Tel: 01723 862146    **£ - P - 5 rooms**
Village Inn 5 miles from Scarborough

WESTOW
**Blacksmiths Arms**
Main Street, Westow, York, North Yorkshire
Tel: 01653 618365    **£ - P - 6 rooms**
Email: blacksmithsinn@cwcom.net
Family Pub caters for special needs

WEST WITTON, WENSLEYDALE
**The Wensleydale Heifer Inn**
See main entry on page 37

WHITBY
**Beehive Inn**
New Holm, Whitby,
North Yorkshire YO21 3QY
Tel: 01947 602703    **£ - P - 3 rooms**
A 15th century drovers Inn 2 miles from
Whitby

**The Eskdale Inn**
Station Road, Castleton, Whitby,
North Yorkshire YO21 2EU
Tel: 01287 660234    **£ - P - 3 rooms**
Village Inn 5 minutes drive from Castletown

**The Flask Inn**
Robin Hoods Bay, Whitby,
North Yorkshire YO22 4QH
Tel: 01947 880305    **£ - P - 6 rooms**
Email: flaskinn@aol.com
Web: www.flaskinn.com
16th century Inn located on the A171 close to
North Yorkshire Moors National Park

**Ye Horseshoe Inn**
Egton, Whitby, North Yorkshire YO21 1TZ
Tel: 01947 895274    **£ - P - 3 rooms**
Lovely village Inn 7 miles from Whitby

WIGGLESWORTH, SKIPTON
**The Plough Inn**
See main entry below

WRELTON, PICKERING
**The Huntsman Hotel**
Main Street, Wrelton, Pickering,
North Yorkshire YO18 8PG
Tel: 01751 472530    **£ - P - 3 rooms**
Email: howard@thehuntsman.freeserve.co.uk
Web: www.europage.co.uk/huntsman
Special needs are catered for, also offers
bargain breaks

YORK
**The Bay Horse Inn**
York Road, Green Hammerton, York,
North Yorkshire YO26 8BN
Tel: 01423 331113    **£ - P - 10 rooms**
Email: bayhorsepc@aol.com
Web: www.thebayhorse.com
Village Inn 8 miles from York

**Burton Stone Inn**
34 Clifton, York, North Yorkshire YO30 6AW
Tel: 01904 622945    **£ - P - 5 rooms**
Village Inn 5 minutes walk from York walls

**Clifton Hotel**
Water Lane, York, North Yorkshire YO30 6PL
Tel: 01904 692923    **£ - P - 4 rooms**
Local Pub with a childrens play area 15min-
utes walk from the city centre

**Cross Keys Hotel**
34 Goodramgate, York,
North Yorkshire YO1 7LS
Tel: 01904 686941    **££ - P - 3 rooms**
Situated right next to York Minster

---

# The Plough Inn

*Wigglesworth, Skipton, North Yorkshire BD23 4RJ*

**P**

**Tel: 01729 840243**
Email: sue@ploughinn.info   Web: www.ploughinn.info

Located in the peaceful village of Wigglesworth, The Plough Inn has magnificent views of Pen-
y-ghent and Ingleborough and is ideally situated for exploring the wonderful countryside of the
Yorkshire Dales National Park and the Forest of Bowland Area of Outstanding Natural Beauty.
There are 12 comfortable, well-appointed *en suite* rooms (all rooms are non-smoking).

# The Old Grey Mare

*Clifton Green, York, North Yorkshire YO30 6LH*

**£ - P - R - BG - rooms**

Tel: 01904 654485     Fax: 01904 679703
Email: terryoldgreymare@tinyworld.co.uk
Web: www.oldgreymare.com

Just 10 minutes walk to the centre of the historic City of York, this former coaching inn dates back to the 17th Century, The Old Grey Mare provides ideal accommodation with a friendly family run atmosphere, candlelit restaurant and games room, beer garden and open fireplaces. Our tastefully decorated rooms have *en suite* facilities, colour television, tea and coffee facilities. Children are more than welcome to stay in our large family rooms.

**The Crown**
Roecliffe, York, North Yorkshire YO51 9LY
Tel: 01423 322578     **£ - P - 9 rooms**
Email: crownroecliffe@btinternet.com
Located in a pretty hamlet 18 miles from York

**The Foresters Arms**
Kilburn, York, North Yorkshire YO6 4AH
Tel: 01347 868386     **££ - P - 10 rooms**
Email: forresters@destination-england-co.uk
Web: www.destination-england.co.uk/foresters

Local village Inn located around 6 miles from Thirsk

**Old Black Bull Inn**
Raskelf, York, North Yorkshire YO6 3LF
Tel: 01347 821431     **£ - P - 6 rooms**
Email: pjacksobbull@bizonline.co.uk
Village Inn 8 miles from Thirsk

**The Old Grey Mare**
See main entry above

# SOUTH YORKSHIRE

Barnsley     Doncaster
South Yorkshire
Hope Valley     Rotherham
• Sheffield

## ATTERCLIFFE, SHEFFIELD
**The Noose and Gibbet Inn**
97 Broughton Lane, Attercliffe, Sheffield,

South Yorkshire S9 2DE
Tel: 01142 617182     **£ - 14 rooms**
Town Pub just 10 minutes tram ride to the centre

## BARNSLEY
**Bottom Mill Inn**
Park Road, Barnsley,
South Yorkshire S70 5LJ
Tel: 01226 282639     **£ - P - 7 rooms**
Email: jimboloftus@aol.com
Inn with a restaurant, within a Country Park, 2 miles from Barnsley

# Churchills Hotel

*1 High Street, Wombwell, Barnsley, South Yorkshire S73 0DA*

Tel: 01226 340099    Fax: 01226 211126
Email: churchillshotel@btconnect.com
Web: www.churchillshotel-wombwell.co.uk

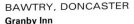

At Churchills we combine good old-fashioned Yorkshire hospitality with the highest standards of accommodation, good food, friendly service and competitive tariffs. The hotel has recently been extensively refurbished, and all 15 rooms are provided with *en suite* facilities. Our twin and double tariff starts from £39.50. We have a number of executive suites that can be offered at special rates.

At Churchills we pride ourselves on our food, whether you prefer a quiet meal in our beautiful Spencer Suite restaurant, or a steak in the Squires Bar, you can be assured of good food, great value, great atmosphere and first class service.

Our lively Squires Bar, situated on the ground floor, is open throughout the year. There is a wide variety of entertainment four evenings a week.

---

BAWTRY, DONCASTER
**Granby Inn**
High Street, Bawtry, Doncaster, South
Yorkshire DN10 6JA
Tel: 01302 710219    **£ - P - 8 rooms**
Village Inn 9 miles from Doncaster

BRADFIELD
**The Strines Inn**
Bradfield Dale, Bradfield,
South Yorkshire S6 6JE
Tel: 01142 851247    **££ - P - 3 rooms**
Country Inn 15 minute drive to Sheffield

CHAPELTOWN, SHEFFIELD
**Coach and Horses**
13 Station Road, Chapeltown, Sheffield,
South Yorkshire S35 2XE
Tel: 01142 467595    **£ - P - 8 rooms**
Village Pub 7 miles from Sheffield

CUBLEY, PENISTONE
**Cubley Hall**
Mortimer Road, Cubley, Penistone, South
Yorkshire S36 9DF
Tel: 01226 766086    **££ - P - Rooms**

Email: cubley.hall@ukonline.co.uk
18th century Inn set in its own grounds

DODWORTH, BARNSLEY
**Travellers Inn**
23 Green Road, Dodworth, Barnsley,
South Yorkshire S75 2RR
Tel: 01226 284173    **£ - P - 4 rooms**
Email: jeremy@travellersinn.freeserve.co.uk
Village Inn 3 miles from Barnsley

BARRTHALL, PARKGATE
**Fitzwilliam Arms**
Taylors Lane, Barrthall, Parkgate, Rotherham,
South Yorkshire S62 5EE
Tel: 01709 522744    **£ - P - 18 rooms**
Local Pub 4 miles from Rotherham

INGBIRCHWORTH, PENISTONE
**Fountain Inn**
Wellthorne Lane, Ingbirchworth, Penistone,
Sheffield, South Yorkshire S36 7GJ
Tel: 01226 763125    **££ - P - 10 rooms**
Email: reservations@fountain-inn.co.uk
Web: www.fountain-inn.co.uk
Country Inn 10 minutes drive to Barnsley

ROTHERHAM
**Moulders Rest Hotel**
Masborough Street, Rotherham, South
Yorkshire S60 1EG
Tel: 01709 560095   **Rooms**
Town bar

SHALESMOOR, SHEFFIELD
**Nags Head**
Shalesmoor, Sheffield,
South Yorkshire S3 8UJ
Tel: 01142 726626   **Rooms**
Town centre Pub

SHEFFIELD
**Norfolk Arms**
Chapeltown, Sheffield,
South Yorkshire S35 2YG
Tel: 01142 468414   **£ - P - 10 rooms**
Village Inn, nr J35a of the M1

**Wagon and Horses**
Langsett, Stocksbridge, Sheffield,
South Yorkshire S36 4GY
Tel: 01226 763147   **£ - P - 3 rooms**
Email: info@langsettinn.com
Web: www.langsettinn.com
Village Inn midway between Sheffield and
Barnsley

**Wortley Arms Hotel**
Halifax Road, Wortley Village, Sheffield,
South Yorkshire S35 7DB
Tel: 01142 882245   **£ - P - 3 rooms**
Village Inn located between Sheffield and
Barnsley

WOMBWELL, BARNSLEY
**Churchills Hotel**
See main entry on page 40

# TYNE & WEAR

HEATON
**The Corner House**
Heaton Road, Heaton, Newcastle-upon-Tyne,
Tyne-and-Wear NE6 5RP
Tel: 01912 659602   **£ - P - 9 rooms**
Traditional Inn 2 miles from the city centre

NEWBURN,
NEWCASTLE-UPON-TYNE
**The Keelman's Lodge**
Grange Road, Newburn, Newcastle-upon-
Tyne, Tyne-and-Wear NE15 8NL
Tel: 01912 671689   **£ - P - 6 rooms**
Email: admin@petersen-stainless.co.uk
Web: www.petersen-stainless.co.uk
Riverside Lodge, next to "The Big Lamp
Brewery and Pub"

NEWCASTLE-UPON-TYNE
**Bellegrove Hotel**
19–20 Bellegrove Terrace, Newcastle-upon-
Tyne, Tyne-and-Wear NE2 4LL
Tel: 01912 325837   **£ - P - 5 rooms**
Located 2 minutes from the town centre

**The Edgefield Lodge**
Edgefield Avenue, Newcastle-upon-Tyne,
Tyne-and-Wear
Tel: 01912 858174   **£ - P - 10 rooms**
Local Pub, short Metro ride to the city centre

WHITLEY BAY
**Caprice Hotel**
14–16 South Parade, Whitley Bay, Tyne-and-Wear NE26 2RG
Tel: 01912 530141    **£ - P - 20 rooms**
Hotel with Pub 300 yards from the sea

**The Waterford Arms**
Collywell Bay Road, Whitley Bay,
Tyne-and-Wear NE26 4QZ
Tel: 01912 370450    **££ - Rooms**
Located near the fishing harbour. Good sea views

# WEST YORKSHIRE

Tel: 01274 721784    **£ - P - 13 rooms**
Town Pub 10 minutes walk from the centre

**Prince of Wales**
Harrowgate Road, Bradford, West Yorkshire
Tel: 01274 638729    **£ - Rooms**
Local town Pub on the Outskirts of Bradford

**Victoria Hotel**
10 Cottinley Road, Bradford,
West Yorkshire BD15 9JP
Tel: 01274 823820    **£ - P - 6 rooms**
Village Inn 4 miles from Bradford

BIRSTALL
**Oakwell Motel**
Lower Lane, Birstall,
West Yorkshire WF17 9HD
Tel: 01924 441514    **£ - P - Rooms**
Motel with a public bar on the main road to Birstall

BRADFORD
**Castle Hotel**
20 Grattan, Bradford, West Yorkshire BD1 2LU
Tel: 01274 393166    **£ - P - 8 rooms**
Located in the centre of Bradford

**The Melborn Hotel**
104 White Abbey Road, Bradford,
West Yorkshire
Tel: 01274 726867    **£ - P - 5 rooms**
Down to earth music Pub. 1 mile from Bradford city centre

**New Beehive Inn**
171 Westgate, Bradford,
West Yorkshire BD1 3AA

BRIGHOUSE
**The Black Bull**
46 Briggate, Thornton Square, Brighouse,
West Yorkshire HD6 1EF
Tel: 01484 714816    **£ - P - 6 rooms**
Email: katrina@bitmember.net
Web: www.westel.co.uk/blackbull
Town centre hotel / Pub

CLECKHEATON
**Wickham Arms**
15 St Peg Lane, Cleckheaton,
West Yorkshire BD19 3SA
Tel: 01274 873936    **££ - P - 10 rooms**
Located in a small town 7 miles from Bradford, off the M62

CLIFTON
**Black Horse Inn**
Clifton, West Yorkshire HD6 4HJ
Tel: 01484 713862    **££ - P - 21 rooms**
Quaint village Inn located 15 minutes from Leeds

CROSS HILLS
**Dalesway Inn**
Skipton Road, Cross Hills, West Yorkshire
Tel: 01535 633618      **£ - P - 5 rooms**
Village Inn 3 miles from Skipton

DEWSBURY
**Beer Street**
2 Kowells Yard, Boothroyd Lane, Dewsbury,
West Yorkshire WF13 2RE
Tel: 01924 466207      **£ - P - rooms**
Town centre Pub, ideal workers' low cost
accommodation

**Jack D's**
33 Westgate, Dewsbury,
West Yorkshire WF13 1JQ
Tel: 01924 456209      **£ - 9 rooms**
Busy town centre Pub

GREETLAND, HALIFAX
**Rose and Crown**
98 Rochdale Road, Greetland, Halifax,
West Yorkshire HX4 8HR
Tel: 01422 373017      **£ - P - 4 rooms**
Old traditional rural Pub 3 miles from Halifax

HALIFAX
**The Grove Inn**
Burnley Road, Brearley Luddenfoot, Halifax,
West Yorkshire HX2 6HS
Tel: 01422 883235      **£ - P - 3 rooms**
Village Inn 5 miles from Halifax

**The Rock Inn Hotel**
Holywell Green, Halifax,
West Yorkshire HX4 9BS
Tel: 01422 379721      **££ - P - 30 rooms**
Large  bar / restaurant / hotel set in a scenic
valley 3 miles from Halifax

HAREWOOD
**Harewood Arms Hotel**
Harrogate Road, Harewood,
West Yorkshire  LS17 9LH
Tel: 01132 886566      **££ - P - 23 rooms**
A former old coaching Inn 7 miles from Leeds

HAWORTH
**3 Sisters Hotel**
Brow Top Road, Haworth,

West Yorkshire BD22 9PH
Tel: 01535 643458      **£ - P - 9 rooms**
Small country hotel / Inn 5 minute drive to
Bradford

**Howarth Old Hall**
Sun Street, Haworth, nr Keighley,
West Yorkshire
Tel: 01535 642709      **Rooms**
An historic Inn at the foot of the cobbled main
street

**Old Sun Hotel**
79 West Lane, Haworth, Keighley,
West Yorkshire BD22 8EL
Tel: 01535 642780      **£ - P rooms**
Country Inn 3 miles from Keighley

**The Old White Lion Hotel**
Main Street, Haworth,
West Yorkshire BD22 8DU
Tel: 01535 642313      **££ - P - 14 rooms**
Email: enquiries@theoldwhitelionhotel
Village Inn 4 miles from Keighley

HEBDEN BRIDGE
**Hinchcliffe Arms**
Cragg Vale, Hebden Bridge,
West Yorkshire HX7 5TA
Tel: 01422 883256      **£ - P - 3 rooms**
Web: www.hinchcliffearms.com
Country Inn 4 miles from Hebden Bridge

HOLMFIRTH, HUDDERSFIELD
**Red Lion Inn**
Sheffield Road, Jackson Bridge, Holmfirth,
Huddersfield, West Yorkshire HD7 7HS
Tel: 01484 683499      **£ - 6 rooms**
Located close to the Peak District and
Yorkshire Dales

HORBURY
**Quarry Inn and Cottages**
70 Quarry Hill, Horbury,
West Yorkshire WF4 5NE
Tel: 01924 272523      **£ - P - 4 rooms**
Village Inn 10 minutes drive from Wakefield

HUDDERSFIELD
**O'Neill's**
29 Queensgate, Huddersfield, West Yorkshire

Tel: 01484 412931    **£ - 6 rooms**
Huddersfield town centre near the University

**KIRKBURTON**
**Woodman Inn at Thunderbridge**
Kirkburton, nr Huddersfield,
West Yorkshire HD8 0PX
Tel: 01484 605778    **££ - P - 12 rooms**
Email: thewoodman@connectfree.co.uk
Village Inn 4 miles from Huddersfield

**LIVERSEDGE**
**Lillibets**
Leeds Road, Liversedge,
West Yorkshire WF15 6HX
Tel: 01924 404911    **£ - P - 6 rooms**
Local town Pub 2 miles from Dewsbury

**MARSDEN, WEST YORKSHIRE**
**The Olive Branch**
Manchester Road, Marsden,
West Yorkshire HD7 6LU
Tel: 01484 844487    **££ - P - 3 rooms**
Village Inn 5 minute drive to Marsden

**MARSH, HUDDERSFIELD**
**Croppers Arms**
136 Westbourne Road, Marsh, Huddersfield,
West Yorkshire HD1 47F
Tel: 01484 421522    **£ - P - 6 rooms**
Family run country Inn 2 miles from
Huddersfield

**MORLEY, LEEDS**
**Nelson Arms**
84 Victoria Road, Morley, Leeds,
West Yorkshire LS27 8LS
Tel: 01132 533527    **£ - P - 5 rooms**
Town Pub

**OGDEN**
**Moorlands Inn**
Keighley Road, Ogden,
West Yorkshire HX2 8XD
Tel: 01422 248943    **Rooms**
Town Pub

**OULTON, LEEDS**
**New Masons Arms**
26 Aberford Road, Oulton, Leeds,
West Yorkshire LS26 8JR

Tel: 01132 822334    **£ - P - Rooms**
Semi-rural Pub 5 miles from Leeds centre

**PONTEFRACT**
**Horse Vaults**
2 Horse Fair, Pontefract,
West Yorkshire WF8 1PD
Tel: 01977 702672    **£ - P – Rooms**
Town Pub located in the centre of Pontefract

**Old Church Tavern**
Northbaileygate, Pontefract,
West Yorkshire WF8 2JG
Tel: 01977 798899    **£ - P - Rooms**
Local Pub on the outskirts of town

**POOL-IN-WHARFEDALE**
**Half Moon Inn**
Main Street, Pool, West Yorkshire LS21 1LH
Tel: 01132 842878    **£ - P - 5 rooms**
Village Inn 8 miles from Leeds

**ROBERTTOWN, LIVERSEDGE**
**New Inn**
Robert Town Lane, Roberttown, Liversedge,
West Yorkshire WF15 7NP
Tel: 01924 402069    **££ - P rooms**
Village Pub with restaurant 5 miles from
Huddersfield

**SHELF, HALIFAX**
**Duke of York Inn**
West Street, Shelf, Halifax,
West Yorkshire HX3 7LN
Tel: 01422 202056    **£ - P - 6 rooms**
Email: dukeofyork@england.com
Web: www.dukeofyork.co.uk
Village Inn 2 miles from Halifax

**SHELLEY, HUDDERSFIELD**
**The Three Acres Inn**
Roydhouse, Shelley, Huddersfield,
West Yorkshire HD8 8LR
Tel: 01484 602606    **££ - P - 20 rooms**
Email: 3acres@globalnet.co.uk
Village Inn close to the cities and motorways

**STANBURY, KEIGHLEY**
**The Old Silent Inn**
Hob Lane, Stanbury, Keighley,
West Yorkshire BD22 0HW

Tel: 01535 647437    **££ - P - 9 rooms**
Traditional village Inn with open log fires

**WAINSTALLS, HALIFAX**
**Crossroad Inn**
Mount Tabor Road, Wainstalls, Halifax,
West Yorkshire HX2 7BV
Tel: 01422 245316    **£ - P - 7 rooms**
Country inn with spectacular viewsx

**WAKEFIELD**
**Bolands Bar**
2 Union Street, Wakefield, West Yorkshire
Tel: 01924 372036    **£ - 4 rooms**
Town centre pub

**Elephant and Castle**
109 Westgate, Wakefield, West Yorkshire
Tel: 01924 376610    **£ - 4 rooms**
Local Pub on the outskirts of Wakefield

**Kirkland Hotel**
605 Leeds Road, Wakefield,
West Yorkshire WF1 2LU
Tel: 01924 826666    **£ - P - 6 rooms**
Email: kirkland@rapidmail.co.uk
Local pub 2 miles from Wakefield
town centre

**Whitehart**
77 Westgate End, Wakefield,
West Yorkshire WF2 9RL
Tel: 01924 375887    **£ - P - 8 rooms**
Local pub on the outskirts of Wakefield

**WIDDOP**
**Pack Horse Inn**
Widdop, West Yorkshire HX7 7AT
Tel: 01422 842803    **£ - P - 3 rooms**
Countryside Inn located 5 miles from
Hebden

# Central England

## CAMBRIDGESHIRE

**ELY**
**The Flyer Hotel**
69 Newnham Street, Ely, Cambs CB7 4PQ
Tel: 01353 669200      **£ - P - 6 rooms**
Email: grahem@flyerhotel.co.uk
Web: www.flyerhotel.co.uk
Located 100 yards from Ely town centre

**GODMANCHESTER**
**Black Bull**
32 Post Street, Godmanchester,
Cambs PE18 8AQ
Tel: 01480 453310      **£££ - P - 8 rooms**
18th century coaching house 10 minute walk
to the town centre

**GRANTCHESTER**
**The Blue Ball Inn**
57 Broadway, Grantchester, Cambs
Tel: 01223 840679      **££ - 2 rooms**
Email: johnroos@ntlworld.com
Rural village within working distance to
Cambridge city centre

**HILTON, HUNTINGDON**
**The Prince Of Wales**
Potton Road, Hilton, Huntingdon,
Cambs PE18 9NG
Tel: 01480 830257      **££ - P - 4 rooms**
Email: princeofwales.hilton@talk21.com
Village Inn close to Huntingdon, CAMRA listed

**HOLYWELL**
**The Old Ferryboat Inn**
Holywell, Cambs PE17 3TG
Tel: 01480 463227      **££ - P - 7 rooms**
Riverside Inn 3 miles from St Ives

**HORSEHEATH**
**The Old Red Lion**
Linton Road, Horseheath, Cambs CB1 6QF
Tel: 01223 892909      **££ - P - 12 rooms**
Village Inn close to M11 5 miles from Haverhill

**BUCKDEN, ST NEOTS**
**George Coaching Inn**
High Street, Buckden, St Neots,
Cambs PE19 5XA
Tel: 01480 810307      **£ - P - 16 rooms**
Village Inn 5 miles from Huntingdon

**EATON SOCON, ST NEOTS**
**White Horse Inn**
103 Great North Road, Eaton Socon, St Neots,
Cambs PE19 8EL
Tel: 01480 474453      **££ - P - 3 rooms**
Village Inn 1 mile from St Neots

**ELLINGTON**
**The Mermaid**
High Street, Ellington, Cambs
Tel: 01480 891450      **£ - 2 rooms**
Village Pub 5 miles from Huntingdon

**ELTISLEY**
**The Leeds Arms**
See main entry opposite

# The Leeds Arms

*The Green, Eltisley, Huntingdon, Cambs PE19 6TG*

Reservations: 01480 880283   Guests: 01480 880516 / 7
Fax: 01480 880379

The Leeds Arms was built towards the end of the 18th Century. Constructed in the style of a "T" class building it has a central entrance and chimneys at each end of the range. Used as a coach stop in early times it has changed from a dwelling and public house to its current status of a village Free House Motel. A log fire completes the atmosphere of those early times.

Situated just off the A428 St Neots to Cambridge road, the Leeds Arms is sited on the village green overlooking the cricket clubhouse, which has an unusual thatched roof structure. The accommodation consists of three twin bedrooms with bath and six single rooms with shower, all rooms have colour television, coffee / tea facilities and telephone. The Motel rooms are separate from the main building.

## HUNTINGDON
**The Old Bridge House**
1 High Street, Huntingdon, Cambs PE18 6TQ
Tel: 01480 452681     **£££ - Rooms**
Stylish town house next to the river

## NEEDINGWORTH
**Pike and Eel Hotel and Marina**
Needingworth, nr St Ives, Cambs PE17 3TW
Tel: 01480 463336     **££ - P - 9 rooms**
Email: pikeandeel@btinternet.com
Riverside hotel and bar with restaurant

## PETERBOROUGH
**Prince of Wales**
Eastfield Road, Peterborough, Cambs PE1 4AN
Tel: 01733 319677     **Rooms**
Town Pub

## ST IVES
**Golden Lion Hotel**
Market Hill, St Ives, Cambs
Tel: 01480 492100     **£ - P - 20 rooms**
Email: goldenlion@netscape.co.uk
Town centre location

**White Hart Inn**
1 Sheep Market, St Ives, Cambs
Tel: 01480 463275     **£ - P - 3 rooms**
Town centre Inn

## SAINT NEOTS
**Kings Head**
South Street, Saint Neots, Cambs PE19 2BW
Tel: 01480 474094     **£ - 5 rooms**
Located in the centre of St Neots

## STILTON, nr PETERBOROUGH
**The Bell Inn**
Great North Road, Stilton, nr Peterborough,
Cambs PE7 3RA
Tel: 01733 241066     **££ - P - 19 rooms**
Where Stilton cheese was born

## STRETHAM, ELY
**The Red Lion**
47 High Street, Stretham, Ely, Cambs CB6 3JQ
Tel: 01353 648132     **£ - P - 12 rooms**
Email: frank.hayes@gateway.net
Web: www.redlion.org
Refurbished village Inn 4 miles from Ely

## SUTTON GAULT, ELY
**The Anchor Inn**
Bury Lane, Sutton Gault, Ely, Cambs CB6 2BD
Tel: 01353 778537     **££ - 2 rooms**
Riverside Inn specialising in fine food

## SWAFFHAM BULBECK
**The Black Horse**
High St, Swaffham Bulbeck, Cambs CB5 0HP

Tel: 01223 811366    **£ - P - 7 rooms**
Village Inn 6 miles from Newmarket

### TYDD ST GILES, WISBECH
**Crown and Mitre**
Tydd St Giles, Wisbech, Cambs PE13 5LF
Tel: 01945 870808    **£ - P - 2 rooms**
Village Inn 8 miles from Wisbech

### UPWELL, NEW WISBECH
**Five Bells Hotel**
1 New Rd, Upwell, New Wisbech, Cambs
PE14 9AA
Tel: 01945 772222    **££ - P 7 rooms**
Family Run, 5 miles from Wisbech

### WHITTLESEY
**George Hotel**
10 Market Place, Whittlesey, Peterborough,
Cambs PE7 1AB
Tel: 01733 202516    **£ - P - 4 rooms**
Situated in the centre of this market town

**Hero of Aliwal**
75 Church Street, Whittlesey, Cambs
Tel: 01733 203736    **£ - P - 5 rooms**

Located 200 yards from the town centre

**New Crown**
58 High Causeway, Whittlesey, Peterborough,
Cambs PE7 1QA
Tel: 01733 205134    **£ - P - 1 room**
Busy town Pub 5 minutes walk from town
centre

**Old Crown**
11 - 13 Gracious Street, Whittlesey,
Peterborough, Cambs PE7 1AP
Tel: 01733 203652    **£ - P - Rooms**
Town centre Pub

### WISBECH
**Angel Hotel**
45 Alexandra Road, Wisbech, Cambs PE13 1HT
Tel: 01945 589794    **£ - P - 4 rooms**
Town Pub 2 minutes walk from town centre

**Rose and Crown Hotel**
23–24 Market Place, Wisbech,
CambsPE13 1DG
Tel: 01945 589800    **££ - P - 30 rooms**
Town centre hotel with a busy public bar

# DERBYSHIRE

AMBERGATE, BELPER
**The Lord Nelson Inn**
Bullbridge, Ambergate, Belper,
Derbys DE56 2EW
Tel: 01773 852037    **£ - P - 5 rooms**
Country Pub 3 miles from Ripley

ASHBOURNE
**Bowling Green Inn**
North Avenue, Ashbourne, Derbys DE6 1EZ
Tel: 01335 342511    **£ - P - 3 rooms**
Rural Pub 500 yards from Ashbourne

**Ye Olde Vaults**
Market Place, Ashbourne, Derbys DE6 1EU
Tel: 01335 346127    **£ - P - 4 rooms**
Small town centre Pub

ASHBOURNE
**The Dog and Partridge Country Inn**
Swinscoe, Ashbourne, Derbys DE6 2HS
Tel: 01335 343183    **££ - P - 25 rooms**
17th century Inn near Alton Towers

**The Green Man**
St Johns Street, Ashbourne, Derbys DE6 1GH
Tel: 01335 345783    **£ - P - 18 rooms**
Town centre coaching Inn

BAKEWELL
**The Castle Inn**
Castle Street, Bakewell, Derbys DE45 1DU
Tel: 01629 812103    **£ - P - 4 rooms**
Located in the centre of Bakewell

**The Lathkil Hotel**
Over Haddon, Bakewell, Derbys DE45 1JE
Tel: 01629 812501    **££ - P - 4 rooms**
Email: info@lathkil.co.uk
Web: www.lathkil.co.uk
In a peaceful village 2 miles from Bakewell

**The Monsal Head Hotel**
Monsal Head, Bakewell, Derbys DE45 1NL
Tel: 01629 640250    **££ - P - 7 rooms**
Email: christine@monsalhead.com
Web: www.monsalhead.com
Village Inn / hotel 3 miles from Bakewell

**The Rutland Arms Hotel**
The Square, Bakewell, Derbys DE45 1BT

Tel: 01629 812812    **££ - P - 35 rooms**
Email: rutland@bakewell.demon.co.uk
Located in the centre of town. Pets accepted

BAMFORD IN THE HIGH PEAK
**The Yorkshire Bridge Inn**
See main entry below

BAMFORD, HOPE VALLEY
**Derwent Hotel**
Main Road, Bamford, Hope Valley, Derbys
Tel: 01433 651395    **££ - P - 12 rooms**
Village Inn 12 miles from Derbyshire

BARLOW
**Peacock Hotel**
Hackney Lane, Barlow, Derbys S18 7TD
Tel: 01142 890296    **£ - P - 1 room**
Village Inn 1.5 miles from Chesterfield

BIRCH VALE
**The Waltzing Weasel Inn**
New Mills Road, Birch Vale, Derbys
Tel: 01663 743402    **££ - P - 8 rooms**
Traditional Inn 20 minutes from Stockport

BRADLEY
**Jinglers Inn – The Fox and Hounds**
Belper Rd, Bradley, Ashbourne,
Derbys DE6 3EN
Tel: 01335 370855    **PW - Rooms**
Pets welcome

# The Yorkshire Bridge Inn

*Ashopton Road, Bamford in the High Peak, The Hope Valley, Derbys S33 0AZ*

**££ - P - 14 rooms**

Tel/Fax: 01433 651361    Email: mr@ybridge.force9.co.uk    Web: www.yorkshire-bridge.co.uk

The Yorkshire Bridge Inn, set in the heart of the Derbyshire Peak District, is one of the finest residential Inns in this region and is famous for It's food, hospitality and comfort. There are fourteen beautifully furnished *en suite* bedrooms offering double, twin or family accommodation.

Although not specifically designed for the disabled, a number are located on the ground floor, thus being suitable for those having difficulty with stairs. All are well equipped with remote control colout televisions, beverage making facilities, telephone and hairdryer. We also offer a wonderful four-poster room for special occasions.

BRADWELL
**The Bowling Green**
Smalldale, Bradwell, Derbys
Tel: 01433 620450    **£ - P - 6 rooms**
Village Inn 16 miles from Sheffield

BRASSINGTON
**Miners Arms**
Miners Hill, Brassington, Derbys DE4 4HA
Tel: 01629 540792    **rooms**
Village Inn

BRETON, HOPE VALLEY
**Barrel Inn**
Breton, nr Eyam, Hope Valley, Derbys
Tel: 01433 630856    **££ - P - 1 room**
Country hilltop Inn 2 miles from Eyam

BUXTON
**The Devonshire Arms**
Peak Forest, Buxton, Derbys SK17 8EJ
Tel: 01298 23875    **£ - P - 3 rooms**
Web: www.devarms.com
Traditional Inn in Peak District walking country

**The Queens Head Hotel**
High Street, Buxton, Derbys SK17 6EU
Tel: 01298 23841    **£ - P - 6 rooms**
Five minutes walk from Buxton town centre

BUXWORTH
**The Navigation Inn**

Brookside Road, Buxworth, Derbyshire
Tel: 01663 732072    **£ - P - 6 rooms**
e-ail: lynda@navigationinn.co.uk
200 year old country Pub + restaurant

CASTLETON
**The Castle Hotel**
Castle Street, Castleton, Derbys
Tel: 01433 620578    **P - 9 rooms**
Set in the Peak District National Park

**Ye Olde Cheshire Cheese Inn**
See main entry below

DARLEY BRIDGE, MATLOCK
**Square and Compass**
Station Road, Darley Bridge, Matlock,
Derbys DE4 2EQ
Tel: 01629 733255    **£ - P - 5 rooms**
Village Inn 3 miles from Matlock

NORTH DARLEY, DALE
**Whitworth Hotel**
Dale Rd, North Darley, Dale, Derbys DE4 2FT
Tel: 01629 733568    **£ - P - 6 rooms**
Village Inn two miles from Matlock

DERBY
**Mr Grundys Pub Tavern**
Ashbourne Road, Derby, Derbys DE22 3AD
Tel: 01332 340279    **22 rooms**
Tavern bar In town

# Ye Olde Cheshire Cheese Inn

*How Lane, Castleton, Hope Valley, Derbys S33 8WJ*

**£ - P - R - BM - 9 rooms**

Tel: 01433 620330    Fax: 01433 821847
Email: kslack@btconnect.com
Web: www.peakland.com/cheshirecheese

Set deep in the heart of the Peak District National Park, Ye Olde Cheshire Cheese Inn is a strik-
ing building which dates back to 1660, and is truly beautiful with half timbered walls, flower-
filled window boxes and hanging baskets. Inside you'll find black Oak beams, log fires and a
wealth of gleaming brass, but the Inn is so much more than a place to eat and drink ...
It also offers some of the best accommodation in the area. There are 10 beautifully appointed
*en suite* rooms, some even have four-poster beds ! All are individually styled and are competi-
tively priced.

# The Bentley Brook Inn

*Fenny Bentley, Ashbourne, Derbys DE6 1LF*

**P - 10 rooms**

Tel: 01335 350278    Fax: 01335 350442
Email: all@bentleybrookinn.co.uk
Web: www.bentleybrookinn.co.uk

In The Bentley Brook Inn there are ten comfortable bedrooms, all of which were created within the old building that was first a thatched medieval farmhouse. Each room has colour TV, radio, direct dial telephone, hair dryers, tea and coffee making facilities and individually controlled radiators. Other facilities offered for resident guests include a full laundry service, shoe cleaning equipment and a welcome for well behaved dogs.

Open all day, the bar serves a selection of real ales and cider, some of which are brewed by our on site brewery 'Leatherbritches'. This is a small traditional craft brewery, owned and operated by youngest son Bill Allingham.

EYAM
**Miners Arms**
Water Lane, Eyam, Derbys S32 5RG
Tel: 01433 630853    **££ - P - 7 rooms**
Village Inn 12 milews from Chesterfield

FOOLOW
**The Bulls Head Inn**
Foolow, Derbys
Tel: 01433 630873    **££ - P - 3 rooms**
Village Inn 30 minutes drive into Chesterfield

FENNY BENTLEY
**The Bentley Brook Inn**
See main entry above

FROGGAT EDGE, nr CALVER
**Chequers Inn**
Froggatt Edge, nr Calver, Derbys S30 1ZB
Tel: 01433 630231    **£ - P - 5 rooms**
Email: info@chequers-froggatt.com
Country Inn 8 miles from Sheffield

GREAT HUCKLOW, nr TIDESWELL
**Queen Anne Inn**
Great Hucklow, nr Tideswell,
Derbys SK17 8RF
Tel: 01298 871246    **£ - Rooms**
Email: malcolm_hutton@bigfoot.com
Situated in the heart of the Peak District

GRINDLEFORD
**The Maynard Arms**
Main Road, Grindleford, Derbys
Tel: 01433 630321    **££ - P - 10 rooms**
Country house hotel 12 miles from Sheffield

HARDSOFT, CHESTERFIELD
**The Weeping Ash**
Hardstoft, Chesterfield, Derbys S45 8AF
Tel: 01246 850276    **£ - P - 15 rooms**
Residental country Inn 8 miles from
Chesterfield

HARTINGTON
**The Manifold Inn**
Hulme End, Hartington, Derbys SK17 0EX
Tel: 01298 84537    **££ - P - 5 rooms**
Country Inn 11 miles from Buxton

HATHERSAGE
**The Millstone Inn**
Sheffield Road, Hathersage, Derbys, S32 1DA
Tel: 01433 650258    **££ - P - 7 rooms**
Set in the Peak Park near to Sheffield

HOGNASTON
**The Red Lion Inn**
Main Street, Hognaston, Derbys DE6 1PR
Tel: 01335 370396    **££ - P - 3 rooms**
Village Inn 5 miles from Ashbourne

HOPE
**Cheshire Cheese Inn**
Edale Road, Hope, Derbys S33 6ZF
Tel: 01433 620381    **££ - P - 1 Room**
Country Pub 15 miles from Sheffield

**The Poachers Arms**
95 Castleton Road, Hope, Derbys S33 6SB
Tel: 01433 620380    **££ - P - 6 rooms**
Set within the Peak District National Park

HOPE VALLEY
**Woodroofe Arms Hotel**
1 Castletown Rd, Hope Valley, Derbys S33 65B
Tel: 01433 620351    **£ - P - 3 rooms**
Village Inn 8 miles from Sheffield

HULLAND WARD, ASHBOURNE
**The Black Horse Inn**
Main Road, Hulland Ward, Ashbourne,
Derbys DE6 3EE
Tel: 01335 370206    **££ - P - 4 rooms**
17th century Inn 4 miles from Ashbourne

KIRK IRETON, ASHBOURNE
**Barley Mow Inn**
Main Street, Kirk Ireton, Ashbourne,
Derbys DE6 3JP
Tel: 01335 370306    **£ - P - 5 rooms**
Country Pub 6 miles from Ashbourne

LEADMILL BRIDGE
**The Plough Inn**
See main entry below

LITTLE HAYFIELD, HIGH PEAK
**The Lantern Pike**
Glossop Rd, Little Hayfield, High Peak, Derbys
Tel: 01663 747590    **£ - P - 5 rooms**
Small Village Inn located just 5 miles from
Glossop

LONGNOR, BUXTON
**Crewe and Harper Arms Hotel**
Longnor, Buxton, Derbys SK17 0NS
Tel: 01298 83205    **£ - P - 6 rooms**
Village Inn 5 miles from Buxton

LOWER PILSLEY, nr CHESTERFIELD
**Coach And Horses Inn**
Locko Road, Lower Pilsley, nr Chesterfield,
Derbys S45 8DN
Tel: 01291 622626    **£ - P - 4 rooms**
Village Inn 5 miles from Chester

MATLOCK
**Old English Hotel**
77 Dale Road, Matlock, Derbys DE4 3LT
Tel: 01629 55028    **£ - P - Rooms**
Large town Pub which also includes a
nightclub

---

# The Plough Inn

*Leadmill Bridge, Hathersage, Hope Valley,
Derbys S32 1BA*

**£££ - P - 6 rooms**

Tel: 01433 650319    Email: theploughinn@leadmillbridge.fsnet.co.uk
Web: theploughinn-hathersage.com

This privately owned 16th century Inn, in 9 acres of its own land set in idyllic surroundings on
the banks of the River Derwent, is situated in the Peak National Park, making it an ideal base
from which to explore this beautiful part of Derbyshire. The Plough Inn offers tasteful and comfortable accommodation, cosy open fires and delicious home-cooked meals. All of our bedrooms are *en suite* with tea and coffee making facilities, colour television and hairdryers. A full
English breakfast is included.

Our luxury Doubles are in our newly converted Cottage, with full bathrooms, Video, Hi-Fi and
sitting area. They have been restored using local materials, leaving many exposed beams and
stonework.

**The White Lion Inn**
195 Starkholmes Rd, Matlock, Derbys DE4 5JA
Tel: 01629 582511    **£ - P - 3 rooms**
Email: whitelion@ntlworld.com
Web: www.rihgtfast.com/whitelion
Good views across Matlock

**MILLERS DALE, BUXTON**
**Anglers Rest**
Millers Dale, Buxton, Derbys SK17 8SN
Tel: 01298 871323    **£ - P - Rooms**
Country Inn 6 miles from Buxton

**NEW MILLS**
**The Pack Horse Inn**
Mellor Road, New Mills, Derbys
Tel: 01663 742365    **£ - P - 5 rooms**
Email: info@packhorseinn.co.uk
Country Pub located just 2 miles from New Mills

**NEWBOLD, CHESTERFIELD**
**Olde House Trading Post**
Lowndsley Green Road, Newbold,
Chesterfield, Derbys S40 4RN
Tel: 01246 274321    **£ - Rooms**
Family Pub situated just on the outskirts of town

**NEWTON SOLNEY,**
**BURTON-UPON-TRENT**
**The Unicorn Inn**
Repton Road, Newton Solney, Burton-upon-Trent, Derbys
Tel: 01283 703324    **£ - P - 8 rooms**
Email: unicorn.newtonsolney@barbox.net
Village Inn 3 miles from Burton

**PADFIELD, GLOSSOP**
**Peels Arms**
6–12 Temple Street, Padfield, Glossop,
Derbys SK13 1EX
Tel: 01457 852719    **£ - P - Rooms**
Email: peels@talk21.com
Village Pub 2 miles from Glossop

**ROWARTH**
**Little Mill Inn**
Rowarth, Derbys
Tel: 01663 743178    **£ - P - 3 rooms**
Village Inn 2 miles from New Mills

**SHARDLOW**
**The Old Crown**
Cavendish Bridge, Shardlow,
Derbys DE72 2HL
Tel: 01332 792392    **£ - P - 2 rooms**
Village Inn 6 miles from Derby

**SHELDON, nr BAKEWELL**
**Cock and Pullet**
Main Street, Sheldon, nr Bakewell,
Derbys DE45 1QS
Tel: 01629 814292    **£ - P - 3 rooms**
Village Inn 2 miles from Bakewell

**SMALLEY**
**The Bell Inn**
Main Road, Smalley, Derbys
Tel: 01332 880635    **££ - P - 3 rooms**
Village Pub 4 miles from Derby

**SOUTH NORMANTON**
**White Swan Inn**
Castle Eden East, South Normanton,
Derbys DE55 2DY
Tel: 01773 811457    **£ - P - 3 rooms**
On Junction 28 of the M1

**STAVELEY, CHESTERFIELD**
**Foresters Arms**
Market Street, Staveley, Chesterfield,
Derbys S43 3UT
Tel: 01246 477455    **£ - P - Rooms**
Email: info@theforesters.co.uk
Web: www.theforesters.co.uk
Village Inn located just 4 miles from Chesterfield

**TICKNALL, DERBY**
**The Staff of Life**
7 High St, Ticknall, Derby,
Derbys DE73 1JH
Tel: 01332 862479    **£ - P - 5 rooms**
Web: www.thestaffoflife.com
Village Inn 25 miles from Derby

**YOULGREAVE, BAKEWELL**
**The Farmyard Inn**
Main Street, Youlgreave, Bakewell,
Derbys DE45 1UW
Tel: 01629 636221    **£ - P - 3 rooms**
Village Inn 2 miles from Bakewell

# HEREFORD AND WORCESTER

Tel: 01432 830252    **£ - P - 6 rooms**
Village Inn 5 miles from Hereford

## CRASWALL
**The Bulls Head**
Craswall, Herefordshire HR2 0PN
Tel: 01981 510616    **£ - 3 rooms**
Country Inn 5 miles from Hay-on-Wye

## CROPTHORNE, EVERSHAM
**The Bell Inn**
Main Road, Cropthorne, Evesham,
Worcs WR10 3NE
Tel: 01386 860255    **£ - P - 4 rooms**
Village Inn 3 miles from Evesham

## ECKINGTON, nr PERSHORE
**Anchor Inn and Restaurant**
Cotheridge Lane, Eckington, nr Pershore,
Worcs WR10 3BA
Tel: 01386 750356    **££ - P - 5 rooms**
Email: anchoreck@aol.com
Web: www.anchoreckington.co.uk
Traditional village Inn convenient for
Worcester

## ELMLEY CASTLE, PERSHORE
**The Old Mill Inn**
Mill Lane, Elmley Castle, Pershore,
Worcs WR10 3HP
Tel: 01386 710407    **££ - P - 6 rooms**
Email: oldmilin@dircon.co.uk
Web: www.elmleymill.com
Rural Inn 5 miles from Pershore

## EVESHAM
**The Crown Inn**
Waterside, Evesham, Worcs WR11 IJ2
Tel: 01386 446151    **£ - P - 6 rooms**
Local village Inn

**George and Dragon**
Bendley Street, Evesham, Worcs WR11 4AD
Tel: 01386 446362    **£ - P - 4 rooms**
2 minutes walk from Evesham town centre

## ABBERLEY
**The Manor Arms Country Inn**
Abberley, Worcester, WorcsWR6 6BN
Tel: 01299 896507    **£ - P - 10 rooms**
Email: themanorarms@btconnect.com
Web: www.themanorarms.com
Village Inn 7 miles from Stourport

## ASHPERTON, LEDBURY
**The Hopton Arms**
Ashperton, Ledbury, Herefordshire HR8 2SE
Tel: 01531 670520    **£ - P - 10 rooms**
Email: peter@hoptonarms.co.uk
Web: www.hoptonarms.co.uk
Village Inn 5 miles from Ledbury

## AYMESTREY
**Riverside Inn**
Aymestrey, Herefordshire, HR6 9ST
Tel: 01568 708440    **££ - P - 5 rooms**
Inn by the river 8 miles from Ludlow

## BROADWAY
**The Crown and Trumpet Inn**
Church Street, Broadway, Worcs WR12 7AE
Tel: 01386 853202    **££ - P - 5 rooms**
Email: ascott@cotswoldholidays.co.uk
Web: www.cotswoldholidays.co.uk
Traditional 17th century Inn

## CANON
**The Nags Head Inn**
Canon Pyon, Hereford, Herefordshire HR4 8NY

**Ye Olde Red Horse**
Bine Street, Evesham, Worcs WR11 4JE
Tel: 01386 442784    **£ - P - 5 rooms**
Located close to the town centre

**FLADBURY**
**Chequers Inn**
Chequers Lane, Fladbury, Worcs WR10 2PZ
Tel: 01386 860276    **££ - P - 8 rooms**
Village Inn 4 miles from Evesham

**FLYFORD, FLAVELL**
**The Boot Inn**
Radford Road, Flyford, Flavell, Worcester,
Worcs WR7 4BS
Tel: 01386 462658    **£ - P - 5 rooms**
Email: thebootinn@yahoo.com
Village Inn 15 minute drive to Worcester

**FOWNHOPE**
**The Green Man Inn**
Fownhope, Herefordshire, HR1 4PE
Tel: 01432 860243    **££ - P - 23 rooms**
Country Inn 6 miles from Hereford

**GOODRICH, nr ROSS-ON-WYE**
**The Inn on the Wye**
Kerne Bridge, Goodrich, nr Ross-on-Wye,
Herefordshire HR9 5QS
Tel: 01600 890872    **P - Rooms**
Email: gkgardiner.attheinn@virgin.net
Web: www.theinnonthewye.co.uk
18th century riverside coaching Inn near
Goodrich Castle

**Ye Hostelrie**
Goodrich, nr Ross-on-Wye,
Herefordshire HR9 6HX
Tel: 01600 890241    **£ - P - 7 rooms**
Email: info@ye-hostelrie.co.uk
Village Inn 5 miles from Ross-on-Wye

**GREAT MALVERN**
**Great Malvern Hotel**
Grahem Road, Great Malvern,
Worcs WR14 2HN
Tel: 01684 563411    **£ - P - 14 rooms**
Email: sutton@great-malvern-hotel.co.uk
Hotel with popular public bar in the centre of
town

**HADLEY HEATH, nr DROITWICH**
**The Hadley Bowling Green Inn**
Hadley Heath, nr Droitwich, Worcs WR9 0AR
Tel: 01905 620294    **££ - P - 13 rooms**
Email: hadleybowlinggreeninn@btopenworld.com
Old coaching Inn 5 miles from Droitwich

**INKBERROW**
**Bulls Head Inn**
The Village Green, Inkberrow, Worcs  WR7 4DY
Tel: 01386 792233    **£ - P - 5 rooms**
Village Inn 6 miles from Redditch

**KINGSLAND, LEOMINSTER**
**The Corners Inn**
Kingsland, Leominster, Herefordshire HR6 9RY
Tel: 01568 708385    **£ - P - 3 rooms**
Email: enq@cornersinn.co.uk
Web: www.cornersinn.co.uk
16th century black and white village Inn 4
miles from Leominster

**KINGTON**
**Oxford Arms**
Duke Street, Kington, Herefordshire HR5 3DR
Tel: 01544 230322    **£ - P - Rooms**
Local market town Pub 18 miles from
Hereford

**The Queens Head**
Bridge Street, Kington, Herefordshire HR5 3DW
Tel: 01544 231106    **£ - P - 3 rooms**
Local Pub near the centre of Kington

**KNIGHTWICK**
**The Talbot**
Knightwick, Worcs WR6 5PH
Tel: 01886 821235    **££ - P - 11 rooms**
Email: info@the-talbot.co.uk
Unique country Inn 12 miles from Worcester

**LEDBURY**
**The Talbot**
14 New St, Ledbury, Herefordshire HR8 2DX
Tel: 01531 632963    **£ - P - 7 rooms**
Town centre Pub

**LEDGEMOOR, nr WEOBLEY**
**Marshpools Country Inn**
Ledgemoor, nr Weobley, Herefordshire HR4 8RN

Tel: 01544 318215    **£ - P - 3 rooms**
Email: burgoyne@marshpools.freeserve.co.uk
Web: www.country-inn.co.uk
Remote Pub 8 miles from Hereford

## LEOMINSTER
**Black Swan Hotel**
West St, Leominster, Herefordshire HR6 8EP
Tel: 01568 612020    **£ - P - 10 rooms**
Town centre coaching Inn

## LINTON, ROSS-ON-WYE
**Alma Inn**
Linton, Ross-on-Wye, Herefordshire HR9 7RY
Tel: 01989 720355    **P - 2 rooms**
Village Inn 5 miles from Ross-on-Wye

## LITTLE COWARNE, BROMYARD
**The Three Horseshoes Inn**
Little Cowarne, Bromyard,
Herefordshire HR7 4RQ
Tel: 01885 400276    **£ - P - 2 rooms**
Village Inn 6 miles from Bromyard

## MALVERN
**The Malvern Hills Hotel**
See main entry below

## MALVERN WELLS
**Foley Arms Hotel**
14 Worcester Road, Malvern Wells,

Worcs WR14 4QS
Tel: 01684 573397    **£££ - P - 28 rooms**
Town centre hotel that also has a busy
public bar

**Wyche Inn**
74 Wyche Road, Malvern Wells,
Worcs WR14 4EQ
Tel: 01684 575396    **£ - P - 5 rooms**
Located high above Malvern with outstanding
views

## MARTLEY
**The Admiral Rodney**
See main entry opposite

## PENCOMBE
**The Wheelwright Arms**
Pencombe, Herefordshire
Tel: 01885 400358    **P - 1 self catering
                            cottage**
Village Inn 4 miles from Bromyard Cottage,
price on request

## PERSHORE
**White Horse Hotel**
Pershore, Worcestershire
Tel: 01386 552689    **£ - P - 5 rooms**
Town Pub just 2 minutes walk to the town
centre

# The Malvern Hills Hotel

*Jubilee Drive, Upper Colwall, Malvern,
Herefordshire WR13 6DW*

**£££ - P**

Tel: 01684 540237
Email: malhilhotl@aol.com
Web: malvernhillshotel.co.uk

The Malvern Hills Hotel is an old style coaching Inn nestling on the majestic slopes of the
Malverns in the heart of an area of outstanding natural beauty where you can enjoy leisurely
walks with breathtaking scenery. There are comfortable, *en suite* single, double, twin, family
and ground floor bedrooms available, one being a four-poster.

Excellent home-made bar food is served by friendly staff in a lively oak panelled lounge with a
variety of rel ales (CAMRA recommended), or dine in the elegance of our fine fixed price candlelit restaurant, all in the traditions of a hostelry with a heritage of half a millennium.

# The Admiral Rodney Inn

*Berrow Green, Martley, Nr Worcester WR6 6PL*

**P - 3 rooms**

Tel: 01886 821375
Email: sqrighol@aol.com

Situated in beautiful West Worcestershire countryside with wonderful views.

All rooms with King Sized beds (one a four poster), excellent facilities include en-euite and Full English Breakfast. The pub serves Real Ales and bar food, and there is also a fine dining Restaurant.

## RUCKHALL
**The Ancient Camp Inn**
Ruckhall, Hereford, Herefordshire HR2 9QX
Tel: 01981 250449     **££ - P - 5 rooms**
Quiet country Pub situated 4 miles from Hereford

## ST OWEN'S CROSS
**The New Inn**
St Owen's Cross, Herefordshire HR2 8LQ
Tel: 01989 730274     **££ - P - 2 rooms**
Old coaching Inn 4 miles from Ross-on-Wye

## STAUNTON-ON-WYE
**Portway Inn**
Brecon Road, Staunton-on-Wye,
Herefordshire HR4 7NH
Tel: 01981 500474     **£ - Rooms**
16th century Inn 10 miles from Hereford

## TRUMPET, LEDBURY
**The Trumpet Inn**
Trumpet, Ledbury, Herefordshire HR8 2RA
Tel: 01531 670277     **P - 1 apartment**
Email: trumpetinn@aol.com
Web: www.trumpetinn.com
Traditional oak beamed English Pub

## UPTON SNODSBURY
**The French House Inn**
Worcester Road, Upton Snodsbury,
Worcs WR7 4NW
Tel: 01905 381631     **£ - P - Rooms**
French cuisine, 5 miles from Worcester

## WHITNEY-ON-WYE
**Rhydspence Inn**
Whitney-on-Wye, Herefordshire HR3 6EU
Tel: 01497 831262     **££ - P - 7 rooms**
14th century Inn 3 miles from Hay-on-Wye

## WILTON, ROSS-ON-WYE
**The White Lion**
Wilton Lane, Wilton, Ross-on-Wye,
Herefordshire HR9 6AQ
Tel: 01989 562785     **£ - P - 3 rooms**
Email: lois@thewhitelion.fsbusiness.co.uk
Riverside Inn, the restaurant is an old jail

## WOOLHOPE
**The Butchers Arms**
Woolhope, Herefordshire HR1 4RF
Tel: 01432 860281     **£ - P - 2 rooms**
Email: peter@thebutchersarms.org.uk
Small country Inn 7 miles from Hereford and 5 miles from Ledbury

# LEICESTERSHIRE

## ASHBY-DE-LA-ZOUCH
**Plough Inn**
The Green, Ashby-de-la Zouch, Leicestershire
Tel: 01530 412817    **Rooms**
Local town Pub

## DESFORD
**Blue Bell Inn**
39 High Street, Desford, Leics LE9 9JF
Tel: 01455 822901    **£ - P - 5 rooms**
Email: tcclarke@msn.com
Web: www.thebluebellinn.com
Village / country Inn 8 miles from Leicester

## EAST LANGTON
**The Bell Inn**
Main Street, East Langton, Leics LE16 7TW
Tel: 01858 545278    **£ - P - 2 rooms**
Email: achapman@thebellinn.co.uk
Web: www.thebellinn.co.uk
Rural Village Inn 4 miles from Market
Harborough

## GLOOSTON
**The Old Barn Inn and Restaurant**
Andrews Lane, Glooston, Leics LE16 7ST
Tel: 01858 545215    **£ - P - 2 rooms**
Rural village Inn 4 miles from Market
Harborough

## HINKLEY
**Branagans**
23 Regent Street, Hinkley, Leics LE10 0AZ
Tel: 01455 611230    **£ - P - 4 rooms**
Town Pub, bar and diner

**The Railway Hotel**
Station Road, Hinkley, Leics LE10 1AP
Tel: 01455 615285    **£ - P - 4 rooms**
Located 5 minutes walk to the town centre

## LEICESTER FOREST, LEICESTER
**The Red Cow**
Hinckley Rd, Leicester Forest, Leics LE3 3PG
Tel: 01162 387878    **£ - P - 31 rooms**
Country Inn 20 minutes drive to Leicester

## GADDESBY, LEICESTER
**Cheney Arms**
Gaddesby, Leicester, Leics LE7 4XE
Tel: 01664 840260    **£ - P - 4 rooms**
Rural Inn 6 miles from Melton Mowbray

## LOUGHBOROUGH
**Peacock Inn**
26 Factory St, Loughborough, Leics LE11 1AL
Tel: 01509 214215    **£ - P - Rooms**
Local Pub 5 minutes walk to Loughborough

**The Swan in the Rushes**
See main entry opposite

## LUTTERWORTH
**The Greyhound Coaching Inn**
9 Market Street, Lutterworth, Leics LE17 4EJ
Tel: 01455 553307    **£ - P - 37 rooms**
Email: bookings@greyhoundinn.fsnet.co.uk
Web: www.greyhoundinn.co.uk
Town hotel with a public bar

## MARKET BOSWORTH
**Dixie Arms Hotel**
6 Main St, Market Bosworth, Leics CV13 0JW
Tel: 01455 290218    **££ - P - 4 rooms**
Old coaching Inn in this historic market town

# The Swan in the Rushes

*21 The Rushes, Loughborough, Leics LE11 5BE*

**P - 2 rooms**

Tel: 01509 217014    Web: www.tynemill.co.uk

The Swan has recently refurbished rooms (2 *en suite*), 2 bars featuring 10 real ales, Home-cooked fare, Car park, is 2 minutes walk from the town centre and 20 minutes walk from the train station, credit / debit cards welcome.

**The Red Lion**
1 Park St, Market Bosworth, Leics CV13 0LL
Tel: 01455 291713    **£ - P - 5 rooms**
Email: eddieandliz@theredlion.dabsol.co.uk
Traditional town centre English Inn

MARKET HARBOROUGH
**The George**
Great Oxendon, Market Harborough,
Leics LE16 8NA
Tel: 01858 465205    **£ - P - 3 rooms**
Village Inn 3 miles from Market Harborough

**Greyhound Inn**
Kettering Road, Market Harborough,
Leics LE16 8AW
Tel: 01858 462324    **£ - P - 4 rooms**
Country Pub 2 minutes from the town centre

MARSTON TRUSSEL
**The Sun Inn**
Main Street, Marston Trussel, Market
Harborough, Leics LE16 9TY
Tel: 01858 465531    **££ - P - 20 rooms**
Country Pub 3 miles from Market Harborough

MEDBOURNE
**The Nevill Arms**
12 Waterfall Way, Medbourne,
Leics LE16 8EE
Tel: 01858 565288    **£ - P - 8 rooms**
Village Inn 6 miles from Market Harborough

NEWBOLD, COLEORTON
**Cross Keys Inn**
9 Worthington Lane, Newbold, Coleorton,
Leics LE67 8PJ

Tel: 01530 224799    **£ - P - 2 rooms**
Country Inn with open fires 3 miles from
Ashby-de-la-Zouch

OADBY
**Horse and Hounds**
Glen Rise, Oadby, Leics LE2 4RG
Tel: 08707 001519    **P - Rooms**
Large road side Inn, slightly upmarket

PINWALL
**The Red Lion**
Main Road, Pinwall, Leics CV9 3NB
Tel: 01827 712223    **£ - P - 6 rooms**
Village Inn 2 miles from Atherstone

REDMILE
**Peacock Inn**
Church Corner, Redmile, Leics NG13 0GA
Tel: 01949 842554    **££ - P - 10 rooms**
Email: peacock@redmile.fsbusiness.co.uk
Country Inn/restaurant 10 near to Grantham

SUTTON IN THE ELMS
**The Mill on the Soar**
Coventry Road, Sutton in the Elms,
Leics LE9 6QD
Tel: 01455 282419    **££ - P - 25 rooms**
Email: themill@work.gb.com
Country Inn 8 miles from Liecester

WILBARSTON
**The Fox Inn**
Church Street, Wilbarston, Market
Harborough, Leics LE16 8QG
Tel: 01536 771270    **£ - P - 4 rooms**
Village Inn 4 miles from Corby

# LINCOLNSHIRE

## ALLINGTON
**The Welby Arms**
The Green, Allington, Lincs NG23 2EA
Tel: 01400 281361     **££ - P - 3 rooms**
Traditional village Inn 5 miles from Grantham

## ASWARBY, SLEAFORD
**The Tally Ho Inn**
Aswarby, Sleaford, Lincs NG34 8SA
Tel: 01529 455205     **£ - P - 6 rooms**
A 17th century Inn located just 4 miles from
Sleaford

## BARROW HAVEN,
## BARROW-UPON-HUMBER
**Haven Inn**
Ferry Road, Barrow Haven, Barrow-upon-
Humber, North Lincs DN19 7EX
Tel: 01469 530247     **Rooms - PW**
Email: dmhav123@aol.com
Web: www.haveninn.com
Pets welcome

## BENINGTON
**Admiral Nelson**
Main Road, Benington, Lincs PE22 0BT
Tel: 01205 760460     **£ - P - 2 rooms**
Country Pub located just 5 miles from Boston

## BLYTON, GAINSBOROUGH
**Black Horse Inn**
93 High Street, Blyton, Gainsborough,
Lincs DN21 3JX
Tel: 01427 628277     **£ - P - 2 rooms**
Rural traditional Pub located on the A159 4
miles from Gainsborough

## BOSTON
**The Kings Arms**
13 Horncastle Road, Boston, Lincs PE21 9BU
Tel: 01205 364296     **Rooms**
Cosy open log fires meals served

**The Robin Hood**
104 High Street, Boston, Lincs PE21 8TA
Tel: 01205 356696     **Rooms**
Town Pub with beer garden

## BRANSTON
**Moor Lodge Hotel**
Sleaford Road, Branston, Lincs LN4 1HU
Tel: 01522 791366     **Rooms**
Village Inn

## BRIGG
**The Woolpack Hotel**
See main enrty opposite

## BURGH-LE-MARSH
**The Bell Hotel**
High Street, Burgh-le-Marsh, Skegness,
Lincs PE24 5JP
Tel: 01754 810318     **Rooms**
Meals, open fire, beer garden, function room

## CLAYPOLE, NEWARK-ON-TRENT
**Five Bells Public House**
95 Main Street, Claypole, Newark-on-Trent,
Lincs NG23 5BJ
Tel: 01636 626561     **£ - P - 3 rooms**
Village Pub 5 miles from Newark

## COLLY, nr STAMFORD
**Collyweston Slater**

# The Woolpack Inn

*4 The Market Place, Brigg, Lincs DN20 8HA*

**£ - P - BG - 5 rooms**

Tel: 01652 655649
Email: harry@woolpack488.freeserve.co.uk
Web: www.woolpack-hotel.co.uk

The Woolpack Hotel is situated in the centre of the picturesque market town of Brigg and is a public house with a warm, friendly welcome and homely accommodation. The town, and the pub, is close to the M180, Humberside International Airport and The Humber Bridge making for easy access. Nearby, there are also local amenities, including convenient golf courses and course fishing sites.

Also offered at The Woolpack Hotel: Live Entertainment, Super league Pool Tables, Big Screens Live Sports and a Friday night disco. Special accommodation rates for contractors / groups.

87 Main Street, Colly, nr Stamford,
Lincs PE9 3PQ
Tel: 01780 444288    **£ - 4 rooms**
Email: info@btinternet.com
Village Inn 3 miles from Stamford

## CONINGSBY
**The Lea Gate Inn**
Leagate Road, Coningsby, Lincs LN4 4RS
Tel: 01526 342370    **££ - P - 8 rooms**
Email: enquiries@theleagateinn.co.uk

Web: www.theleagateinn.co.uk
Village Inn 10 miles from Boston

**The White Bull Inn**
See main entry below

## CORBY GLEN
**The Coachman**
Corby Glen, Lincs NG33 4NS
Tel: 01476 550316    **£ - P - 4 rooms**
Countryside Inn 8 miles from Grantham

# The White Bull Inn

*55 High Street, Coningsby, Lincs LN4 4RB*

**£ - P - R - BM - PW - C - 4 rooms**

Tel: 01526 342439    Fax: 01526 342818
Email: whitebullinn@amserve.com
Web: www.smoothhound.co.uk/hotels/whitebul.html

The White Bull is a riverside family pub with large play area and beer garden. All accommodation is *en suite* with tea / coffee making facilities and colour TV. There is also a four poster bridal suite. A Full English breakfast is served in the restaurant. The restaurant is named after the Battle of Britain Memorial flight and provides hot and cold food between 11.00am to 11.00pm everyday. The pub has a full children's certificate and also includes facilities for the disabled.

**CORRINGHAM, GAINSBOROUGH**
**The Becket Arms**
25 High Street, Corringham, Gainsborough,
Lincs DN21 5QP
Tel: 01427 838201    **£ - P - 4 rooms**
Village Inn 3 miles from Gainsborough

**DONINGTON-ON-BAIN**
**The Black Horse**
Main Road, Donington-on-Bain, Lincs
LN11 9TJ
Tel: 01507 343640    **£ - P - 8 rooms**
Village Inn 7 miles from Louth

**DYKEBOURNE**
**The Wishing Well Inn**
Main Street, Dykebourne, Lincs PE10 0AF
Tel: 01778 422970    **£ - P - 12 rooms**
A wishing well, oak beams and log fires

**EASTON-ON-THE-HILL, STAMFORD**
**The Oak Inn**
48 Stamford Road, Easton-on-the-Hill,
Stamford, Lincs PE9 3PA
Tel: 01780 752286    **£ - P - 6 rooms**
Email: peter@klippon.demon.co.uk
Village Inn 2 miles from Stamford

**EAST WATER, ROTHENDALE**
Commercial Hotel
1085 Burnley Road, East Water,
Rothendale, Lincs
Tel: 01706 216043    **£ - P - 2 rooms**
Village Pub 5 miles from Burnley

**EWERBY**
**Finch Hatton Arms**
43 Main Street, Ewerby, Lincs NG34 9PH
Tel: 01529 460363    **££ - P - 8 rooms**
Village Pub / hotel 4 miles from Sleaford

**FULBECK**
**The Hare and Hounds Country Inn**
See main entry below

**GAINSBOROUGH**
**White Hart Hotel and Pub**
49 Lord Street, Gainsborough, Lincs DN21 2DD
Tel: 01427 612018    **£ - P - 14 rooms**
Email: white.hart@tesco.net
Town centre hotel, Pub and restaurant

**GRANTHAM**
**Five Bells**
79 Brook Street, Grantham, Lincs NG31 6RY
Tel: 01476 400555    **£ - 4 rooms**
Town Pub 5 minutes from the town centre

**GREAT LIMBER**
**The New Inn**
High Street, Great Limber, Lincs
Tel: 01469 560257    **£ - P - 7 rooms**
Village Inn 5 miles from Grimsby

**GRIMTHORPE, BOURNE**
**The Black Horse Inn**
Grimsthorpe, Bourne, Lincs PE10 0LY
Tel: 01778 591247    **££ - P - 6 rooms**
Village Inn 5 minutes drive to Bourne

# The Hare and Hounds Country Inn

*The Green, Fulbeck, Grantham, Lincs NG32 3JJ*

**£ - P - BM - BG - PW - 8 rooms**

Tel: 01400 272090    Fax: 01400 273663
Email: stay@hareandhoundsfulbeck.co.uk
Web: www.hareandhoundsfulbeck.co.uk

The Hare and Hounds is an award winning 17th century free house and restaurant. The accommodation consists of 8 *en suite* bedrooms. All rooms have colour TV, tea and coffee facilities, and are set around a pretty courtyard. The busy bar serves traditional real ale and has an extensive wine list. 3 star AA and ETB. The restaurant is no smoking and there is also a no smoking area off the main bar.

## HARGATE, HOLBEACH, SPALDING
**The Bull Inn**
Old Main Road, Fleet, Hargate, Holbeach,
Spalding, Lincs PE12 8LH
Tel: 01406 426866 **£ - P - 3 rooms**
Listed Pub on the road that goes around The
Wash

## HORBLING, SLEAFORD
**Plough Inn**
4 Spring Lane, Horbling, Sleaford,
Lincs NG34 0PF
Tel: 01529 240263 **P - Rooms**
Country Inn 8 miles from Sleaford

## HORNCASTLE
**Fighting Cocks Inn**
West Street, Horncastle, Lincs LN9 5JF
Tel: 01507 527307 **£ - P - 3 rooms**
Small market town Pub

## LINCOLN
**Barbican Hotel**
11 St Mary's Street, Lincoln, Lincs LN5 7EQ
Tel: 01522 543811 **£ - P - 14 rooms**
Town centre Pub

**Duke William**
44 Bailgate, Lincoln, Lincs LN1 3AP
Tel: 01522 533351 **££ - P - 11 rooms**
Historical Pub in the old part of Lincoln

**Ye Olde Crowne Inn**
Clasketgate, Lincoln, Lincs
Tel: 01522 542896 **£ - P - 10 rooms**
Town centre Inn

## LITTLE BYTHAM, GRANTHAM
**The Willoughby Arms**
Station Road, Little Bytham, Grantham,
Lincs NG33 4RA
Tel: 01780 410276 **P - 3 rooms**
Email: willo@willoughbyarms.co.uk
Web: www.willoughbyarms.co.uk
Old village Inn 6 miles from Stamford

## LOUTH
**Boars Head**
12 Newmarket, Louth, Lincs LN11 9HH
Tel: 01507 603561 **Rooms**
Batemans Pub, open fires meals served

**Packhorse Hotel**
65–67 Eastgate, Louth, Lincs LN11 9PL
Tel: 01507 603848 **££ - P - Rooms**
Town Pub

**Masons Arms**
Cornmarket, Louth, Lincs LN11 9PY
Tel: 01507 609525 **£ - 10 rooms**
Email: justin@themasons.co.uk
Web: www.themasons.co.uk
Located in the centre of this old market town

## LUDFORD
**The White Hart Inn**
Magna Mile, Ludford, Lincolnshire
Tel: 01507 313489 **£ - P - 4 rooms**
Village Inn 6 miles from Louth

## MARKET RASEN
**Nettleton Lodge Inn**
Off Moortown Road, Market Rasen,
Lincs LN7 6HX
Tel: 01472 851829 **£ - P - 3 rooms**
Country Inn 12 miles from Grimsby

## MARSTON, GRANTHAM
**Thorold Arms**
Main Street, Marston, Grantham,
Lincs NG32 2HH
Tel: 01400 250899 **P - 2 rooms**
Village Inn 7 miles from Grantham

## NORTH COTES, GRIMSBY
**The Fleece Inn**
Lock Road, North Cotes, Grimsby,
Lincs DN36 5UP
Tel: 01472 388233 **£ - P - 3 rooms**
Village Inn 10 miles from Grimsby

## OLD LEAKE, BOSTON
**The Bricklayers Arms**
Main Road, Old Leake, Boston,
Lincs PE22 9HT
Tel: 01205 870657 **Rooms**
Inn with open log fire meals served

## PARTNEY
**Red Lion Inn**
Partney, Lincs PE23 4PG
Tel: 01790 752271 **£ - P - 3 rooms**
Village Inn 10 miles from Skegness

# The Blue Cow Inn

*South Witham, Nr Grantham, Lincs NG33 5QB*

**£ - P - 6 rooms**

Tel: 01572 768432
Email: richard@thirlwell.fslife.co.uk
Web: www.thebluecowinn.co.uk

This 13th Century Inn with its Oak beams, stone floors and open fires can be found just off the A1 in the picturesque village of South Witham. The Inn boasts its very own Brewery and serves only its own ales. The well-appointed accommodation includes colour TV, hair dryer, direct dial phone, PC point and tea / coffee making facilities. Prices, to include full English breakfast, start at £40 single / £45 double Our bar is open all day every day, and Bar and Restaurant food is available every lunchtime and evening.

---

**RAITHBY**
**Red Lion Inn**
Main Street, Raithby, Lincs PE23 4DS
Tel: 01790 753727    **£ - P - 3 rooms**
Email: alcaprawn@aol.com
Village Inn 3 miles from Spilsby

**nr SOMERCOTES, LOUTH**
**Axe and Cleaver**
Keeling Street, nr Somercotes, Louth,
Lincs LN11 7PR
Tel: 01507 358738    **£ - P - 3 rooms**
Village Pub 10 miles from Lough

**SKEGNESS**
**The Vine Hotel**
Vine Road, Skegness, Lincs PE25 3DB
Tel: 01754 763018    **Rooms**
Open fires and beer garden. Meals served

**SOUTH FERRIBY**
**The Nelthorpe Arms**
School Lane, South Ferriby, Lincs DN18 6AW
Tel: 01652 635235    **£ - P - 3 rooms**
Village Inn 2 miles from Barton

**SOUTH WITHAM**
**The Blue Cow Inn**
See main entry above

**SPALDING**
**The Lincoln Arms**
4 Bridge Street, Spalding, Lincs

Tel: 01775 722691    **£ - P - 4 rooms**
Traditional local Pub 2 minutes walk to the town centre

**Ship Albion**
Albion Street, Spalding, Lincs PE11 2AJ
Tel: 01775 769644    **Rooms**
Beer garden and meals served

**SPILSBY**
**Shades**
Church Street, Spilsby, Lincs PE23 5LP
Tel: 01790 752200    **Rooms**
Meals served, beer garden

**White Hart Hotel**
4 Cornhill, Spilsby, Lincs PE23 5JD
Tel: 01790 752244    **£ - P - 6 rooms**
Web: www.spilsby.co.uk
Small country Inn 14 miles from Skegness

**SUTTON BRIDGE**
**New Inn**
Sutton Bridge, Lincs PE12 9UA
Tel: 01406 351032    **£ - Rooms**
Town centre Pub

**SWAYFIELD, GRANTHAM**
**The Royal Oak Inn**
High Street, Swayfield, Grantham,
Lincs NG33 4LL
Tel: 01476 550247    **£ - P - 5 rooms**
Country Pub 10 miles from Grantham

# The Marquis of Granby

*High Street, Wellingore, Lincs LN5 0HW*

**£ - P**

Tel: 01522 810442     Fax: 01522 810740

Email: marquisofgranby@aol.com   Web: www.marquisofgranby.fsnet.co.uk

Welcome to The Marquis of Granby. We are a friendly family run village Inn set in the heart of rural Lincs with close links to the major towns of Lincoln, Grantham, Newark and Sleaford and boasts superb accommodation and modern facilities, including a restaurant that seats 40, a spacious bar, and lounge area with an open fire.

We offer a full range of accommodation types, all *en suite*, and a variety of dishes including home-cooked dishes, traditional Sunday lunches and bar meals.

TETFORD
**The White Hart Inn**
East Road, Tetford, Lincs LN9 6UU
Tel: 01507 533255    **£ - P - 7 rooms**
600 year old village Inn 7 miles from Horncastle

THORNTON CURTIS
**The Thornton Hunt Inn**
17 Main Street, Thornton Curtis,
Lincs DN39 6XW
Tel: 01469 531252    **£ - P - 3 rooms**
Email: peter@thorntoninn.com
Village Inn located just 10 miles from Barton

TIMBERLAND
**Penny Farthing Inn**
Station Road, Timberland, Lincs LN4 3SA
Tel: 01526 378359    **£ - P - 8 rooms**
300 year old village Inn 15 miles from Lincoln

TORKSEY
**The Castle Inn**
Station Road, Torksey, Lincolnshire
Tel: 01427 718212    **£ - P - 4 rooms**
Village 7 miles from both Lincoln and Gainsborough

WADDINGTON
**Horse and Jockey Inn**
High Street, Waddington, Lincs LN5 9RF
Tel: 01522 720224    **£ - P - 4 rooms**
Village Inn 5 miles from Lincoln

WAINFLEET ALL SAINTS,
SKEGNESS
**The Royal Oak**
73 High Street, Wainfleet All Saints,
Skegness, Lincs PE24 4BZ
Tel: 01754 880328    **Rooms**
Pub features a popular beer garden and open fires

**The Woolpack Hotel**
39 High Street, Wainfleet All Saints,
Skegness, Lincs PE24 4BJ
Tel: 01754 880353    **Rooms**
Batemans hostelry, selection of bar meals served

WELLINGORE
**The Marquis of Granby**
See main entry above

WINTERTON
**Cross Keys Hotel**
King Street, Winterton, Lincs DN15 9RN
Tel: 01724 732215    **£ - P - 3 rooms**
Centre of village and a short drive to Scunthorpe

WOODHALL SPA
**Railway Hotel**
Kirkstead, Woodhall Spa, Lincs LN10 6QX
Tel: 01526 352580    **P - Rooms**
Pub that also has a touring and static caravan park

# NORFOLK

## ACLE
**East Norwich Inn**
47 Old Road, Acle, Norfolk NR13 3QN
Tel: 01493 751112     **P - 10 rooms**
Village Inn 10 miles from both Norwich and
Great Yarmouth

## ATTLEBOROUGH
**Breckland Lodge**
London Road, Attleborough, Norfolk NR17 1AY
Tel: 01953 455202     **£ - P - 21 rooms**
Large Inn / restaurant on the A11 near
Snetterton racecourse

## BEACHAMWELL
**Great Danes Country Inn**
The Green, Beachamwell, nr Swaffham,
Norfolk PE37 8BG
Tel: 01366 328443     **£ - P - 4 rooms**
Email: corole@gtdanes.fsnet.co.uk
Web: www.countryinns.co.uk
Traditional village Inn 6 miles from Swaffham

## BINHAM
**Chequers Inn**
Front Street, Binham, Norfolk NR21 0AL
Tel: 01328 830297     **£ - P - 2 rooms**
Quaint village Pub 10 miles from Fakenham

## BLAKENEY
**White Horse Hotel**
4 High Street, Blakeney, Norfolk NR25 7AL
Tel: 01263 740574     **££ - P - 10 rooms**
Village Inn 5 miles from Holt

## BURGH CASTLE, GREAT YARMOUTH
**Church Farm**
Church Road, Burgh Castle, Great Yarmouth,
Norfolk NR31 9QG
Tel: 01493 780251     **£ - P - 6 rooms**
Village Pub with restaurant, 3 miles from
Great Yarmouth

## BURNHAM MARKET, KINGS LYN
**Hoste Arms**
Market Place, Burnham Market, Kings Lyn,
Norfolk PE31 8HD
Tel: 01328 738257     **£££ - P - 28 rooms**
Email: thehostearms@compuserve.com
Web: www.hostearms.co.uk
Award winning Inn, pets welcome

## COLTISHALL
**Kings Head**
26 Wroxham Rd, Coltishall, Norfolk NR12 7EA
Tel: 01603 737426     **£ - P - 4 rooms**
Village Inn 7 miles from Norwich

## DERSINGHAM, KINGS LYN
**Coach and Horses Hotel**
77 Manor Road, Dersingham, Kings Lyn,
Norfolk PE31 6LN
Tel: 01485 540391     **£ - P - 3 rooms**
Village Inn located just 10 miles from Kings
Lynn

## DISS
**Crossways Public House**
Bridge Road, Diss, Norfolk IP21 4DJ
Tel: 01379 740638     **P - 3 rooms**
Village Inn 1 mile from Diss

## EAST BARSHAM, FAKENHAM
**White Horse Inn**
Fakenham Road, East Barsham, Fakenham,
Norfolk NR21 0LH
Tel: 01328 820645     **£ - P - 3 rooms**
Village Inn ideal for travellers, 3 miles from
Fakenham

## EATON
**Red Lion**
Eaton Street, Eaton, Norfolk
Tel: 01603 454787    **£ - P - 6 rooms**
17th century village Inn 5 miles from Norwich

## ERPINGHAM, AYLSHAM
**Saracen's Head**
Wolterton, Erpingham, Aylsham,
Norfolk NR11 7LX
Tel: 01263 768909    **££ - P - 4 rooms**
Web: www.broadland.com/saracenshead
Delightfully hidden in a corner of a field

## FOULDEN, THETFORD
**The White Hart Inn**
White Hart Street, Foulden, Thetford,
Norfolk IP26 5AW
Tel: 01366 328638    **£ - P - 3 rooms**
Email: sylviachisholm@virgin.net
Village inn, with accommodation in a former
barn

## FAKENHAM
**The Boar Inn**
Great Ryburgh, Fakenham, Norfolk NR21 0DX
Tel: 01328 829212    **£ - P - 5 rooms**
Email: boarinn@aol.com
Web: www.ourworld.compuserve.com/
    homepages/
Village Inn with restaurant near Fakenham

## GREAT YARMOUTH
**Dukes Head Hotel**
13 Hall Quay, Great Yarmouth,
Norfolk NR20 1HP
Tel: 01493 859184    **£ - P - 9 rooms**
Harbourside Inn

**White Horse Inn**
13 Northgate Street, Great Yarmouth, Norfolk
Tel: 01493 859560    **£ - P - 10 rooms**
Located close to the town centre and 5 minutes walk to the sea

## GRIMSTON, KINGS LYN
**The Bell Inn**
1 Gayton Road, Grimston, Kings Lynn,
Norfolk PE32 1BG
Tel: 01485 601156    **£ - P - 6 rooms**
Village Inn 8 miles from Kings Lyn

## HEVINGHAM, NORWICH
**Marsham Arms**
Hevingham, Norwich, Norfolk NR10 5NP
Tel: 01603 754268    ££ - P - 8 rooms
Email: nigelbradley@marshamarms.co.uk
Web: www.marshamarms.co.uk
Village Inn close to the Norfolk Broads

## HOLT
**Feathers Hotel**
6 Market Place, Holt, Norfolk NR25 6BW
Tel: 01263 712318    **££ - P - 16 rooms**
Town hotel with a public bar

## KINGS LYNN
**Kings Head Hotel**
See main entry on page 66

**The Stuart House Hotel**
See main entry on page 66

**The Tudor Rose Hotel**
St Nicholas Street, Kings Lynn,
Norfolk PE30 1LR
Tel: 01553 762824    **££ - P - 14 rooms**
Hotel / Inn near the centre of town

## LANGLEY
**The Beauchamp Arms**
Buckenham Ferry, Langley, Norfolk
Tel: 01508 480247    **£ - P - 5 rooms**
Riverside country Inn 10 minute drive to
Loddon

## LARLING
**Angel Inn**
Larling, Norfolk NR16 2QU
Tel: 01953 717963    **£ - P - 5 rooms**
Village Inn 6 miles from Attleborough

## MARSHAM
**Flags Free House**
Old Norwich Rd, Marsham, Norfolk NR10 5PS
Tel: 01263 735000    **££ - P - 12 rooms**
Village Inn 2 miles from Aylsham

## NORWICH
**Bakers Arms**
St Leonards, Norwich, Norfolk NR1 4JF
Tel: 01603 610684    **£ - P - 6 rooms**
Village Inn less than 1mile from Norwich

# Kings Head Hotel

*Great Bircham, Kings Lynn, Norfolk PE31 6RJ*

P

Tel: 01485 578265
Web: www.smoothhound.co.uk/hotels/kingsheadhotel.html

On the edge of the Royal Sandringham Estate beside the B1153, The King's Head Hotel is ideally placed for a whole host of holiday activities in this beautiful unspoilt part of Norfolk. The hotel has five charming bedrooms all with *en suite*, beverage making facilities and TV.

# The Stuart House Hotel

*35 Goodwins Road, King's Lynn, Norfolk PE30 5QX*

**££ - P - rooms**

Tel: 01553 772169    Fax: 01553 774788
Email: stuarthousehotel@btinternet.com
Web: www.stuart-house-hotel.co.uk

Quietly situated, close to the town centre, yet The Stuart House Hotel is far from the madding crowd. The refurbished bedrooms have been individually furnished to make every guest's stay an extremely pleasant and comfortable one. The Honeymoon Suite boasts a superb Four-Poster Bed and Jacuzzi, most room are *en suite* and have tea / coffee making facilities, satellite TV and direct dial telephones. Regular, plus a large selection of guest beers always available in our CAMRA *Good Beer Guide* listed bar. The Kings Lynn Beer Festival is held in the grounds in July.

**The Buckinghamshire Arms**
Blickling, Norwich, Norfolk NR11 6NF
Tel: 01263 732133    **££ - P - 3 rooms**
17th century traditional village Inn

**Worlds End**
Norwich Road, Norwich, Norfolk NL14 8JT
Tel: 01508 570205    **£ - P - 2 rooms**
Country Pub situated just 5 miles from Norwich

OLD HUNSTANTON
**Neptune Inn**
85 Old Hunstanton Road, Old Hunstanton, Norfolk PE36 6HZ
Tel: 01485 532122    **£££ - P - 7 rooms**
Village Inn 1 mile from Hunstanton

POTTER HEIGHAM, GREAT YARMOUTH
**Falgate Inn**
Ludham Road, Potter Heigham, Great Yarmouth, Norfolk NR29 5HZ
Tel: 01692 670003    **£ - P - 5 rooms**
Email: mailber@cypress72.freeserve.co.uk
Village Inn 10 miles from Great Yarmouth

RICKINGHALL, DISS
**The Bell Inn**
See main entry opposite

ROUGHTON, NORWICH
**New Inn**
Norwich Road, Roughton, Norwich, Norfolk NR11 8SJ

# The Bell Inn

*The Street, Rickinghall, Diss, Norfolk IP22 1BN*

**P - Rooms**

Tel: 01379 898445
Email: bell-inn@rickinghall.fsworld.co.uk
Web: www.thebellrickinghall.com

The Bell is a delightful 17th Century Coaching Inn located in a peaceful village setting, overlooking the surrounding countryside. With ample Free Parking and Patio Garden. All bedrooms are centrally heated, Fully En-Suite and individually furnished in keeping with the character and atmosphere of the Inn. They are equipped with a Colour Television, Radio Alarm Clock, Hair Dryer and Tea & Coffee making facilities.

Tel: 01263 761389    **£ - P - rooms**
Country Inn 18 miles from Norwich

### RUSHALL, DISS
**Half Moon Inn**
The Street, Rushall, Diss, Norfolk IP21 4QD
Tel: 01379 740793    **£ - P - 11 rooms**
Email: stay@rushallhalfmooninns.co.uk
Web: www.rushallhalfmooninns.co.uk
Traditional local village Inn located 4 miles from Diss

### SALHOUSE, NORWICH
**The Lodge Inn**
Vicarage Road, Salhouse, Norwich,
Norfolk NR13 6HD
Tel: 01603 782828    **££ - P - 3 rooms**
Email: thelodgeinn@salhouse.f.s.business.co.uk
Situated 1 mile from Wroxham

### SNETTISHAM, KINGS LYNN
**The Rose and Crown**
Old Church Road, Snettisham, Kings Lyn,
Norfolk PE31 7LX
Tel: 01485 541382    **££ - P - 11 rooms**
Web: www.14th-century-inn.co.uk
Village Inn 4 miles from Hunstanton

### SOUTH WOOTON, KINGS LYNN
**Farmers Arms Inn**
South Wootton, Kings Lyn, Norfolk PE30 3HQ
Tel: 01553 675566    **£££ - P - 61 rooms**
Large country Inn 4 miles from Kings Lyn

### SPROWSTON, NORWICH
**The Blue Boar**
See main entry on page 70

### TASBURGH, nr NORWICH
**Countryman**
Ipswich Road, Tasburgh, nr Norwich,
Norfolk NR15 1NS
Tel: 01508 470946    **£ - P - 2 rooms**
Country style Inn, main road location

### THOMPSON, THETFORD
**The Chequers Inn**
See main entry on page 70

### THORNHAM, NORFOLK
**The Lifeboat Inn**
See main entry on page 71

### THORPE MARKET, NORWICH
**Green Farm Hotel**
North Walsham Road, Thorpe Market,
Norwich, Norfolk NR11 8TH
Tel: 01263 833602    **££ - P - 14 rooms**
16th century farmhouse hotel close to the
Norfolk Broads

### TITCHWELL
**Titchwell Manor Hotel**
Titchwell, Norfolk PE31 8BB
Tel: 01485 210221    **££ - P - 15 rooms**
A manor hotel with a public bar 10 minutes
drive to Hunstanton

# The Blue Boar Inn

NORWICH

*259 Wroxham Road, Sprowston, Norwich, Norfolk NR7 8RL*

**£ - P - 5 rooms**

Tel: 01603 426803
Fax: 01603 487749
Email: enquiries@blueboarnorwich.co.uk
Web: www.blueboarnorwich.co.uk

The Blue Boar Inn is situated on the main A1151 fron Norwich to Wroxham just one mile from the ring road and ten minutes drive from the City centre.

Room Rate per night, not per person, including English breakfast served in your room

| | | |
|---|---|---|
| Room 1 | £45.00 | Single £35.00 (double bed, adjacent private bathroom) |
| Rooms 2 and 4 | £50.00 | Single £40.00 (2 double beds in each) |
| Room 5 | £60.00 | Single £50.00 (1 double bed and lounge furniture) |
| Room 3 | £70.00 | Single £60.00 (2 double beds and lounge furniture) |

NB: rooms 1 and 2 can be linked to provide a family suite, 3 double beds.

---

# The Chequers Inn

*Griston Road , Thompson, Thetford, Norfolk IP24 1PX*

**££ - P - R - BM - PW - BG - C**

Tel: 01953 483360        Fax: 01953 488092
Email: themcdowalls@barbox.net
Web: www.thompsonchequers.com (under construction)

The Chequers Inn is ideally situated for visitors who enjoy walking and exploring beautiful countryside, and is hidden amongst the trees on the edge of Thompson Village. The well-appointed purpose built accommodation offers everything for the modern traveller, including telephone, television, hairdryer, modem point, tea and coffee making facilities. One room is furnished for the disabled.

The Inn has a fine no smoking restaurant, as well as a bar snack menu, There is a large garden and ample parking.

Well-behaved dogs are welcome in the public bar and garden

---

TIVETSHALL ST MARY
**The Old Ram Coaching Inn**
Ipswich Road, Tivetshall St Mary,
Norfolk NR15 2DE
Tel: 01379 676794    **££ - P - 11 rooms**
Country Inn 5 miles from Diss

TOFT MONKS
**Toft Lion**
Toft Monks, Norfolk NR34 0EP
Tel: 01502 677702    **£ - P - 2 rooms**
Quiet Village Inn located just 3 miles from
Beccles

# Lifeboat Inn

*Ship Lane, Thornham, Norfolk PE36 6LT*

**P - 14 rooms**

Tel: 01485 512236
Email: reception@lifeboatinn.co.uk
Web: www.lifeboatinn.co.uk

The original character of this 16th Century Alehouse has been retained while offering modern comforts for a more relaxing stay. All bedrooms are *en suite*, have beverage making facilities, TV and direct dial telephones. Most have spectacular views over Thornham harbour to the sea.

UPPER SHERINGHAM
**The Red Lion Inn**
The St, Upper Sheringham, Norfolk NR26 8AD
Tel: 01263 825408 **£ - P - 3 rooms**
400 year old Pub with views of the sea 1 mile from Sheringham

WEST BECKHAM
**The Wheatsheaf**
Manor Farm, Church Road, West Beckham,
Norfolk NR25 6NX
Tel: 01263 822110 **P - 3 rooms**
Village Inn 3 miles from Sherringham

WISBECH
**The Princess Victoria Country Inn**
Market Lane, Walpole St Andrew, Wisbech,
Norfolk PE14 7LP
Tel: 01945 780888 **£ - P - 2 rooms**
Email: carole@princessvictoria.fsnet.co.uk
Country Inn 10 minutes drive to Wisbech

WAREHAM ALL SAINTS
**Three Horseshoes**
Bridge Street, Wareham All Saints,
Norfolk NR23 1NL
Tel: 01328 710547 **£ - P - 3 rooms**
Village Inn 2 miles from Wells

WINTERTON-ON-SEA
**Fishermans Return**
The Lane, Winterton-on-Sea,
Norfolk NR29 4BN
Tel: 01493 393305 **Rooms**
A 300 year old pub built from traditional brick and flint

WYMONDHAM
**Cross Keys Inn**
11–13 Market Place, Wymondham,
Norfolk NR18 0AX
Tel: 01953 602152 **£ - 4 rooms**
Town centre Pub

# NORTHAMPTONSHIRE

BADBY
**The Windmill**
Main Street, Badby, Northants NN11 3AN
Tel: 01327 702363    **££ - P - 10 rooms**
Traditional thatched, stone, Inn / hotel 2 miles
from Daventry

ASHBY ST LEDGER
**The Old Coach House**
Main Street, Ashby St Ledger,
Northants CV23 8UN
Tel: 01788 890349    **££ - P - 6 rooms**
Email: info@theoldecoachhouse.co.uk
Web: www.theoldecoachhouse.co.uk
Country village Inn 3 miles from Daventry

BARNWELL
**Montagu Arms**
Barnwell, Northants PE8 5PH
Tel: 01832 273726    **£ - P - 3 rooms**
Village Pub 3 miles from Oundle

BRACKLEY
**The Red Lion**
11 Market Place, Brackley,
Northants N13 7AB
Tel: 01280 702228    **£ - P - 3 rooms**
Town centre location

CLIPSTON
**The Bulls Head**
Harborough Road, Clipston,
Northants LE16 9RT
Tel: 01858 525268    **£ - P - 3 rooms**
Village Inn 3 miles from Market Harborough

DAVENTRY
**Abercom Hotel**
101 Warwick, Daventry, Northants NN11 4AJ
Tel: 01327 703741    **£ - P - 20 rooms**
Hotel / Pub 12 miles from Rugby

DESBOROUGH
**The George**
79 High Street, Desborough,
Northants NN14 2NB
Tel: 01536 760271    **£ - P - 5 rooms**
Town centre Pub

EAST HADDON, NORTHAMPTON
**The Red Lion Hotel**
East Haddon, Northampton,
Northants NN6 8BU
Tel: 01604 770223    **££ - P - 5 rooms**
Village Inn 7 miles from J18 off the M1

GAYTON
**The Queen Victoria Inn**
See main entry opposite

HARRINGTON
**The White Swan**
Seaton Road, Harringworth,
Northants NN17 3AF
Tel: 01572 747543    **££ - P - 6 rooms**
Three miles from Rockingham racing circuit

HARRINGWORTH
**The White Swan**
See main entry opposite

HELLIDON, DAVENTRY
**The Red Lion**
Hellidon, Daventry, Northants NN11 6LE

# The Queen Victoria Inn

*10 High Street, Gayton, Northants NN7 3HD*

**£ - P - R - BM - 4 rooms**

Tel / Fax: 01604 858878

The Queen Victoria Inn is centrally located just 5 miles from Northampton town centre, 3 miles from Junction 15A of the M1 and 4 miles from Towester. The bar serves Tanglefoot and Eagle IPA ales as well as a large selection of fine wines. Lots of homemade dishes, using local produce, are served either in the bar or restaurant. The home made sweets and puddings are a speciality. As well as the steak menu there is also a snack menu at lunchtime.

Accommodation consists of three twin rooms (from £55 per night) and 1 single room (£35 per night) all rooms are *en suite*. There is plenty of car parking, disabled facilities and a heated outside patio area. Friday to Sunday open all day.

# The White Swan

*Seaton Road, Harringworth, Northants NN17 3AF*

Tel: +44(0)01572 747543
Email: thewhiteswan@fsmail.net
Web: www.thewhite-swan.com

The White Swan provides six recently refurbished *en suite* comfortable bedrooms, each individually designed in attractive country style, all have full central heating, colour television, radio alarm, tea and coffee making facilities and hairdryer.

The restaurant is usually busy – a sign that our food goes down well with our customers. We often change our menu adding new dishes, as well as keeping the more traditional ones like our roast Sunday lunch.

The White Swan, which has been serving the local community since the 16th century, is a free house and serves a good selection of beers as well as keeping a larger than usual range of wines for the connoisseur to choose from.

Tel: 01327 261200     **££ - P - 8 rooms**
Email: j.daffurn@aol.com
Village Inn 6 miles from Daventry

### IRTHLINGBOROUGH
**Oliver Twist**
96 High Street, Irthlingborough,
Northants NN9 5PX
Tel: 01933 650353     **£ - P - 5 rooms**
Local village Pub 3 miles from Wellingborough

### KILSBY
**The George**
11–13 Watling Street, Kilsby,
Northants CV23 8YE
Tel: 01788 822229     **£ - P - 6 rooms**
Village Inn 2 miles from J18 off the M1

### LOIS WEEDON
**The Globe Hotel**
Watling Street, Lois Weedon,

Northants NN7 4QD
Tel: 01327 340336    **££ - P - 18 rooms**
Email: info@theglobeatweedon.co.uk
Country hotel 3 miles from Daventry

**MORTON PINKNEY**
**Englands Rose**
Upper Green, Morton Pinkney, nr Daventry,
Northants NN11 3SG
Tel: 01295 760353    **£ - P - 8 rooms**
Village Inn 10 miles from Daventry

**NETHER HAYFORD**
**The Foresters Arms**
22 The Green, Nether Hayford,
Northants NN7 3LE
Tel: 01327 340622    **£ - P - 3 rooms**
Village Pub 7 miles from Towcester

**SIBBERTOFT**
**The Red Lion**
Wellend Rise, Sibbertoft, Northants LE16 9UD
Tel: 01858 880011    **£ - P - 2 flats**
Village Inn 6 miles from Market Harborough

**SULGRAVE**
**The Star Inn**
Manor Road, Sulgrave, Northants OX17 2SA
Tel: 01295 760389    **££ - P - 3 rooms**
17th century ivy clad Inn 6 miles from Banbury

**SYRESHAM, nr BRACKLEY**
**The Kings Head**
2 Abbey Road, Syresham, nr Brackley,
Northants NN13 5HW
Tel: 01280 850280    **££ - P - 5 rooms**
Email: kingshead@aol.com
Small village Inn 4 miles from Brackley and 2
miles from Silverstone

**TOWCESTER**
**The Saracens Head Hotel**
219 Watling Street, Towcester,
Northants NN12 6BX
Tel: 01327 350414    **££ - P - 2 rooms**
Old coaching Inn 7 miles from Northampton

**WEST TOWCESTER**
**The Winning Post**
97 Watling Street, west Towcester,
Northants NN12 6AG

Tel: 01327 353891    **£ - P - 10 rooms**
Local town Pub

**The Monk and Tipster**
36 Watling Street, Towcester,
Northants NN12 6AF
Tel: 01327 350416    **£ - 9 rooms**
Located 200 yards from the town centre

**UPPER BENFIELD, CASTLE ASHBY**
**Falcon Hotel**
Upper Benefield, Castle Ashby,
Northants NN7 1LF
Tel: 01604 696200    **£££ - P - 16 rooms**
Holds the highest AA award for Inns

**UPPER BENFIELD,**
**PETERBOROUGH**
**Benefield Wheatsheaf Hotel**
Upper Benefield, Peterborough,
Northants PE8 5AN
Tel: 01832 205254    **£ - P - 9 rooms**
Menu changes seasonally

**WEEDON LOIS, NORTHAMPTON**
**Heart of England Hotel**
High Street, Weedon Lois, Northampton,
Northants NN7 4QD
Tel: 01327 340335    **£ - P - 13 rooms**
Village Inn 7 miles from Towcester

**WEEDON LOIS, NORTHAMPTON**
**The Narrow Boat Inn**
Stow Hill, Weedon Lois, Northampton,
Northants NN7 4RZ
Tel: 01327 340536    **£ - P - 7 rooms**
Next to the canal 7 miles from Northampton

**WHITFIELD**
**Sun Inn**
Farrer Close, Whitfield, Northants NN13 5TG
Tel: 01280 850232    **£ - P - 10 rooms**
Email: suninn00@hotmail.com
Village Inn 4 miles from Brackley

**WHITLLEBURY**
**The Fox and Hounds**
44 High Street, Whitllebury,
Northants NN12 8XJ
Tel: 01327 857210    **£ - P - 4 rooms**
Village Inn close to Silverstone race track

# NOTTINGHAMSHIRE

Tel: 01909 591213　**£ - P - 7 rooms**
Village Inn 5 miles from Worksop

**BUNNY, NOTTINGHAM**
**Rancliffe Arms**
Loughborough Road, Bunny, Nottingham,
Notts NG11 6QT
Tel: 01159 844727　**£ - P - 4 rooms**
Village Inn 11 miles from Nottingham

**DUNHAM-ON-TRENT**
**The Bridge Inn**
Main Street, Dunham-on-Trent, Notts
Tel: 01777 228385　**P - Rooms**
Village local on the A57, good ales

**EDWINSTOWE**
**Forest Lodge Hotel**
2–4 Church Street, Edwinstowe,
Notts NG21 9QA
Tel: 01623 824443　**£ - P - 8 rooms**
Email: ed@forestlodge.co.uk
Village Inn 2 miles from Mansfield

**BARNABY-IN-THE-WILLOWS,**
**NEWARK**
**Willow Tree Inn**
Front Street, Barnby-in-the-Willows, Newark,
Notts NG24 2SA
Tel: 01636 626613　**£ - P - 7 rooms**
Email: info@willowtreeinn.co.uk
Web: www.wiilowtreeinn.co.uk
Village Inn 4 miles from Newark

**EDWINSTOWE, MANSFIELD**
**The Black Swan**
High Street, Edwinstowe, Mansfield,
Notts NG21 9QR
Tel: 01623 822598　**£ - P - 3 rooms**
Email: blackswan@fsbusiness
Located in the centre of Edwinstowe

**BESTHORPE**
**The Lord Nelson**
Main Road, Besthorpe, Notts NG23 7HR
Tel: 01636 892265　**£ - P - 3 rooms**
Village Inn 7 miles from Newark

**FLINTHAM, EWARK**
**The Boot and Shoe**
Main Street, Flintham, Ewark,
Notts NG23 5LA
Tel: 01636 525246　**£ - P - 5 rooms**
17th century Inn 6 miles from Newark

**BINGHAM**
**Chesterfield Arms**
Church Street, Bingham, Notts NG13 8AL
Tel: 01949 837342　**£ - P - 3 rooms**
Village Inn 7 miles from Nottingham

**KEGWORTH**
**The Station Hotel**
Station Road, Kegworth, Notts DE74 2GE
Tel: 01509 672252　**£ - P - 4 rooms**
Old fashioned country Pub close to J24
off the M1

**BLYTH**
**The Angel Inn**
Bawtry Road, Blyth, Notts

KELHAM, NEWARK
**Red House Country Manor Hotel**
Main Street, Kelham, Newark,
Notts NG23 5QP
Tel: 01636 705266    **££ - P - 8 rooms**
Country Inn 3 miles from Newark town centre

KIMBERLEY
**Nelson and Railway Inn**
12 Station Road, Kimberley, Notts NG16 2NR
Tel: 01159 382177    **£ - P - 3 rooms**
Village Inn 5 miles from Nottingham

NETHER LANGWITH, MANSFIELD
**The Jug and Glass**
Queens walk, Nether Langwith, Mansfield,
Notts NG20 9EW
Tel: 01623 742283    **£ - P – R – BM - BG**
Email: carolhill@btinternet.com
Beautiful rural setting - The Pub by the stream

NEWARK
**The Mailcoach**
13 London Road, Newark, Notts NG24 1TN
Tel: 01636 605164    **£ - P - 8 rooms**
Traditional Inn 2 minute walk to Newark town
centre

**The Watermill**
67 Millgate, Newark, Notts NG24 4JU
Tel: 01636 703385    **£ - P - 2 rooms**
Local community Pub 5 minutes walk to the
town centre

NORMANTON-ON-TRENT
**The Square and Compass**
Eastgate, Normanton-on-Trent,
Notts NG23 6RN
Tel: 01636 821439    **£ - P - 3 rooms**
Village Pub 12 miles from Newark

NOTTINGHAM
**Framptons Bar and Bistro**
11 St James Terrace, Nottingham,
Notts NG1 6FW
Tel: 01159 411997    **£ - 6 rooms**
Bar bistro in the centre of Nottingham

RAWLSTON, NEWARK
**The Crown Inn**
Staythorpe Road, Rawlston, Newark,
Notts NG25 5SG
Tel: 01636 814358    **£ - P - 5 rooms**
Village Inn with restaurant 4 miles from
Newark

RETFORD
**Black Boy Inn**
14 Moorgate, Retford, Notts DN22 6RH
Tel: 01777 702758    **£ - P - 3 rooms**
Local Pub on the outskirts of Retford

RETFORD
**Newcastle Arms**
37 Bridge Gate, Retford, Notts DN22 7UX
Tel: 01777 702446    **£ - P - rooms**
Town Pub just 100 yards from the town cen-
tre

SOUTHWELL
**Crown Hotel**
11 Market Place, Southwell,
Notts ND25 0HE
Tel: 01636 812120    **£ - P - 7 rooms**
Town Pub 13 miles from Nottingham city

**Reindeer Inn**
26 Westgate, Southwell,
Notts NG25 0JH
Tel: 01636 813257    **£ - P - 3 rooms**
Village Inn 7 miles from Newark

UNDERWOOD, NOTTINGHAM
**Hole In the Wall**
Main Road, Underwood, Nottingham,
Notts NG16 5GQ
Tel: 01773 713936    **££ - P - 12 rooms**
Village Inn 20 minutes drive to Nottingham

WEST STOCKWITH
**Waterfront**
Canal Lane, West Stockwith, Nottinghamshire
Tel: 01427 891223    **£ - P - 1 flat**
Village Inn opposite the Marina 7 miles from
Gainsborough

# SHROPSHIRE

Tel: 01746 763977    **£ - P - 2 rooms**
Email: sugarloaf@globalnet.co.uk
Web: www.bassavilla.com
16thC Inn with award winning restaurant

**The Friars Inn**
3 St Mary's Street, Bridgnorth,
Shropshire WV16 4DW
Tel: 01746 762396      **6 rooms**
Town Inn 2 minutes walk from the centre

**The Golden Lion**
83 High St, Bridgnorth, Shropshire WV16 4DS
Tel: 01746 762016    **£ - P - 4 rooms**
Web: www.midlandspubs.co.uk/
        bridgnorth/goldenlion
Located on Bridgnorth high street

## BISHOP'S CASTLE
**The Castle Hotel**
The Square, Bishop's Castle,
Shropshire SY9 5BN
Tel: 01588 638403      **££ - P - 5 rooms**
Web: www.bishops-castle.co.uk/castlehotel
CAMRA listed, Ideal for walkers

**Three Tuns**
Salop Street, Bishop's Castle,
Shropshire SY9 5BW
Tel: 01588 638797      **££ - P - 4 rooms**
Located 2 minutes walk from the town centre

## BORASTON, TENBURY WELLS
**Peacock Inn**
Worcester Road, Boraston, Tenbury Wells,
Shropshire, WR15 8LL
Tel: 01584 810506      **££ - P - 3 rooms**
Email: juidler@fsbdial.co.uk
Web: smoothhound.co.uk/hotels/peacockinn.html
One mile from Tenbury Wells

## BRIDGNORTH
**Bassa Villa Bar and Grill**
48 Cartway, Bridgnorth,
Shropshire WV16 4BG

## BRIMFIELD, LUDLOW
**The Roebuck Inn**
Brimfield, Ludlow, Shropshire SY8 4NE
Tel: 01584 711230      **££ - P - 3 rooms**
Between Ludlow and Leominster

## BROSELEY, NR IRONBRIDGE
**The Pheasant Inn**
See main entry on page 78

## BURLTON, SHREWSBURY
**The Burlton Inn**
Burlton, Shrewsbury, Shropshire SY4 5TB
Tel: 01939 270284      **££ - P - 6 rooms**
Email: bean@burltoninn.co.uk
Web: www.burltoninn.co.uk
Country Inn 7 miles from Shrewsbury

## BUTTERCROSS, LUDLOW
**The Church Inn**
See main entry on page 78

## CANDY, OSWESTRY
**The Old Mill Inn**
Candy, Oswestry, Shropshire
Tel: 01691 657058      **£ - P - 5 rooms**
Original Millhouse Pub 2 miles from Oswestry

# The Pheasant Inn

*56 Church Street, Broseley, nr Ironbridge,*
*Shropshire TF12 5BX*

**£ - P - 5 rooms**

Tel / Fax: 01952 884499
Email: susan.vasey@btopenworld.com
Web: www.virtual-shropshire.co.uk/pheasant/

Located in the centre of the rural Shropshire town of Broseley, close to the Ironbridge Gorge,
you are assured of a warm welcome by the owners
Clive and Sue Vasey. Four *en suite* bedrooms are spacious and individually decorated, offering
all the amenities and comfort guests have come to expect from this quality Inn, which clearly
benefits from Clive and Sue's twenty-five years experience.

Dining at The Pheasant is a rare treat. Using only fresh ingredients in all the dishes, the menu is
both varied and imaginative. In the cooler months log fires complete the warm and friendly
atmosphere in the dinning area, or guests can take their meals al fresco on the rear patio during
the summer months.

The Pheasant Inn is located in the rural town of Broseley, close to Ironbridge and Telford. We
are easily accessible via the nearby motorway network (M54).

# The Church Inn

*Buttercross, Ludlow, Shropshire SY8 1AW*

**£ - P - 9 rooms**

Tel: 01584 872174      Fax: 01584 877146
Email: reception@thechurchinn.com      Web: www.thechurchinn.com

The Church Inn has nine rooms, all *en suite* ~ with their own tea making
facilities and colour television. As well as a range of traditional beers,
including a regularly changed "guest" beer, there is a wide choice of wines, spirits, cocktails and
soft drinks.

The restaurant seats 24, and it is often worthwhile booking a table as our reputation for carefully chosen ingredients and freshly cooked dishes usually ensures a full house.

Double / Twin *en suite*                          £50.00 / room
Single occupancy (Monday to Thursday inc)    £30.00 / room
Family *en suite* room (double and single bed) £60.00 / room

CHELMARSH, BRIGNORTH
**The Bulls Head Inn**
Chelmarsh, Bridgnorth, Shropshire, WV16 6BA
Tel: 01746 861469      **£ - P - 9 rooms**

Email: dave@bullshead.fsnet.co.uk
Web: www.virtual-shropshire.co.uk/bulls-head-inn
A 17th century Inn located 4 miles south of
Bridgnorth

## CHELMARSH, BRIGNORTH
**Unicorn Inn**
Hampton Loade, Chelmarsh, Bridgnorth,
Shropshire WV16 6BN
Tel: 01746 861515     **£ - P - 9 rooms**
Email: unicorninn.bridgnorth@virginnet.co.uk
Web: www.freespace.virginnet.co.uk/unicorninn
Located in the Severn Valley, ideal for walking
and fishing

## CHETWIND END, NEWPORT
**Bridge Inn**
Lower Bar, Chetwind End, Newport,
Shropshire TF10 7JB
Tel: 01952 811785     **£ - P - 5 rooms**
Town Pub situated half a mile from the town
centre

## CHURCH STRETTON
**Longmynd Hotel**
Cunnery Road, Church Stretton,
Shropshire SY6 6AG
Tel: 01694 722244     **Rooms**
Pets welcome in hotel accommodation

## CLEOBURY MORTIMER
**The Crown at Hopton**
Hopton Wafers, Cleobury Mortimer,
Shropshire DY14 0NB
Tel: 01299 270372     **££ - P - 7 rooms**
Email: desk@crownathopton.co.uk
Web: www.go2.co.uk/crownathopton
Village Inn 8 miles from Ludlow

## CLEOBURY MORTIMER
**The Kings Arms Hotel**
Cleobury Mortimer, Shropshire DY14 8BS
Tel: 01299 270252     **£ - 5 rooms**
Town centre Pub with rooms

## CLEOBURY MORTIMER
**Redfern Hotel**
Cleobury Mortimer, Shropshire
Tel: 01299 270395     **PW - Rooms**
Pets welcome

## CLUN
**Sun Inn**
High Street, Clun, Shropshire SY7 8JB
Tel: 01588 640277     **£ - P - 7 rooms**
On the high street in the small town of Clun

## COALBROOKDALE, TELFORD
**The Grove Inn**
10 Wellington Road, Coalbrookdale, Telford,
Shropshire TF8 7DX
Tel: 01952 433269     **£ - P - 4 rooms**
Email: frog@fat-frog.co.uk
Web: www.fat-frog.co.uk
Traditional Inn near the famous Ironbridge

## CRAVEN ARMS
**Stokesay Castle Coaching Inn**
School Road, Craven Arms, Shropshire SY7 9PE
Tel: 01588 672304     **££ - P - 12 rooms**
Email: stokesaycastlecoachinginn@talk21.com
Local Pub 8 miles from Ludlow

## CRAVEN ARMS
**Craven Arms Hotel**
Tewsbury Road, Craven Arms, Shropshire
Tel: 01588 673331     **£ - P - 8 rooms**
Town Pub located in the centre of town

## CRESSAGE
**The Cholmondeley Riverside Inn**
Cressage, Shropshire SY5 6AF
Tel: 01952 510900     **££ - P - 7 rooms**
17th century riverside rural Pub / restaurant

## EDGMOND, NEWPORT
**Lamb Inn**
29 Shrewsbury Road, Edgmond, Newport,
Shropshire TF10 8HU
Tel: 01952 810421     **£ - P - 3 rooms**
Rural Pub 1 mile from Newport

## FORTON, NEWPORT
**The Swan at Forton**
Eccleshall Road, Forton, Newport,
Shropshire TF10 8BY
Tel: 01952 812169     **£ - P - 9 rooms**
Village Inn 4 miles from Newport

## FRANKWELL, SHREWSBURY
**Ye Olde Bucks Head Inn**
Frankwell, Shrewsbury. Shropshire SY3 8JR
Tel: 01743 369392     **£ - P - 10 rooms**
Email: jennyhodges@onetel.net.uk
Local Pub half a mile from the town centre

## HANMER, NR WHITCHURCH
**Hanmer Arms**
See main enrty on page 80

# Hanmer Arms

*Hanmer, nr Whitchurch, Shropshire SY13 3DE*

**££ - P - R - BM - BG - C - WTB 3 stars - 28 rooms**

Tel: 01948 830532    Fax: 01948 830740
Email: enquiry@hanmerhotel.co.uk
Web: www.hanmerhotel.co.uk

The Hanmer Arms Hotel is a quiet, family-run establishment where guests can be assured of a warm welcome and first-class service throughout their stay. Most of the staff are local to the area and will be happy to help you plan your holiday if required. There are 25 bedrooms, most of which are located outside the main building allowing guests the freedom and privacy to come and go as they please, children are most welcome. There is also a ground floor apartment for elderly or disabled guests.

The Hanmer Hotel is licensed to hold civil wedding ceremonies and has superb conference facilities for local businesses. They also run a popular Sunday Carvery lunch and the restaurant is renowned for its excellent food and friendly service. The Hanmer Arms Hotel also boasts ample car parking, beer garden and a gym room.

---

## HARLEY, nr SHREWSBURY
**Plume of Feathers**
Harley, nr Shrewsbury, Shropshire SY5 6LP
Tel: 01952 727360    **£ - P - rooms**
Country Inn 5 minutes walk into Harley

## HODNET
**The Bear Hotel**
Hodnet, Shropshire TF9 3NH
Tel: 01630 685214    **££ - P - 8 rooms**
Known for its medieval banquets

## IRONBRIDGE GORGE, TELFORD
**Bird in Hand Inn**
Waterloo Street, Ironbridge Gorge, Telford,
Shropshire TF8 7HG
Tel: 01952 432226    **££ - P - 6 rooms**
18th century Inn, in the Ironbridge Gorge

## IRONBRIDGE GORGE, TELFORD
**The Golden Ball Inn**
Newbridge Road, Ironbridge Gorge, Telford,
Shropshire TF8 7BA
Tel: 01952 432179    **££ - P - 4 rooms**
Email: matrowland@hotmail.com
Web: www.thegoldenballinn.com
Traditional Inn 500 yards from Iron Bridge

## LLANFAIR WATERDINE
**The Waterdine**
Llanfair Waterdine, Shropshire LD7 1TU
Tel: 01547 528214    **££ - P - 3 rooms**
Country Inn with restaurant 5 miles from
Knighton

## LONGVILLE-IN-THE-DALE
**Longville Arms**
Longville in the Dale, Much Wenlock,
Shropshire TF13 6DT
Tel: 01694 771206    **£ - P - 4 rooms**
Authentic 18th century Inn

## LUDFORD BRIDGE, LUDLOW
**Charlton Arms Hotel**
Ludford Bridge, Ludlow, Shropshire SY8 1PJ
Tel: 01584 872813    **££ - P - 6 rooms**
Riverside Inn 5 minutes walk from the town
centre

## LUDLOW
**The Wheatsheaf Inn**
Lower Broad St, Ludlow, Shropshire SY8 1PQ
Tel: 01584 872980    **£ - 5 rooms**
17th century Inn 100 yards from the town
centre

**The Bull Hotel**
14 The Bull Ring, Ludlow, Shropshire SY8 1AD
Tel: 01584 873611     **£ - P - 4 rooms**
Email: bull.ludlow@btinternet.com
Web: www.ludlow.org.uk/bullhotel
Oldest Pub in Ludlow dating to the 14thC

**LYDBURY NORTH**
**The Powis Arms**
Lydbury North, Shropshire SY7 8AU
Tel: 01588 680254     **££ - P - 3 rooms**
An Inn on a lake 3 miles from Bishops Castle

**MELVERLEY**
**The Tontine Inn**
See main entry below

**MUCH WENLOCK**
**Gaskell Arms Hotel**
Much Wenlock, Shropshire TF13 6AQ
Tel: 01952 727212     **££ - P - 13 rooms**
Email: maxine@gaskellarms.co.uk
Web: www.smoothhound.co.uk/gaskell/hotel
Hotel 5 minutes walk to the town centre

**The Talbot Inn**
See main entry on page 82

**MUNSLOW**
**The Crown**
Munslow, Shropshire SY7 9ET

Tel: 01584 841205     **£ - P - 3 rooms**
Country Inn 7 miles from Ludlow

**NORTHGATE, BRIDGNORTH**
**The Bear Inn**
Northgate, Bridgnorth, Shropshire WV16 4ET
Tel: 01746 763250     **£ - P - 3 rooms**
Located in the centre of Northgate

**OSWESTRY**
**The Bear Hotel**
Salop Road, Oswestry, Shropshire SY11 2NR
Tel: 01691 652093     **££ - P - 10 rooms**
Small town hotel with a malt whisky bar

**Greyhound Hotel**
Willow St, Oswestry, Shropshire SY11 1AJ
Tel: 01691 653392     **£ - P - 3 rooms**
Edge of town rural Pub, short walk to the
town centre

**PICKLESCOTT**
**Bottle and Glass Inn**
Picklescott, Shropshire SY6 6NR
Tel: 01694 751345     **£ - P - 3 rooms**
Deep in the country Inn 10 miles from
Shrewsbury

**SHREWSBURY**
**Cromwells Hotel and Wine Bar**
11 Dogpole, Shrewsbury, Shropshire SY1 1EN

# Tontine Inn

*Melverley, Nr Shrewsbury, Shropshire SY40 8PJ*

**£ - P - 3 rooms**

Tel: 01691 682258
Email: tontine.inn@btinternet.com
Web: www.tontineinn.co.uk

The Tontine Inn is situated on the Welsh Border. The Public House serves Real Ale, Good Food, and also offers three luxuriously furnished *en suite* bedrooms to those wishing to stay in this area of castles, myths and legends.

The well stocked bar offers an endless selection of beers, spirits and an ever-growing selection of fine malt whiskies, wines, aperitifs and soft drinks. It is also equipped with a large Library and a three-piece suite seating area for your comfort.

Each room provides: Power Shower · Hair Dryer · Colour TV · Dual Voltage Shaver Point · Tea and Coffee

# The Talbot Inn

*High Street, Much Wenlock, Shropshire TF13 6AA*

**P - 6 rooms**

Tel: 01952 727077    Fax: 01952 728436
Email: maggie@talbotinn.dps.co.uk
Web: www.the-talbot-inn.com

The Talbot Inn is a delightful old tavern; it is approached through an archway that leads into a charming courtyard. Overlooking the courtyard, the former Malt House of 1762 has been converted into 6 spacious en suite bedrooms, all attractively appointed and equipped with television, hair dryer, hospitality tray and telephone / modem.

The inn, with its old beams and open log fire, is full of character and atmosphere, and the much-praised food lives up to its reputation. All dishes are based on prime quality local ingredients, carefully prepared, attractively presented and served by courteous and efficient staff.

---

Tel: 01743 361440    **£ - 7 rooms**
Email: theresa@cromwellsinn.co.uk
Web: www.cromwellshotel.co.uk
Wine bar / restaurant / rooms located in the centre of Shrewsbury

## ST GEORGES, TELFORD
**Albion Inn**
Station Hill, St Georges, Telford,
Shropshire TF2 9AD
Tel: 01952 614193    **£ - P - 2 rooms**
Village Pub 1 mile from Telford

## TRENCH
**Old Shawbirch Inn**
Trench Road, Trench, Shropshire TF2 7DX
Tel: 01952 605711    **£ - P - 3 rooms**
Town centre Pub

## UPPER AFFCOT, CHURCH STRETTON
**The Travellers Rest Inn**
See main entry opposite

## WALCOT WELLINGTON, TELFORD
**Allscott Inn**
Walcot Wellington, Telford, Shropshire TF6 5EQ
Tel: 01952 248484    **P - 4 rooms**
Email: allscottinn@telfordlife.co.uk
Village Inn 4 miles from Wellington

## WENLOCK EDGE, MUCH WENLOCK
**Wenlock Edge Inn**
Hilltop, Wenlock Edge, Much Wenlock,
Shropshire TF13 6DJ
Tel: 01746 785678    **££ - P - 3 rooms**
Email: info@wenlockedgeinn.co.uk
Web: www.wenlockedgeinn.co.uk
Country Inn 4 miles from Much Wenlock

## WENTNOR, BISHOP'S CASTLE
**The Crown Inn**
Wentnor, Bishop's Castle, Shropshire SY9 5EE
Tel: 01588 650613    **££ - P - 3 rooms**
Email: crowninn@wentnor.com
Web: www.wentnor.com
16thC Inn central for fishing, riding, walking

## WENTNOR, BISHOP'S CASTLE
**The Inn on the Green**
Wentnor, Bishop's Castle, Shropshire SY9 5EF
Tel: 01588 650105    **£ - P - 6 rooms**
Email: thegreen@redhotant.com
Rural Pub 6 miles from Bishops Castle

## WOODSEVES, MARKET DRAYTON
**Four Alls**
Woodseves, Market Drayton,
Shropshire TF9 2AG
Tel: 01630 652995    **£ - P - 9 rooms**
Country Inn 1 mile from Market Drayton

# The Travellers Rest Inn

*Upper Affcot, Church Stretton, Shropshire SY6 6RL*

**£ - P - BM - P - C - ETB /RAC 3 diamond - 12 rooms**

Tel: +44 (0) 1694 781275   Fax: +44 (0) 1694 781555
Email: reception@travellersrestinn.co.uk
Web: www.travellersrestinn.co.uk/

The Travellers Rest is a traditional Inn offering good food, real ale, good accommodation and good company in South Shropshire, it is situated alongside the A49 in an area of hills and valleys - part of South Shropshire - with unspoilt views, peaceful villages and market towns steeped in history.

Here at The Travellers Rest Inn we have 12 very well appointed *en suite* rooms, all are furnished to a high standard and have television / radio and tea / coffee making facilities. The rooms are located away from any 'sounds' of the Inn, and access to your room can be straight from the car park, which makes entry easy. Two of the six ground floor rooms are suitable for accompanied wheelchair users.

Not being 'tied' to any brewery we always have many cask ales to choose from ... one can tell that the Bar has a well-stocked feel. The wine list and fine array of spirits and liqueurs add to the welcome for all travellers from far and wide.

The Travellers Rest Inn's recommended food is available throughout the day, from lunchtime until the last orders taken - allowing the final meals to be served by 9.00 pm.

# STAFFORDSHIRE

ABBOTS BROMLEY
**The Coach and Horses**
High St, Abbots Bromley, Staffs  WS15 3BN
Tel: 01283 840256    **£ - P - 2 rooms**
Village Inn 6 miles from Uttoxeter

ABBOTS BROMLEY
**The Crown Inn**
Market Place, Abbots Bromley, Staffs WS15 3BS
Tel: 01283 840227    **£ - P - 6 rooms**
Email: f.j.crown@aol.com
Web: www.thecrowninn.net
Village 20 minutes drive to Alton Towers

ALTON, STOKE-ON-TRENT
**Bulls Head Inn**
High St, Alton, Stoke-on-Trent, Staffs  ST10 4AQ

Tel: 01538 702307    **££ - P - 7 rooms**
Email: janet@alton.freeserve.co.uk
Web: www.thebullsheadinn.freeserve.co.uk
Village Inn 7 miles from Uttoxeter

**The Peakstones Inn**
Cheadle Road, Alton, Stoke-on-Trent,
Staffs ST10 4DH
Tel: 01538 755776    **£ - P - 6 rooms**
Country Inn 4 miles from Cheadle

**Royal Oak**
Alton, Stoke-on-Trent, Staffs ST10 4BH
Tel: 01538 702625    **£ - P - 3 rooms**
Email: eng@royaloak-alton.co.uk
Web: www.royaloak-alton.co.uk
Village Inn 15 miles from Stoke-on-Trent

BLACKSHAW MOOR, LEEK
**Three Horseshoes Inn**
Blackshaw Moor, Leek, Staffs ST13 8TW
Tel: 01538 300296    **£ - P - 6 rooms**
Email: info@threeshoesinn.co.uk
Web: www.threeshoesinn.co.uk
Award winning country Pub located2 miles
from Leek

BRIGTOWN
**Bridgtown Tavern**
192 Walsall Rd, Bridgtown, Staffs WS11 3JI
Tel: 01543 462310    **£ - P - 4 rooms**
Located on the outskirts of town

CHARPLEY HEATH, HELVESTON
**Bird In Hand**
Sandon Road, Charpley Heath, Helveston,
Staffs ST15 8RG
Tel: 01889 505237    **£ - P - 5 rooms**
Country Pub 5 miles from Helveston

CHEADLE
**The Royal Oak**
69 High Street, Cheadle, Staffs ST10 1AN
Tel: 01538 753116    **££ - P - 11 rooms**
Town centre Pub

FROGHALL, STOKE-ON-TRENT
**The Railway Inn**
Froghall, Stoke-on-Trent, Staffs ST10 2HA
Tel: 01538 754782    **£ - P - 5 rooms**
Country Pub 3 miles from Cheadle

HANDSACRE, RUGELEY
**The Olde Peculiar**
The Green, Handsacre, Rugeley,
Staffs WS15 4DP
Tel: 01543 491891    **£ - P - 2 rooms**
Village Pub 4 miles from Lichfield

HOARCROSS,
BURTON-UPON-TRENT
**Meynell Ingram Arms**
Abbotts Bromley Road, Hoarcross,
Burton-Upon-Trent, Staffs DE13 8RB
Tel: 01283 575202    **Rooms**
Village Inn

HOLLINGTON, STOKE-ON-TRENT
**The Raddle Inn**
Quarry Bank, Hollington, Stoke-on-Trent,
Staffs ST10 4HQ
Tel: 01889 507278    **£ - P - 5 rooms**
Email: peter@logcabin.co.uk
Web: www.logcabin.co.uk
Village Inn 3 miles from Cheadle

LAKE BROOK, nr LEEK
**Travellers Rest**
Lake Brook, nr Leek, Staffs ST13 7DR
Tel: 01538 382186    **£ - P - 3 rooms**
Village Inn situated 20 minute drive to Alton
Towers

NEEDWOOD,
BURTON-UPON-TRENT
**The New Inn**
Five Lanes End, Burton Road, Needwood,
Burton-upon-Trent, Staffs DE13 9PB
Tel: 01283 575392    **£ - P - 4 rooms**
Email: barry@newinn.co.uk
Web: www.newinn.co.uk
Country Inn 5 miles from Buxton

POLESWORTH, nr TAMWORTH
**Fosters Yard**
12 Market Street, Polesworth, nr Tamworth,
Staffs B78 1HW
Tel: 01827 899313    **£ - P - 11 rooms**
Village Inn 4 miles from Tamworth

OAKAMOOR, STOKE-ON-TRENT
**The Lord Nelson**
See main entry opposite

# The Lord Nelson

*Carr Bank, Oakamoor, Stoke-on-Trent, Staffs ST10 3DQ*

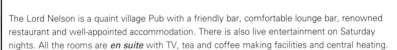

**£ - P - R - BG - BM - P - C - 3 rooms**

Tel: 01538 702242

The Lord Nelson is a quaint village Pub with a friendly bar, comfortable lounge bar, renowned restaurant and well-appointed accommodation. There is also live entertainment on Saturday nights. All the rooms are *en suite* with TV, tea and coffee making facilities and central heating.

We are only one mile from Alton Towers, five miles from Dovedale and the Peak District National park, nine miles from Stoke-on-Trent and the Potteries Museum, and close to the delightful market towns of Cheadle, Leek, Uttoxeter and Ashbourne. If you like walking Oakamoor is on The Staffordshire Way, and there are many other scenic walks in the area.

SANDON, nr STAFFORD
**Dog and Doublet Inn**
Sandon, nr Stafford, Staffs ST18 0DJ
Tel: 01889 508331 **£ - P - 4 rooms**
Country Pub 3 miles from Stafford

STOW-BY-CHARTLEY
**The Plough Inn**
Amerton, Stowe-by-Chartley, Stafford,
Staffs ST18 0LA
Tel: 01889 270308 **£ - P - 6 rooms**
Countryside Inn 5 miles from Staffordshire

TAMWORTH
**Globe Inn**
Lower Gungate, Tamworth, Staffs B79 7AW
Tel: 01827 60455 **£ - P - 18 rooms**
Town centre Pub

**Tamworth Arms**
Litchfield Street, Tamworth, Staffs B79 7QL
Tel: 01827 67056 **£ - P - 20 rooms**
Email: dawnmwalker@btinternet.com
Located 2 minutes walk to Tamworth town
centre

TUTBURY
**Ye Olde Dog and Partridge Inn**
High Street, Tutbury, Staffs DE13 9LS
Tel: 01283 813030 **££ - P - 20 rooms**
Village Inn 10 minutes drive to Burton-on-Trent

WATERHOUSES,
STOKE-ON-TRENT
**Ye Olde Crown Hotel**
See main entry on page 86

WATERHOUSES,
STOKE-ON-TRENT
**The Cross Inn**
Cauldon Low, Waterhouses, Stoke-on-Trent,
Staffs ST10 3EX
Tel: 01538 308338 **£ - P - 8 rooms**
Email: adrian_weaver@hotmail.com
Web: www.crossinn.co.uk
Pub with its own caravan park 8 miles from
Cheadle

WHITTINGTON, LICHFIELD
**The Dog Inn**
Main Street, Whittington, Lichfield,
Staffs WS14 9JU
Tel: 01543 432252 **£ - P - 5 rooms**
Email: thedoginn@leighnadi.freeserve.co.uk
Village Inn 2 miles from Lichfield

# Ye Olde Crown Hotel

*Leek Road, Waterhouses, Stoke-on-Trent,*
*Staffs ST10 3HL*

**£ - P - 7 rooms**

Tel: 01538 308204

Stan and Kay Stevens extend a warm friendly welcome to their 17th Century Coaching Inn. Situated in the picturesque village of Waterhouses near the bank of the River Hamps, on the edge of the beautiful Peak District National Park and the Staffordshire Moor lands.

The accommodation comprises of one double and a triple room with *en suite* facilities and one single room with its own bathroom. All rooms have colour television with tea / coffee making facilities. In addition to our famous traditional breakfasts we also provide a full lunch and evening menu.

In addition we have a cottage that is situated next-door comprising two double, a twin and a family room with *en suite* facilities.

# SUFFOLK

Lowestoft •

Brome •

Bury St Edmunds •

Pettistree •

Ipswich •

Felixstow •

## ALDEBURGH
**The Mill Inn**
Market Cross Place, Aldeburgh,
Suffolk IP15 5BJ
Tel: 01728 452563     **£ - 4 rooms**
Town Pub 3 minutes walk to the town centre

## ALDRINGHAM
**Parrot and Punchbowl Inn**
Aldringham Lane, Aldringham, Suffolk IP16 4PY
Tel: 01728 830221     **£ - P - 1 room**
Email: info@parrotandpunchbowl.co.uk

Web: www.parrotandpunchbowl.co.uk
Country Inn 3 miles from Aldborough

## BARDWELL, BURY ST EDMUNDS
**The Six Bells at Bardwell**
The Green, Bardwell, Bury St Edmunds,
Suffolk IP31 1AW
Tel: 01359 250820     **££ - P - 10 rooms**
16th century Inn with rooms set around a courtyard

## BARNHAM, IPSWICH
**The Sorrel Horse Inn**
Old Norwich Road, Barnham, Ipswich,
Suffolk IP6 0PG
Tel: 01473 830327     **£ - P - 8 rooms**
Email: matt@sorrelhorse.freeserve.co.uk
Web: www.sorrelhorse.freeserve.co.uk
Country Inn 4 miles from Ipswich

## BECCLES
**The Kings Head**
New Market, Beccles, Suffolk NR34 9HA

Tel: 01502 712147 **££ - P - 12 rooms**
Email: enquiries@kingsheadhotel-uk.co.uk
Web: www.kingsheadhotel-uk.co.uk
17thC Inn located in Beccles town centre

**BECK ROW, MILDENHALL**
**Rose and Crown**
82 Holmsey Green, Beck Row, Mildenhall,
Suffolk IP28 8AD
Tel: 01638 713407 **£ - P - 3 rooms**
Village Inn 10 minutes drive to Mildenhall

**BILDENSTON**
**The Crown Hotel**
High Street, Bildeston, Suffolk IP7 7EB
Tel: 01449 740510 **£ - P - 13 rooms**
14thC coaching Inn 6 miles from Stowmarket

**BLAXHALL, WOODBRIDGE**
**The Ship Inn**
Blaxhall, Woodbridge, Suffolk IP12 2DY
Tel: 01728 688316 **£ - P - 4 rooms**
Traditional 17th century Inn

**BLYFORD**
**Queen's Head Inn**
Southwold Road, Blyford, Suffolk IP19 9JY
Tel: 01502 478404 **£ - P - 3 rooms**
Village Inn 3 miles from Halesworth

**BROME, NR EYE**
**The Brome Grange Hotel**
See main entry below

**BROME**
**Cornwallis Arms**
Brome, Suffolk IP23 8AJ
Tel: 01379 870326 **£££ - P - 16 rooms**
Country hotel with bar 7 miles from Diss

**BUNGAY**
**Angel**
1 Lower Olland St, Bungay, Suffolk NR35 1BY
Tel: 01986 892507 **£ - P - 3 rooms**
Small town centre Pub

**DUNWICH**
**The Ship Inn**
St James Street, Dunwich, Suffolk IP17 3DT
Tel: 01728 648219 **££ - P - 4 rooms**
Busy village Inn 5 miles from Halesworth

**EASTBRIDGE**
**The Eels Foot Inn**
Eastbridge, Suffolk IP16 4SN
Tel: 01728 830154 **£ - P - 1 room**
Village Inn 3 miles from Leiston

**EYKE, WOODBRIDGE**
**Elephant and Castle**
Eyke, Woodbridge, Suffolk
Tel: 01394 460241 **£ - P - 4 rooms**
Local village Inn 5 miles from Woodbridge

**FELIXSTOWE**
**Dolphin Hotel**
41 Beach Station Road, Felixstowe, Suffolk

# Brome Grange Hotel

*Norwich Road, Brome, Nr Eye, Suffolk IP23 8AP*

**££ - P - 22 rooms**

Tel: 01379 870456    Fax: 01379 870921
Email: bromegrange@fastnet.co.uk
Web: www.bromegrange

The Grange, founded in the 17th Century, is set in delightful countryside midway between the market towns of Diss in Norfolk and Eye in Suffolk. All 20-courtyard bedrooms offer every modern day comfort and convenience, and are set in a quadrangle overlooking the hotel's gardens. Facilities include newspapers, iron and ironing board, fax machine and photocopier.

Dining at Brome Grange is an experience to savour. The restaurant serves the very best of English and international cuisine using only the finest local grown produce.

# The Three Kings

*Hengrave Road, Fornham All Saints, Bury St Edmunds, Suffolk IP28 6LA*

### P - 12 rooms

Tel: 01284 766979    Fax: 01284 723308
Email: c.conway@tinyworld.co.uk

The Three Kings is proud to offer superior courtyard, *en suite*, accommodation in beautifully converted Class II listed outbuildings to make your stay a memorable one. We also have a comfortable, renowned restaurant and offer excellent pub meals, and are within easy reach of Bury St Edmunds and three well-known golf clubs! For further information about our 4 twin-bedded, 5 double bedded, 2 family and 1 disabled suited bedrooms, please contact us.

Tel: 01394 282261    **£ - P - 9 rooms**
Seaside Pub

## FORNHAM ALL SAINTS, BURY ST EDMUNDS
**The Three Kings**
See main entry above

## FRAMLINGHAM
**Crown and Anchor Inn**
4 Church St, Framlingham, Suffolk IP13 9PQ
Tel: 01728 723611    **£ - 3 rooms**
Town Pub, Ipswich is 15 miles away

## FRAMSDEN
**The Doberman Inn**
The Street, Framsden, Suffolk IP14 6HJ
Tel: 01473 890461    **£ - P - 1 Room**
Village Inn 11 miles from Ipswich

## HADLEIGH, IPSWICH
**White Hart**
46 Bridge Street, Hadleigh, Ipswich
Suffolk, IP7 6DB
Tel: 01473 822206    **££ - P - 4 rooms**
Email: enquiries@whiteharthadleigh.co.uk
Web: www.whiteharthadleigh
16th century Inn on the outskirts of Hadleigh

## HALESWORTH
**The Angel Hotel**
Thoroughfare, Halesworth, Suffolk IP19 8AH
Tel: 01986 873365    **££ - P - 7 rooms**
Email: angel@halesworth.ws

Web: www.halesworth.ws/angel/
16th century Inn in the centre of Halesworth

## HAVERHILL
**Rose and Crown**
1 Withersfield Rd, Haverhill, Suffolk CB9 9LA
Tel: 01440 708446    **£ - P - 10 rooms**
Located in the centre of town, public bar / hotel / restaurant

## HUNDON, nr SUDBURY
**The Plough Inn**
Brockley Green, Hundon, nr Sudbury, Suffolk CO10 8DT
Tel: 01440 786789    **££ - P - 8 rooms**
Country Inn with views of the Stour Valley

## IPSWICH
**The Brewers Arms**
See main entry opposite

## LAVENHAM
**Angel Hotel**
Market Place, Lavenham, Suffolk CO10 9QZ
Tel: 01787 247388    **££ - P - 8 rooms**
15th century Inn in the town centre

## LONG MELFORD, SUDBURY
**George and Dragon**
Han Street, Long Melford, Sudbury, Suffolk CO10 9JB
Tel: 01787 371285    **££ - P - 8 rooms**
Email: geodrg@mail.globalnet.co.uk
Village Inn 10 miles from Sudbury

# Brewers Arms

*18–20 Orford Street, Ipswich, Suffolk IP1 3NS*

**£ - P - BM - BG - 5 rooms**

Tel / Fax: 01473 400361          Email: shaundesilva@aol.com

Traditional small town centre family run pub. Located close to most amenities and just 5 minutes walk from Ipswich football Stadium and 10 minutes walk from the railway station. Adjacent to the pub is the 5 bed roomed guest house with the accommodation. The Brewers Arms facilities include car parking and a beer garden. Bar meals are also available.

The room tariff starts at:   Single = £20.00 / Double = £35.00 / Triple = £50.00
Long-term contractors rates available

## LOWESTOFT
**Barmoosh**
Munroes and Co, High Street, Lowestoft,
Suffolk NR32 1HP
Tel: 01502 572617      **P - Rooms**
Town Pub

## MILDENHALL
**White Hart Hotel**
21 High Street, Mildenhall, Suffolk IP28 7EA
Tel: 01638 713894      **££ - P - 10 rooms**
Located in the centre of town

## ORFORD
**Jolly Sailor Inn**
Quay Street, Orford, Suffolk IP12 2NU
Tel: 01394 450243      **£ - 3 rooms**
Country village Inn 10 miles from Woodbridge

## PETTISTREE, WOODBRIDGE
**The Three Tuns Coaching Inn**
See main entry on page 90

## RAMSHOLT, WOODBRIDGE
**Ramsholt Arms**
Dock Road, Ramsholt, Woodbridge,
Suffolk IP12 3AB
Tel: 01394 411229      **££ - P - 4 rooms**
On the tidal estuary of the Deban River

## SNAPE
**The Crown Inn**
Bridge Road, Snape, Suffolk IP17 1SL
Tel: 01728 688324      **££ - P - 3 rooms**
Village Inn 10 miles from Woodbridge

## SOUTHWOLD
**The Angel Inn**
39 High Street, Wangford, Southwold,
Suffolk NR34 8RL
Tel: 01502 578636      **££ - P - 7 rooms**
Email: inn@wangford.freeserve.co.uk
Web: www.angel-wangford.co.uk
Family run village Inn 3 miles from Southwold

**Crown Hotel**
The High Street, Southwold, Suffolk IP18 6DP
Tel: 01502 722275      **£££ - P - 14 rooms**
Email: crown.hotel@adnams.co.uk
Inn / hotel owned by local brewer Adnams,
located near the town centre

## SPEXHALL, HALESWORTH
**Huntsman and Hounds**
Stone Street, Spexhall, Halesworth,
Suffolk IP19 0RN
Tel: 01986 781341      **£ - P - 3 rooms**
Email: huntsmanspexhall@aol.com
Beautifully kept 15th century Inn

## STOKE ASH, EYE
**The White Horse Inn**
Stoke Ash, Eye, Suffolk IP23 7ET
Tel: 01379 678222      **£ - P - 7 rooms**
Email: whitehorse@stokeash.fsbusiness.co.uk
On A140 between Ipswich and Norwich

## STOKE-BY-NAYLAND, COLCHESTER
**The Angel Inn**
Polstead Street, Stoke-by-Nayland, Colchester,

# Three Tuns Coaching Inn

*Main Road, Pettistree, Woodbridge, Suffolk IP13 0HW*

**££ - P - 11 rooms**

Tel: 01728 747979    Fax: 01728 746244
Email: jon@threetuns-coachinginn.co.uk
Web: www.threetuns-coachinginn.co.uk

Whether to enjoy a drink at the bar, a meal in the restaurant or just to relax in the warm and friendly atmosphere of the exceptionally well-appointed lounge with its comfy sofas and, on cooler evenings, welcoming open log fires, all visitors will find something special here. Those wishing to stay for longer can spoil themselves in one of the 11 delightful *en suite* guest bedrooms equipped to the highest standards of comfort and quality. Disabled facilities.

Close to the Heritage coast and many of the region's sights and attractions, The Three Tuns is an ideal place to take a break from shopping or sightseeing, or to use as a base for exploring the area.

Suffolk CO6 4SA
Tel: 01206 263245    **££ - P - 6 rooms**
Web: www.angelhotel.com
Village Inn sited at the centre of Constable country

## THORNHAM MAGNA
**The Four Horses**
Wickham Road, Thornham Magna,
Suffolk IP23 8DH
Tel: 01379 678777    **££ - P - 8 rooms**
12th century village Inn 7 miles from Diss

## WENHASTON, nr SOUTHWOLD
**The Compasses Inn**
Wenhaston, nr Southwold, Suffolk IP19 9EF
Tel: 01502 478319    **PW - Rooms**
Pets welcome

## WESTLETON
**White Horse Inn**
Darshan Road, Westleton, Suffolk IP17 3AH
Tel: 01728 648222    **£ - P - 3 rooms**
Local village Inn 7 miles from Leiston

## WITHERSFIELD
**The White Horse Inn**
Hollow Hill, Withersfield, Suffolk CB9 7SH
Tel: 01440 706081    **££ - P - 5 rooms**
Village Inn 2 miles from Haverhill

## WOOLPIT, BURY ST EDMUNDS
**The Bull Inn and Restaurant**
The Street, Woolpit, Bury St Edmunds,
Suffolk IP30 9SA
Tel: 01359 240393    **£ - P - 4 rooms**
Email: trevor@howling.fsbusiness.co.uk
In the village centre with its own restaurant

**Swan Inn**
The Street, Woolpit, Bury St Edmunds,
Suffolk IP30 9QN
Tel: 01359 240482    **£ - P - 5 rooms**
14th century coaching Inn 8 miles from Bury St Edmunds

## WORLINGTON, BECCLES
**The Colville Arms**
Lowestoft Road, Worlington, Beccles,
Suffolk NR34 7EF
Tel: 01502 712571    **£ - P - 10 rooms**
Email: pat@thecolvillearms.freeserve.co.uk
Motel style, 5 minutes from the Broads

## YOXFORD, SAXMUNDHAM
**Blois Arms**
High Street, Yoxford, Saxmundham,
Suffolk IP17 3EP
Tel: 01728 668238    **£ - P - 2 rooms**
Email: nigel.trapp@btopenworld.com
Village Inn 4 miles from Saxmundham

# WARWICKSHIRE

Tel: 01608 685223　　**££ - P - 6 rooms**
12th century village coaching Inn 12 miles
from Stratford-upon-Avon

## BROOM, nr ALCESTER
**Broom Hall Inn**
Bidford Road, Broom, nr Alcester,
Warks B50 4HE
Tel: 01789 773757　　**££ - P - 12 rooms**
Village Inn 7 miles from Stratford

## EASONHALL, RUGBY
**The Golden Lion**
Easonhall, Rugby, Warks CV23 0JA
Tel: 01788 832265　　**££ - P - 12 rooms**
Email: goldenlioninn@aol.com
Web: www.goldenlion-easonhall.co.uk
Traditional old Inn located just 4 miles from
Rugby

## ETTINGTON
**The Houndshill**
Banbury Road, Ettington, Warks CV37 7NS
Tel: 01789 740267　　**£ - P - 8 rooms**
Rural Inn 4 miles from Stratford-upon-Avon

## ETTINGTON,
## STRATFORD-UPON-AVON
**White Horse Inn**
Banbury Road, Ettington, Stratford-upon-Avon,
Warks CV37 7SU
Tel: 01789 740641　　**£ - P - 4 rooms**
Village Inn 6 miles from Stratford-upon-Avon

## GREAT WOLFORD
**The Fox and Hounds Inn**
See main entry on page 92

## HALFORD, SHIPSTON-ON-STOUR
**Halford Bridge Inn**
Fosseway, Halford, Shipston-on-Stour,
Warks CV36 5BN
Tel: 01789 740382　　**£ - P - 7 rooms**
Village country Inn 6 miles from Stratford-
upon-Avon

## ALDERMINSTER
**The Bell**
Alderminster, Warks CV37 8NY
Tel: 01789 450414　　**£ - P - 7 rooms**
Email: thebellalderminster@tiscali.co.uk
Coaching Inn 3 miles from Stratford

## ANSLEY VILLAGE, NUNEATON
**The Boot Inn**
Birmingham Road, Ansley Village, Nuneaton,
Warks CV10 9PL
Tel: 02476 392349　　**£ - P - 5 rooms**
Village Inn 5 miles from Nuneaton

## ARMSCOTE,
## STRATFORD-UPON-AVON
**Fox and the Goose**
Armscote, Stratford-upon-Avon,
Warks CV37 8DD
Tel: 01608 682293　　**££ - P - 4 rooms**
Small local village Inn with restaurant

## BRAILES
**The George Hotel**
High Street, Brailes, Warks OX15 5HN

# Fox and Hounds Inn

*Great Wolford, Warks CV36 5NQ*

**££ - P - R - BM - Pets - 3 rooms**

Tel: 01608 674220     Fax: 01608 684871
Email: info@thefoxandhoundsinn.com
Web: www.thefoxandhoundsinn.com

The Fox & Hounds Inn remains one of the few unspoilt village hostelries nestling in glorious countryside on the edge of the North Cotswolds. A warm welcome, roaring log fires, traditional ales and well over 180 different whiskies as well as delicious food, using the best local produce, await you in this honey coloured stone Inn.

With our traditional Sunday lunches, blackboard specials and bar menu, there is something for everyone – or if it is a special occasion we can accommodate up to 24 guests with your own menu in part of the Inn. All recently refurbished, our *en suite*, comfortable rooms each have colour TV, complimentary toiletries, coffee / tea making facilities and no early morning call!

HENLEY-IN-ARDEN
**White Swan**
100 High Street, Henley-in-Arden,
Warks CV95 5BY
Tel: 01564 792623     **££ - P - 10 rooms**
Country Inn located in this market town

KENILWORTH
**The Cottage Inn**
36 Stoneleigh Road, Kenilworth, Warwickshire
Tel: 01926 853900     **£ - P - 5 rooms**
Located on the outskirts of Kenilworth

KILSBY, RUGBY
**Halfway House**
Watling St, Kilsby, Rugby, Warks CV23 8YE
Tel: 01788 822888     **£ - P - 7 rooms**
Country Pub 3 miles from Rugby,

KINETON
**The Castle Inn**
Edgehill, Kineton, Warwickshire
Tel: 01295 670255     **££ - P - 3 rooms**
Email: castleedgehill@msn.com
Web: www.our-Web-site.com/the-castle-inn
Village Inn built to look like a castle

LITTLE COMPTON
**The Red Lion**
Little Compton, Moreton-in-Marsh, Warks
Tel: 01608 674397     **£ - P - 3 rooms**

Email: david@redlioninn.freeserve.co.uk
Village Inn 4 miles from Moreton-in Marsh

LONG ITCHINGTON
**Cuttle Inn**
Foutham Road, Long Itchington, Warks
Tel: 01926 812314     **P - Rooms**
Village Inn 7 miles from Leamington

LOWER GREEN, ILMINGTON
**The Howard Arms**
See main entry opposite

LOWER QUINTON,
STRATFORD-UPON-AVON
**The Collage Arms Inn**
See main entry opposite

MANCETTER, nr ATHERSTONE
**The Blue Boar**
Watling Street, Mancetter, nr Atherstone,
Warks CV9 1NE
Tel: 01827 716166     **£ - P - 5 rooms**
Located just 200 yards from the town centre

PAILTON, nr RUGBY
**White Lion Inn**
Pailton, nr Rugby, Warks CV23 0QD
Tel: 01788 832359     **££ - P - 9 rooms**
Web: www.whitelionpailton.co.uk
Village coaching Inn 6 miles from Rugby

# Howard Arms

*Lower Green, Ilmington, Warks CV36 4LT*

**P - 3 rooms**

Tel / Fax: 01608 682226
Email: howard.arms@virgin.net   Web: www.howardarms.com

The Howard Arms has enjoyed an idyllic location on the village green in Ilmington, just south of Stratford-upon-Avon, for over 400 years. Complimenting The Howard Arms traditional function of eating and drinking are three delightful bedrooms, all decorated and furnished in antique country style. Each non-smoking room is *en suite.*

# College Arms Inn

*Lower Quinton, Stratford-upon-Avon, Warks CV37 8SG*

**£ - P - 4 rooms and a period cottage**

Tel: (+44) 01789 720342   Fax: (+44) 01789 720404
Email: collegearms@easicom.com
Web: www.thecollegearms.co.uk

An historic 16th Century Inn on the edge of the beautiful Cotswolds giving easy access to Stratford upon Avon, Cheltenham, Oxford and Warwick. The College Arms, reeking of history, gives you superb accommodation, excellent food and hospitality. The inn was owned originally by Henry VIII and later purchased by Magdalene College, Oxford and remained under it's ownership for 400 years. Because of this connection The College Arms is the only public house in England permitted legally to display the College Coat of Arms.

Accommodation consists of four superb, non smoking, *en suite* rooms with TV and tea and coffee making facilities. Included is a full English, or continental style, breakfast served in the dining room which boasts an extensive menu with dedicated non smoking areas.

PRINCETHORPE
**The Three Horseshoes**
Southam Road, Princethorpe,
Warks CV23 9PR
Tel: 01926 632345   **£ - P - 5 rooms**
Recently refurbished country Pub 5 miles from
Rugby

PRIORS MARSTON, SOUTHAM
**Holly Bush Inn**
Holly Bush Lane, Priors Marston, Southam,
Warks CV47 7RW
Tel: 01327 260934   **££ - P - 8 rooms**
Country Inn 5 miles from Southam

RATLEY
**The Rose and Crown**
Ratley, Warwickshire
Tel: 01295 678148   **£ - P - 2 rooms**
Village Inn 8 miles from Banbury

SHIPTON-ON-STOUR
**The Red Lion**
Main Street, Shipston-on-Stour, Warks
Tel: 01608 684221   **£ - P - 4 rooms**
Village Pub 7 miles from Shipston-on-Stour

**The White Bear**
See main entry on page 94

# White Bear Hotel

*High Street, Shipton on Stour, Warks CV36 4AJ*

**£ - P - 10 rooms**

Tel: 01608 661558
Fax: 01608 662612
Email: whitebearhot@hotmail.com
Web: www.whitebearhotel.co.uk

The Georgian facade of The White Bear Hotel, known locally as 'The Bear', faces the centre of the bustling Market Square of this small town, which nestles on the edge of The Cotswolds, and is within easy reach of Stratford-upon-Avon (10 miles) and Oxford (28 miles). The Bear boasts traditional public and lounge bars, both with open fires and wooden settles. A range of real ales is available, together with usual keg beers, a selection of fine wines from the cellar, and an interesting collection of malt whiskies.

Dining at The White Bear is a delicious experience. Choose between casual dining in the bar, or in the relaxed ambience of the recently refurbished restaurant.

The hotel has ten comfortable *en suite* bedrooms, all with colour TV, tea / coffee facilities and direct dial telephones.

---

## STRATFORD-UPON-AVON
**Queens Head**
54 - 53 Ely Street, Stratford-upon-Avon,
Warks CV37 6LM
Tel: 01789 204914     **££ - Rooms**
Email: richard@distinctivepubs.freeserve.co.uk
Web: www.distinctivepubs.co.uk
Town centre location

## STUDLEY
**Nags Head Inn**
33 Redditch Road, Studley, Warks B80 7AU
Tel: 01527 852405     **5 rooms**
Village Inn

## SUTTON CHENEY, NUNEATON
**Royal Arms**
Main Street, Sutton Cheney, Nuneaton,
Warks CV13 0AG
Tel: 01455 290263     **£ - P - 15 rooms**
Web: www.royalarms.co.uk
Village Inn 5 miles from Hinckley

## TEMPLE GRAFTON
**The Blue Boar Inn**
See main entry opposite

## TWYCROSS
**Curzon Arms**
29 Main Road, Twycross, Warks CV9 3PL
Tel: 01827 880334     **£ - P - 4 rooms**
Country Pub 5 miles from Atherstone

## WARWICK
**Black Horse Inn**
62 The Saltisford, Warwick, Warks CV34 4TD
Tel: 01926 403989     **£ - P - 18 rooms**
Town Pub 3 minutes from the town centre

**Crown and Castle Inn**
2–4 Coventry Road, Warwick, Warks CV34 4NT
Tel: 01926 492087     **££ - P - 14 rooms**
Town centre Inn

**The Seven Stars**
Friars Street, Warwick, Warks CV34 6HD
Tel: 01926 492658     **££ - P - 3 rooms**
Email: sevenstars@gofornet.co.uk
Web: www.smoothhound.co.uk
Olde Worlde town centre Inn

**The Tilted Wig**
11 Market Place, Warwick, Warks CV34 4SA

# The Blue Boar

*Temple Grafton, Warks B49 6NR*

**££ - P - 15 rooms**

Tel: 01789 750010     Fax: 01789 750635
Email: blueboar@covlink.co.uk
Web: www.blueboarinn.co.uk

The Blue Boar Inn, a quintessential English hostelry, rests in the village of Temple Grafton close to Stratford-upon-Avon. Landlord and owner, Mr Sean Brew has invested substantially, yet tastefully, to provide 15 rooms all with *en suite* facilities. Tariffs are £45.00 for a single room and £65.00 for a double room per night including breakfast. There are also family rooms as children are most welcome.

The Blue Boar Inn combines the traditional atmosphere of an English country tavern, with fine hearty food and excellent accommodation, providing the ideal stop over for the business visitor, an informal, yet private meeting-place for a local club or group, a pillow for the weary traveller or simply a good, cask-conditioned pint.

Tel: 01926 410466     **££ - P - 4 rooms**
Town centre Inn

**The Tudor House Inn**
90 - 92 West Street, Warwick, Warks
Tel: 01926 495447     **££ - 9 rooms**
Web: www.oldenglish.co.uk
15th century Inn by Warwick Castle entrance

WILMCOTE,
STRATFORD-UPON-AVON
**Mary Arden Inn**
The Green, Wilmcote, Stratford-upon-Avon,
Warks CV37 9XJ
Tel: 01789 267030     **££ - P - 11 rooms**
Village Inn just 3 miles from Stratford-upon-Avon

# WEST MIDLANDS

BRIERLEY HILL, DUDLEY
**Saltwells Inn**
Saltwells Lane, Brierley Hill, Dudley,
West Midlands DY5 1AX
Tel: 01384 569224     **£ - P - 15 rooms**
Located in a nature reserve in the town

CLENT
**The French Hen**
Bromsgrove Rd, Clent, West Midlands DY9 9PY
Tel: 01562 883040     **£ - P - Rooms**
French atmosphere, ideal location for south Birmingham area

COLESHILL
**The George and Dragon**
Coventry Rd, Coleshill, West Midlands B46 3EH
Tel: 01675 466586     **£ - P - 7 rooms**
Village Inn 10 minutes drive to the NEC

COVENTRY
**Brewer and Baker**
East St, Coventry, West Midlands CV1 5OS
Tel: 02476 229013     **£ - 9 rooms**
Town Pub

DUDLEY
**The Bush**
2 Buffery Road, Dudley, West Midlands
Tel: 01384 253753     **£ - P - 4 rooms**
Town Pub just 5 minutes from Dudley town
centre

**The Lamp Tavern**
116 Lower High Street, Dudley, West
Midlands DY1 1QT
Tel: 01384 254129     **Rooms**
Owned by local brewer Bathams, excellent
traditional ales

KINGSWINFORD, DUDLEY
**The Old Courthouse Hotel**
High Street, Kingswinford, Dudley, West
Midlands DY6 8AX

Tel: 01384 833456     **£ - P - 4 rooms**
Village Inn 5 minutes walk to Kingswinford
centre

MERIDEN, COVENTRY
**The Bulls Head**
Main Road, Meriden, Coventry, West
Midlands CV7 7NL
Tel: 01676 523798     **££ - P - 13 rooms**
Country Inn 5 miles from Coventry

NUNEATON
**The Rugger Tavern**
121 Attleborough Road, Nuneaton, West
Midlands CV11 4JQ
Tel: 02476 356326     **£ - P - 9 rooms**
Town Pub half a mile from the city centre

SEDLEIGH
**Swan Inn**
Gospel End Street, Sedleigh, West Midlands
Tel: 01902 884922     **£ - P - 4 rooms**
Town centre Pub

WHITLEY, COVENTRY
**The Royal Oak**
London Road, Whitley, Coventry, West
Midlands CV3 4AL
Tel: 02476 501077     **£ - P - 4 rooms**
10 minute walk to Coventry town centre

# South-East England
## BEDFORDSHIRE

ASTWICK
**Tudor Oaks**
1 Taylors Road, Astwick, Beds
Tel: 01462 834133    **P - Rooms**
Web: www.tudoroaks.co.uk
Real ale Pub on the A1 between Letchworth
and Biggleswade

DUNSTABLE
**The Highwayman**
Dunstable, Beds
Tel: 0800 917 3085    **££ - P rooms**
Old English Inns. Reservations 0800 917 3085

HARROLD
**The Oakley Arms**
High Street, Harrold, Beds MK43 7BH
Tel: 01234 720478    **£ - P - 4 rooms**
Village Inn 9 miles from Bedford

HEATH AND REACH
**Axe and Compass**
Leighton Road, Heath and Reach,
Beds LU7 0AA
Tel: 01525 237394    **£ - P - 9 rooms**
Village Inn 1.5 miles from Leighton Buzzard

IRELAND, nr SHEFFORD
**Black Horse**
Ireland, nr Shefford, Beds SG17 5QL
Tel: 01462 811398    **£ - P - 2 rooms**
Country Inn 1 mile from Shefford

LANNINGHAM
**Park Hotel**
6 Oak Road, Lanningham, Beds
Tel: 01274 546262    **£ - P - Rooms**
Local Pub on the outskirts of Lanningham

LEIGHTON BUZZARD
**Hunt Hotel**
19 Church Road, Leighton Buzzard, Beds
Tel: 01525 374692    **P - Rooms**
Comfortable rooms once used by Edward
Prince of Wales and Mrs. Simpson

LITTLE BRICKHILL
**The George Inn**
Whatling Street, Little Brickhill,
Beds MK17 9NB
Tel: 01525 261298    **££ - P - 4 rooms**
Email: info@georgeinnmk.co.uk
Web: www.georgeinnmk.co.uk
Village Inn 10 minutes drive to Milton Keynes

LUTON
**Euphoria**
9 Chapel Street, Luton, Beds LU1 2SE
Tel: 01582 720427    **£ - 4 rooms**
Town centre Pub with restaurant

**Wheelwrights Arms**
34 Guildford Street, Luton, Beds LU1 2NR
Tel: 01582 759321    **£ - P - 7 rooms**
Town centre Pub

nr BEDFORD
**The Queens Head**
Near Bedford, Beds
Tel: 0800 917 3085    **££ - P - Rooms**
Old English Inns. Reservations 0800 917 3085

POTTON
**The Old Coach House**
12 Market Street, Potton, Beds SG19 2NP
Tel: 01767 260221     **£ - P - 12 rooms**
Country Inn located in the centre of Potton

SALFORD
**Red Lion Hotel**
Wavendon Road, Salford, Beds
Tel: 0800 917 3085     **P - Rooms**
rooms have four poster beds

SHEFFORD
**The Red Lion Lodge**
Dead Mans Cross, Shefford, Beds SG17 5QQ
Tel: 01234 381381     **£ - P - 8 rooms**
Village Inn 8 miles from Bedford

**White Hart**
2 North Bridge Street, Shefford,
Beds SG17 5DH
Tel: 01462 811144     **£ - P - 4 rooms**
In the centre of this small market town

STREATLEY, LUTON
**The Chequers**
171 Sharpenhoe Road, Streatley, Luton,
Beds LU3 3PS
Tel: 01582 882072     **£ - P - 4 rooms**
Village Inn 10 minutes drive to Luton

TODDINGTON
**The Griffin Hotel**
Station Road, Toddington, Beds LU5 6BN
Tel: 01525 872030     **£ - P - 6 rooms**
Village Inn 6 miles from Milton Keynes and
Luton

**Sow and Pigs**
19 Church Square, Toddington, Beds
Tel: 01525 873089     **P - Rooms**
Web: www.sowandpigs.co.uk
CAMRA listed popular local Inn

TURVEY
**The Three Cranes**
High Street, Loop, Turvey, Beds MK43 8EP
Tel: 01234 881305     **P - Rooms**
17th century coaching Inn

WOBURN
**The Bell Hotel**
Woburn, Beds
Tel: 0800 917 3085     **££ - P - Rooms**
Old English Inns. Reservations 0800 917 3085

**Herold Leisure Magpie Hotel**
18 Bedford Street, Woburn, Milton Keynes,
Beds MK17 9QB
Tel: 01525 290219     **££ - Rooms**
Comfortable Pub in the centre of the village

# BERKSHIRE

## ASTON
**The Flower Pot**
Ferry Lane, via Aston Lane, Aston,
Berks RG9 3DG
Tel: 01491 574721    **£ - P - 3 rooms**
Village Inn 3 miles from Henley-on-Thames

## BALL HILL, NEWBURY
**The Furze Bush Inn**
Hatt Common, Ball Hill, Newbury,
Berks RG20 0NQ
Tel: 01635 253228    **££ - P - 10 rooms**
Email: info@thefurzeinn.co.uk
Country Inn just a 10 minute drive from
Newbury

## BEENHAM, READING
**The Six Bells**
Beenham Village, Beenham, Reading,
Berks RG7 5NX
Tel: 01189 713368    **£ - P - 4 rooms**
Village Inn 8 miles from Reading

## BOXFORD
**The Bell at Boxford**
Lambourn Road, Boxford, Berks RG2 8DD
Tel: 01488 608721    **££ - P - 11 rooms**
Email: bellatboxford@lycos.co.uk
Award winning country Inn 4 miles from
Newbury

## BRACKNELL
**The Admiral Cunningham**
Priestwood Court Road, Bracknell, Berks
Tel: 01344 483052    **£ - P - 2 rooms**
Located just a 5 minute walk from the town
centre

## BURGHFIELD, READING
**The Hatch Gate**
Reading Road, Burghfield, Reading,
Berks RG3 3TH
Tel: 01189 832059    **£ - P - 2 rooms**
400 year old country Inn 4 miles from Reading

## NORTH HEATH, CHIEVELEY
**The Blue Boar Inn**
Wantage Road, North Heath, Chieveley,
Berks RG20 8UE
Tel: 01635 248236    **££ - P - 15 rooms**
16thC country Inn 4 miles from Newbury

## COMPTON, nr NEWBURY
**The Compton Swan Hotel**
Compton, nr Newbury, Berks RG20 6NJ
Tel: 01635 578269    **££ - P - 6 rooms**
Country Inn 7 miles from Newbury

## EAST GARSTON
**Queens Arms Hotel**
Newbury Rd, East Garston, Berks RG17 7ET
Tel: 01488 648757    **££ - P - 14 rooms**
Country hotel 7 miles from Newbury

## EAST ILSLEY, nr NEWBURY
**The Swan**
High Street East Ilsley, nr Newbury,
Berks RG20 7LF
Tel: 01635 281238    **££ - P - 5 rooms**
Village Inn 10 miles from Newbury

## HAMSTEAD MARSHA, NEWBURY
**The White Hart Inn**
Kintbury Road, Hamstead Marsha, Newbury,
Berks RG20 0HW
Tel: 01488 658201    **££ - P - 3 rooms**
Village Inn specializing in Italian food

## HIGHCLERE
**The Yew Tree**
Andover Road, Hollington Cross, Highclere,
Berks RG20 9SE
Tel: 01635 253360    **£ - P - 5 rooms**

Email: yewtree@theoldmonk.co.uk
Traditional country inn 5 miles from Newbury

## HUNGERFORD
**The Lamb Inn**
5 Charnham St, Hungerford, Berks RG17 0EP
Tel: 01488 686390    **£ - P - 5 rooms**
Town Pub close to the town centre

## INKPEN
**The Crown and Garter**
Great Common, Inkpen, Hungerford,
Berks RG17 9QR
Tel: 01488 668325    **££ - P - 8 rooms**
Web: www.crownandgarter.com
16th century Inn ideal for walking and cycling

**The Swan Inn**
See main entry below

## KINTBURY
**The Dundas Arms**
53 Station Road, Kintbury, Berks RG17 9UT
Tel: 01488 658263    **££ - P - 5 rooms**
River and canal-side Pub with its own jetty

## KNOWL HILL
**Bird in the Hand Country Inn**
Bath Road, Knowl Hill, Berks RG10 9UP

Tel: 01628 826622    **£££ - P - 15 rooms**
Country Inn 5 miles from Maidenhead

## MAINDENS GREEN, WINKFIELD
**The Cottage Inn**
Winkfield Street, Maidens Green, Winkfield,
Windsor, Berks SL4 4SW
Tel: 01344 882242    **£££ - P - 10 rooms**
Country Inn 10 minutes from Windsor

## NEWBURY
**The Bacon Arms**
10 Oxford Street, Newbury, Berks RG14 1JB
Tel: 01635 31822    **££ - P - 14 rooms**
Town centre olde coaching Inn

**The Coopers Arms**
39 Bartholomew Street, Newbury,
Berks RG14 5LL
Tel: 01635 47469    **£ - P - 4 rooms**
Locals Pub on the edge of town

**The Ship Inn**
Ashford Hill, Newbury, Berks RG19 8BD
Tel: 01189 814504    **£ - P - 9 rooms**
Village Inn 7 miles from Newbury

## SONNING
**Bull Inn**
High Street, Sonning, Berks RG4 6UP

# The Swan Inn

*Craven Road, Lower Green, Inkpen, Hungerford,*
*Berks RG17 9DX*

**££ - P - 10 rooms**

Tel: +44 (0)1488 668326
Email: enquiries@theswaninn-organics.co.uk
Web: www.theswaninn-organics.co.uk

The Swann Inn is a perfect venue for an evening meal, a conference, a weekend exploring the
Berkshire countryside or a longer relaxing stay. The tastefully extended 17th century village inn
has 10 *en suite* bedrooms including a spacious bridal suite which is beautifully furnished.
Family rooms are also spacious and 2 extra beds for children for up to 10 year of age can be
provided. All rooms are complete with direct dial telephone and modem connection, colour television, trouser press, hair dryer, tea and coffee making facilities.

The, 'Campaign for Real Food' restaurant has a varied menu using fresh home grown organic
produce, which is GMO free, with vegetarian options.

Tel: 01189 693901     **£££ - P - 7 rooms**
Traditional Inn just 15 minutes drive to
Reading

SONNING COMMON, nr READING
**Bird-In-Hand**
Peppard Road, Sonning Common, nr Reading,
Berks RG4 9NP
Tel: 01189 723230     **£ - P - 6 rooms**
16th century coaching Inn with restaurant 2
miles from Reading

STREATLY, READING
**The Bull At Streatley**
Reading Road, Streatly, Reading,
Berks RG8 9JT
Tel: 01491 872392     **££ - P - 6 rooms**
Village Inn 9 miles from Reading

THATCHAM
**The Swan**
Station Road, Thatcham, Berks RG13 4QL
Tel: 01635 862084     **££ - P - 6 rooms**
Village Inn 4 miles from Newbury

THATCHAM, NEWBURY
**The Kings Head**
59 The Broadway, Thatcham, Newbury,
Berks RG19 3HP
Tel: 01635 862145     **£ - P - 3 rooms**
Town centre Pub 3 miles from Newbury

**The White Hart**
2 High Street, Thatcham, Newbury,
Berks RG19 3JD
Tel: 01635 863251     **£ - P - 6 rooms**
Email: des@deswilliams.demon.co.uk
Country Inn in the centre of Thatcham 3 miles
from Newbury

WARGRAVE
**The Bull Hotel**
See main entry below

WASH WATER, NEWBURY
**The Woodpecker**
Wash Water, Newbury, Berks RG20 0LU
Tel: 01635 43027     **££ - P - 3 rooms**
Rural Inn 3 miles from Newbury

WHITCHURCH
**The Ferryboat Inn**
High Street, Whitchurch, Berks RG8 7DB
Tel: 01189 842161     **£ - P - 2 rooms**
Country Pub 5 minutes drive to Pangbourne

WINDSOR FOREST, WINKFIELD
**Rose and Crown**
Woodside, Windsor Forest, Winkfield,
Berks SL4 2DP
Tel: 01344 882051     **£ - P - 2 rooms**
Country Inn, with restaurant, within a mile
from Ascot

# The Bull Hotel

*High Street, Wargrave, Berks RG10 8DD*

**££ - P - rooms**

Tel: 0118 9403120
Email: jw@thebullatwargrave.co.uk
Web: www.thebullatwargrave.co.uk

Situated in the centre of Wargrave, a picturesque riverside village, The Bull Hotel has a warm
friendly welcome that greets you when you visit our beamed pub with cosy corners, amusing
pictures, odd levels and a large working inglenook fireplace providing a huge crackling log fire
during the winter months.

All our rooms are of a high standard and enjoy *en suite* facilities. Tastefully decorated and comfortable they offer a relaxing end to your day.

**WOODSPEEN, NEWBURY**
**The Five Bells**
Belmont, Lambourne Road, Woodspeen,
Newbury, Berks RG20 8BN
Tel: 01635 48763     **£ - P - 2 rooms**
Village Inn 2 miles from Newbury

**YATTENDON**
**The Royal Oak Hotel**
The Square, Yattendon, Berks RG18 0UG
Tel: 01635 201325     **£££ - Rooms**
Village Inn situated to the north east of
Newbury

# BUCKINGHAMSHIRE

**ADSTOCK, BUCKINGHAM**
**The Folly Inn**
Buckingham Road, Adstock, Buckingham,
Bucks MK18 2HS
Tel: 01296 712671     **£ - P - 12 rooms**
Village Inn 2 miles from Buckingham

**AMERSHAM OLD TOWN**
**Saracens Head Inn**
38 Whielden Street, Amersham Old Town,
Bucks HP7 0HU
Tel: 01494 721958     **££ - 5 rooms**
Email: eamonn@thesaracensheadinn.com
Web: www.thesaracensheadinn.com
Traditional coaching Inn, in the centre of Old
Amersham Town

**ASHERDON**
**The Gate Hangers**
Lower End, Ashendon, Bucks HP18 0HE
Tel: 01296 651296     **£ - P - 5 rooms**
Village Inn 5 minutes drive to Aylesbury

**AYLESBURY**
**Royal Oak Inn**
Wingrave Road, Aston Abbotts, Aylesbury,
Bucks HP22 4LT
Tel: 01296 681262     **£ - 5 rooms**
Email: moulty.towers@btinternet.com
Village Inn 10 miles from Aylesbury

**BENNET END, RADNAGE**
Three Horseshoes Inn
Horseshoe road, Bennett End, Radnage,
Bucks HP14 4EB
Tel: 01494 483273     **£ - P - 3 rooms**
Country Inn 15 minutes to High Wycombe

**BRILL**
**The Pheasant Inn**
Windmill Street, Brill, Bucks HP18 9TG
Tel: 01844 237104     **££ - P - 3 rooms**
Web: www.thepheasant.co.uk
Accommodation situated in the old bakery

**BUCKINGHAM**
**White Hart Hotel**
Market Square, Buckingham, Bucks MK18 1NL
Tel: 01280 815151     **£ - P - 20 rooms**
Town centre Inn / hotel

**CHALFONT ST GILES**
**The White Hart**
Three Households, Chalfont St Giles,

Bucks HP8 4LP
Tel: 01494 872441    **£££ - P - 11 rooms**
Village Pub with a brand new 7 bedroom
lodge

## CHESHAM
**The Gamekeepers Lodge**
Bellingdon Road, Chesham, Bucks HP5 2NN
Tel: 01494 793491    **£ - P - 3 rooms**
Email: patricia.miller@btopenworld.com
Locals Pub on the outskirts of town 7 minutes
walk to the town centre

## DOWNLEY, HIGH WYCOMBE
**The Bricklayers Arms**
High Street, Downley, High Wycombe,
Bucks HP13 5XJ
Tel: 01494 520597    **£ - P - 3 rooms**
Community village Pub 5 minutes drive to
High Wycombe

## DRAYTON PARSLOW, MILTON KEYNES
**Three Horseshoes**
10 Main Road, Drayton Parslow, Milton
Keynes, Bucks MK17 0JS
Tel: 01296 720296    **£ - P - 9 rooms**
Email: 3shoes@threehorseshoes.idps.co.uk
Web: www.threehorseshoes.free-online.co.uk
Village Inn 4 miles from Bletchley

## FAWLEY
**The Walnut Tree**
Fawley, Bucks RG9 6JE
Tel: 01491 638360    **££ - Rooms**
Village Inn north of Henley

## GREAT MISSENDEN
**The George Inn**
94 High Street, Great Missenden,
Bucks HP16 0BG
Tel: 01494 862084    **££ - P - 6 rooms**
Village Inn 6 miles from Andover

## HADDENHAM, AYLESBURY
**The Rose and Thistle**
6 Station Road, Haddenham, Aylesbury,
Bucks HP17 8AJ
Tel: 01844 291451    **£ - P - 2 rooms**
Country Inn 4 miles from Thame

## HAMBLEDEN
**Stag and Huntsman Inn**
Hambleden, Bucks RG9 6RP
Tel: 01491 571227    **££ - P - 3 rooms**
Village Inn 6 miles from Henley-on-Thames

## HIGH WYCOMBE
**The Terriers**
133 Amersham Road, High Wycombe,
Bucks HP13 5AD
Tel: 01494 523827    **£ - P - 3 rooms**
Less than 2 miles from the town centre

## IBSTONE
**The Fox**
The Common, Ibstone, Buckinghamshire
Tel: 01491 638289    **££ - P - 18 rooms**
The quintessential village Inn 10 minutes drive
to High Wycombe

## IVER
**The Bull**
7 High Street, Iver, Bucks SL0 9ND
Tel: 01753 651115    **£ - P - 3 rooms**
Mainly caters for workers. Village Inn 1 mile
from Uxbridge

## LITTLE TINGEWICK, nr FINMERE
**The Red Lion**
Little Tingewick, nr Finmere, Bucks MK18 4AG
Tel: 01280 848285    **P - 2 rooms**
Village Inn 4 miles from Buckingham

## LONG CRENDON
**The Angel Inn**
47 Bicester Road, Long Crendon,
Bucks HP18 9EE
Tel: 01844 208268    **££ - P - 3 rooms**
Village Inn 1 mile from Thame

## LONGWICK, PRINCES RISBOROUGH
**The Red Lion**
Thame Road, Longwick, Princes Risborough,
Bucks HP27 9SG
Tel: 01844 344980    **£ - P - 6 rooms**
Country Pub 1 mile from Princes Risborough

## MARLOW
**The Prince of Wales**
1 Mill Road, Marlow, Bucks SL7 1PX

# The White Hart

*1 Gun Lane, Sherington, Newport Pagnell, Bucks MK16 9PE*

**££ - P - R - BM - BG - PW - C**

Tel: 01908 611953          Fax: 01908 618109

Email: whitehartresort@aol.com

Web: www.whitehartsherington.com

This well-known hostelry is about 300 years old and stands in the pretty village of Sherington. The village location makes it perfect for touring the surrounding area, just 3 miles from junction 14 of the M1 and within easy reach of Milton Keynes.

The White Hart offers luxury en suite accommodation for the whole family. The rooms, many with exposed beams, are situated within a converted barn just across the courtyard from the main building. The restaurant, with its high-beamed ceiling and tall stonewalls make this a most charismatic place to eat. On cold winter nights the open fire is a welcome addition! There is also a beer garden; plenty of parking, well-behaved pets are welcome.

---

Tel: 01628 482970    **££ - P - 6 rooms**
Town Pub close to the river

## MOULSOE
**The Carrington Arms**
Cranfield Road, Moulsoe, Bucks MK16 0HB
Tel: 01908 218050    **££ - P - 8 rooms**
Food orientated country Pub 4 miles from Milton Keynes

## PADBURY
**Black Bird**
Main Street, Padbury, Bucks MK18 2AY
Tel: 01280 813017    **£ - P - 6 rooms**
17th century country Inn with restaurant 2 miles from Buckingham

## PRINCES RISBOROUGH
**The George and Dragon**
74 High Street, Princes Risborough,
Bucks HP27 0AX
Tel: 01844 343087    **££ - P - 7 rooms**
Situated right n the centre of Princes Risborough

## SALFORD, MILTON KEYNES
**Red Lion Hotel**
Wavendon Rd, Salford, Milton Keynes, Bucks
Tel: 01908 583117    **Rooms**
Four posters, log fire, good food

## SAUNDERTON, nr PRINCES RISBOROUGH
**Rose and Crown Hotel**
Saunderton, nr Princes Risborough,
Bucks HP27 9NP
Tel: 01844 345299    **P - 17 rooms**
Well appointed wayside Inn between Aylesbury and High Wycombe

## SHERINGTON
**The White Hart**
See main entry above

## SKIRMETT
**The Frog**
Skirmett, Bucks RG9 6TG
Tel: 01491 638996    **Rooms**
Rural local north east of Henley

## STONY STRATFORD
**Bull Hotel**
64 High Street, Stony Stratford, Bucks
Tel: 01908 567104    **£ - P - 14 rooms**
Old coaching Inn located in the centre of town

**The Old George**
41 High Street, Stony Stratford, Milton Keynes, Bucks MK11 1AA
Tel: 01908 562181    **££ - P - 11 rooms**
Olde Worlde Pub / hotel in the centre of town

WADDESDON
**The Five Arrows Hotel**
High Street, Waddesdon, Bucks HP18 0JE
Tel: 01296 651727    **££ - Rooms**
On the Rothchild estate north west of
Aylesbury

WEST WYCOMBE
**The George and Dragon Hotel**
High St, West Wycombe, Bucks HP14 3AB
Tel: 01494 464414    **££ - 11 rooms**
Situated in the National Trust village of West
Wycombe, 3 miles from High Wycombe

WESTON TURVILLE,
nr AYLESBURY
**The Five Bells**
40 Main Street, Weston Turville, nr Aylesbury,
Bucks HP22 5RW
Tel: 01296 613131    **££ - P - 16 rooms**
Owned by Inn Keepers Lodge

WHADDON, MILTON KEYNES
**Lowndes Arms and Motel**
High Street, Whaddon, Milton Keynes,
Bucks MK17 0NA

Tel: 01908 501706    **££ - P - 11 rooms**
16th century village Inn 3 miles from Milton
Keynes

WHITELEAF, PRINCES
RISBOROUGH
**Red Lion**
Upper Icknield Way, Whiteleaf, Princes
Risborough, Bucks HP27 0LL
Tel: 01844 344476    **£ - P - 4 rooms**
Village Inn 1 mile from Princes Risborough

WOOBURN COMMON
**Chequers Inn**
Kiln Lane, Woodburn Common,
Bucks HP10 0JQ
Tel: 01628 529575    **£££ - Rooms**
Traditional rural Inn north of Maidenhead

WOOBURN GREEN
**The Old Bell**
Town Lane, Wooburn Green, Bucks HP10 0PL
Tel: 01628 520406    **££ - P - 6 rooms**
Email: peterlim@oldbell.co.uk
Web: www.oldbell.co.uk
Local Pub 10 minutes drive to High Wycombe

# EAST SUSSEX

ALCISTON
**Rose Cottage Inn**
Alciston, East Sussex BN26 6UW
Tel: 01323 870377    **£ - P - 1 flat**
Village Inn 5 miles from Lewes

BARCOMBE
**The Anchor Inn**
Anchor Lane, Barcombe, East Sussex BN8 5BS
Tel: 01273 400414    **££ - P - 3 rooms**
Idyllic riverside Inn 5 miles from Lewis

BURWASH
**Bell Inn**
High Street, Burwash, East Sussex TN19 7EH
Tel: 01435 882304    **£ - P - 1 room**
Traditional village Inn 18 miles from Hastings

**Rose and Crown Inn**
Ham Lane, Burwash, East Sussex TN19 7ER
Tel: 01435 882600    **£ - P - 3 rooms**
Email: info@roseandcrownburwash.co.uk
Web: www.roseandcrownburwash.co.uk
Village Inn 2 miles off the A21

COWDEN, nr EDENBRIDGE
**White Horse Inn Hotel**
Holtye, Cowden, nr Edenbridge,
East Sussex TN8 7ED
Tel: 01342 850640     **£ - P - 11 rooms**
Country Inn 3 miles from East Grinstead

EAST DEAN, nr ESASTBOURNE
**Birling Gap Hotel**
Birling Gap, East Dean, nr Eastbourne,
East Sussex BN20 0AB
Tel: 01323 423197     **£ - P - 9 rooms**
Traditional Inn 5 miles from Eastbourne

EWHURST GREEN
**The White Dog Inn**
Village Street, Ewhurst Green,
East Sussex TN32 5TD
Tel: 01580 830264     **£ - P - 3 rooms**
Country Inn 10 miles from Hastings

FLETCHING
**The Griffin Inn**
High Street, Fletching, East Sussex TN22 3SS
Tel: 01825 722890     **££ - P - 8 rooms**
Email: nigelpullan@thegriffininn.co.uk
Web: www.thegriffininn.co.uk
16thC Inn with large garden

**Rose and Crown**
High street, Fletching, nr Uckfield, East
Sussex TN22 3ST
Tel: 01825 722039     **££ - P - 3 rooms**
Email: rose.and.crown@talk21.com
16th century village Inn 3 miles from Uckfield

HARTFIELD
**Anchor Inn**
Church Street, Hartfield, East Sussex TN7 4AG
Tel: 01892 770424     **£ - P - 2 rooms**
14thC Inn on the edge of the Ashdown Forest

HASTINGS
**Churchills Hotel**
3 St Helens Crescent, Hastings,
East Sussex TN34 2EN
Tel: 01424 439359     **£ - P - 8 rooms**
Town hotel with 10 minutes from the sea

**Pissarros Bar**
9–10 South Terrace, Hastings,
East Sussex TN34 1SA
Tel: 01424 213633     **£ - Rooms**
Town centre bar

HORAM
**The Horam Inn**
See main entry below

HOVE
**Hangleton Manor Inn**
Hangleton Valley Drive, Hove,
East Sussex BN3 8AN
Tel: 01273 413266     **££ - P - 3 rooms**
Listed country Inn just 5 minute drive to Hove

IDEN, nr RYE
**Bell Inn**
Church Lane, Iden, Rye, East Sussex TN31 7PU
Tel: 01797 280242     **£ - P - 2 rooms**
Traditional village Inn 3 miles from Rye

# The Horam Inn

*The High Street, Horam, East Sussex TN21 0EL*

**£ - P - R - BG - C - 6 rooms**

**Tel: 01435 812692**

The Horam Inn is situated in the heart of Horam village at the junction of the main roads to
Heathfield, London and Eastbourne. This charming village Inn is ideally located just 5 miles from
Heathfield, 15 miles from the coast and is close to the Cuckoo Trail.

The average room price is £35 for a single room, £50 for a double room and £65 for a family
room. Children are most welcome. The Inn boasts a comfortable restaurant, bar meals are also
served, beer garden, car parking.

## LEWES
**The Crown Inn**
High Street, Lewes, East Sussex BN7 2NA
Tel: 01273 480670    **££ - P - 8 rooms**
Email: sales@crowninn-lewes.co.uk
Web: www.crowninn-lewes.co.uk
Family run town centre Inn

## MAYFIELD
**Rose and Crown Inn**
Fletching St, Mayfield, East Sussex TN20 6TE
Tel: 01435 872200    **P - 5 rooms**
Village Inn 5 miles from Crowborough

## PILTDOWN, UCKFIELD
**The Piltdown Man**
Piltdown, Uckfield, East Sussex TN22 5XL
Tel: 01825 723563    **££ - P - 3 rooms**
Email: enquiries@thepiltdownman.com
Web: www.thepiltdownman.com
Country Inn 2 miles from Uckfield

## ROBERTSBRIDGE
**Ostrich Hotel**
Station Road, Robertsbridge,
East Sussex DN32 5DG
Tel: 01580 881737    **£ - P - Rooms**
Village Pub 5 miles from Battle

## RYE
**Cinque Ports Hotel**
26 Cinque Port Street, Rye,
East Sussex TN31 7AN
Tel: 01797 222319    **£ - P - 3 rooms**
Town centre Pub between the centre and the
railway station, large beer garden

**Queens Head Hotel**
19 Landgate, Rye, East Sussex TN31 7LH
Tel: 01797 222181    **£ - Rooms**
By the Land Arch 2 minutes walk into town

**The Mermaid Inn**
Mermaid Street, Rye, East Sussex TN31 7EY
Tel: 01797 223065    **£££ - P - 31 rooms**
One of England's oldest Inns

**The Hare and Hounds**
Main Road, Rye, East Sussex TN31 7ST
Tel: 01797 230483    £ - 4 rooms
Village Inn 3 minutes drive to Rye

## SIDLEY, BEXHILL-ON-SEA
**Pelham Hotel**
Holliers Hill, Sidley, Bexhill-on-Sea, East
Sussex TN40 2DD
Tel: 01424 210269    **Rooms**
Newly refurbished seaside hotel with a
public bar

## SOUTHOVER, LEWES
**The Kings Head**
High Street, Southover, Lewes,
East Sussex BN7 1AS
Tel: 01273 474628    **Rooms**
One of the Pubs n Bars Group

## ST LEONARDS
**Old England**
45 London Road, St Leonards,
East Sussex TN37 6AJ
Tel: 01424 722154    **Rooms**
Seaside Pub

## TICEHURST
**The Bull Inn**
Three Leg Cross, Ticehurst, Wadhurst, East
Sussex TN5 7HH
Tel: 01580 200586    **£ - P - 4 rooms**
Email: michael@thebullinn.co.uk
Web: www.thebullinn.co.uk
Rural Inn 10 miles from Tunbrdge Wells

**Cherry Tree Inn**
Dale Hill, Ticehurst, East Sussex TN5 7DG
Tel: 01580 201229    **£ - P - 3 rooms**
Email: leondiane@aol.com
Country Inn by Dale Hill golf course

## WADHURST
**Best Beech Inn**
Best Beech, Mayfield Lane, Wadhurst, East
Sussex TN5 6JH
Tel: 01892 782046    **£ - P - 7 rooms**
Web: www.bestbeechinn.com
Rural Inn 7 miles from Tonbridge Wells

## WINCHELSEA
**The New Inn**
German St, Winchelsea, East Sussex TN36 4EN
Tel: 01797 226252    **££ - P - 6 rooms**
Email: newinnwsea@aol.com
18thC Inn located in the centre of town

# ESSEX

## BRENTWOOD
**18th Century Inn**
See main entry below

## BURNHAM-ON-CROUCH
**Ship Inn**
52 High Street, Burnham-on-Crouch, Essex
Tel: 01621 785057     **£ - P - 3 rooms**
Email: brendatof@ukonline.co.uk
A village style pub located right on the High
Street

**Ye Olde White Hart Hotel**
See main entry on page 109

## CLACTON-ON-SEA
**Plaza Hotel Public House / Restaurant**
5 Marine Parade East, Clacton-on-Sea,
Essex CO15 1PT
Tel: 01255 476021     **£ - rooms**
Seafront Pub

## CLAVERING, SAFFRON WALDEN
**The Cricketers**
Clavering, Saffron Walden, Essex CB11 4QT
Tel: 01799 550442     **£££ - P - 8 rooms**
Email: cricketers@lineone.net
Web: www.thecricketers.co.uk
Village Pub 10 minutes from Saffron Walden

## DEDHAM, nr COLCHESTER
**The Marlborough Head Hotel**
Mill Lane, Dedham, nr Colchester,
Essex CO7 6DH
Tel: 01206 323250     **££ - 3 rooms**
Traditional village Inn 5 miles from Colchester

## DOVERCOURT
**Queens Hotel**
119 The High St, Dovercourt, Essex CO12 3AP
Tel: 01255 502634     **Rooms**
Country hotel on the outskirts of town

## DOVERCOURT, HARWICH
**Phoenix Hotel**
Lower Marine Parade, Dovercourt, Harwich,
Essex CO12 3ST
Tel: 01255 502071     **£ - Rooms**
Seaside Pub right on the coast

## FEEING, COLCHESTER
**The Old Anchor**
132 Feering Hill, Feering, Colchester,
Essex CO5 9PY
Tel: 01376 572855     **££ - P - 6 rooms**
Traditional English Inn

---

# 18th Century Inn

*In the heart of Brentwood Town Centre, Essex*

Tel: 01277 202430     Email: linton_27@yahoo.com

This friendly local Inn offers affordable, basic accommodation. It is an ideal place for contractual
workers. All rooms have central heating and TV, there are shared facilities ie bathroom, kitchen
and public car parking. The bar is a great place to eat and drink, and has frequent entertainment.
Also there is a function room for 45 available.

# Ye Olde White Hart Hotel

*The Quay, Burnham-On-Crouch, Essex CM0 8AS*

**£ - P - 19 rooms**

Tel / Fax: 01621 782106

The Hotel, built with character in the 1600s, overlooks the River Crouch and has its own jetty and pier. The situation is ideal for exploring the pleasant Riverside Walks and experience the peaceful Essex countryside and villages. Eleven of the comfortable bedrooms are *en suite* with TV and tea / coffee making facilities, eight with shared facilities.

Rates from: Single £19.80, Double £37.00 per night

---

## FINCHINGFIELD
**The Red Lion Inn**
6 Church Hill, Finchingfield, Braintree,
Essex CM7 4NN
Tel: 01371 810400     **£ - P - 3 rooms**
Email: franktyler_new.uk@excite.co.uk
Web: www.red-lion-finchingfield.com
16th century village Inn 9 miles from Braintree

## GREAT BROMLEY, COLCHESTER
**Old Courthouse Inn**
Harwich Road, Great Bromley, Colchester,
Essex CO7 7JG
Tel: 01206 250322     **££ - P - 5 rooms**
Email: oldcourthouseinn@21.com
Located just off A120 fairly near to Harwich

## HALSTEAD
**White Hart Inn**
15 High Street, Halstead, Essex CO9 2AA
Tel: 01787 475657     **£ - P - 3 rooms**
15th century town centre coaching Inn

## HARWICH
**Alma Inn**
25 Kingshead St, Harwich, Essex CO12 3EE
Tel: 01255 503474     **£ - P - 4 rooms**
Victorian Pub in old Harwich town

**The Hanover Inn**
See main entry on page 110

## HATFIELD PEVEREL, CHELMSFORD
**The Swan Inn**
The Street, Hatfield Peverel, Chelmsford,
Essex CM3 2DW

Tel: 01245 380238     **£ - P - 4 rooms**
Located in a small town 6 miles from
Chelmsford

## HORNDON-ON-THE-HILL
**Bell Inn and Hill House**
High Rd, Horndon-on-the-Hill, Essex SS17 8LD
Tel: 01375 642463     **££ - P - 15 rooms**
15th Century coaching Inn 3 miles from
Stamford le Hope

## LITTLE DUNMOW
**Flitch of Bacon**
The Street, Little Dunmow, Essex CM6 3HT
Tel: 01371 820323     **££ - P - 3 rooms**
Village Inn 5 miles from Great Dun

## LITTLE WALTHAM
**The Windmill Motor Inn**
Chatham Green, Little Waltham, Chelmsford,
Essex CM3 3LE
Tel: 01245 361188     **££ - P - 9 rooms**
Email: a131windmill.essex@virgin.net
A cosy country Pub just 5 miles from
Chelmsford

## MALDEN
**Jolly Sailor**
Hythe Quay, Malden, Essex CM9 5HP
Tel: 01621 853463     **£ - P - 4 rooms**
Great views across the harbour

## NORTH FAMBRIDGE
**The Ferry Boat Inn**
See main entry on page 110

# Hanover Inn

*65 Church Street, Harwich, Essex CO12 3DR*

**£ - Letting rooms**

Tel: 01255 502927    Fax: 07031 151597
Email: baz.mackness@easynet.co.uk
Bookings: bookings@hanover-inn-harwich.co.uk
Web: www.hanover-inn-harwich.co.uk

The Hanover Inn is a local fisherman's tavern offering an informal and friendly atmosphere sited in the heart of historic Old Harwich, and is an ideal stopover for ferry and cruise passengers using Harwich International Port, providing comfortable accommodation, a selection of real ales and a rather special breakfast experience.

Guests can explore the narrow streets and follow the Heritage Trail or take a conducted tour of the town to enjoy the carefully preserved and restored buildings that date back to the 15thC. Old Harwich offers a selection of restaurants serving freshly landed fish, crab and lobster dishes.

# The Ferryboat Inn

*Ferry Lane, North Fambridge, Essex CM3 6LR*

**£ - P - Rooms**

Tel: +44(0)1621 740208
Email: sylviaferryboat@aol.com
Web: www.ferryboatinn.net

The Ferry Boat is a 500 year old riverside freehouse pub offering accommodation for just £40 per double room per night as well as serving renowned beers (principal beers being Shepherd Neame Bishops Finger, Spitfire and Best Bitter), food (fresh local produce) and hospitality. This away-from-it-all friendly locals pub is located by the Essex Wildlife Trust's 600 acre sanctuary in North Fambridge.

The purpose built accommodation is all on the ground floor, set in a courtyard behind the Inn and is rated Three Diamonds by the English Tourism Council. All rooms have TV, tea / coffee making facilities, and cots are available. One room is equipped to allow disabled access.

**RADWINTER, SAFFRON WALDEN**
**The Plough**
Sampford Road, Radwinter, Saffron Walden,
Essex CB10 2TL
Tel: 01799 599222    **£ - P - 3 rooms**
Rural 17thC Inn 4 miles from Saffron Walden

**SAFFRON WALDEN**
**Cricketers Arms**
Rickling Green, Saffron Walden,

Essex CB11 3YG
Tel: 01799 543210    **££ - P - 10 rooms**
Traditional Inn overlooking the town's cricket green

**Queen Elizabeth**
2 East St, Safron Waldon, Essex CV10 1LS
Tel: 01799 520065    **£ - Rooms**
Small town Pub in the centre of Saffron Waldon

# Cap and Feathers Inn

*South Street, Tillingham, Essex CM0 7TH*

**P - Letting rooms**

Tel and Fax: 01621 779212

The Cap & Feathers is a 16th Century Inn which has welcoming bed and breakfast rooms and resident ghost, Captain Cook. We have freshly cooked home made food prepared with local produce – Vegetarians catered for – Traditional Sunday roast – Noted home made pies and sausages. There are also no-smoking rooms.

Cyclists and ramblers welcome, children and dogs welcome.

Award winning Real Ales are always available, including Crouch Vale, and other guest beers. Meetings Welcome!

THAXTED, DUNMOW
**The Farmhouse Inn**
Monk St, Thaxted, Dunmow, Essex CM6 2NR
Tel: 01371 830864    **£ - P - 10 rooms**
Rural Inn 8 miles from Stanstead Airport

TILLINGHAM
**The Cap and Feathers**
See main entry above

WALTON-ON-THE-NAZE
**Queens Head Hotel**
76 High Street, Walton-on-the-Naze,
Essex CO14 8AD
Tel: 01255 675763    **£ - Rooms**
A traditional seaside Pub located right in the town centre

# GREATER LONDON

## CARSHALTON
**Greyhound Hotel**
2 High Street, Carshalton, London SN5 3PE
Tel: 02086 471511     **£ - P - 21 rooms**
Email: thegreyhound@youngs.co.uk
In the centre of Carshalton

## CHARLTON
**McDonnells Free House**
Woolich Road, Charlton, London SE7 8SU
Tel: 02088 530143     **£ - 10 rooms**
Handy for Charlton railway station

## CHINGFORD
**Molly K's**
Kings Head Hill, Chingford, London E4 7ES
Tel: 02085 295773     **£ - P - 8 rooms**
Local Pub 800 yards from the railway station

## CHISLEHURST
**Bull's Head**
Royal Parade, Chislehurst, London
Tel: 02084 671727     **££ - P - 5 rooms**
In a residential area

## CLAPHAM COMMON, SOUTHSIDE
**The Windmill on the Common**
Clapham Common, Southside, London SW4 9DE
Tel: 02086 734578     **£££ - P - 29 rooms**
Email: windmillhotel@youngs.co.uk
The London hotel with a country feel, owned
by Youngs Brewery

## CRANFORD
**Jolly Gardeners**
144 High Street, Cranford, London
Tel: 02088 976996     **£ - P - 2 rooms**
Two miles from Heathrow

## CROYDON
**The Swan and Sugarloaf**
1 Brighton Rd South, Croydon, London CR2 6EA
Tel: 02086 887888     **Rooms**
One of the Pubs n Bars group of Inns

## EALING
**Kings Arms**
55 The Grove, Ealing, London W5 5DX
Tel: 02085 670606     **££ - P - 7 rooms**
Local town Pub 500 yards from Ealing centre

## EAST SHEEN
**The Plough Inn**
42 Christchurch Road, East Sheen,
London SW14 7AF
Tel: 02088 767833     **££ - Rooms**
A 16thC Inn located very near to Richmond
Park

## ELEPHANT AND CASTLE
**Elephant and Castle**
Newington Causeway, Elephant and Castle,
London SE1 6BN
Tel: 02073 579134     **Rooms**
One of the Pubs n Bars group of Inns

## GREENWICH
**The Mitre Inn**
291 Greenwich High Road, Greenwich,
London SE10 8NA
Tel: 02083 556760     **Rooms**
Three bar traditional pub with function room

**The Pilot**
68 River Way North, Greenwich,
London SE10 0BE
Tel: 02088 585910     **££ - P - 7 rooms**
Busy Pub just 100 yards from the Dome

HAMMERSMITH
**Brook Green Hotel**
170 Shepherds Bush Road, Hammersmith
Tel: 02076 032516    **££ - 14 rooms**
Email: brookgreen@youngs.co.uk
Opposite Brook Green Park

HAMPTON HILL
**The Roebuck**
72 Hampton Road, Hampton Hill,
London TW12 1JN
Tel: 02082 558133    **£ - 4 rooms**
Centre of Hampton Hill

KENSINGTON
**Earl Derby**
50 Bosworth Road North, Kensington,
London W10 5UG
Tel: 02089 692879    **8 rooms**
Traditional London Pub

KINGS CROSS
**Dun-a-ri**
19 Caledonian Road, Kings Cross, London
Tel: 02078 374863    **£ - 5 rooms**
Late license town Pub near Kings Cross

LAMBETH
**The Windmill**
44 Lambeth High Street, Lambeth,
London SE1 7JS
Tel: 02077 351698    **£ - 7 rooms**
In the centre of Lambeth, serves real ale

PADDINGTON
**Kings Arms Hotel**
254 Edgware Road, Paddington,
London W2 1DS
Tel: 02072 628441    **£ - 16 rooms**
Email: kingsarmshotel@compuserve.com
Hotel and bar, nr Edgware Road station

PECKHAM
**Montpellier**
Choumert Road, Peckham, London SE15 4AR
Tel: 02076 391736    **£ - 9 rooms**
Local town Pub

SOUTHWARK
**Mad Hatter Hotel**
3–7 Stamford Street, Southwark,

London SE1 9NY
Tel: 02074 019222    **£££ - 30 rooms**
Situated close to Waterloo Station

TOOTING
**The Railway Bell**
284 Micham Road, Tooting,
London SW17 9NT
Tel: 02086 722777    **Rooms**
One of the Pubs n Bars group of Inns

**The Wheatsheaf**
2 Upper Tooting Road, Tooting,
London SW17 7PG
Tel: 02086 722805    **Rooms**
One of the Pubs n Bars group

WALWORTH, KENNINGTON
**Liam Ogs**
374 Walworth Road, Walworth,
London SE17 2NF
Tel: 02077 033295    **££ - 6 rooms**
Local Pub 10 minutes by bus to the West End

WANDSWORTH
**The Brewers Inn**
147 East Hill, Wandsworth, London SW18 2QB
Tel: 02088 744128    **££ - P - 16 rooms**
Email: brewersinn@youngs.co.uk
Web: www.youngs.co.uk
Large bar / bistro, Youngs Brewery Inn

**The Grosvenor Arms**
204 Garrett Lane, Wandsworth,
London SW18 4ED
Tel: 02088 742709    **4 rooms**
Local Pub 500yards from Earlsfield Station

WESTMINSTER
**Sanctuary House**
33 Tothill Street, Westminster, London
Tel: 02077 994044    **£££ - 34 rooms**
Email: sanctuary@fullers.co.uk
Large Fullers Brewery Pub, 10 minutes walk
to Victoria station

WOOLWICH
**Roses Free House**
49 Hare Street, Woolwich, London SE18 6NE
Tel: 02088 541538    **£ - P - 4 twin rooms**
Located in the centre of Woolwich

# HAMPSHIRE

## ALDERSHOT
**Duke of York**
248 Weybourne Road, Aldershot,
Hants GU11 3NF
Tel: 01252 321150      **£ - P - 5 rooms**
Local urban Pub 5 minutes drive to Aldershot
centre

## ALTON
**Dukes Head**
Butts Road, Alton, Hants GU34 1LH
Tel: 01420 82331      **P - 3 rooms**
Town Pub 300 yards from the town centre

## ANDOVER
**Amport Inn**
Amport, Andover, Hants SP11 8AE
Tel: 01264 710371      **££ - P - 9 rooms**
Village Inn 10 minutes drive to Andover

**White Hart Hotel**
Bridge Street, Andover, Hants SP10 1BH
Tel: 01264 352266      **££ - P - 27 rooms**
Email: whiteharthotel.andover@eldridge-
pope.co.uk
Web: www.eldridge-pope.co.uk
Large Inn / hotel near the centre of Andover

## BARTON STACEY, WINCHESTER
**The Swan Inn**
Barton Stacey, Winchester, Hants SO21 3RL
Tel: 01962 760470      **£ - P - 3 rooms**
Village Inn 10 minute drive to Winchester

## BROOK, LYNDHURST
**The Bell Inn**
Brook, Lyndhurst, Hants SO43 7HE
Tel: 02380 812214      **££ - P - 25 rooms**
In the heart of the New Forest. Owned by the
same family for 200 years

## BURITON, PETERSFIELD
**The Master Robert**
Buriton, Petersfield, Hants GU31 5SW
Tel: 01730 267275      **6 rooms**
Email: masterrobertinn@aol.com
Family run Pub near Queen Elizabeth Country
Park

## CHERITON
**The Flower Pots Inn**
Cheriton, Hants SO24 0QQ
Tel: 01962 771318      **££ - P - 4 rooms**
Village Inn 3 miles from New Alresford

## DAMERSHAM, FORDINGBRIDGE
**The Compasses Inn**
Damerham, Fordingbridge, Hants SP6 3HQ
Tel: 01725 518231      **££ - P - 6 rooms**
Village Inn 3 miles from Fordingbridge

## DROXFORD, SOUTHAMPTON
**White Horse Inn**
Southill, Droxford, Southampton, Hampshire
Tel: 01489 877490      **£ - P - 3 rooms**
Village Inn 9 miles from Fareham

## DUNBRIDGE, ROMSEY
**The Mill Arms**
Barley Mill, Dunbridge, Romsey,
Hants SO51 0LF
Tel: 01794 340401      **£ - P - 6 rooms**
Email: the-mill-arms@river-dun.demon.co.uk
Web: www.river-dun.demon.co.uk/
Village Inn 6 miles from Romsey

## EAST MEON, nr PETERSFIELD
**Ye Olde George Inn**
Church Street, East Meon, nr Petersfield,

Hants GU32 1NH
Tel: 01730 823481     **££ - P - 5 rooms**
Riverside 15th century coaching Inn

EAST TYTHERLEY
**Star Inn**
East Tytherley, Hants SO51 1EG
Tel: 01794 340225     **££ - P - 3 rooms**
Email: info@starinn.co.uk
Web: www.starinn.co.uk
Country / village Inn 6 miles from Romsey

EASTON
**Cricketers Inn**
Easton, Hants SO21 1EJ
Tel: 01962 779353     **£ - P - 4 rooms**
Email: thecricketersinn138@aol.com
Village Inn 4 miles from Winchester

FACCOMBE
**Jack Russell Inn**
Faccombe, Hants SP11 0DS
Tel: 01264 737315     **££ - P - 3 rooms**
Village Inn 8 miles from Newbury and Andover

FAREHAM
**Roundabout Hotel**
46 Wallingtonshore Road, Fareham, Hants
Tel: 01329 822542     **££ - P - 16 rooms**
Email: info@theroundabouthotel.co.uk
Web: www.theroundabouthotel.co.uk
Hotel with a public bar just off the M27

FAWLEY, nr SOUTHAMPTON
**Falcon Hotel**
The Square, Fawley, nr Southampton,
Hants SO4 1DD
Tel: 02380 891005     **£ - P - 3 rooms**
Local Pub centre of Fawley

FORDINGBRIDGE
**The Crown Inn**
62 High Street, Fordingbridge, Hants SP6 1AX
Tel: 01425 652552     **£ - 3 rooms**
Email: candm.bell@ukgateway.net
Old coaching Inn close to the New Forest

**The Ship Inn**
68 High Street, Fordingbridge, Hants SP6 1AX
Tel: 01425 651820     **£ - P - 4 rooms**
Town centre Inn

LONGPARISH
**The Plough Inn**
Longparish, Hants SP11 6PB
Tel: 01264 720358     **£ - P - 2 rooms**
Traditional village Inn 5 miles from Andover

LYMINGTON
**Angel Inn**
108 High Street, Lymington, Hants SO41 9AP
Tel: 01590 672050     **££ - P - 12 rooms**
Web: www.stayhere.uk.com
Olde traditional town centre Inn

**The Mayflower Inn**
Kings Saltern Road, Lymington, Hants
Tel: 01590 672160     **££ - P - 6 rooms**
Village Inn with restaurant 5 minutes walk to
the town centre

MIDDLE WALLOP, STOCKBRIDGE
**The George Inn**
The Crossroads, Middle Wallop, Stockbridge,
Hants SO20 8EG
Tel: 01264 781224     **££ - P - 3 rooms**
Email: joanne.george@virgin.net
Village restaurant / bar 6 miles from Andover

OLD PORTSMOUTH
**Duke of Buckingham**
119 High Street, Old Portsmouth,
Hants PO1 2HW
Tel: 02392 827067     **£ - 4 rooms**
Lively students' Pub in the old town

OVERTON
**White Hart Hotel**
London Road, Overton, Hants RG25 3NW
Tel: 01256 770237     **£ - P - 6 rooms**
Village Inn 8 miles from Basingstoke

PORTSMOUTH
**Avenue Hotel**
314 Twyford Avenue, Portsmouth,
Hants PO8 2NT
Tel: 02392 660554     **£ - 10 rooms**
Town sports Pub near the port

**Sally Port Inn**
57-58 High St, Portsmouth, Hants PO1 2LU
Tel: 02392 821860     **££ - 11 rooms**
Olde Worlde Pub in Portsmouth old town

RINGWOOD
**The Original White Hart**
Market Place, Ringwood, Hants BH24 1AW
Tel: 01425 472702　　**££ - P - 15 rooms**
Town centre Inn

SELBOURNE, ALTON
**The Queens and The Limes**
High St, Selbourne, Alton, Hants GU34 3JJ
Tel: 01420 511454　　**££ - P - 13 rooms**
Email: enquiries@queens-selbourne.co.uk
Web: www.queens-selbourne.co.uk
Village Inn 6 miles from Alton

SETLEY, BROCKENHURST
**The Filly Inn**
Lymington Road, Setley, Brockenhurst,
Hants SO42 7UF
Tel: 01590 623449　　**£ - P - 6 rooms**
Email: pub@fillyinn.co.uk
Web: www.fillyinn.co.uk
Village Inn 2 miles from Brockenhurst

ST MARY BOURNE
**The George Inn**
St Mary Bourne, Hants SP11 6BG
Tel: 01264 738340　　**££ - P - 2 rooms**
A traditional village Inn just a10 minute drive
from Andover

STOCKBRIDGE, nr WINCHESTER
**White Hart Inn**
Stockbridge, nr Winchester, Hants SO20 6HF
Tel: 01264 810663　　**££ - P - 14 rooms**
Email: whitehart@accommodation-inns.co.uk
Web: www.accommodation-inns.co.uk
Located just outside town 12 miles from
Winchester

STUCKTON, nr FORDINGBRIDGE
**The Three Lions**
Stuckton, nr Fordingbridge, Hants SP6 2HF
Tel: 01425 652489　　**£££ - P - 3 rooms**
Email: the3lions@btinternet.com
Excellent restaurant, amongst the highest
rated Inns in Britain

TADLEY, BASINGSTOKE
**The Treacle Mine Hotel**
Filchester Road, Tadley, Basingstoke,
Hants RG26 3PX
Tel: 01189 814857　　**£ - P - 7 rooms**
Village Inn 5 minutes walk to Tadley town
centre

WHICHURCH
**White Hart Hotel**
Newbury Street, Whitchurch,
Hants RG28 7DN
Tel: 01256 892900　　**£ - P - 20 rooms**
Old coaching Inn / hotel in the centre of
Whitchurch

WHITWAY, nr NEWBURY
**The Carnarvon**
Winchester Road, Whitway, nr Newbury,
Hants RG20 9LE
Tel: 01635 278222　　**££ - P - 12 rooms**
Contemporary Pub 4 miles from Newbury

WINCHESTER
**Old Coach House Inn**
156–157 The High Street, Winchester,
Hants SO23 9BA
Tel: 01962 852985　　**£ - P - Rooms**
Olde Worlde town centre Pub

**Wykeham Arms**
75 Kingsgate Street, Winchester,
Hants SO23 9PE
Tel: 01962 853834　　**£££ - P - 14 rooms**
Email: doreen@wykehamarms.fsnet.co.uk
A country Pub in the town 5 minutes walk to
Winchester town centre

WOODFALLS, SALISBURY
**The Woodfalls Inn**
The Ridge, Woodfalls, Salisbury,
Hants SP5 2LN
Tel: 01725 513222　　**££ - P - 10 rooms**
Email: woodfallsi@aol.com
Web: www.woodfallsinn.co.uk
Traditional Inn on the edge of the New Forest

# www.stayinapub.com

# HERFTORDSHIRE

## ALDBURY
**The Greyhound Inn**
19 Stocks Road, Aldbury, Herts HP23 5RT
Tel: 01442 851228    **££ - P - 9 rooms**
Country Inn 10 minute drive to Tring

## ASHWELL, BALDDOCK
**Three Tuns Hotel**
6 High St, Ashwell, Baldock, Herts SG7 5NL
Tel: 01462 742107    **££ - P - 6 rooms**
Country Inn 3 miles from Baldock

## BALDOCK
**The White Lion**
40 The High Street, Baldock, Herts SG7 6BJ
Tel: 01462 892875    **£ - P - 6 rooms**
Town centre Pub

## BAYFORD
**The Bakers Arms**
9 Ashendene Road, Bayford, Herts SG13 8PX
Tel: 01992 511578    **££ - P - 6 rooms**
Village Inn 6 miles from Hertford

## CHIPPERFIELD
**The Windmill**
The Common, Chipperfield, Herts WD4 9BU
Tel: 01923 264310    **£ - P - 2 rooms**
Village Inn 6 miles from Hemel Hampstead

## CHIPPERFIELD, KINGS LANGLEY
**The Two Brewers**
The Common, Chipperfield, Kings Langley,
Herts WD4 9BS

Tel: 01923 265266    **££ - P - 20 rooms**
Well appointed country Inn 4 miles from
Hemel Hampstead

## CODICOTE
**The Bell Inn**
See main entry on page 118

## EAST BARNET
**The Bailey**
187 Victoria Rd, East Barnet, Herts EN4 9SG
Tel: 02084 419044    **£ - P - 5 rooms**
Village Pub 7 miles from London

## GUSTARD WOOD
**The Cross Keys**
Ballslough Hill, Gustard Wood, Herts AL4 8LA
Tel: 01582 832165    **£ - P - 3 rooms**
Country Pub 6 miles from St Albans

## HARTINGFORDBURY
**The Prince of Wales**
244 Hartingfordbury Road, Hartingfordbury,
Herts SG14 2LG
Tel: 01992 581149    **£ - P - 5 rooms**
Village Inn 15 minutes drive to Hertford

## HEMEL HEMPSTEAD
**The Midland Hotel**
Midland Rd, Hemel Hempstead, Herts HP2 5BS
Tel: 01442 253218    **£ - P - 7 rooms**
Family Pub 5 minutes from the centre

**The Queens Head**
34 Lawn Lane, Hemel Hampstead,
Herts HP3 9HL
Tel: 01442 240169    **£ - 4 rooms**
Just 200 yards from the centre of town

## HERTFORD
**Ram Inn**
108 Fore street, Hertford, Herts SG14 1AB
Tel: 01992 583876    **£ - P - 4 rooms**
Email: henry.maasdorp@btclick.com
400 year old locals town centre Pub

# Bell Inn and Motel

*65 High Street, Codicote, Herts SG4 8XD*

**££ - P - 25 rooms**

Tel: 01438 821600    Fax: 01438 821700
Email: info@thebellmotel.co.uk
Web: www.thebellmotel.co.uk

Situated in the Hertfordshire village of Codicote, The Bell Inn and Motel offers 25 individual bungalow style rooms all with *en suite* facilities: Satellite TV, direct dial telephones, ironing facilities, hair drier, tea and coffee courtesy tray.

Our traditional Pub offers an exciting choice of fine ales and beers. The bar meals are all freshly prepared, generous and very reasonable in price. Major sports events are shown on a big-screen. Free entertainment is provided in the bar Fridays and Saturdays. Located just 26 miles from London with good transport links to mainline train stations.

HERTFORD HEATH, HERTFORD
**The Jolly Pinder**
40 London Road, Hertford Heath, Hertford,
Herts SG13 7PW
Tel: 01992 500668    **£ - P - 9 rooms**
Village Inn 2 miles from Hertford

LONDON COLNEY
**The Colney Fox**
1 Barnet Road, London Colney, Herts AL9 1BL
Tel: 01727 823698    **£ - P - 12 rooms**
Village Inn 4 miles from St Albans

NEW BARNET
**The Hadley Hotel**
113 Hadley Rd, New Barnet, Herts EN5 5QN
Tel: 02084 490161    **£ - P - 6 rooms**
Email: thehadley@aol.com
On the edge of town in a residential area

NUTHAMSTEAD
**Woodman Inn**
Nuthampstead, Herts
Tel: 01763 848328    **£ - P - 4 rooms**
Email: woodman.inn@virgin.net
Web: www.thewoodman-inn.co.uk
Village Inn 7 miles from Royston

ROYSTON
**The Old Bull Hotel**
56 High Street, Royston, Herts SG8 9AW

Tel: 01763 242003    **££ - P - 11 rooms**
Recently refurbished town Inn just off from
the centre

SAINT ALBANS
**Black Lion Inn**
198 Fishpool Street, Saint Albans,
Herts AL3 4SB
Tel: 01727 851786    **££ - P - 10 rooms**
Village Inn located 10 minutes walk from St
Albans centre

ST IPPOLYTS, HITCHIN
**The Greyhound Inn**
See main entry opposite

TONWELL
**Robin Hood and Little John**
14 Ware Road, Tonwell, Herts SG12 0HN
Tel: 01920 463352    **£ - P - 8 rooms**
Traditional village Inn just 2 miles from
Hertford

WADESMILL, WARE
**The Feathers Inn**
49 Cambridge Road, Wadesmill, Ware,
Herts SG12 0TN
Tel: 01920 462606    **££ - P - 3 rooms**
Email: thefeathersinn@
ware8152905.freeserve.co.uk
Village Inn 2 miles north of Ware

# The Greyhound

*London Road, St Ippolyts, Hitchin, Herts SG4 7NL*

**££ - P - R - BM - 4 rooms**

Tel: 01462 440989
Email: greyhound@freenet.co.uk

Since re-opening this derelict Pub in 1992 we have become a benchmark for quality and service in hospitality, beer and food. We use fresh meat, fish and vegetables from local suppliers to produce a wide, varied menu.

Ideally placed for all of Herts Bedford, Luton, Cambridge and London. There are many nearby historical sites and beautiful walks in the area.

A pair of shotguns hangs over the bar, it is said they once belonged to Albert Ebenezer and Ebenezer Albert Fox, the notorious twins who were poachers of note, and who once used the King as an alibi to escape prosecution for poaching.

Our comfortable, *en suite*, rooms are centrally heated and have TV / radio, ironing, hairdryer and tea / coffee facilities. We have a 3-diamond rating from the AA and the (EETB) tourist board. Personal service is the key to our success, and we advise booking to make sure you receive it. So please feel free to drop in, you will be welcome.

## WARE

**The Victoria**
2–4 Star Street, Ware, Herts SG12 7AA
Tel: 01920 462565    **£ - P - 3 rooms**
Traditional town public house with two public bars

## WARESIDE

**The Chequers Inn**
Much Hadham-Ware Road, Wareside, Herts
Tel: 01920 467010    **£ - P - 4 rooms**
Email: brcook.chequersinn@virgin.net
Village Inn 3 miles from Ware

## WATFORD

**Bedford Arms**
26 Langley Road, Watford, Herts WD1 3PT
Tel: 01923 440047    **£ - 8 rooms**
Local Pub 10minute walk to the town centre

**Dunnings**
153 St Albans, Watford, Herts WD24 5BD
Tel: 01923 442500    **£ - P - 7 rooms**
Community local less than 10 minute walk to the town centre

**Wellington Arms**
2 Woodford Road, Watford, Herts WD1 71PA
Tel: 01923 253091    **£ - P - 14 rooms**
Located 5 minutes walk from Watford town centre

## WHEATHAMPSTEAD

**The Tin Pot Inn**
33 Gustard Wood, Wheathampstead,
Herts AL4 8RR
Tel: 01582 833134    **££ - P - 7 rooms**
Country Inn located just 4 miles from Harpenden

# ISLE OF WIGHT

Tel: 01983 293393    **£ - P - 2 rooms**
Rural Pub very close to Cowes

## FRESHWATER
**The Vine Inn**
School Green Road, Freshwater,
Isle of Wight PO40 9UP
Tel: 01983 752959    **£ - P - 2 rooms**
Village Inn near the centre of Freshwater

## LAKE, SANDOWN
**The Stag Inn**
45 Sandown Road, Lake, Sandown, Isle of
Wight PO36 9JL
Tel: 01983 403149    **£ - P - 4 rooms**
Village Inn 10 minutes walk to Sandown

## BEMBRIDGE
**The Crab and Lobster Inn**
32 Forelands Field Road, Bembridge, Isle of
Wight PO35 5TR
Tel: 01983 872244    **££ - P - 5 rooms**
Village Inn 20 minutes to the town centre

## CHALE, VENTNOR
**Clarendon Hotel White Mouse Inn**
Church Place, Chale, Ventnor, Isle of Wight,
PO38 2HA
Tel: 01983 730431    **££ - P - 15 rooms**
Village Pub with hotel rooms above, 5 miles
from Ventnor

## COWES
**The Anchor Inn**
1 High Street, Cowes, Isle of Wight
Tel: 01983 292823    **££ - 7 rooms**
Located in the centre of Cowes

**The Duke of York**
Mill Hill Road, Cowes, Isle of Wight PO31 7PT
Tel: 01983 295171    **££ - P - 12 rooms**
Olde style marine Pub situated at the top of
Cowes

**Fountain Hotel**
High Street, Cowes, Isle of Wight PO31 7AW
Tel: 01983 292397    **££ - 20 rooms**
Town hotel with a public bar

**The Kingston Arms**
176 Newport Road, Cowes, Isle of Wight
PO31 7PS

## RYDE
**The Crown Hotel**
10 St Thomas Square, Ryde,
Isle of Wight PO33 2PJ
Tel: 01983 562080    **15 rooms**
Town Inn / hotel with a busy bar

**Ryde Castle**
Ryde, Isle Of Wight PO33 1JA
Tel: 01983 563755    **£££ - P - 21 rooms**
Hotel with public bar on the outskirts of Ryde

## SANDPIPERS
**The Fat Cat Bar**
Sandpipers, Coastguard Lane, Isle of Wight
Tel: 01983 753634    **£ - P - 12 rooms**
Email: info@fatcattrading.co.uk
Country Inn with restaurant 1 mile from
Freshwater

## SEAVIEW
**Seaview Hotel and Restaurant**
High street, Seaview, Isle of Wight PO34 5EX
Tel: 01983 612711    **£££ - P - 16 rooms**
Email: reception@seaviewhotel.co.uk
Web: www.seaviewhotel.co.uk
Village Inn ideal for yachting 10 minutes drive
from Ryde

# Highdown Inn

*Highdown Lane, Totland, Isle of Wight PO39 0HY*

**£ - P - rooms**

Tel: 01983 752450
Email: mail@highdowninn.fsnet.co.uk
Web: www.netguides.co.uk/wight/highdown.html

The Highdown Inn is in a unique rural situation within easy reach of beaches at Freshwater, close to Tennyson Down, The Needles, Alum Bay and is an ideal base for some of the finest walks on The Isle of Wight. Once a smugglers' haunt, the Highdown is set in its own attractive gardens, backed by open farmland, with ample off road parking.

The small, well-appointed restaurant is open daily, offering home-cooked produce with locally caught seafood available in season.

En-suite Bed and Breakfast accommodation is available throughout the year. We will be glad to offer daily or weekly rates on request. There is also a lovely Beer Garden and a superb Children's Activity Centre.

SHANKLIN
**The Steamer Inn**
18 The Esplanade, Shanklin,
Isle of Wight PO37 6BS
Tel: 01983 862641      **£ - 8 rooms**
Traditional seaside pub ocated very close to
the beach

TOTLAND
**The Highdown Inn**
See main entry above

VENTNOR
**The Lansdowne Arms**
High Street, Ventnor, Isle of Wight PO38 1LZ
Tel: 01983 855371      **£ - 4 rooms**
Town Pub just 3 minutes from the centre

**The Spyglass Inn**
The Esplanade, Ventnor,
Isle of Wight PO38 1JX
Tel: 01983 855338      **£ - P - 3 rooms**
Seaside Inn very close to the sea

# KENT

Email: whitehorse@shepherd-neame.co.uk
Web: www.shepherd-neame.co.uk
Country Inn 2 miles from Faversham, ideal for
the channel ferry

## BRENCHLEY, TONBRIDGE
**The Bull**
High Street, Brenchley, Tonbridge,
Kent TN12 7NQ
Tel: 01892 722701      **££ - P - 7 rooms**
Web: www.users.globalnet.co.uk/~bullinn/
Village Inn 8 miles from Tonbridge

## ASHFORD
**O'Briens**
111New Street, Ashford, Kent TN24 8TP
Tel: 01233 620745      **£ - P - Rooms**
Town centre Pub

## BRENZETT, ROMNEY MARSH
**Fleur De Lys**
Brenzett, Romney Marsh, Kent
Tel: 01797 344234      **P - Rooms**
Village Inn 6 miles from Romney Marsh

## BAPCHILD, SITTINGBOURNE
**Fox and Goose**
2 Fox Hill, Bapchild, Sittingbourne,
Kent ME9 9AD
Tel: 01795 472095      **£ - P - 5 rooms**
Family country Inn 1 mile from Sittingbourne

## BROADSTAIRS
**Wrotham Arms**
9 Ramsgate Rd, Broadstairs, Kent CT10 1QQ
Tel: 01843 861788      **£ - 6 rooms**
Local Pub 100 yards from the centre and sea

## BARHAM, nr CANTABURY
**Old Coach House**
Dover Road, Barham, nr Canterbury,
Kent CT4 6SA
Tel: 01227 831218      **££ - P - 10 rooms**
17th century coaching Inn on the Dover road

## CANTERBURY
**The Kings Head**
204 Wincheap, Canterbury, Kent CT1 3RY
Tel: 01227 462885      **£ - P - 3 rooms**
Local Pub just outside the city wall

## BENENDON
**The Bull**
The Street, Benendon, Cranbrook,
Kent TN17 4DE
Tel: 01580 240054      **££ - P - 3 rooms**
Email: thebullatbenenden@btinternet.com
Village Inn 5 miles from Cranbrook

## CHARING, ASHFORD
**Royal Oak Inn**
5 High St, Charing, Ashford, Kent TN27 0HU
Tel: 01233 712612      **££ - P - 10 rooms**
Email: theroyal-oak.charingtn27@barbox.net
Local village Pub that travellers will love

## BOUGHTON STREET,
## nr FAVERSHAM
**White Horse Inn**
Boughton Street, nr Faversham,
Kent ME13 9AX
Tel: 01227 751700      **££ - P - 13 rooms**

## CHILHAM, CANTERBURY
**The Woolpack Inn**
High St, Chilham, Canterbury, Kent CT4 8DL
Tel: 01227 730208      **£££ - P - 14 rooms**
Email: woolpack@shepherd-neame.co.uk
Web: www.shepherd-neame.co.uk
15th century village Inn close to Canterbury

**CRANBROOK**
**White Horse Inn**
High Street, Cranbrook, Kent TN17 3EX
Tel: 01580 712615    **£ - P - 4 rooms**
Large Pub in the centre of the village

**DARTFORD**
**Fulwich Hotel**
150 St Vincent Road, Dartford, Kent DA1 1XE
Tel: 01322 223683    **£ - 5 rooms**
Local Pub 10 minutes walk from Dartford

**DEAL**
**The Kings Head**
9 Beach Street, Deal, Kent CT14 7AH
Tel: 01304 368194    **£ - 15 rooms**
Seaside Pub 50 yards from the Beach

**DOVER**
**The Swingate Inn and Hotel**
Deal Road, Dover, Kent CT15 5DP
Tel: 01304 204043    **£ - P - 14 rooms**
Email: terry@swingate.com
Web: www.swingate.com
Country Inn 5 minutes drive to Dover

**DYMCHURCH, ROMNEY MARSH**
**The Ship Inn**
118 High Street, Dymchurch, Romney Marsh,
Kent TN29 0LD
Tel: 01303 872122    **£ - P - 8 rooms**
Email: bookings@theshipinn.co.uk
Web: www.theshipinn.co.uk
Village Inn located in the centre of Dymchurch

**EASTLING**
**The Carpenters Arms**
See main entry below

**EAST SUTTON, MAIDSTONE**
**The Shant Hotel**
Charlton Lane, East Sutton, Maidstone,
Kent ME17 3DT
Tel: 01622 842235    **££ - P - 16 rooms**
Fine ales, extensive wines, good food

**EDENBRIDGE**
**Ye Old Crown**
74–76 High Street, Edenbridge, Kent TN8 5AR
Tel: 01732 867896    **£ - P - 6 rooms**
Web site: www.lionheartinns.co.uk
Traditional town Pub

**ELHAM**
**The Rose and Crown**
High Street, Elham, Kent CT4 6TD
Tel: 01303 840226    **£ - P - 6 rooms**
Email: info@roseandcrown.co.uk
Web: www.roseandcrown.co.uk
Village Inn 10 minutes drive from Canterbury

**GROOMBRIDGE, TUNBRIDGE
WELLS**
**The Crown Inn**
The Green, Groombridge, Tunbridge Wells
(Royal), Kent TN3 9QH
Tel: 01892 864742    **£ - P - 4 rooms**
Web: www.thecrowngroombridge.co.uk
16thC Inn 3 miles from Tunbridge Wells

# The Carpenters Arms

*The Street, Eastling, Kent  ME13 0AZ*

**£ - P**

Tel: 01795 890234
Email: carpenters-arms@lineone.net
Web: www.carpenters-arms.com

We have comfortable, modern rooms in a building adjoining our welcoming main bar and renowned restaurant. All our rooms have *en suite* facilities: TV, Tea and coffee making facilities, Ironing facilities, Hairdryer and Telephone available.

Single B&B: £41.50. Double/Twin B&B: from £49.50–£52.00 per room.

HAWKHURST
**Queens Inn**
Rye Road, Hawkhurst, Kent TN18 4EY
Tel: 01580 753577   **Rooms**
Country Inn just 8 miles from Tunbridge Wells

HYTHE
**White Hart Hotel**
71 High Street, Hythe, Kent CT21 5AJ
Tel: 01303 263121   **£ - 4 rooms**
Village Inn 5 miles from Folkstone

LADDINGFORD, MAIDSTONE
**Chequers**
The Street, Laddingford, Maidstone,
Kent ME18 6BP
Tel: 01622 871266   **£ - P - 1 room**
Village Inn 7 miles from Maidstone

LADYWELL, DOVER
**The Park Inn**
1–2 Park Place, Ladywell, Dover,
Kent CT6 1DQ
Tel: 01304 203300   **££ - P - 5 rooms**
Email: theparkinn@cs.com
Web: www.theparkinnatdover.co.uk
A beautifully appointed Inn and restaurant

LENHAM
**Who'd a Thought It**
Grafty Green, Lenham, Kent ME17 2AR
Tel: 01622 858951   **£ - P - 13 rooms**
Web: www.whodathoughtit.com
A very Individual 16thC house

LENHAM, MAIDSTONE
**The Dog and Bear Hotel**
The Square, Lenham, Maidstone,
Kent ME17 2PG
Tel: 01622 859415   **££ - P - 24 rooms**
Email: dogbear@shepherd-neame.co.uk
Web: www.shepherd-neame.co.uk
Large 15thC coaching Inn close to Leeds
Castle

LITTLEBOURNE
**King William IV**
4 high Street, Littlebourne, Kent CT3 1ST
Tel: 01227 721224   **££ - P - 7 rooms**
Village inn that used to be an old brewery and
Oast-house

LONGFORD
**The Rising Sun Inn**
Fawkham Green, Longfield, Kent DA3 8NL
Tel: 01474 872291   **££ - P - 7 rooms**
Village Inn 30 minutes drive to Dartford

NEWENDEN
**White Hart**
Rye Road, Newenden, Kent
Tel: 01797 252166   **£ - P - 6 rooms**
Village Inn (A28) 10 miles from Tenterden

nr LENHAM, MAIDSTONE
**The Harrow Inn**
Warren Street, nr Lenham, Maidstone,
Kent ME17 2ED
Tel: 01622 858727   **£ - P - 14 rooms**
17thC Inn on the Old Pilgrims Way

nr ROMNEY MARSH
**Captain Howey Hotel**
Little Stone Road, nr Romney Marsh, Kent
Tel: 01797 362187   **£ - P - 9 rooms**
Local town Pub near the station

OLD ROMNEY, ROMNEY MARSH
**The Rose and Crown Inn**
Swamp Road, Old Romney, Romney Marsh,
Kent TN29 9SQ
Tel: 01797 367500   **£ - P - 5 rooms**
Village Inn 3 miles from Romney Marsh

PLUCKLEY
**The Dering Arms**
Station Road, Pluckley, Kent TN27 0RR
Tel: 01233 840371   **£ - P - 3 rooms**
Village Inn next to the rural station.

PRESTON, FAVERSHAM
**The Windmill Inn**
Canterbury Road, Preston, Faversham,
Kent ME13 8LT
Tel: 01795 536505   **£ - P - 4 rooms**
Email: terry@thewindmillinn.free-online.co.uk
Village Inn on the edge of Faversham

RINGLESTONE HAMLET
**The Ringlestone Inn**
Ringlestone Hamlet, Maidstone, Kent ME17 1NX
Tel: 01622 859900   **£££ - P - 3 rooms**
16thC Inn with many original features

RIPPLE
**The Plough Inn**
Church Lane, Ripple, Kent
Tel: 01304 360209     **£ - P - 2 rooms**
Village Inn 4 miles from Deal

SALTWOOD, HYTHE
**Castle Hotel**
The Green, Saltwood, Hythe, Kent CT21 4AJ
Tel: 01303 266311     **£ - P - 6 rooms**
Village Inn 1 mile from Hythe

SANDWICH
**The Fleur-De-Lis**
6 - 8 Delf Street, Sandwich, Kent CT13 9BZ
Tel: 01304 611131     **££ - 10 rooms**
Web: www.verinitaverns.co.uk
17thC coaching Inn in the centre of town

SARRE, BIRCHINGTON
**The Crown Inn**
Ramsgate Rd, Sarre, Birchington, Kent CT7 0LF
Tel: 01843 847808     **££ - P - 12 rooms**
Email: crown@shepherd-neame.co.uk
Web: www.shepherd-neame.co.uk
Ideal for Canterbury and ferry ports

SMARDEN
**The Chequers Inn**
The Street, Smarden, Kent TN27 8QA
Tel: 01233 770217     **££ - P - 4 rooms**
14thC Inn, 5 golf courses close by

STAPLE, CANTERBURY
**The Three Tuns Inn**
Staple, Canterbury, Kent CT3 1LN
Tel: 01304 812317     **££ - P - 8 rooms**
Email: johngunner@totalise.co.uk
Web: www.three-tuns-staple.freeserve.co.uk
A village Inn located just 5 miles from
Sandwich

TENTERDEN
**Eight Bells**
43 High Street, Tenterden, Kent TN30 6BJ
Tel: 01580 762788     **£ - 5 rooms**
Local high street town Pub

**White Lion Hotel**
High Street, Tenterden, Kent TN30 6BD
Tel: 01580 765077     **££ - P - 15 rooms**
17thC Inn in the centre of this local market
town

TILMANSTONE
**Plough and Harrow**
Dover Rd, Tilmanstone, Deal, Kent CT14 0HX
Tel: 01304 617582     **£ - P - 4 rooms**
Village Inn 15 minute drive to Dover

TONBRIDGE
**Ye Olde Chequers Inn**
122 High Street, Tonbridge, Kent TN9 1AS
Tel: 01732 358957     **£ - P - 4 rooms**
Old traditional town centre Inn

---

# The Bridge Hotel

*13–15 St Mildreds Road, Westgate-on-Sea,
Kent CT8 8RE*

**££ - P - 18 rooms**

Tel: 01843 831023     Fax: 01843 835564
Email: bridge@hotelwestgate.freeserve.co.uk
Web: www.smoothhound.co.uk/hotels/bridgew.html

The Bridge Hotel is situated in the quiet and small suburb of Westgate, within yards of beaches, putting greens and tennis courts, and a public golf course, cinema, shops, the main railway are all within a short distance and Margate is just two miles away.

Our 18 bedrooms are well fitted out for your every convenience, including tea and coffee making facilities, colour TV, direct dial telephone, clock radio, full *en suite* with bath and shower, trouser press. Hairdryers on request and a Night Porter for 24 hour service. The hotel is friendly and family run.

## TUNBRIDGE WELLS
**George and Dragon Inn**
School Hill, Lamberhurst, Tunbridge Wells,
Kent TN3 8DQ
Tel: 01892 890277    **££ - P - 4 rooms**
Olde Worlde traditional Inn. Seafood is a spe-
ciality. Just a 15 minute drive to Tunbridge
Wells

**Royal Wells Inn**
Mount Ephraim, Tunbridge Wells (Royal),
Kent TN4 8BE
Tel: 01892 511188    **£££ - P - 18 rooms**
Email: info@royalwells.co.uk
A short walk from Tunbridge Wells town
centre

## WESTGATE-ON-SEA
**The Bridge Hotel**
See main entry on page 125

## WORTH, DEAL
**The Blue Pigeons Inn**
The Street, Worth, Deal, Kent CT14 0DE
Tel: 01304 613245    **£ - P - 9 rooms**
Quiet village Inn 2 minutes walk to Sandwich

## WROTHAM, SEVENOAKS
**The Bull Inn Hotel**
Wrotham, Sevenoaks, Kent TN15 7RF
Tel: 01732 789800    **££ - P - 11 rooms**
Web: www.bullinnhotel.co.uk
14thC village Inn off J2 of the M20

## WYE, ASHFORD
**New Flying Horse Inn**
Upper Bridge Street, Wye, Ashford,
Kent TN25 5AN
Tel: 01233 812297    **££ - P - 10 rooms**
Web: www.shepherd-neame.co.uk
17thC Inn located in the Wye Valley

# OXFORDSHIRE

## ABINGDON
**Machine Man Inn**
Long Whittenham, Abingdon, Oxon OX14 4QP
Tel: 01865 407835    **£ - P - 5 rooms**
Email: crispinevans@aol.com
Village Inn 4 miles from Abingdon

## ALDERBURY, BANBURY
**The Bell Inn**
High St, Alderbury, Banbury, Oxon OX17 3LS
Tel: 01295 810338    **£ - P - 1 room**
Email: tim@thebell-alderbury.com
Web: www.thebell-alderbury.com
Village Inn 3 miles from Banbury

## APPLETON
**Plough Inn**
Eaton Road, Appleton, Oxon OX13 5JR
Tel: 01865 862441    **£ - P - Rooms**
Country Inn 8 miles from Oxford

## ASTHALL
**The Maytime Inn**
Asthall, Oxon OX18 4HW
Tel: 01993 822068    **££ - P - 6 rooms**
Village Inn 5 miles from Whitney

## BAMTON
**Elephant and Castle**
Bridge Street, Bampton, Oxon OX18 2HA

Tel: 01993 850316    **£ - P - 3 rooms**
Village Inn 5 miles from Whitney

**The Romany Inn**
Bridge Street, Bampton, Oxon OX18 2HA
Tel: 01993 850237    **11 rooms**
Lively village Inn 7 miles from Whitney

BENSON, WALLINGFORD
**The Crown Inn**
52 High Street, Benson, Wallingford,
Oxon OX10 6RP
Tel: 01491 838247    **££ - P - 5 rooms**
Newly refurbished town centre Inn

BLEDINGTON
**The Kings Head Inn**
The Green, Bledington, Glos/Ocon OX7 6HD
Tel: 01608 658365
*See Gloucestershire for the main entry*

BLEWBURY, DIDCOT
**The Barley Mow**
London Rd, Blewbury, Didcot, Oxon OX11 9NU
Tel: 01235 850296    **££ - P - 5 rooms**
Village Inn just off A34

BUCKLAND, FARINGDON
**The Lamb at Buckland**
Lamb Lane, Buckland, Faringdon,
Oxon SN7 8QN
Tel: 01367 870484    **£ - P - 4 rooms**
Country Inn 25 minutes drive from Oxford and
Swindon

**The Trout Inn**
Tadpole Bridge, Buckland, Faringdon,
Oxon SN7 8RF
Tel: 01367 870382    **££ - P - rooms**
Email: info@trout-inn.co.uk
Web: www.trout-inn.co.uk
Riverside Inn

BURFORD
**The Inn for All Seasons**
The Barringtons, Burford, Oxon OX18 4TN
Tel: 01451 844324    **£££ - P - 10 rooms**
Old coaching Inn

**Lamb Inn**
Sheep Street, Burford, Oxon OX18 4LR

Tel: 01993 823155    **£££ - P - 16 rooms**
15thC Inn returns you to a gentler time

**Old Bull Hotel**
105 High Street, Burford, Oxon OX18 4RG
Tel: 01993 822220    **P - 15 rooms**
Town centre Inn

CHACOMBE, BANBURY
**George and Dragon**
1 Silver Street, Chacombe, Banbury,
Oxon OX17 2JR
Tel: 01295 711500    **££ - P - 2 rooms**
Village Inn 3 miles from Banbury

CHARLBURY
**The Bell House**
Church Street, Charlbury, Oxon OX7 3PP
Tel: 01608 810278    **£££ - P - 12 rooms**
Country hotel / bar / restaurant

**Bull Inn**
Sheep Street, Charlbury, Oxon OX7 3RR
Tel: 01608 810689    **££ - P - 3 rooms**
16th century Inn and restaurant situated in a
small town

CHIPPING NORTON
**The Falkland Arms**
See main entry on page 128

**Kings Arms Hotel**
18 West St, Chipping Norton, Oxon OX7 5AA
Tel: 01608 642668    **£ - P - 13 rooms**
Town centre Pub with rooms

**Oxford House**
18 Horsefare, Chipping Norton, Oxon OX7 5AQ
Tel: 01608 642918    **£ - rooms**
Large town centre Pub

CHURCH ENSTONE
**Crown Inn**
Mill Lane, Church Enstone, Oxon OX7 4NN
Tel: 01608 677262    **£ - P - 2 rooms**
Village Inn 6 miles from Woodstock and
Chipping Norton

CLIFTON HAMPDEN
**Plough Inn**
Abingdon Rd, Clifton Hampden, Oxon OX14 3EG

# The Falkland Arms

*Great Tew, Chipping Norton, Oxon OX7 4DB*

**P - Rooms**

Tel: 01608 683653
Email: sjcourage@btconnect.com          Web: www.falklandarms.org.uk

Set in the Cotswold village of Great Tew in the heart of rural Oxfordshire, The Falkland Arms stands opposite the village green. The six, recently refurbished, *en suite*, antique furnished bedrooms are reached via the original stone spiral staircase, have beverage making facilities and remote control TV. All are non-smoking.

Tel: 01865 407811     **££ - 8 rooms**
Village Inn 3 miles from Abingdon

### DEDDINGTON
**Deddington Arms**
Horsefair, Deddington, Oxon OX15 0SM
Tel: 01869 338364     **£££ - P - 27 rooms**
Email: deddarms@aol.com
Village Inn 15 miles from Banbury

**The Unicorn Inn**
Market Place, Deddington, Banbury,
Oxon OX15 0QH
Tel: 01869 338838     **£ - P - 6 rooms**
Located 7 miles from Banbury

### DRAYTON, BANBURY
**The Roebuck Inn**
Drayton, Banbury, Oxon OX15 6EN
Tel: 01295 730542     **P - 2 rooms**
Village Inn 5 minute walk into Banbury

### DUNS TEW
**The White Horse Inn**
Duns Tew, Oxon OX6 4JS
Tel: 01869 340272     **££ - P - 10 rooms**
Village Inn 7 miles from Banbury

### EYNSHAM
**The White Hart**
See main entry on page 129

### FIFIELD, nr BURFORD
**Merrymouth Inn**
Stow Road, Fifield, nr Burford, Oxon OX7 6HR
Tel: 01993 831652     **££ - P - 9 rooms**

Email: info@cotswoldinn.co.uk
Web: www.cotswoldinn.co.uk
Rural Inn in the middle of the Cotswolds, 4
miles from Burford

### FREELAND, OXFORD
**Shepherds Hall Inn**
Whitney Rd, Freeland, Oxford, Oxon OX8 8HQ
Tel: 01993 881256     **£ - P - 5 rooms**
Located on the A4095 Oxford to Whitney road

### GORING
**Miller of Mansfield**
High Street, Goring, Oxon
Tel: 01491 872829     **££ - P - 10 rooms**
Web: www.millerofmansfield.co.uk
This is a lovely ivy covered Inn with Oak
beams and a log fire

**The John Barleycorn Inn**
Manor Road, Goring, Oxon
Tel: 01491 872509     **£ - 6 rooms**
16th century village Inn 12 miles from Reading

### GREAT BARRINGTON, BURFORD
**The Fox Inn**
Great Barrington, Burford, Oxon OX18 4QA
Tel: 01451 844385     **££ - P - 4 rooms**
Village Inn 3 miles from Burford

### HAILEY, WITNEY
**Bird in Hand**
Whiteoak Green, Hailey, Witney, Oxon OX8 5XP
Tel: 01993 868321     **££ - P - 16 rooms**
Web: www.oxfordpages.co.uk/birdinhand
Residential Country Inn 4 miles from Whitney

# The White Hart Inn

*Newland Street, Eynsham, Oxon OX29 4LB*

**££ - P - BM - BG - ETB 4 diamonds - 3 rooms**

Email: whiteharteynsham@aol.com

Situated in the ancient village of Eynsham, close to the Thames, and midway between Oxford and Witney, just off the A40. Originally constructed in the mid-14th century, the White Hart was converted into a Coach House in 1836, with the addition of a stable block, to which sympathetic conversion has resulted in three attractive *en suite* letting rooms off the courtyard. Roaring fires on those cold winter nights, and a beautiful garden for balmy summer days, complement the many original features of this historic Inn.

Offering lunch and evening Restaurant facilities, conference and function room, overnight accommodation and a well stocked bar. Come and see us soon, enjoy a meal or a snack, take a drink or two, and if you can't bear to leave us then stay the night!

---

## HENLEY
**The Bull**
Bell Street, Henley, Oxon
Tel: 01491 574821    **Rooms**
Town Pub close to the town centre

## HENLEY-ON-THAMES
**The Old White Horse**
100 North Field End, Henley-on-Thames,
Oxon RG9 2JN
Tel: 01491 575763    **££ - P - 4 rooms**
Traditional country Pub 1 mile from Henley

**The Rose and Crown Inn**
56 New Street, Henley-on-Thames,
Oxon RG9 2BT
Tel: 01491 578376    **££ - 3 rooms**
Located in the town centre

## HOOK NORTON
**Pear Tree Inn**
Scotland End, Hook Norton, Oxon OX15 5NU
Tel: 01608 737482    **£ - P - rooms**
Small cottage Inn with Hook Norton ales

## KIDLINGTON, OXFORD
**The Wise Alderman Inn**
249 Banbury Road, Kidlington, Oxford,
Oxon OX5 1BF
Tel: 01865 372281    **£ - P - 7 rooms**
Village Inn 6 miles from Oxford

## KINGHAM, OXFORD
**The Plough Inn**
17 The Green, Kingham, Oxford,
Oxon OX7 6YD
Tel: 01608 658327    **£ - P - 5 rooms**
Village Inn situated 6 miles from Chipping
Norton

## LEWKNOR, WATLINGTON
**Lambert Arms**
London Road, Lewknor, Watlington,
Oxon OX9 5SQ
Tel: 01844 351496    **££ - P - 5 rooms**
Village Inn 5 miles from Thame

## MINSTER LOVELL
**Mill and Old Swan**
Minster Lovell, Oxon OX8 5RN
Tel: 01993 774441    **£ - P - 63 rooms**
Built in the 14th century, with log fires, oak
beams

## NETTLEBED,
## nr HENLEY-ON-THAMES
**The White Hart Hotel**
28 High Street, Nettlebed, nr Henley-on-
Thames, Oxon RG9 5DD
Tel: 01491 641245    **£££ - P - 12 rooms**
Email: info@whiteharthotel.com
Country Inn and hotel 5 minutes drive from
Henley

NORTH NEWINGTON, BANBURY
**The Blinking Owl**
Main Street, North Newington, Banbury,
Oxon OX15 6AE
Tel: 01295 730650     **££ - P - 3 rooms**
Village Inn 3 miles from Banbury

OXFORD
**The Cock and Camel**
24–26 George Street, Oxford, Oxon OX1 2AE
Tel: 01865 203705     **£££ - 8 rooms**
Email: cockandcamel@youngs.co.uk
Web: www.youngs.co.uk
Modern hotel and bar in Oxford town centre

**The Old Black Horse Hotel**
102 St Clements, Oxford, Oxon OX4 1AR
Tel: 01865 244691     **££ - P - 10 rooms**
Located just outside the city centre

PILSHILL
**The Crown Inn**
Pishill, Oxon RG9 6HH
Tel: 01491 638364     **££ - P - 1 Cottage**
15thC Olde Worlde Pub 4 miles from Henley

SHENINGTON
**The Bell**
Shenington, Oxon OX15 6NQ
Tel: 01295 670274     **£ - 3 rooms**
Country Pub 6 miles from Banbury

SHILLINGTON, WALLINGFORD
**The Kingfisher Inn**
27 Henley Road, Shillingford, Wallingford,
Oxon OX10 7EL
Tel: 01865 858595     **££ - P - 6 rooms**
Web: www.kingfisher-inn.co.uk
Village Inn 2 miles from Wallingford

SHIPTON-UNDER-WYCHWOOD
**The Lamb Inn**
High Street, Shipton-under-Wychwood,
Oxon OX7 6DQ
Tel: 01993 830465     **£££ - P - 5 rooms**
Web: www.thelambinn.net
Cotswold Inn 8 miles from Chipping Norton

SOULDERN, BICESTER
**The Fox Inn**
Fox Lane, Souldern, Bicester, Oxon

Tel: 01869 345284     **£ - P - 4 rooms**
Traditional country Inn located in the centre of
the village

STONOR, HENLEY-ON-THAMES
**The Stoner Arms**
Stonor, Henley-on-Thames, Oxon RG9 6HE
Tel: 01491 638866     **£££ - P - 10 rooms**
Dining here is a gourmet experience

THAME
**Black Horse**
11 Corn Market, Thame, Oxon OX9 2BL
Tel: 01844 212886     **£ - P - 9 rooms**
Town centre Pub

WALLINGFORD
**The Coachmakers Arms**
37 St Mary's St, Wallingford, Oxon OX10 0EU
Tel: 01491 839382     **£ - 3 rooms**
Town centre Pub

**The Dolphin**
2 St Mary's St, Wallingford, Oxon OX10 0EL
Tel: 01491 837377     **£ - P - 4 rooms**
Town centre Pub

WANTAGE
**The Star Inn**
Watery Lane, Wantage, Oxon OX12 9PL
Tel: 01235 751539     **££ - P - 8 rooms**
Email: thestarinn@starsholt111.fs.net.co.uk
Country Inn 4 miles from Wantage

WARMINGTON
**Wobbly Wheel Inn**
Warwick Road, Warmington, Banbury,
Oxon OX16 1JJ
Tel: 01295 690214     **£ - P - 15 rooms**
Premier Lodge motel 5 miles from Banbury

WITNEY
**The Court Inn**
See main entry on page 131

WHEATLY
**Bat and Ball Inn**
28 High Street, Wheatly, Oxon OX44 9HJ
Tel: 01865 874379     **££ - P - 7 rooms**
Email: tony@fsbusiness.co.uk
Village Inn 5 miles from Oxford

# The Court Inn

*Bridge Street, Witney, Oxon OX8 6DA*

**P - 10 rooms**

Tel: 01993 703228
Email: info@courtinn.co.uk

Situated within minutes of the town centre, and only 12 miles from Oxford, The Court Inn is the convenient choice for business people and tourists. All 10 rooms are comfortably furnished and centrally heated, with Colour TV, radio / alarm, telephone and beverage making facilities. There are also hair dryers, ironing facilities and a children's cot is available.

# The Killingworth Castle Inn

*Glympton Road, Wooton, Oxon OX20 1EJ*

**P - Letting rooms**

Tel / Fax: 01993 811401     Email: wiggiscastle@aol.com     Web: www.killingworthcastle

Built in 1637 in the picturesque village of Wooton on the main London - Aberystwyth road, the Killingworth Castle Inn retains much of it's character and original features. In the main bar area there are beamed ceilings, a beautiful beech floor and two large stone fireplaces. The Inn is a recipient of the new Cask Marque accreditation for quality real ales. Just two miles from Blenheim Palace and Woodstock the area offers many outstanding walks.

WOLFSTONE, nr FARINGDON
**White Horse Inn**
Wolfstone, nr Faringdon, Oxon SN7 7QL
Tel: 01367 820726     **Rooms**
Village Inn 20 minutes drive to Swindon

WOODCOTE
**The Highwayman Inn**
Exlade Street, Woodcote, Oxon RG8 0UA
Tel: 01491 682020     **££ - P - 4 rooms**
Village Inn 10 minutes drive to Reading

WOODSTOCK
**The Punch Bowl**
12 Oxford Street, Woodstock, Oxford,
Oxon OX20 1TR
Tel: 01993 811218     **££ - P - 10 rooms**
Email: info@punchbowl-woodstock.co.uk
Web: www.punchbowl-woodstock.co.uk
Located in the centre of Woodstock

WOOTON
**The Killingworth Castle Inn**
See main entry above

**Kings Head Inn**
Chapel Hill, Wootton, Woodstock,
Oxon OX20 1DX
Tel: 01993 811340     **Rooms**
Email: t.fay@kings-head.co.uk
Web: www.kings-head.co.uk
Quiet village Inn and restaurant 2 miles from Woodstock

# SURREY

ADDLESTONE
**Crouch Oak**
138 Station Rd, Addlestone, Surrey KT15 2BE
Tel: 01932 842562     **£ - P - 8 rooms**
Town centre Pub

ALBURY
**The Drummond Arms Inn**
The Street, Albury, Surrey GU5 9AG
Tel: 01483 202039     **£ - P - 11 rooms**
Village Inn 6 miles from Guildford

BLETCHINGLY
**Whyte Harte Hotel**
11–21 High St, Bletchingly, Surrey RH1 4PB
Tel: 01883 743231     **£ - P - 12 rooms**
Located in a small village 4 miles from Redhill
near J6 of the M25

BRAMLEY
**Blue Anchor**
155 High Road, Byfleet, Surrey KT14 7RL
Tel: 01932 346301     **£ - P - 15 rooms**
Email: info@kestrelpubs.com
Web: www.kestrelpubs.com
Village Pub 7 miles from Woking

**Jolly Farmer Inn**
High Street, Bramley, Surrey GU5 0HB
Tel: 01483 893355     **££ - P - 22 rooms**
Village Inn 3 miles from Guildford

CHERTSEY
**Coach and Horses**
14 St Annes Rd, Chertsey, Surrey KT16 9DG

Tel: 01932 563085     **££ - P - 3 rooms**
Community town Pub

CHIDDINGFOLD
**The Crown Inn**
The Green, Chiddingfold, Surrey GU8 4TX
Tel: 01428 682255     **££ - P - 8 rooms**
Country Inn 30 minute drive to Guildford

COLDHARBOUR
**Plough Inn**
Coldharbour, Surrey RH5 6HD
Tel: 01306 711793     **££ - P - 6 rooms**
Village Inn 5 miles from Dorking

COMPTON
**The Harrow Inn**
The Street, Compton, Surrey GU3 1EG
Tel: 01483 810379     **£ - P - 4 rooms**
Country Pub 15 minute drive to Guildford

EGHAM
**Foresters Arms**
1 North Street, Egham, Surrey
Tel: 01784 432625     **££ - P - 8 rooms**
Quiet residential area 10 minutes walk to
Egham centre

EPSOM
**Caspers Wine Bar**
11–13 Upper High St, Epsom, Surrey KT17 4QY
Tel: 01372 727752     **£ - P - 8 rooms**
Wine bar 2 minute walk from the town centre

ESHER
**The Bear Inn**
71 High Street, Esher, Surrey KT10 9LQ
Tel: 01372 469786     **£££ - 7 rooms**
Located in the centre of Esher

EWELL
**Queen Adelaide**
272 Kingston Road, Ewell, Surrey KT19 0SH
Tel: 02083 932666     **P - Rooms**
A National Premier Lodge roadside Inn

EWHURST
**Bulls Head Hotel**
The High Street, Ewhurst, Surrey GU6 7DE
Tel: 01483 277447    **£ - P - 5 rooms**
Village Inn 3 miles from Cranleigh

FARNHAM
**The Elmtree**
14 Weybourne Rd, Farnham, Surrey GU9 9EF
Tel: 01252 313050    **££ - P - 5 rooms**
Village Inn 1 mile from both Farnham and
Aldershot

**The Exchange**
Station Hill, Farnham, Surrey GU9 8AD
Tel: 01252 726673    **££ - 6 rooms**
Town local near the railway station

HASLEMERE
**The Wheatsheaf Inn**
See main entry below

HEATHEND, FARNHAM
**Royal Arms Hotel**
172 Farnborough Road, Heathend,
Farnham, Surrey
Tel: 01252 320149    **£ - P - 5 rooms**
Village Inn 2 miles from Aldershot

HERSHAM, WALTON-ON-THAMES
**The Bricklayers Arms**
6 Queens road, Hersham, Walton-on-Thames,
Surrey KT12 5LS
Tel: 01932 220936    **££ - 2 rooms**
A village Inn situated in the very centre of
Hersham

NEWHAW LOCK, nr WOKING
**White Hart**
Newhaw Lock, nr Woking, Surrey KT15 2DS
Tel: 01932 842927    **££ - P - 4 rooms**
Friendly canal side pub and restaurant just10
minutes drive from Woking, and 20 from
Heathrow

OCKLEY, DORKING
**The Kings Arms Inn**
Stane St, Ockley, Dorking, Surrey RH2 5TP
Tel: 01306 711224    **££ - P - 6 rooms**
Country Pub 6 miles from Dorking

OLD WOKING
**The Queens Head**
40 High Street, Old Woking, Surrey GU22 9ER
Tel: 01483 728833    **Rooms**
Rural Pub

REIGATE
**Prince of Wales**
2 Holmesdale Road, Reigate, Surrey RH2 0BQ
Tel: 01737 243112    **£ - Rooms**
In the suburbs of Riegate 10 minutes walk to
town centre

RICHMOND
**The Dukes Head**
42 The Vineyards, Richmond,
Surrey TW10 6AW
Tel: 02089 484557    **££ - P - 11 rooms**
Email: thedukeshead@yahoo.com
Web: www.dukeshead.com
Friendly local 10 minutes walk from Richmond
Station

RICHMOND
**Red Cow**
59 Sheen Road, Richmond, Surrey TW9 1YJ
Tel: 02089 402511      **££ - P - 4 rooms**
Edge of Richmond near Twickenham

TANDRIDGE, nr OXTED
**Barley Mow**
Tandridge Lane, Tandridge, nr Oxted,
Surrey RH9 8NJ
Tel: 01883 713770      **£ - P - 3 rooms**
Village Inn 3 miles from Oxted

VIRGINIA WATER
**The Wheatsheaf Hotel**
London Road, Virginia Water,
Surrey GU25 4QF
Tel: 01344 842057      **£££ - P - 17 rooms**
Country Inn / hotel 1 mile from Egham

WORMLEY
**Wood Pigeon**
Station Approach, Wormley, Surrey GU8 5TB
Tel: 01428 682362      **£ - P - 3 rooms**
Village Inn 12 miles from Guildford

# WEST SUSSEX

AMBERLEY
**The Sportsman**
See main entry on page 135

BALLS CROSS, PETWORTH
**The Stag Inn**
Balls Cross, Petworth, West Sussex GU28 9JP
Tel: 01403 820241      **£ - 2 rooms**
Remote Olde Worlde village Inn 3 miles from
Petworth

BILLINGHURST
**The Half Moon Inn**
Kirdford, Billingshurst, West Sussex RH14 0LT
Tel: 01403 820223      **£££ - P - 2 rooms**
Web: www.the-halfmoon-inn.com
16th century Inn off the A272 3 miles from
Petworth

BOGNOR REGIS
**Belle Vue Hotel**
Waterloo Regis, Bognor Regis,
West Sussex PO21 1TA
Tel: 01243 863434      **£ - 12 rooms**
1 minute walk to the sea

BRAMBER, STEYNING
**Castle Inn Hotel**
Bramber, Steyning, West Sussex BN44 3WE
Tel: 01903 812102      **££ - P - 11 rooms**
Village Inn 2 miles from Steyning

CHICHESTER
**George and Dragon**
North Street, Chichester,
West Sussex PO19 1NQ
Tel: 01243 785660      **££ - P - 10 rooms**
18th century Inn near the centre of Chichester

**The Horse and Groom**
See main entry on page 135

COPTHORNE
**Hunters Moon Inn**
Copthorne Bank, Copthorne,
West Sussex RH10 3JF
Tel: 01342 713309      **£ - P - 10 rooms**
Email: enquiries@huntersmooninn.co.uk
Country Inn with a great pub atmosphere 10
minute drive to Gatwick Airport

# The Sportsman Inn

*Rackham Road, Amberley, Nr Arundel, West Sussex BN18 9NR*

**P - Rooms**

Tel: 01798 831787    Fax: 01798 839177
Email: contact@thesportsmanamberley.co.uk
Web: www.thesportsmanamberley.co.uk

The Sportsman is located on the fringe of Amberley "the pearl of the South Downs", and has five guest bedrooms, three double and two twins, each with *en suite* bathroom, offering comfortable accommodation and hearty English or continental breakfast. One bathroom is fully fitted to accommodate disabled access. Also, find out more about The Miserable Old Buggers' Club

# Horse and Groom

*East Ashling, Chichester, West Sussex*

**P - Rooms**

Tel: 01243 575339    Fax: 01243 575560
Email: horseandgroomea@aol.com
Web: www.horseandgroom.sageWeb.co.uk

The Horse & Groom Inn has an original flint barn which has been carefully and tastefully converted into five twin / double *en suite* rooms whilst three new *en suite* twin / double rooms have been added this year.

The bar area retains the charm of a country pub complete with a cast iron range, whilst the 60 cover restaurant has the intimacy of tables for two and the availability of catering for large parties and special functions.

Goodwood Racecourse and Motor Circuit are close by, making the Horse and Groom a popular place to stay in the comfortable bed and breakfast accommodation.

COULTERSHAW BRIDGE, PETWORTH
**Badgers Tavern**
Coultershaw Bridge, Petworth,
West Sussex GU28 0JF
Tel: 01798 342651    **££ - P - 3 rooms**
Country Inn 1.5 miles from Petworth

CUCKFIELD, HAYWARDS HEATH
**The Wheatsheaf Inn**
Broad Street, Cuckfield, Haywards Heath,
West Sussex RH17 5DW
Tel: 01444 454078    **££ - P - 10 rooms**
Village Inn 10 miles from Haywards Heath

DIAL POST, nr HORSHAM
**Crown Inn**
Worthing Road, Dial Post, nr Horsham,
West Sussex RH13 8NH
Tel: 01403 710902    **£ - P - 4 rooms**
Rural Pub 7 miles from Horsham

ELSTED
**The Elsted Inn**
See main entry on page 136

FITTLEWORTH, PULBOROUGH
**Swan Inn**
Lower Street, Fittleworth, Pulborough,

# The Elsted Inn

*Elsted Marsh, Elsted, Midhurst, West Sussex GU29 0JT*

**££ - P - 4 rooms**

Tel / Fax: 01730 813662      Web: www.elstedinn.co.uk

The Elsted is a traditional Inn offering quality local fresh foods, real ales, wines, garden, car park and a warm welcome. Accommodation consists of four quality *en suite* bedrooms in a detached Coach House beside the Inn. The Inn is surrounded by glorious countryside, close to the South Downs for walking, riding, cycling and touring. Located between Stedham and the Hartings, two miles south of the A272, Chichester, Goodwood, Petersfield, Midhurst, Petworth and the sea are all within an easy drive.

Double £65 – Single £45 inclusive of full English breakfast and VAT

---

West Sussex RH20 1EN
Tel: 01798 865429      **££ - P - 15 rooms**
Email: info@hotel'swaninn.com
Web: www.swaninn.com
Award winning Inn in the village centre

## HALFWAY BRIDGE
**Halfway Bridge Inn**
Halfway Bridge, West Sussex GU28 9BP
Tel: 01798 861281      **££ - P - 8 rooms**
Midway between Midhurst and Petworth

## COWFOLD, HORSHAM
**The Coach House**
Horsham Road, Cowfold, Horsham,
West Sussex RH13 8BT
Tel: 01403 864247      **£ - P - 15 rooms**
Email: coachhousecowfold@talk21.com
Roadside Inn situated only 7 miles from
Horsham

## ITCHENOR, CHITCHESTER
**The Ship Inn**
The Street, Itchenor, Chichester,
West Sussex PO20 7AH
Tel: 01243 512284      **£ - P - 3 rooms**
Village Inn 6 miles from Chichester

## LINGFIELD
**The Star Inn**
Church Rd, Lingfield, West Sussex RH7 6AH
Tel: 01342 832364      **££ - 7 rooms**
Email: thestarinn@breathEmail.net
Web: www.starinnlingfield
15th century Inn set in the heart of the village

## LITTLEHAMPTON
**Arun View Inn**
Wharf Road, Littlehampton,
West Sussex BN17 5DD
Tel: 01903 722335      **£ - P - 6 rooms**
Riverside Inn on the outskirts of Littlehampton

## MANNINGS HEATH, HORSHAM
**Dun Horse Inn**
Brighton Road, Mannings Heath, Horsham,
West Sussex RH13 6HZ
Tel: 01403 265783      **P - 3 rooms**
Village Pub 2 miles from Horsham

## RUDGWICK, NR HORSHAM
**The Mucky Duck Inn**
See main entry on page 137

## SAYERS COMMON
**Duke of York Inn**
Old London Road, Sayers Common, West
Sussex BN6 9HY
Tel: 01273 832262      **£ - P - 4 rooms**
Located 10 miles north of Brighton

## SHOREHAM-BY-SEA
**Bridge**
87 High Street, Shoreham-by-Sea, West
Sussex BN43 5DE
Tel: 01273 452477      **£ - P - 4 rooms**
Riverside Pub in town

## STEYING
**Chequer Inn**
41 High St, Steyning, West Sussex BN44 3RE

# Mucky Duck Inn

*Tismans Common, Loxwood Road, Rudgwick, Nr Horsham, West Sussex RH12 3BW*

**P - Rooms**

Tel: 01403 822300      Email: mucky_duck_pub@msn.com
Web: www.mucky-duck-inn.co.uk

The Mucky Duck is a traditional Country Inn with a roaring log fire in the winter and sunny gardens for the summer. All comfortable rooms are *en suite* with TV, radio, tea and coffee facilities and hair dryer. We are wheelchair friendly with direct access from large car park.

Tel: 01903 814437      **£ - P - 3 rooms**
Email: chequerinn@btinternet.com
Village Inn 5 miles from Worthing

### SUTTON, PULBOROUGH
**White Horse Inn**
The Street, Sutton, Pulborough,
West Sussex RH20 1PS
Tel: 01798 869221      **££ - P - 6 rooms**
Village Inn 10 minute drive to Petworth

### TILLINGTON, PETWORTH
**The Horse Guards Inn**
Tillington, Petworth, West Sussex GU28 9AF
Tel: 01798 342332      **£ - P - Rooms**
Email: mail@horseguardsinn.co.uk
Web: www.horseguardsinn.co.uk
Village Inn 1 mile from Petworth

## www.stayinapub.com

# South-West England

## AVON AND BRISTOL

Web: www.huntersrest.co.uk
Converted hunting lodge with beautiful views

### HALLATROW
**The Old Station Inn**
Wells Road, Hallatrow, Bristol BS39 6EN
Tel: 01761 452228     **£ - P - 4 rooms**
Email: steveandtracy@lycos.co.uk
Country Pub 9 miles from Bath

### HOTWELLS
**The Bear Inn**
261 - 263 Hotwells Road, Hotwells,
Bristol BS8 4SF
Tel: 01179 877796     **£ - P - 5 rooms**
City centre Inn

**Nova Scotia**
Nova Scotia Place, Hotwells, Bristol BS1 6XJ
Tel: 01179 297994     **£ - P - 2 rooms**
Old traditional waterfront Inn

**Rose of Denmark**
6 Dowry Place, Hotwells, Bristol BS8 4QL
Tel: 01179 405866     **£ - P - 3 rooms**
Town Pub 3 miles from the town centre

### nr RINGTON
**Darlington Arms**
On the A38, nr Rington, Bristol
Tel: 01934 862247     **£ - P - 6 rooms**
Country Pub 2 miles from Bristol airport

### PENSFORD
**The Carpenters Arms**
Stanton Wick, Pensford, Bristol
Tel: 01761 490202     **££ - 12 rooms**
Email: carpenters@dial.pipex.com
Country Inn 8 miles from Bath

### RICKFORD
**The Plume of Feathers**
Rickford, Bristol
Tel: 01761 462682     **£ - 3 rooms**

### AVONMOUTH
**Royal Hotel**
28 Gloucester Road, Avonmouth,
Bristol BS11 9AD
Tel: 01179 822847     **£ - P - 30 rooms**
Hotel with a Pub, close to the M5, 20 minute
drive to Bristol centre

### AXBRIDGE
**The Lamb Inn**
The Square, Axbridge, Bristol BS26 2AP
Tel: 01934 732253     **Rooms**
Town hotel part owned by Butcombe Brewery

### BLAGDON
**The Live and Let Live Inn**
Bath Road, Blagdon, Bristol
Tel: 01761 462403     **£ - P - 8 rooms**
Country Pub 12 miles from both Bristol and
Wells

### CLIFTON
**Channings**
20 Pembroke Road, Clifton, Bristol BS8 3BB
Tel: 01179 733970     **££ - 11 rooms**
Located in a residential area 15minute walk
from Bristol centre

### CLUTTON HILL
**The Hunters Rest**
King Lane, Clutton Hill, Bristol
Tel: 01761 452303     **££ - P - 4 rooms**
Email: paul@huntersrest.co.uk

Email: plumeoffeathers@aol.com
Country Inn 10 miles from Bristol

TEMPLE CLOUD
**The Temple Inn**
Main Road, Temple Cloud, Bristol
Tel: 01761 452244    **£ - P - 2 rooms**
Village Inn 10 miles from Bristol and Bath

WEST HARPTREE
**The Blue Bowl Inn**
Bristol Road, West Harptree, Bristol BS18 6HJ
Tel: 01761 221269    **£ - P - 3 rooms**
Country Pub 12 miles from Bristol

**Wellsway Inn**
Harptree Hill, West Harptree,
Bristol BS18 6EJ
Tel: 01761 221382    **Rooms**
One of the Pubs n Bars group

YATTON
**The Prince of Orange Inn**
17 High Street, Yatton, Bristol BS19 4JD
Tel/Fax: 01934 832193 **£ - P - 5 rooms**
Village Inn located 10 miles from Weston
Supermare

# CHANNEL ISLANDS

Alderney

Channel

Guernsey

Sark

Islands

Jersey

**GUERNSEY**

CASTEL
**Fleur Du Jardin**
Kings Mill, Castel, Guernsey GY5 7JT
Tel: 01481 257996    **££ - P - 17 rooms**
Large tourist Pub and hotel

**Hougue du Pommier**
Hougue du Pommier Road, Castel,
Guernsey GY5 7FQ
Tel: 01481 256531    **££ - P - 43 rooms**
Email: hotel@houguedupommier.guernsey.net
Quiet hotel with an oak beamed public bar

VALE
**Chandlers Hotel**
Braye Road, Vale, Guernsey GY3 5QL
Tel: 01481 244280    **£ - P - 15 rooms**
Pub / hotel 10 minute drive to St Peter Port

FOREST
**Deerhound Inn**
Forest Road, Forest, Guernsey
Tel: 01481 238585    **££ - P - 6 rooms**
Country Inn 4 miles from St Peter Port

ST PIERRE DY BOIS
**Loungfrie Inn**
Royte De Loungfrie, St Pierre Dy Bois,

**ALDERNEY**

LE HURET
**Rose and Crown**
Le Huret, Aldernay GY9 32R
Tel: 01481 823414    **££ - 6 rooms**
Located near the centre of St Marys

NEW TOWN ROAD
**Harbour Lights**
New Town Road, Aldernay GY9 3YR
Tel: 01481 822168    **££ - P - 16 rooms**
Email: harbour.lights@virgin.net
Located near the harbour. Families with
children welcome

Guernsey GY7 9RX
Tel: 01481 263107     **££ - P - 5 rooms**
Country Inn 4 miles from St Peter Port

## JERSEY

### ST AUBINS HABOUR
**Old Court House Inn**
St Aubins Harbour, Jersey JE3 8AB
Tel: 01534 746433     **££ - P - 9 rooms**
Email: ochstaubins@jerseymail.co.uk
15thC Inn with views across the harbour

# CORNWALL

### BALNOON, SAINT IVES
**Noahs Inn**
Old Coach Road, Balnoon, Saint Ives,
Cornwall TR26 3JB
Tel: 01736 797572     **£ - P - rooms**
Country Pub located just 3 miles away from St
Ives

### BODINNICK, nr FOWEY
**Old Ferry Inn**
Bodinnick, nr Fowey, Cornwall PL23 1LX
Tel: 01726 870237     **£ - P - rooms**
Family run Inn with an *à la carte* restaurant

### BODMIN
**White Hart Hotel**
Saint Teath, Bodmin, Cornwall PL30 3JX
Tel: 01208 850281     **£ - P - 2 rooms**
Olde worlde village Inn 6 miles from
Wadebridge

### BOLVENTOR, LAUNCESTON
**Jamaica Inn**
Bolventor, Launceston, Cornwall PL15 7TS
Tel: 01566 86250     **££ - P - 7 rooms**
Email: jamaciainn@eclipse.co.uk
Ideal stopover located on Bodmin Moor

### BOSCASTLE
**The Wellington Hotel**
See main entry on page 141

### BUDE
**The Brendon Arms**
Bude, Cornwall EX23 8SD
Tel: 01288 354542     **£ - P - 11 rooms**
Two minutes walk to Bude town centre

### CHARLESTOWN
**The Rashleigh Arms**
Charlestown Road, Charlestown,
Cornwall PL25 3NJ
Tel: 01726 73635     **££ - P - 5 rooms**
Lively village Inn and restaurant 1.5 miles from
St Austell

# The Wellington Hotel

*Old Road, Boscastle, Cornwall PL35 0AQ*

**££ - P - 16 rooms**

Tel: 01840 250202    Fax: 01840 250621
Email: vtobutt@enterprise.net  Web: www.wellingtonboscastle.co.uk

The Wellington Hotel is an historic 16th century Coaching Inn set in ten acres of woodland with a garden and aviary in glorious National Trust countryside close to an Elizabethan harbour. The Anglo / French restaurant specialises in regional cuisine and seafood. The free house bar has a log fire and serves real ales, lagers, malt whiskies, fine wines and exceptional bar food.

# The Galleon Inn

*12 Fore Street, Fowey, Cornwall PL23 1AQ*

**7 rooms**

Tel: 01726 833014    Fax: 01726 833663
Email: sqrighol@aol.com

Situated in an enviable position on the Fowey River. All bedrooms have King Sized beds and excellent facilities including *en suite*. Reasonable rates include Full English Breakfast. Real Ales and Good Food served in the pub or on the riverside patio.

CRACKINGTON HAVEN
**Coombe Barton Inn**
Crackington Haven, Cornwall EX23 0TG
Tel: 01840 230345    **£ - P - 6 rooms**
Email: info@coombebartoninn.com
Village Inn 11 miles from Bude

CRAFTHOLE, TORPOINT
**Liscawn Inn**
Crafthole, Torpoint, Cornwall PL11 3BD
Tel: 01503 230863    **P - Rooms**
14th century Inn 6 miles from Torpoint

CREMYLL, TORPOINT
**The Edgcumbe Arms**
Cremyll, Torpoint, Cornwall PL10 1NX
Tel: 01752 822294    **££ - P - 6 rooms**
Country Pub 10 miles from Torpoint

FOWEY
**The Galleon Inn**
See main entry above

**The Ship Inn**
Trafalgar Square, Fowey, Cornwall PL23 1AZ
Tel: 01726 832230    **£ - P - 6 rooms**
Town Pub in Fowey

FROGPOOL, TRURO
**Cornish Arms**
Frogpool, Truro, Cornwall TR4 8RP
Tel: 01872 863445    **£ - P - 1 room**
Family friendly Inn 6 miles from Truro

GOLANT
**The Fishermans Arms**
Fore Street, Golant, Cornwall
Tel: 01726 832453    **£ - P - 1 room**
Riverside Inn 5 miles from Fowey

GUNNISLAKE
**The Rifle Volunteer Inn**
St Anns Chapel, Gunnislake, Cornwall
Tel: 01822 832508    **£ - P - 6 rooms**
Village Inn 3 miles from Callington

GUNWALLOE, HELSTON
**The Halzephron Inn**
Gunwalloe, Helston, Cornwall TR12 7QB
Tel: 01326 240406    **££ - P - 2 rooms**
Country Inn 4 miles from Helston

HARLYN BAY, PADSTOW
**The Harlyn Inn**
Harlyn Bay, Padstow, Cornwall PL28 8SB
Tel: 01841 520207    **£ - P - 9 rooms**
Email: harlyninn@aol.com
Village Inn 3 miles from Padstow

HAYLE
**White Hart Hotel**
10 Foundry Square, Hayle,
Cornwall TR24 4HQ
Tel: 01736 752322    **£ - P - 15 rooms**
More of a hotel with a public bar. Near the
centre of town

HESSENFORD, TORPOINT
**Copley Arms**
Hessenford, Torpoint, Cornwall PL11 3HJ
Tel: 01503 240209    **££ - P - 5 rooms**
Village Inn 8 miles from Torpoint

KINGSAND
**The Halfway House Inn**
Fore Street, Kingsand, Torpoint,
Cornwall PL10 1NA
Tel: 01752 822279    **££ - P - 6 rooms**
Email: halfway@eggconnecy.net
Web: www.crappot.co.uk
Seaside Pub 10 miles from Plymouth

LANLIVET, nr BODMIN
**The Crown Inn**
Lanlivet, nr Bodmin, Cornwall PL30 5BT
Tel: 01208 872707    **£ - P - 2 rooms**
Country Inn 7 miles from Bodmin

LANNER, REDRUTH
**Lanner Inn**
The Square, Lanner, Redruth,
Cornwall TR16 6EH
Tel: 01209 215611    **£ - P - 6 rooms**
Email: lannerinn@btconnect.com
Web: www.lannerinn.com
Friendly real ale village Inn 3 miles from
Redruth

LANREATH, LOOE
**Punch Bowl Inn**
Lanreath, Looe, Cornwall PL13 2NX
Tel: 01503 220218    **££ - Rooms**
Country Inn 8 miles from Looe

LAUNCESTON
**Bakers Arms**
Southgate Street, Launceston, Cornwall
Tel: 01566 772510    **£ - 7 rooms**
Rustic town Pub with a country feel

**White Hart Hotel**
15 Broad Street, Launceston,
Cornwall PL15 8AA
Tel: 01566 772013    **£ - P - 27 rooms**
Large town centre hotel with a busy bar

**The White Horse Inn**
14 Newport Square, Launceston, Cornwall
Tel: 01566 772084    **P**
Located just outside of Launceston town
centre

LELANT, ST IVES
**Badger Inn**
Lelant, St Ives, Cornwall TR26 3JT
Tel: 01736 752181    **£ - P - 6 rooms**
Village Inn 3 miles from St Ives

LERRYN, LOSTWITHIEL
**Ship Inn**
Lerryn, Lostwithiel, Cornwall PL22 0PT
Tel: 01208 872374    **££ - P - 4 rooms**
Village Inn 3 miles from Lostwithiel

LONGROCK, PENZANCE
**Mount View Hotel**
Longrock, Penzance, Cornwall TR20 8JJ
Tel: 01736 710416    **Rooms**
Village Inn

LOSTWITHIEL
**Royal Oak Inn**
Duke Street, Lostwithiel, Cornwall,PL22 0AH
Tel: 01208 872552    **££ - P - 6 rooms**
Town Pub in Lostwithiel

MARAZION
**The Godolphin Arms**
See main entry opposite

# Godolphin Arms

*Marazion, Cornwall TR17 0EN*

**££ - P - 10 rooms**

Tel: +44 (0)1736 710202    Fax: +44 (0)1736 710171
Email: enquiries@godolphinarms.co.uk
Web: www.godolphinarms.co.uk

The Godolphin Arms is situated on the edge of the sand facing St Michael's Mount at Marazion and is truly one of the most enviable locations in the county of Cornwall with magnificent views across Mounts Bay and beyond. After a refurbishment, The Godolphin Arms now has 10 *en suite* rooms, most with sea views (2 of which have disabled access). We offer our guests a warm and friendly atmosphere, and pride ourselves on our attentive service

# The Merrymore Inn

*Mawgan Porth, Newquay, Corwall TR8 4BA*

**P - 7 rooms**

Tel: 01637 860258
Email: info@merrymoorinn.com    Web: www.merrymoorinn.com

The Merrymoor Inn is a fully licensed freehouse which has been run by our family since 1961. Although many things have changed since then our aims remain the same. We offer comfortable accommodation, comprising of seven rooms all with *en suite* facilities: hair dryer, TV, direct dial phone and hospitality tray, and good food and drink in a friendly relaxed atmosphere. The inn offers exceptionally good value and is only fifty yards from Mawgan Porth Beach. We are within a twenty-minute drive of the spectacular Eden Project, a must for all visitors to the area.

MEVAGISSEY
**The Fountain Inn**
3 Cliff Street, Mevagissey, Cornwall
Tel: 01726 842320    **£ - P - 3 rooms**
Located in a fishing village close to the harbour

MAWGAN PORTH, NEWQUAY
**The Merrymoor Inn**
See main entry above

MOUSEHOLE
**Ship Inn**
Mousehole, Cornwall TR19 6QX
Tel: 01736 731234    **£ - 2 rooms**
Village Inn 3 miles from Penzance

NANCENOY, CONSTANTINE
**Trengilly Wartha**
Nancenoy, Constantine, Cornwall TR11 5RP
Tel: 01326 340332    **£ - P - 8 rooms**
One mile from Constantine village

NEW POLZEATH, WADEBRIDGE
**Atlantic House Hotel**
New Polzeath, Wadebridge,
Cornwall PL27 6UG
Tel: 01208 862208    **££ - P - 30 rooms**
Seaside bar / hotel

PADSTOW
**London Inn**
Lanadwell St, Padstow, Cornwall PL28 8AN

Tel: 01841 532554 **£ - 3 rooms**
Friendly local near the centre of Padstow

**PELYNT, nr LOOE**
**Jubilee Inn**
Pelynt, nr Looe, Cornwall PL13 2JZ
Tel: 01503 220312 **£ - P - 11 rooms**
16thC Inn complete with bridal suite

**PENDEEN**
**Trewellard Arms Hotel**
Trewellard Rd, Pendeen, Cornwall TR19 7TA
Tel: 01736 788634 **£ - P - 4 rooms**
Country Inn 3 miles from St Just

**PENDEEN, PENZANCE**
**North Inn**
The Square, Pendeen, Penzance,
Cornwall TR19 7DN
Tel: 01736 788417 **£ - P rooms**
Coastal village Pub 7 miles from Penzance

**PENDOGGETT**
**The Cornish Arms**
Pendoggett, Cornwall PL30 3HH
Tel: 01208 880263 **££ - P - 8 rooms**
Local village Inn 3 miles from Port Isaac

**PENZANCE**
**Kings Arms Inn**
Paul, Penzance, Cornwall TR19 6TZ
Tel: 01736 731224 **£ - P - 3 rooms**
Village Inn 3 miles from Penzance

**PILLATON, SALTASH**
**The Weary Friar Inn**
Pillaton, Saltash, Cornwall PL12 6QS
Tel: 01579 350238 **£ - P - 13 rooms**
Village Inn 2 miles west of A388

**POLPERRO**
**Crumplehorn Inn**
Crumplehorn, Polperro, Cornwall PL13 2RJ
Tel: 01503 272348 **££ - P - 3 rooms**
Old fashioned 16th century Inn

**POLZEATH, WADEBRIDGE**
**Oyster Catcher**
Polzeath, Wadebridge, Cornwall
Tel: 01208 862371 P - 8 Rooms
Beach bar with self-contained apartments

**PORT GAVERNE, PORT ISAAC**
**The Port Gaverne Inn**
Port Gaverne, Port Isaac, Cornwall PL29 3SQ
Tel: 01208 880244 **££ - P - 16 rooms**
Old coastal Inn by a secluded cove

**PORTCUONO**
**Cable Station Inn**
The Valley, Porthcuono, Cornwall TR19 6JX
Tel: 01736 810479 **P – 11 cottages**
Families with children welcome, Penzance is
10 miles

**Mariners Lodge**
Porthcurno, Penzance, Cornwall TR19 6JU
Tel: 01736 810236 **Rooms**
Village Inn

**PORTH, NEWQUAY**
**Porth Lodge Hotel**
Porth Dean Road, Porth, Newquay,
Cornwall TR7 2TL
Tel: 01637 874483 **£ - P - 20 rooms**
Local Pub just outside Newquay, half a mile
Porth Beach

**PORTHLEVEN**
**The Harbour Inn**
Porthleven, nr Helston, Cornwall TR13 9JB
Tel: 01326 573876 **££ - P - 10 rooms**
Located on Porthleven Harbour

**PORTLOE**
**The Ship Inn**
Portloe, Cornwall
Tel: 01872 501356 **£ - P - 2 rooms**
Village Inn 12 miles from Truro

**PORTMELLON COVE, MEVAGISSEY**
**Rising Sun Inn**
Portmellon Cove, Mevagissey,
Cornwall PL26 6PL
Tel: 01726 843235 **££ - P - 7 rooms**
Country Inn 6 miles from St Austell

**RUAN MINOR, HELSTON**
**Kennack Sands Inn**
Kuggar, Ruan Minor, Helston,
Cornwall TR12 7LX
Tel: 01326 290547 **£ - P - 10 rooms**
Traditional village Inn 10 miles from Helston

SALTASH
**Holland Inn**
Hatt, Saltash, Cornwall PL12 6PJ
Tel: 01752 844044    **£ - P - 30 rooms**
Email: hollandinnhotel@freenetname.co.uk
Large wayside Inn on the main road

ST AGNES
**Driftwood Spars**
See main entry below

SAINT AUSTELL
**Duke of Cornwall Hotel**
98 Victoria Road, Saint Austell,
Cornwall PL25 4QD
Tel: 01726 72031    **£ - P - 6 rooms**
On the outskirts of town

SAINT DENNIS, nr SAINT AUSTELL
**Boscawen Hotel**
Fore Street, Saint Dennis, nr Saint Austell,
Cornwall PL26 8AD
Tel: 01726 822275    **£ - P - 5 rooms**
Web: www.boscawenhotel.co.uk
Pub / hotel near the Eden Project

SAINT ISSEY, WADEBRIDGE
**Ring 'O' Bells**
Church Town, Saint Issey, Wadebridge,
Cornwall PL27 7QA
Tel: 01841 540251    **£ - P - 2 rooms**

Email: ringersstissey@freeserve.co.uk
Village Inn 5 miles from Padstow

SAINT JUST
**Commercial Hotel**
Market Square, Saint Just, Cornwall TR19 7HE
Tel: 01736 788455    **£ - P - 7 rooms**
Village Inn 7 miles from Penzance

**Star Inn**
Saint Just, Cornwall TR17 7LL
Tel: 01736 788767    **£ - 2 rooms**
Handy for airport to the Scillies

SAINT MAWGAN, NEWQUAY
**The Falcon Inn**
Saint Mawgan, Newquay, Cornwall TR8 4EP
Tel: 01637 860225    **££ - P - 4 rooms**
Email: abanks@cwcom.net
Web: www.falcon-inn.net
17thC village Inn 5 miles from Newquay

SAINT MINVER
**The Fourways Inn**
Churchtown, Saint Minver, Cornwall
Tel: 01208 862384    **££ - P - 9 rooms**
Village Inn 5 miles from Wadebridge

SAINT NEOT, LISKEARD
**The London Inn**
Saint Neot, Liskeard, Cornwall PL14 6NG

# Driftwood Spars Hotel

*Trevaunance Cove, St Agnes, Cornwall TR5 0RT*

**P - Rooms**

Tel: 01872 552428 / 553323    Fax: 01872 553701
Email: driftwoodspars@hotmail.com
Web: www.driftwoodspars.com

Originally built as a marine warehouse and fish cellar, the Driftwood Spars was converted into a hotel in the 1930's and used to house evacuees during the war. With constant sensitive modernisation there are now 15 *en suite* bedrooms, all with TV, phone, refreshment trays etc and some have dramatic sea views. Spacious garden rooms have been added which are very popular with families and pet owners. As well as the contrasting, dark, mysterious, atmospheric lower bars there are upstairs eating areas, and a carvery, very popular with locals and tourists, young and old, who come with healthy appetites for good food, real ale and live music - and above all a good natter! The latest additions are a microbrewery and a seaside theme gift shop.

Tel: 01579 320263    **£ - P - 3 rooms**
Village Inn 5 miles from Liskeard and Bodmin

STRATTON
**The Kings Arms**
Howells Road, Stratton, Cornwall
Tel: 01288 352396    **£ - P - 3 rooms**
Village Inn 2 miles from Bude

TINTAGEL
**The Cornishman**
Fore Street, Tintagel, Cornwall PL34 0DB
Tel: 01840 770238    **£ - P - 10 rooms**
Email: info@cornishmaninn.com
Web: www.cornishmaninn.com
Village Inn 30 minutes drive to Wadebridge

**The Port William**
Trebarwith Strand, Tintagel,
Cornwall PL34 0HB
Tel: 01840 770230    **££ - P - 6 rooms**
Email: william@eurobell.co.uk
Village local 4 miles from Tintagel

TORPOINT
**Carbeile Inn**
Trevol Road, Torpoint, Cornwall PL11 2NJ
Tel: 01752 814102    **£ - P - 5 rooms**
Local Pub on the outskirts of Torpoint

**Inn On the Shore**
Downderry, Torpoint, Cornwall PL11 3JY
Tel: 01503 250210    **£ - P - 5 rooms**
Village Inn on the beach with a continental feel

TREGADILLET
**Eliot Arms (Square and Compass)**
Tregadillet, Cornwall PL15 7EU
Tel: 01566 772051    **£ - P - 2 rooms**
Village Inn 2 miles from Launceston

TREMATON
**The Crooked Inn**
Trematon, Cornwall
Tel: 01752 848177    **££ - P - 15 rooms**
Traditional country Inn 1 miles from Saltash

TRURO
**The City Inn**
Pydar Street, Truro, Cornwall TR1 3SP
Tel: 01872 272623    **£ - P - 4 rooms**

Country Pub in the town. Good food, Real ales

**The New Inn**
Veryan, Truro, Cornwall TR2 5QA
Tel: 01872 501362    **£ - 3 rooms**
Village Pub 12 miles from Truro

WADEBRIDGE
**The Inn For All Seasons**
c/o 38 Talmena Avenue, Wadebridge, nr
Bodmin, Cornwall PL27 7RR
Tel: 07970 643844    **P - 12 rooms**
Country house Inn

**Molesworth Arms Hotel**
Molsworth Street, Wadebridge,
Cornwall PL27 7DP
Tel: 01208 812055    **Rooms - PW**
Pets welcome

WIDEMOUTH BAY, BUDE
**Bay View Inn**
Marine Drive, Widemouth Bay, Bude, North
Cornwall EX23 0AW
Tel: 01288 361273    **P - 8 rooms**
Country Inn by the sea 2.5 miles from Bude

**Brocksmoor Hotel**
Widemouth Bay, Bude, Cornwall EX23 0DF
Tel: 01288 361207    **£ - P - 7 rooms**
Seaside Pub / hotel with restaurant

WIDEMOUTH, BUDE
**Widemouth Manor Hotel**
Widemouth, Bude, Cornwall EX23 0DE
Tel: 01288 361263    **£ - P - 8 rooms**
Beside the sea on Widemouth Bay

ZELAH
**The Hawkins Arms**
High Road, Zelah, Cornwall
Tel: 01872 540339    **£ - P - 2 rooms**
Located on the A30 16 miles past Bodmin

# DEVON

## BAMTON, TIVERTON
**Exeter Inn**
Tiverton Road, Bampton, Tiverton,
Devon EX16 9DY
Tel: 01398 331345 **££ - P - 8 rooms**
Email: exeterinn@farmersweekly.net
Web: www.exeterinn.co.uk
Village Inn just outside Bampton

## BANTHAM, nr KINGSBRIDGE
**Sloop Inn**
Bantham, nr Kingsbridge, Devon TQ7 3AJ
Tel: 01548 560489 **££ - P - 5 rooms**
16th century fishing village Inn Pets accepted

## BARBROOK, LYNTON
**Beggars Roost Inn**
Barbrook, Lynton, Devon EX35 6LD
Tel: 01598 752404 **££ - P - 7 rooms**
Email: beggars.roost.inn@tinyworld.co.uk
Web: smoothhound.co.uk/hotels/manorho1.html
Village Inn 3 miles from Lynton

## ALLER MILLS, KINGSKERSWELL
**Barn Owl Inn**
Aller Mills, Kingskerswell, Devon TQ12 5AN
Tel: 01803 872968 **££ - P - 6 rooms**
Suburban local 2 miles from Newton Abbot

## ASHBURTON
**Royal Oak**
5 East Street, Ashburton, Devon
Tel: 01364 652444 **£ - P - 2 rooms**
Olde Worlde town centre Pub

## ASHPRINGTON, TOTNES
**Durant Arms**
Ashprington, Totnes, Devon TQ9 7UP
Tel: 01803 732240 **££ - P - 6 rooms**
Hotel, Inn 2.5 miles from Totnes

## AWLISCOMBE, nr HONITON
**Awliscombe Inn**
Awliscombe, nr Honiton, Devon EX14 0PJ
Tel: 01404 42554 **£ - P - 2 rooms**
Village Inn 3 miles from Honiton

## AYLESBEARE
**The Halfway Inn**
Sidmouth Road, Aylesbeare, Devon
Tel: 01395 232273 **P**
Village Inn 8 miles from Exmouth

## BARNSTAPLE
**The Check Inn**
14 Castle Street, Barnstaple, Devon
Tel: 01271 375964 **£ - P - 2 rooms**
Old fashioned Pub 2 minutes from the centre

## BEER
**The Anchor Inn**
Fore Street, Beer, Devon EX12 3ET
Tel: 01297 20386 **££ - 8 rooms**
Fishing village Inn overlooking the old harbour

## BIDEFORD
**The Joiners Arms**
Market Place, Bideford, Devon
Tel: 01237 472675 **£ - P - 4 rooms**
Traditional Inn by Bideford market place

**The Kings Arms**
The Quay, Bideford, Devon EX39 2HW
Tel: 01237 475196 **£ - 3 rooms**
Local town Pub situated on the quay

**Old Coach Inn**
Market Place, Bideford, Devon EX39 2DU
Tel: 01237 472810        **£ - P Rooms**
Town centre Inn

**The Puffin Inn**
123 Bay View Road, Westward Ho, Bideford,
Devon EX39 1BJ
Tel: 01237 473970        **£ - P - 5 rooms**
Email: thepuffins@breathemail.net
Pub overlooks the Northam Burrows Country
Park

BISHOPSTEIGNTON
**Cockhaven Manor Hotel**
Bishopsteignton, Devon TQ14 9FX
Tel: 01626 775252        **P - 12 rooms**
Hotel / Inn 10 miles from Torquay and Newton
Abbot

BLACKAWTON
**Normandy Arms**
Chapel Street, Blackawton, Devon TQ9 7BN
Tel: 01803 712316        **££ - P - 5 rooms**
Email: normandyarms@hotmail.com
Village local 5 miles from Dartmouth

BOVEY TRACEY
**Cromwell Arms**
Bovey Tracey, Devon TQ13 9AE
Tel: 01626 833473        **£ - P - 12 rooms**
Situated in the town centre

**Riverside Inn**
Bovey Tracey, Devon TQ13 9AF
Tel: 01626 832293        **£ - P - 10 suites**
Email: riversideinn83@hotmail.com
Large Inn with restaurant, function room 5
miles from Newton Abbott

BOWBRIDGE, TOTNES
**The Watermans Arms**
Bowbridge, Totnes, Devon TQ9 7EG
Tel: 01803 732214        **££ - P - 15 rooms**
Country Inn 3 miles from Totnes

BRANSCOMBE
**The Masons Arms**
Branscombe, Devon EX12 3DJ
Tel: 01297 680300        **£ - P - 22 rooms**
Village local 5 miles from Sidmouth

BRENDON
**The Rockford Inn**
Brendon, Devon
Tel: 01598 741214        **£ - P - 6 rooms**
Email: enquiries@therockfordinn.com
Village Inn 5 miles from Lynton

BRIDESTOW
**The White Hart Inn**
Fore Street, Bridestowe, Okehampton,
Devon EX20 4EL
Tel: 01837 861318        **£ - P - 2 rooms**
Email: whitehartinn@aol.com
Web: members.aol.com/whitehartinn/bridestowe
Village Inn 6 miles from Okehampton

BROADHEMPSTON
**The Coppa Dolla Inn**
Broadhempston, Devon
Tel: 01803 812455        **£ - P - 1 room**
Village Inn 5 miles from Totnes

BUCKFASTLEIGH
**Abbey Inn**
30 Buckfast Road, Buckfastleigh,
Devon TQ11 0EA
Tel: 01364 642343        **££ - P - 8 rooms**
Riverside Inn located half a mile from
Buckfastleigh

**Dartbridge Inn**
Totnes Road, Buckfastleigh, Devon TQ11 0JR
Tel: 01364 642214        **££ - P - 11 rooms**
Country Inn located just1 mile From
Buckfastleigh

CHAGFORD, nr NEWTON ABBOT
**Bullers Arms**
Southern Mill Street, Chagford, nr Newton
Abbot Devon TQ13 8AW
Tel: 01647 432348        **£ - 3 rooms**
Market town Inn

**The Globe Inn**
See main entry on page 149

CHERITON BISHOP
**The Old Thatch Inn**
Cheriton Bishop, Devon EX6 6HJ
Tel: 01647 24204        **£ - P - 3 rooms**
Village local 10 miles from Exeter

# The Globe Inn

*High Street, Chagford, Devon TQ13 8AJ*

Tel: 01647 433485
Email: miller@theglobe.org.uk
Web: www.the-globe.org.uk

Chagford nestles in the shadow of Meldon Hill, close to the Teign river within the Dartmoor National Park. The Globe Inn was built in the 16th century as a coaching inn. Our 2 bars and restaurant offer a friendly and relaxing atmosphere. Some of our rooms are en suite and all rooms have colour television and tea making facilities.

Twin or Double for single occupancy from £26.25. Twin or Double from £22.50
All rates are inclusive of VAT at standard rate. Unfortunately we do not have suitable accommodation for young children and babies. Picnic lunches can be provided for your days out.

# The New Inn

*High Street, Clovelly, Nr Bideford, North Devon EX39 5TQ*

**P - Rooms**

Tel: 01237 431303     Fax: 01237 431636
Email: newinn@clovelly.co.uk

All the elegance of times past. All the luxuries of today... The New Inn sits amongst flower-strewn cottages in the heart of the ancient fishing village of Clovelly. The steep, cobbled street tumbles down to the 14th century quay and lifeboat station. All The New Inn rooms are *en suite* and superbly furnished, but very individual, as you would expect in a 17th Century Inn. The food is good too!

---

**CHITTLEHAMHOLT, UMBERLEY**
**Exeter Inn**
Chittlehamholt, Umberley, Devon EX37 9NS
Tel: 01769 540281     **£ - P - 5 rooms**
Traditional Inn 6 miles from South Moulton

**CLOVELLY, NR BIDEFORD**
**The New Inn**
See main entry above

**CLOVELLY**
**The Red Lion**
The Quay, Clovelly, Devon EX39 5TF
Tel: 01237 431237     **££ - P - 11 rooms**
Alongside the unspoilt 14th century quay

**CLYST HONITON, EXETER**
**Exeter Inn**
Clyst Honiton, Exeter, Devon EX5 2NJ
Tel: 01392 367907     **£ - P - 1 cottage**
Lets one cottage which is attached to the Pub

**COMBE MARTIN**
**Pack 'O' Cards Inn**
High Street, Combe Martin, Devon EX34 0ET
Tel: 01271 882300     **£ - P - Rooms**
Web: www.packocards.co.uk
Riverside village Inn 10 miles from Barnstable

**The London Inn**
Lynton Road, Combe Martin, Ilfracombe,

Devon EX34 0NA
Tel: 01271 883409    **£ - P - 8 rooms**
Olde worlde village Inn 12 miles from
Barnstable

**COUNTISBURY, LYNTON**
**The Exmoor Sandpiper Inn**
Countisbury, Lynton, Devon,EX35 6NE
Tel: 01598 741263    **P - Rooms**
Email: clair@exmoorsandpiper.demon.co.uk
Web: www.exmoor-hospitality-inns.co.uk
15th century coaching Inn, pets welcome

**CREDITON**
**Dartmoor Railway Inn**
Station Road, Crediton, Devon EX17 3BX
Tel: 01363 772489    **£ - 2 rooms**
Free house 1 mile from the town centre

**CROYDE**
**Billy Buds**
12 Hobbs Hill, Croyde, Devon EX33 1LZ
Tel: 01271 890606    **££ - P - 6 rooms**
Village Inn 3 miles from Bruton

**CROYDE**
**The Thatched Barn Inn**
14 Hobbs Hill, Croyde, Devon
Tel: 01271 890349    **£ - P - 8 rooms**
Email: info@thethatch.com
Country Pub 9 miles from Barnstable

**CROYDE, BRAUTON**
**Manor House Inn**
St Mary's Road, Croyde, Braunton,
Devon EX33 1PG
Tel: 01271 890241    **£ - P - 2 rooms**
Email: info@themanorcroyde.com
Traditional Inn 3 miles from Braunton

**CULLUMPTON**
**White Hart Inn**
19 Fore Street, Cullompton, Devon EX15 1JS
Tel: 01884 33260    **£ - P - 6 rooms**
Town Pub located in the centre of Cullompton

**DALWOOD, AXMINSTER**
**The Tuckers Arms**
Dalwood, Axminster, Devon EX13 7EG
Tel: 01404 881342    **£ - P - 5 Rooms**
Village Inn 4 miles from Axminster

**DARTINGTON**
**Cott Inn**
Dartington, Devon TQ9 6HE
Tel: 01803 863777    **££ - P - 6 rooms**
Country Pub 2 miles from Totnes

**DITTISHAM, nr DARTMOUTH**
**The Red Lion Inn**
Dittisham, nr Dartmouth, Devon TQ6 0ES
Tel: 01803 722235    **££ - P - 6 rooms**
Village Inn 6 miles from Dartmouth

**DODDISCOMBSLEIGH**
**The Nobody Inn**
Doddiscombsleigh, Devon EX6 7PS
Tel: 01647 252394    **££ - P - 7 rooms**
Village Inn 7 miles from Exeter

**DOLTON, nr WINKLEY**
**The Union Inn**
Fore Street, Dolton, nr Winkley,
Devon EX19 8QH
Tel: 01805 804633    **££ - P - 3 rooms**
Village Inn 20 miles from Barnstable

**DOUSLAND**
**Burrator Inn**
Dousland, Devon
Tel: 01822 853121    **£ - P - 10 rooms**
Country Inn 5 miles from Tavistock

**DREWSTEIGNTON**
**The Drewe Arms**
The Square, Drewsteignton, Devon EX6 6GQ
Tel: 01647 281224    **£ - P - 3 rooms**
Village Inn 10 miles from Okehampton

**EAST ALLINGTON**
**Fortescue Arms**
East Allington, Devon TQ9 7RA
Tel: 01548 521215    **£ - P - 3 rooms**
Village Inn 4 miles from Totnes

**EXETER**
**Crawford Hotel**
107 Alphington Road, Exeter, Devon EX2 8JD
Tel: 01392 668008    ££ - P - 8 rooms
Situated 5 minutes walk from the town centre

**Locomotive Inn**
New North Road, Exeter, Devon EX4 4EP

Tel: 01392 275840 **£ - P - 6 rooms**
Local Pub located near the centre of Exeter

**The Three Tuns Inn**
14 Exeter Road, Silverton, Exeter,
Devon EX5 4HX
Tel: 01392 860352 **£ - P - 5 rooms**
Web: www.threetunsinn.co.uk
Olde Worlde village Pub 6 miles from Exeter

FENNY BRIDGES, HONITON
**Greyhound Inn**
Fenny Bridges, Honiton, Devon EX14 0BJ
Tel: 01404 850380 **££ - P - 10 rooms**
Email: info@greyhound-inn.co.uk
Located on the A30, it is just a 5-minute drive
from Honiton

FRIPHELSTOCK, TORRINGTON
**Clinton Arms**
Friphelstock, Torrington, Devon EX38 8JH
Tel: 01805 623279 **£ - P - 4 rooms**
Web: www.gocitys.com/clintonarms
Country Inn 2 miles from Torrington

FROGMORE, KINGSBRIDGE
**The Globe Inn**
Frogmore, Kingsbridge, Devon TQ7 2NR
Tel: 01548 531351 **£ - P - 6 rooms**
Web: www.theglobeinn.co.uk
Village Inn 2 miles from Kingsbridge

GEORGEHAM
**The Kings Arms**
Chapel Street, Georgeham, Devon EX33 1JJ
Tel: 01271 890240 **£ - 3 rooms**
Village Inn 13 miles from Barnstable

GREAT TORRINGTON
**The Black Horse Inn**
The Square, Great Torrington, Devon EX38 8HN
Tel: 01805 622121 £ - 3 rooms
Email: wasyer@aol.com
16thC coaching Inn 10 miles from Barnstable

HALWELL
**The Old Inn**
Halwell, Devon
Tel: 01803 712329 **£ - P - 3 rooms**
Village Inn 6 miles from Totnes and
Dartmouth

HARBERTON
**The Church House Inn**
Harberton, Devon TQ9 7SF
Tel: 01803 863707 **£ - P - 3 rooms**
Village Inn 2.5 miles from Totnes

HATHERLEIGH
**The Bridge Inn**
Market Street, Hatherleigh, Devon EX20 3JA
Tel: 01837 810947 **£ - P - 5 rooms**
Village Inn 7 miles from Okehampton

**The George**
Market Street, Hatherleigh, Okehampton,
Devon EX20 3JN
Tel: 01837810454 **££ - P - 9 rooms**
15th century coaching, Oak beams, log fires

**Tally Ho Inn and Brewery**
14 Market Street, Hatherleigh,
Devon EX20 3JN
Tel: 01837 810306 **£ - P - 3 rooms**
Country Inn 6 miles from Okehampton

HAYTOR VALE
**The Rock Inn**
Haytor Vale, Devon TQ13 9XP
Tel: 01364 661305 **££ - P - 9 rooms**
Country Inn 5 miles from Bovey Tracey

HEXWORTHY
**The Forest Inn**
See main entry on page 152

HOLBETON
**Mildmay Colours Inn**
Holbeton, Devon PL8 1NA
Tel: 01752 830248 **£ - P - 6 rooms**
Country Inn 5 miles from Plymouth

HOLNE
**Church House Inn**
Holne, Devon TQ13 7SJ
Tel: 01364 631208 **£ - P - 6 rooms**
Village Inn 4 miles from Ashburton

HONITON
**White Lion Inn**
194 High Street, Honiton, Devon EX14 1LA
Tel: 01404 42066 **£ - P - 4 rooms**
Community local at the bottom end of Honiton

# The Forest Inn

*Hexworthy, Princetown, via Yelverton, DevonPL20 6SD*

**£ - P - R - BM - BW - BG - PW - C - 10 rooms**

Tel: 01364 631211          Fax: 01364 631515
Email: info@theforestinn.co.uk
Web: www.theforestinn.co.uk

The Forest Inn, situated in the Dartmoor forest, is a country Inn offering an atmosphere from a more relaxed era. The Inn is an ideal refuge for anyone just looking for an opportunity to enjoy the natural beauty of Dartmoor. The comfortable accommodation includes 10 rooms; all are *en suite* and comprise double, twin and family rooms. There is also a 20-bedded bunkhouse with showers and a kitchenette. The tariff for a double / twin room starts at £26 per person. Muddy paws and boots welcome. The restaurant serves delicious home cooked food, and the bar, with its open log fire, has an emphasis on local Devon beers and ciders.

## HORN'S CROSS
**Hoops Inn**
Horn's Cross, Devon EX39 5DL
Tel: 01237 451222      **£££ - 12 rooms**
800 year old village Inn 10 miles from Bideford

## ILFRACOMBE
**Royal Britannia Hotel**
The Harbour, Ilfracombe, Devon EX34 9EE
Tel: 01271 862939      **£ - 18 rooms**
Olde listed Inn, Nelson and Lady Hamilton
stayed here

## KENTON, nr EXETER
**Devon Arms**
Kenton, nr Exeter, Devon EX6 8LD
Tel: 01626 890213      £ - P - 6 rooms
Email: devon.arms@ukgateway.net
Near Powderham Castle between Exeter and
Dawlish

## KINGSTON
**The Dolphin Inn**
Kingston, Devon,TQ7 4QE
Tel: 01548 810314      **££ - P - 3 rooms**
Country Inn 5 miles from Modbury

## LITTLEHEMPSTON
**Tally Ho Inn**
Littlehempston, Devon TQ9 6NF
Tel: 01803 862316      **££ - 4 rooms**
Village Inn 2 miles from Totnes

## LYDFORD, OKEHAMPTON
**Castle Inn Hotel and Restaurant**
Lydford, Okehampton, Devon EX20 4BH
Tel: 01822 820241      **£££ - P - 9 rooms**
15thC Pub 6 miles from Okehampton

## LYNMOUTH
**Rising Sun Hotel**
Harbourside, Lynmouth, Devon EX35 6EQ
Tel: 01598 753223      **££ - 16 rooms**
Harbourside thatched Inn

**The Village Inn**
19 Lynmouth St, Lynmouth, Devon EX35 6EH
Tel: 01598 752354      **£ - P - 6 rooms**
Village Inn 22 miles from Barnstable

## MODBURY
**Exeter Inn**
Church Street, Modbury, Devon PL21 0QR
Tel: 01548 830239      **£ - P - 4 rooms**
Traditional local Pub 8 miles from Kingsbridge

## NEWTON ABBOT
**Kestor Inn**
Manaton, Newton Abbot, Devon TQ13 9UF
Tel: 01647 221204      **£ - P - 4 rooms**
Email: kiran@zoom.co.uk
Quiet Village Inn 9 miles from Newton Abbot

## NORTH BOVEY
**Ring of Bells Inn**
North Bovey, Devon TQ13 8RB

Tel: 01647 440375 **£ - P - 3 rooms**
Village Inn 13 miles from Exeter

## NORTH TAWTON
**The Railway Inn**
Whiddon Down Road, North Tawton, Devon
Tel: 01837 82789 **£ - P - 1 room**
Rural Inn 1 mile from North Tawton

## nr HOLSWORTHY
**Bradworthy Inn**
The Square, nr Holsworthy, Devon
Tel: 01409 241222 **£ - P - 4 rooms**
Village Inn 7 miles from Holsworthy

## OTTERY ST MARY
**Fairmile Inn**
Fairmile, Ottery St Mary, Devon EX11 1LP
Tel: 01404 812827 **£ - P - 3 rooms**
Village Inn handy for Exeter airport / A30

## PRINCETOWN
**Prince of Wales**
Tavistock Road, Princetown, Devon PL20 6QF
Tel: 01822 890219 **£ - Rooms**
In the heart of Dartmoor, brews its own beer

## PRINCETOWN, TAVISTOCK
**Plume of Feathers Inn**
Princetown, Tavistock, Devon PL20 6QG
Tel: 01822 890240 **£ - P - 3 rooms**
Located near the centre of Princetown

## RACKENFORD, nr TIVERTON
**Stag Inn**
Rackenford, nr Tiverton, Devon EX16 8DT
Tel: 01884 881369 **£ - P - 3 rooms**
Village Inn 8 miles from Tiverton

## SOUTH MOLTON
**London Inn**
Molland, South Molton, Devon EX36 3NG
Tel: 01769 550269 **£ - P - 2 rooms**
Traditional village Inn 5 miles from South
Molton

**The Sportsmans Inn**
Sandyway, South Molton, Devon EX36 3LU
Tel: 01643 831109 **£ - P - 3 rooms**
Email: sportsmans@breathemail.net
Rural Inn 7 miles from South Molton

**The George Hotel**
Broad Street, South Molton, Devon
Tel: 01769 572514
Web: www.s-molton.freeserve.co.uk
Historic posting Inn, Routiers recommended

**Old Coaching Inn**
Queen Street, South Molten, Devon EX36 3BJ
Tel: 01769 572526 **£ - P - 6 rooms**
Located in the centre of town

## SHEEPWASH
**Half Moon Inn**
Sheepwash, Devon EX21 5NE
Tel: 01409 231376 **££ - P - 15 rooms**
Traditional Inn 10 miles from Okehampton

## SIDFORD, nr SIDMOUTH
**Blue Ball Inn**
Stevens Cross, Sidford, nr Sidmouth, Devon
Tel: 01395 514062 **££ - P - 6 rooms**
Village Inn 2 miles Sidmouth

## SLAPTON
**The Tower Inn**
Slapton, Devon TQ7 2PN
Tel: 01548 580216 **£ - P - 3 rooms**
Village Inn 6 miles from Dartmouth

## SOUTH ZEAL
**Oxenham Arms**
South Zeal, Devon EX20 2JT
Tel: 01837 840244 **££ - P - 8 rooms**
Village Inn 4 miles from Okehampton

## SPREYTON, CREDITON
**The Tom Cobley Tavern**
Spreyton, Crediton, Devon EX17 5AL
Tel: 01647 231314 **£ - P - 4 rooms**
Email: fjwfilor@tomcobley.fsnet.co.uk
Village Pub 10 miles from Okehampton

## STAVERTON, NR TOTNES
**The Sea Trout Inn**
See main entry on page 154

## STOCKLAND
**Kings Arms**
Stockland, Devon EX14 9BS
Tel: 01404 881361 **£ - P - 3 rooms**
Village Inn 3 miles from Honiton

# The Sea Trout

*Staverton, nr Totnes, Devon TQ9 6PA*

**££ - P - R - BM - BG - PW - C - 10 rooms**

Tel / Fax: 01803 762274

Email: enquiries@seatroutinn.com　　　Web: www.seatroutinn.com

The Sea Trout is a beautiful 400-year-old Inn, with open fires, fresh flowers and a great welcome. This very popular destination Inn is very close to the river Dart (fishing available). All rooms are *en suite*. The Sea Trout Inn boasts 2 RAC ribbons and 2 AA rosettes for excellence. There is ample car parking; a beer garden and well-behaved children are welcome. The Inn is acclaimed for its high quality West Country food and the attentive level of service. Meals are served either in the bar or the comfortable restaurant.

The average room tariff – Single: £45 - Double: £65 - Family room: £75

# Thelbridge Cross Inn

*Thelbridge, Crediton, Devon EX17 4SQ*

**££ - P - R - BM - BG - C - ETC 4 diamond - 7 rooms**

Tel: 01884 860316　　　Fax: 01884 861318

Email: stay@thelbridgexinn.co.uk　　　Web: www.thelbridgexinn.co.uk

Dating back to the 1700's, when it was a coaching Inn and cider house, the beamed ceilings and open log fires retain that "Olde Worlde" feeling today. The Thelbridge Cross Inn enjoys wonderful countryside views, and on a clear day the hills of Dartmoor can be seen to the south and Exmoor to the north. The central location means most of beautiful Devon, and all it has to offer, is within easy reach. The Inn has a reputation for its superb food; the menu offers a wide selection of home cooked dishes, many of them traditional English recipes. Delicious bar meals are also available. It's excellent accommodation comprises of seven *en suite* bedrooms, all of which are extremely clean and comfortable, offering colour television, direct-dial telephone, tea and coffee making facilities and full central heating.

---

**STONEYCOMBE, KINGSERSWELL**
**Bickley Mill Inn**
Stoneycombe, Kingskerswell, Devon
Tel: 01803 873201　　**££ - P - 7 rooms**
Country Inn 3 miles from Kingkerswell

**THELBRIDGE**
**The Thelbridge Cross Inn**
See main entry above

**THE HOE, PLYMOUTH**
**Yardarm**
159 Citadel Road, The Hoe, Plymouth,
Devon PL1 2HU

Tel: 01752 201568　　**£ - 3 rooms**
Old style Pub with beautiful views

**TIVERTON**
**Prince Regent**
Loman Green, Tiverton, Devon EX16 4LA
Tel: 01884 252882
Town Pub in Tiverton

**TOR BRYAN, NEWTON ABBOT**
**Old Church House Inn**
Tor Bryan, Newton Abbot, Devon TQ12 5UR
Tel: 01803 812180　　**££ - P - Rooms**
Three star hotel with bar in this quiet hamlet

TORQUAY
**Chelston Manor Hotel**
Old Mill Road, Torquay, Devon
Tel: 01803 605142    **£ - P - 14 rooms**
Pub / hotel 1 miles from town centre

TORRINGTON
**West of England Inn**
18 South Street, Torrington, Devon EX38 8AA
Tel: 01805 624949    **£ - 4 rooms**
Located in the centre of town

TRUSHAM
**Cridford Inn**
Trusham, Devon TQ13 0NR
Tel: 01626 853694    **££ - P - 4 rooms**
Village Inn 5 miles from Chudleigh

TUCKENHAY
**The Maltsters Arms**
Tuckenhay, Devon TQ9 7EQ
Tel: 01803 732350    **££ - P - 7 rooms**
Country Pub 3 miles from Totnes

TURF LOCK, EXMINSTER
**Turf Hotel**
Turf Lock, Exminster, Devon EX6 8EE
Tel: 01392 833128    **££ - 2 rooms**
Country Pub 4 miles from Exeter

TURNCHAPEL, PLYMOUTH
**New Inn**
1 Boringdon Road, Turnchapel, Plymouth,
Devon PL9 9TV
Tel: 01752 402765    **£ - P - 5 rooms**
25 minutes walk to Plymouth town centre

TURNCHAPEL
**Boringdon Arms**
Boringdon Terrace, Turnchapel, Plymouth,
Devon PL9 9TQ
Tel: 01752 402053    **£ - P - 6 rooms**
Web: www.bori.co.uk
Real ale Pub 6 miles from Plymouth centre

UFFCULME, CULLOMPTON
**Waterloo Cross Inn**
Waterloo Cross, Uffculme, Cullompton,
Devon EX15 3ES
Tel: 01884 840328    **£ - P - 12 rooms**
Quiet Pub just off J27, M5

UMBERLEIGH
**The Rising Sun Inn**
Umberleigh, Devon EX37 9DU
Tel: 01769 560447    **££ - P - 9 rooms**
Riverside village Inn, just 7 miles from
Barnstable

USSCULME
**Ostler Inn**
The Square, Uffculme, Devon EX15 3EB
Tel: 01884 840260    **£ - Rooms**
Village Inn between Taunton and Exeter

WEST CHALDON, KINGSBRIDGE
**Ashburton Arms**
West Chaldon, Kingsbridge, Devon TQ7 2AH
Tel: 01548 531242    **£ - P - 2 rooms**
Village Inn 2 miles from Kingsbridge

WONSON
**The Northmore Arms**
Wonson, Devon EX20 2JA
Tel: 01647 231428    **£ - P - 2 rooms**
Email: info@northmorearms.co.uk
Web: www.northmorearms.co.uk
Ideal for walkers , situated just 1 mile from
Throwleigh

WOODLAND, nr ASHBURTON
**The Rising Sun**
Woodland, nr Ashburton, Devon TQ13 7JT
Tel: 01364 652544    **££ - P - 3 rooms**
Email: mail@risingsunwoodland.co.uk
Web: www.risingsunwoodland.co.uk
Situated on the edge of beautiful Dartmoor,
ideal for walking

YEALMPTON
**Rose and Crown**
Market Street, Yealmpton, nr Plymouth,
Devon PL8 2EB
Tel: 01752 880223    £ - P - 3 Rooms
Located near the centre of town

ZEAL MONACHORUM
**The Waie Inn**
Zeal Monachorum, Crediton,
Devon EX17 6DF
Tel: 01363 82348    **£ - P - 5 rooms**
Email: waieinn@talk21.com
Village Inn 8 miles from Crediton

# DORSET

Dorset BH12 1DQ
Tel: 01202 769555     **£ - P - 6 rooms**
Victorian Pub on the main road opposite
Branksome railway station

## BRIDPORT
**Bridport Arms Hotel**
West Bay, Bridport, Dorset DT6 4EN
Tel: 01308 422944     **££ - P - 13 rooms**
Located right on the beach

## BEAMINSTER
**The Red Lion**
14 The Square, Beaminster, Dorset DT8 3AX
Tel: 01308 862364     **P - Rooms**
18th century coaching Inn

## BERE REGIS
**The Royal Oak Hotel**
See main entry opposite

## BOURNEMOUTH
**Dean Park Inn**
41 Wimborne Road, Bournemouth,
Dorset BH2 6NB
Tel: 01202 552941     **£ - P - 7 rooms**
Country Inn 15 minutes walk to the beach

## BOURTON
**The White Lion Inn**
High Street, Bourton, Dorset SP8 5AT
Tel: 01747 840866     **£ - P - 2 rooms**
Village Inn 4 miles from Wincanton

## BRADPOLE, BRIDPORT
**The Kings Head**
304 St Andrews Road, Bradpole, Bridport,
Dorset DT6 3DS
Tel: 01308 422520     **P - Rooms**
Family run Pub on the edge of Bridport

## BRANKSOME, POOLE
**Branksome Railway Hotel**
429 Poole Road, Branksome, Poole,

**George Hotel**
South Street, Bridport, Dorset DT6 3NQ
Tel: 01308 423187     **Rooms**
Excellent Pub food in the centre of Bridport

**Half Moon**
Melplash, Bridport, Dorset DT6 3UD
Tel: 01308 488321     **P - Rooms**
Beautiful Inn in the heart of the village

**The Lord Nelson**
52 East Street, Bridport, Dorset DT6 3LL
Tel: 01308 422665     **Rooms**
A traditional beer first Pub in town

**The Toll House**
East Road, Bridport, Dorset DT6 4AG
Tel: 01308 423398     **Rooms**
Riverside Inn with a lovely garden

## CHARMINSTER, DORCHESTER
**Inn For All Seasons**
16 North Street, Charminster, Dorchester,
Dorset DT2 9QZ
Tel: 01305 264694     **P - Rooms**
Village Inn 2 miles from Dorchester

## CHRISTCHURCH
**Avon Causeway Inn**
Hurn, Christchurch, Dorset BH23 6AS
Tel: 01202 482714     **££ - P - 12 rooms**
Email: avoncauseway@wadworth.co.uk
Web: www.avoncausewayhotel.co.uk
Village Inn 5 miles from Christchurch

# The Royal Oak Hotel

*1 West Street, Bere Regis, Wareham, Dorset BH20 7HQ*

Tel / Fax: 01929 471203
Email: info@theroyaloakhotel.co.uk
Web: www.theroyaloakhotel.co.uk

The Royal Oak's relaxed atmosphere and friendly, hassle-free service combine with the newly refurbished bedrooms and a pretty location at the edge of an historic Dorset village to give you... "A perfect place to stay in the midst of timeless Hardy country." All beautifully appointed rooms are *en suite*. Each is named after a town from a Thomas Hardy novel and is provided with colour television, tea and coffee making facilities and hair dryer, trouser press and irons are also available. Families are warmly welcomed, cots or addition beds are available on request.
Breakfast, in keeping with the relaxed ambience of the Royal Oak, is served from 8.30am, so you will never feel rushed – choose from a hearty full English or something simpler.

# The Sheaf of Arrows

*4 The Square, Cranborne, Dorset*

**£ - P**

Tel: 01725 517456

The Sheaf of Arrows is set in the centre of the pretty village of Cranborne close to Cranborne Manor Gardens on the Cranborne Chase; it is an excellent base for hikers, fishermen and tourists.

All rooms are en suite with colour TV and tea and coffee making facilities. Delicious home cooked meals are served in both the lounge and public bars and the public bar also boasts a dartboard, pool table and sky TV.

Tariff from: Single room £35.00, Double room £40.00, Family room £45.00 / £50.00.

**CORFE CASTLE**
**Bankes Arms Hotel**
East Street, Corfe Castle, Dorset BH20 5ED
Tel: 01929 480206    **££ - P - 10 rooms**
Email: bankeshotel.corfecastle@telinco.co.uk
Web: www.dorset-info.co.uk/bankes_arms_hotel
Village Inn 5 miles from Swanage

**CORSCOMBE**
**The Fox Inn**
Corscombe, Dorset DT2 ONS
Tel: 01935 891330    **££ - P - 3 rooms**
Country Inn 8 miles from Yeovil

**CRANBORNE**
**The Fleur De Lys**
5 Wimborne Street, Cranborne, nr Wimborne
Minster, Dorset BH21 5PP
Tel: 01725 517282    **£ - P - 8 rooms**
Web: www.btinternet/fleurdelys
Coaching Inn located close to the New Forest

**The Sheaf of Arrows**
See main entry above

**DORCHESTER**
**Junction Hotel**

42 Great Western Road, Dorchester,
Dorset DT1 1UF
Tel: 01305 268826    **P - Rooms**
Web: www.stayhereuk.com
Busy town centre Pub

**The Three Compasses**
Charminster, Dorchester, Dorset DT2 9QT
Tel: 01305 263618    **£ - P - 4 rooms**
Village Inn 2 miles from Dorchester

## EVERSHOT
**The Acorn Inn**
Fore Street, Evershot, Dorset DT2 0JW
Tel: 01935 83228    **££ - P - 9 rooms**
Email: stay@acorn-inn.co.uk
Web: www.acorn-inn.co.uk
Village Pub 8 miles from Yeovil

## FARNHAM
**Museum Hotel**
Farnham, Dorset DT11 8DE
Tel: 01725 516261    **P - 8 rooms**
Pub includes the famous Shed restaurant

## GILLINGHAM
**The Kings Arms Inn**
East Stour Common, Gillingham,
Dorset SP8 5NB
Tel: 01747 838325    **£ - P - 3 rooms**
Email: jenny@kings-arms.fsnet.co.uk
Country Inn 4 miles from Shaftsbury

## HORTON, WIMBORNE MINSTER
**The Horton Inn**
Cranbourne Road, Horton, Wimborne Minster,
Dorset BH21 5AD
Tel: 01258 840252    **££ - P - 9 rooms**

Email: thehorton@btinternet.com
Web: www.welcome.to/thehortoninn
Village Inn situated close to Wimborne
Minster

## IWERNE MINSTER
**The Talbot Hotel**
See main entry below

## LODERS
**Loders Arms**
Loders, Dorset DT6 3SA
Tel: 01308 422431    **£ - P - 2 rooms**
Village Inn 1.5 miles from Bridport

## LYME REGIS
**Angel Inn**
Mill Green, Lyme Regis, Dorset DT7 3PH
Tel: 01297 443267    **£ - P - 2 rooms**
Traditional Pub serving ale from the barrels

**Cobb Arms**
Marine Parade, Lyme Regis, Dorset DT7 3JF
Tel: 01297 443242    **£ - 3 rooms**
Family pub located on the Cobb

## MILTON ABBAS
**The Hambro Arms**
Milton Abbas, Dorset DT11 0BP
Tel: 01258 880233    **££ - 2 rooms**
Village Inn 7 miles from Blandford

## MORETON, nr DORCHESTER
**Frampton Arms**
Moreton, nr Dorchester, Dorset DT2 8BB
Tel: 01305 852253    **£ - P - 3 rooms**
Country Inn located next to the village railway
station

# The Talbot Hotel

*Iwerne Minster, Blandford Forum, Dorset DT11 8QN*

**£ - P - Rooms**

**Tel: 01747 811269**

This Picturesque Victorian pub on the A350 is ideal for walkers and ramblers. The comfortable
rooms are at affordable prices. There are two bars serving real ales and good home cooked
food. Ample parking.

# Marquis of Lorne

*Nettlecombe, near Bridport, Dorset DT6 3SY*

**££ - P - 6 rooms**

Tel: +44 (0) 1308 485236     Fax: +44 (0) 1308 485666

Email: julie.woodroffe@btinternet.com     Web: www.marquisoflorne.com

The seven double *en suite* rooms (one twin with a bath and shower) in The Marquis of Lorne are extremely well appointed and comfortable, all with central heating, remote control TV, hospitality tray, direct dial telephone and a hair dryer. Families very welcome in the pub and dining rooms. No pets, or children under 10 years of age in the bedrooms.

MOTCOMBE, SHAFTSBURY
**The Coppleridge Inn**
Elm Hill, Motcombe, Shaftsbury,
Dorset SP7 9HW
Tel: 01747 851980     **££ - P - 10 rooms**
Email: thecopperidgeinn@btinternet.com
Web: www.copperidge.com
Country Pub 2 miles from Shaftsbury

NETTLECOMBE, NEAR BRIDPORT
**The Marquis of Lorne**
See main entry above

NORTH WOOTON
**The Three Elms**
North Wootton, Dorset DT9 5JW
Tel: 01935 812881     **£ - P - 1 room**
Village Inn

PIDDLETRENTHIDE
**The Poachers Inn**
Piddletrenthide, Dorchester, Dorset DT2 7QX
Tel: 01300 348358     **££ - P - 18 rooms**
Email: thepoachers@
      piddletrenthide.fsbusiness.co.uk
Web: www.thepoachersinn.co.uk
Country Inn in the Piddle Valley

PIMPERNE, BLANFORD
**Anvil Inn and Hawkins Restaurant**
Salisbury Road, Pimperne, Blandford,
Dorset DT11 8UQ
Tel: 01258 453431     **P - PW - rooms**
Email: info@anvilhotel.co.uk
Web: www.anvilhotel.co.uk
Pets welcome

POOLE
**Potters Arms**
21 Blandford Road, Poole, Dorset BH15 4AS
Tel: 01202 674030     **Rooms**
Town Pub 1 mile from Poole centre

**The Shah of Persia**
173 Longfleet Road, Poole, Dorset BH15 2HS
Tel: 01202 676587     **££ - P - 15 rooms**
Recently refurbished Pub on the outskirts of town

PORTLAND
**Jolly Sailor**
Castletown, Portland, Dorset DT5 1BD
Tel: 01305 822322     **Rooms**
Local Pub well situated for divers

**Mermaid Inn**
Wakeham Road, Portland, Dorset DT5 1HS
Tel: 01305 821062     **Rooms**
Ideal for Portland Bill and the spectacular coast

PUNCKNOWLE
**The Crown Inn**
Church Street, Puncknowle, Dorset DT2 9BN
Tel: 01308 897711     **£ - P - 3 rooms**
Village Inn 6 miles from Bridport

SEMLEY, SHAFTSBURY
**The Bennett Arms**
Semley, Shaftsbury, Dorset SP7 9AS
Tel: 01747 830221     **££ - P - 5 rooms**
Web: www.bennettarms.co.uk
Village Inn 5 miles from Shaftsbury

SHAFTSBURY
**The Grove Arms Inn**
Ludwell, Shaftsbury, Dorset SP7 9ND
Tel: 01747 828328    **£ - P - 6 rooms**
Web: www.wiltshireaccommodation.com
17th century Inn ideal for walkers

**The Kings Arms**
Shaftsbury, Dorset
Tel: 01747 852746    **P - Rooms**
Conveinient for the centre of Shaftsbury

**The Ship Inn**
Bleke Street, Shaftsbury, Dorset
Tel: 01747 853219    **Rooms**
Town centre Inn near Gold Hill, good food and
ales

SHERBOURNE
**The Britannia Inn**
Westbury, Sherbourne, Dorset DT9 3EH
Tel: 01935 813300    **£ - P - 7 rooms**
Village style Inn near the centre of Sherbourne

**Crown Inn**
Green Hill, Sherbourne, Dorset DT9 4EP
Tel: 01935 812930    **£ - P - 4 rooms**
Village Inn on the outskirts of Sherbourne

STUDLAND
**The Bankes Arms Hotel**
Watery Lane, Studland, Dorset BH19 3AU
Tel: 01929 450225    **££ - P - 9 rooms**
Real ale country Inn 2 miles from Swanage

SWANAGE
**Purbeck Hotel**
19 High Street, Swanage, Dorset BH19 2LP
Tel: 01929 425160    **£ - Rooms**
Local town Pub

**White Swan**
The Square, Swanage, Dorset BH19 2LJ
Tel: 01929 423804    **£ - P - 3 rooms**
Located in the town centre by the sea

TARRANT MONKTON
**The Langton Arms**
Tarrant Monkton, Dorset DT11 8RX
Tel: 01258 830225    **££ - P - 6 rooms**
Country Inn 5 miles from Blandford

WAREHAM
**Quay Inn**
The Quay, Wareham, Dorset
Tel: 01929 552735    **£ - P - 3 rooms**
Situated on the river

WEST BEXINGTON
**The Manor Hotel**
Beach Road, West Bexington,
Dorset DT2 9DF
Tel: 01308 897616    **£££ - P - 13 rooms**
Country house Inn with restaurant 7 miles
from Bridport

WEYMOUTH
**The Weatherbury**
See main entry below

# The Weatherbury

*7 Carlton Road North, Weymouth, Dorset DT4 7PX*

**£ - P - 7 rooms**

Tel: 01305 786040    Fax: 01305 760229

All 7 tasteful, comfortable *en suite* bedrooms have central heating,
teletext colour (Sky) TV, tea / coffee making facilities. The light self-
service breakfast is available all day. The popular bar boasts a well-
kept pool table, dartboard and friendly locals.

A free-house pub serving good home (varied menu) cooked food, specialising in real ale and is a
"CAMRA" pub of the year. The pub is situated about 450 metres from the "clean" beach and is
15 minutes stroll, along The Esplanade, to the town centre.

WINKTON, CHRISTCHURCH
**Fishermans Haunt Hotel**
Salisbury Road, Winkton, Christchurch,
Dorset BH23 7AS
Tel: 01202 477283    **££ - P - 18 rooms**
Country house Inn 4 miles from Christchurch

WINTERBOURNE ABBAS, nr
DORCHESTER
**Coach and Horses Inn**
Winterbourne Abbas, nr Dorchester,

Dorset DT2 9LU
Tel: 01305 889340    **£ - P - 5 rooms**
Located on the Bridport / Dorchester main
road 4 miles from Dorchester

YETMINSTER
**White Hart Inn**
High Street, Yetminster, Dorset DT9 6LF
Tel: 01935 872338    **£ - P - 1 cottage**
Village Inn 6 miles from both Yeovil and
Sherbourne

# GLOUCESTERSHIRE

ALVINGTON, nr LYDNEY
**Blacksmiths Arms**
Main Rd, Alvington, nr Lydney, Glos GL15 6AU
Tel: 01594 529657    **£ - P - 2 rooms**
Country Inn and restaurant 2 miles from
Lydney

AMBERLEY, STROUD
**The Amberley Inn**
Culver Hill, Amberley, Stroud, Glos GL5 5AF
Tel: 01453 872565    **££ - P - 15 rooms**
Stone built country Inn.  Old English Pub

BARNSLEY
**The Village Pub**
Barnsley, Glos GL7 5EF
Tel: 01285 740421    **£££ - P - 6 rooms**
Village Inn 3 miles from Cirencester

BECKFORD
**Beckford Inn Hotel**
Cheltenham Road, Beckford, Glos GL20 7AN
Tel: 01386 881254    **££ - P - 7 rooms**
Country Inn & restaurant 7 miles to Evesham

BISLEY
**The Bear Inn**
George Street, Bisley, Glos GL6 7BD
Tel: 01452 770265    **£ - P - 2 rooms**
Village Inn 4 miles from Stroud

BLEDINGTON
**The Kings Head Inn**
See main entry on page 162

BOURTON-ON-THE-WATER
**Coach and Horses**
Fosseway, Bourton-on-the-Water,
Cheltenham, Glos GL54 2HN
Tel: 01451 821064    **££ - P - 5 rooms**
Email: info@coach-horses.co.uk
Web: www.coach-horses.co.uk
Village Inn 20 minute drive from Cheltenham

**The Kingsbridge Inn**
Riverside, Bourton-on-the-Water, Cheltenham,
Glos GL54 2BS
Tel: 01451 820371    **££ - P - 3 rooms**
Email: book@lionheartinns.co.uk
Web: www.lionheartinns.co.uk
Village riverside Inn 17 miles from Cheltenham

# The Kings Head Inn

*The Green, Bledington, Glos / Oxon border OX7 6HD*

Tel: +44 (0) 1608 658365   Fax: +44 (0) 1608 658902
Email: kingshead@orr-ewing.com   Web: www.kingsheadinn.net/

The Kings Head Inn, dating back to the late 1500's, is set back off the village green and is what everyone would imagine a timeless English Inn to look like. The original inglenook fireplace dominates one end of the pub and with the old oak beams, Cotswold stonewalls and low ceilings the main bar exudes warmth and charm.

All our food is prepared in-house, meat is bought from a renowned local butcher and we guarantee that none is imported, in winter game is always on the menu, fish comes fresh from Cornwall daily and the vegetables are all home-grown in the nearby Evesham Vale. There are always excellent vegetarian dishes on the menu.

The delightful bedrooms are all furnished to compliment the unique 16th century character of the Inn. All are *en suite* with colour television, tea / coffee making facilities, radio alarm clocks, telephone, use of the residents' lounge and private roof terrace.

**The Lamb Inn**
Great Rissington, Bourton-on-the-Water,
Cheltenham, Glos GL54 2LP
Tel: 01451 820388   **££ - P - 14 rooms**
Web: www.thelamb-inn.com
Village Inn located just 18 miles from
Cheltenham

**Mousetrap Inn**
Lansdowne, Bourton-on-the-Water,
Cheltenham, Glos GL54 2AR
Tel: 01451 820579   **£ - P - 9 rooms**
Email: mtinn@waverider.co.uk
web: www.mousetrap-inn.co.uk
Small Inn with all rooms *en suite*

**Old Manse Hotel**
Victoria Street, Bourton-on-the-Water,
Glos GL54 2BX
Tel: 01451 820082   **££ - P - 15 rooms**
Town centre Pub

**Old New Inn**
Bourton-on-the-Water, Glos GL54 2AF
Tel: 01451 820467   **££ - P - Rooms**
Email: old_new_inn@compuserve.com
web: www.ourworld.compuserve.com/
   homepages/
Country Inn 15 miles from Cheltenham

BREAM, LYDNEY
**The Hedgehog Inn**
High Street, Bream, Lydney, Glos GL15 6JS
Tel: 01594 562358   **£ - P - 2 rooms**
Village Inn 5 miles from Lydney

BROARDWELL, LECHDALE
**The Five Bells**
Broadwell, Lechlade, Glos GL7 3QS
Tel: 01367 860076   **£ - P - 5 rooms**
Village Inn 11 miles from Whitney

BROCKWEIR
**Brockweir Country Inn**
Brockweir, Glos NP6 7NG
Tel: 01291 689548   **£ - P - 3 rooms**
Village Pub 5 miles from Chepstow

CHELTENHAM
**Bell Inn**
70 Bath Road, Cheltenham, Glos GL53 7JT
Tel: 01242 521977   **£ - P - 4 rooms**
Town Pub 5 minutes walk to the high street

CHIPPING CAMDPEN
**Eight Bells Inn**
Church Street, Chipping Campden,
Glos GL55 6JG
Tel: 01386 840371   **££ - P - 6 rooms**

Web: www.eightbellsinn.co.uk
13thC Inn 9 miles from Stratford-upon-Avon

**The Volunteer Inn**
Lower High Street, Chipping Campden,
Glos GL55 6DY
Tel: 01386 840688    **£ - 5 rooms**
Country village Inn 12 miles from Stratford-
upon-Avon

CHURCHDOWN
**Bat and Ball Inn**
Church Road, Churchdown, Glos GL3 2ER
Tel: 01452 713172    **£ - P - 8 rooms**
Village Pub 4 miles from Gloucester

CIRENCESTER
**The Black Horse**
17 Castle Street, Cirencester, Glos GL7 1QD
Tel: 01285 653187    **£ - 4 rooms**
Located in the centre of Cirencester

**The Oddfellows Arms**
See main entry below

**The Talbot Arms**
14 Victoria Road, Cirencester, Glos GL7 1EN
Tel: 01285 653760    **££ - P - 4 rooms**
3 minutes walk to Cirencester town centre

**White Lion Inn**
8 Gloucester Street, Cirencester,
Glos GL7 2DG
Tel: 01285 654053    **££ - 7 rooms**
Email: roylion@aol.com
Web: www.white-lion-cirencester.co.uk
17thC coaching Inn 3 minutes from the centre

CLEARWELL
**Butchers Arms**
The High Street, Clearwell, nr Coleford,
Glos GL16 8JS
Tel: 01594 834313    **££ - P - 4 rooms**
Local village Pub with restaurant 4 miles from
Colford

COLEFORD
**The Angel**
Market Place, Coleford, Glos GL16 8AE
Tel: 01594 833113
One of the Pubs n Bars group of Pubs

COLESBOURNE
**The Colesbourne Inn**
Colesbourne, Glos GL53 9NP
Tel: 01242 870376    **££ - 9 rooms**
Village Inn 6 miles from Cheltenham

CHELTENHAM
**The Green Dragon Inn**
Cockleford, Cowley, Cheltenham,
Glos GL53 9NW
Tel: 01242 870271    **££ - P - Rooms**
Web: www.green-dragon-inn.co.uk
17thC Inn in the heart of the Cotswolds

DIDMARTON
**The Kings Arms Inn**
See main entry on page 164

DRAKERS ISLAND, EWEN
**Wild Duck Inn**
Drakers Island, Ewen, Glos GL7 6BY
Tel: 01285 770310    **££ - P - 12 rooms**
Village Inn 10 minutes drive to Cirencester

# The Oddfellows Arms

*Chester Street, Cirencester, Glos GL7 1HF*

**££ - P - 4 rooms**

Tel: (01285) 641540    Fax: (01285) 640771
Web: www.oddfellowsarms.com

The Oddfellows Arms is a traditional pub that boasts a comfortable interior, a spacious enclosed garden and a new range of fabulous bed and breakfast rooms. All four Bed and Breakfast rooms are newly refurbished and have televisions and tea/coffee making facilities.

# The Kings Arms

*The Street, Didmarton, Glos GL9 1DT*

**££ - P**

Tel: 01454 238245
Email: stay@kadidmarton.com

The Kings Arms is a lovingly restored 17th Century Coaching Inn on the edge of the Badminton Estate. Our AA, Three Diamond accommodation is of the highest standard, as are our two traditional Camra Award bars. There is also an award-winning restaurant and three supers self-catering cottages.

---

FORD
**Plough Inn**
Ford, Glos GL54 5RU
Tel: 01386 584215      **££ - P - 3 rooms**
Village Inn 7 miles from Stow-on-the-Wold

FORTHAMPTON
Lower Lode Inn
Forthhampton, Glos GL19 4RE
Tel: 01684 293224     **£ - P - 4 rooms**
Riverside Inn 2 miles from Tewksbury

FOSSEBRIDGE
**Fossebridge Inn**
Fossebridge, Glos GL54 3JS
Tel: 01285 720721      **££ - P - 15 rooms**
Country Inn 12 miles from Cheltenham

FRAMPTON MANSELL, STROUD
**The Crown Inn**
Frampton Mansell, Stroud, Glos GL6 8JG
Tel: 01285 760601     **PW - Rooms**
Email: book@lionheartinn.co.uk
Web: www.lionheartinn.co.uk
Pets welcome

FRAMPTON-ON-SEVERN
**The Bell Inn**
The Green, Frampton -on- Severn,
Glos GL2 7EP
Tel: 01452 740346     **£ - P - 3 rooms**
Situated on the longest village green in Britain

GUITING POWER
**The Hollow Bottom**
Winchcombe Road, Guiting Power,

Glos GL54 5UX
Tel: 01451 850392     **£ - P - 3 rooms**
Country Pub 12 miles from Cheltenham

HARESFIELD, STONEHOUSE
**Beacon Inn Hotel**
Haresfield, Stonehouse, Glos GL10 3DX
Tel: 01452 728884     **£ - P - 5 rooms**
Email: beaconinn@aol.com
Web: www.thebeaconinn.co.uk
Village Inn 5 miles from Gloucester

HYDE
**Ragged Cott Inn**
Cirencester Road, Hyde, Glos GL6 8PE
Tel: 01453 884643     **££ - P - 10 rooms**
Email: david-savage@oasis-holdings.com
Web: www.home.btclick.com/ragged_cott
Country Inn 7 miles from Stroud

KINGSCOTE, TETBURY
**Hunters Hall**
Kingscote, Tetbury, Glos GL8 8XZ
Tel: 01453 860393     **P - 12 rooms**
Country Inn 5 miles from Tetbury

KELMSCOTT, LECHLADE
**The Plough Inn**
Kelmscott, Lechlade, Glos GL7 3HG
Tel: 01367 253543     **Rooms**
Village Inn north of Swindon

LECHLADE-ON-THAMES
**The New Inn Hotel**
Market Square, Lechlade-on-Thames,
Lechlade, Glos GL7 3AB

# The Bowl Inn

*Church Road, Lower Almondsbury, Bristol BS32 4DT*

**£ - P - R - BM - PW - C - 13 rooms**

Tel: 01454 612757    Fax: 01454 619910
Email: reception@thebowlinn.co.uk
Web: www.thebowlinn.co.uk

The Bowl Inn is an historic Inn offering superb accommodation, excellent food, fine wines and traditional real ales. The Inn is ideally located in the tranquillity of a small village yet easily accessible via the M4 and M5 (J16).

All our individually furnished rooms are *en suite* and are equipped with telephone, coffee making, Sky television and video player, trouser press and hair dryer. Fine food is served in the cosy environment of our own Lilies Restaurant or the more informal atmosphere of the bar. Children's menu is also available. Well-behaved pets are welcome. Average double room tariff: £71.00

Tel: 01367 252296    **££ - P - 19 rooms**
Email: info@newinnhotel.com
Web: www.newinnhotel.com
Located by the river, with a restaurant

LOWER ALMONDSBURY
**The Bowl Inn**
See main entry above

LOWER ODDINGTON,
MORTON-IN-MARSH
**The Fox Inn**
Lower Oddington, Moreton-in-Marsh,
Glos GL56 0UR
Tel: 01451 870555    **££ - P - 3 rooms**
Email: info@foxinn.net
Web: www.foxinn.net
True British village Inn. Flagstones, beams, fireplaces

MARSHFIELD
**The Lord Nelson Inn**
High Street, Marshfield, Glos
Tel: 01225 891820    **£ - P - 2 rooms**
Located in the village centre

MEYSEY HAMPTON
**The Masons Arms**
28 High St, Meysey Hampton, Glos GL7 5JT
Tel: 01285 850164    **££ - P - 9 rooms**
Email: jane@themasonsarms.freeserve.co.uk

Web: www.smoothhound.co.uk/hotels/mason
Village Inn 5.5 miles from Cirencester

MORETON-IN-MARSH
**The Bell Inn**
See main entry on page 166

**Black Bear Inn**
High St, Moreton-in-Marsh, Glos GL56 0AX
Tel: 01608 652992    **£ - P - 2 rooms**
Located on the street with the biggest street market in Britain

**The Horse and Groom**
Barton-on-the-Heath, Moreton-in-Marsh,
Glos GL56 9AQ
Tel: 01386 700413    **££ - P - 5 rooms**
Two miles from Moreton-in-the-Marsh

NAILSWORTH
**Egypt Mill**
Nailsworth, Glos GL6 0AE
Tel: 01453 833449    **££ - P - 17 rooms**
Country Inn 3 miles from Stroud

NAUNTON
**The Black Horse Inn**
Naunton, Glos GL54 3AD
Tel: 01451 850565    **£ - P - 4 rooms**
Country village Inn about 15 miles from Cheltenham

# The Bell Inn

*High Street, Moreton-in-Marsh, Glos GL56 0AF*

**££ - P - 5 rooms**

Tel: +44 (0) 1608 651688    Fax: +44 (0) 1608 652195
Email: keith.pendry@virgin.net
Web: www.bellinncotswold.com

The Bell is a traditional old Cotswold Coaching Inn ideally placed in the centre of one of the Cotswolds better known market towns, Moreton-in-Marsh. The Inn offers luxury accommodation, facilities for the disabled and home cooked food served in our restaurant, which also offers a non smoking area. The menu caters for all tastes, including vegetarian, and any special dietary needs can be catered for.

During the summer months relax in the old courtyard over a pint or two of traditional ale or join in with the locals in the spacious bar. What better way to relax after a busy day out touring around the Cotswolds.

NIBLEY, nr BLAKENEY
**Cock Inn**
Nibley, nr Blakeney, Glos
Tel: 01594 510239    **£ - P - 6 rooms**
Country Pub 3 miles from Blakeney and 3 miles from Lidney

NORTH CERNEY
**The Bathurst Arms**
North Cerney, Glos GL7 7BZ
Tel: 01285 831281    **££ - P - 5 rooms**
Email: info@thebathhurstarms.co.uk
Web: www.thebathurstarms.co.uk
Country Pub 5 miles from Cirencester

NORTHLEACH, CHELTENHAM
**The Sherbourne Arms**
Market Place, Northleach, Cheltenham,
Glos GL54 3EE
Tel: 01451 860241    **£ - P - 3 rooms**
Located 12 miles from Cheltenham

**Wheatsheaf Hotel**
West End, Northleach, Cheltenham,
Glos GL54 3EZ
Tel: 01451 860244    **££ - P - 8 rooms**
Email: whtshfthl@aol.com
Web: www.glosbp.co.uk/hotels/wheatsheaf.htm
Located 100 yards from the centre of Northleach, good restaurant

NYMPSFIELD, STROUD
**The Rose and Crown**
See main entry opposite

PAINSWICK
**The Falcon Inn**
New Street, Painswick, Glos GL6 6UN
Tel: 01452 814222    **££ - P - 12 rooms**
Country Inn 10 miles from Cheltenham

PARKEND, NR LYDNEY
**The Fountain Inn**
See main entry opposite

OLD SODBURY
**Dog Inn**
See main entry on page 168

PAXFORD, CHIPPING SODBURY
**The Churchill Arms**
Paxford, Chipping Campden, Glos GL55 6XH
Tel: 01386 594000    **££ - 4 rooms**
Village Inn situated 5 miles from Moreton-in-the-Marsh

TORMARTON
**Portcullis Inn**
Tormarton, nr Badminton, South Glos GL9 1HZ
Tel: 01454 218263    **£ - Rooms**
Country Inn 4 miles from Badminton

# Rose and Crown Inn

*The Cross, Nympsfield, Stroud, Glos GL10 3TU*

**££ - P - R - BM - BG - PW - C - 3 rooms**

Tel: 01453 860240    Fax: 01453 861564
Web: www.redrosetaverns.co.uk/html/rosecrown.html

The Rose and Crown Inn retains it's unspoilt Cotswold charm with log fires in the winter and stunning floral displays in the summer. The Inn is very popular with walkers as it is just half a mile from the Cotswold Way. Well-behaved children and pets are welcome.

The beautifully refurbished restaurant with its exposed beamed feature gallery serves locally sourced food, meals are also served in the bar between 12 noon and 9pm daily. There is ample car parking and a pleasant beer garden.

Our three letting rooms are all *en suite* with tea / coffee facilities, TV, iron and hairdryer. Average room tariff Single = £42.50 Double = £55 Family = £72

# The Fountain Inn

*Fountain Way, Parkend, nr Lydney, Royal Forest of Dean, Glos GL15 4JD*

**£ - P - 8 rooms**

Tel: 01594 562189    Fax: 01594 564438
Email: thefountaininn@aol.com
Web: www.thefountaininnandlodge.com

Alan and Michelle welcome you to this traditional village Inn, situated right in the heart of the Royal Forest of Dean, and well known locally for its excellent meals and real ales. The Fountain Inn and Lodge makes an ideal base for sightseeing, or for that quiet weekend away from it all. All eight guest rooms (including one specially adapted for the less able) are *en suite*, decorated and furnished to a high standard, and have television and tea / coffee making facilities. Other facilities include: Parking, bar meals, restaurant, beer garden, pets welcome.

**QUEDGELEY**
**Friar Tucks**
Bristol Road, Quedgeley, Glos GL2 4PQ
Tel: 01452 720312    **P - 8 rooms**
Local town Pub 5 miles from Gloucester

**RUARDEAN**
**The Malt Shovel Inn**
Ruardean, Glos GL17 9TW
Tel: 01594 543028    **£ - P - 8 rooms**
Email: mark@maltshovel.u-net.com

Web: www.maltshovel.u-net.com
One of the oldest village Inns in England

**SOUTH CERNEY**
**The Eliot Arms Hotel**
Clarks Hay, South Cerney, Cirencester,
Glos GL7 5UA
Tel: 01285 860215    **££ - P - 11 rooms**
Email: eliotarm@aol.co.uk
Village 4 miles from Cirencester, 10 miles from Swindon

# The Dog Inn

*Old Sodbury, Chipping Sodbury, South Glos BS37 6LZ*

**£ - P - BM - BG - PW - C - 18 rooms**

Tel: 01454 312006      Fax: 01451 318289

Web: www.cotswold-way.co.uk/doginn

The Dog Inn sits on the Cotswold Way, close to the M4 junction 18. Bath and Cirencester are only a short car journey away. Accommodation is offered in several cottages surrounding the pub.

The cottages are homely, tastefully decorated and beautifully kept, with comfortable beds, washing and drying facilities, sitting rooms, gardens and conservatory. Breakfast is usually in the cottages, however, the four well appointed *en suite* rooms in the pub will be serviced from there.

Rooms: Double: 7 (4 *en suite*), Single: 1, Twin: 6 (2 *en suite*), Family: 2. Tariff: Bed and Breakfast from £25.00. Evening Meal from £5.95. Pets and children welcome in some areas (check first). "Extensive menu (100 meals) Daily specials board, fish a speciality"

## SOUTH CERNEY, CIRENCESTER
**Horse and Groom**
Cricklade Road, South Cerney, Cirencester, Glos GL7 5QE
Tel: 01285 860236      **££ - P - 12 rooms**
Country Inn 4 miles from Cirencester

## STONE, nr BERKLEY
**Berkeley Vale Inn**
Stone, nr Berkeley, Glos GL13 9JY
Tel: 01454 260219      **£ - P - 8 rooms**
Village Inn 17 miles from Bristol

## STOW-ON-THE-WOLD
**Old Stocks Hotel**
The Square, Stow-on-the-Wold, Glos GL54 1AF
Tel: 01451 830666      **Rooms - PW**
Pets welcome

**White Hart Inn**
The Square, Stow-on-the-Wold, Cheltenham, Glos GL54 1AF
Tel: 01451 830674      **££ - P - 5 rooms**
Traditional Pub, centre of Stow-on-the-Wold

## STROUD
**The Clotheirs Arms**
1 Bath Road, Stroud, Glos GL5 3JU
Tel: 01453 763801      **£ - P - 7 rooms**

Email: luciano@clothiersarms.co.uk
Web: www.clothiersarms.co.uk
Cotswold stone Inn 5 minutes walk from town centre

## TEWKSBURY
**The Fleet Inn**
Twyning, Tewkesbury, Glos GL20 6DG
Tel: 01684 274310      **££ - P - 3 rooms**
Email: fleetinn@hotmail.com
Web: www.fleetinn.com
Rooms overlook the river

**Royal Oak Inn**
Main Rd, Bredon, Tewksbury, Glos GL20 7LW
Tel: 01684 772393      **£ - P - 4 rooms**
Village Inn 3 miles from Tewksbury

## ULEY
**The Old Crown Inn**
The Green, Uley, Glos GL11 5SN
Tel: 01453 860502      **£ - P - 3 rooms**
Email: sandra@oldcrownuley.freeserve.co.uk
17thC Inn featuring ales brewed in the village

## UPPER ODDINGTON
**Horse and Groom Inn**
Upper Oddington, Moreton-in-the-Marsh, Glos GL56 0XH

# The White Hart Inn

*High Street, Winchcombe, Cheltenham, Glos GL54 5LJ*

**££ - P - 8 rooms**

Tel: 01242 602359    Fax: 01242 602703
Email: enquiries@the-white-hart-inn.co.uk
Web: www.the-white-hart-inn.co.uk

The White Hart Inn and Restaurant is a charming 17th Century family run Coaching Inn offering eight individually decorated *en suite* bedrooms.

The award-winning Restaurant serves modern English cuisine with a Scandinavian influence and the 'Pub' Bar provides an extensive bar menu throughout the day. The Inn offers friendly attentive service in an informal atmosphere and "a taste of Sweden in the Cotswolds"

---

Tel: 01451 830584    **££ - P - 7 rooms**
Village Inn located in the heart of the Cotswolds just 3 miles from Stow-on-the-Wold

## WINCHCOMBE, CHELTENHAM
**The Plaisterers Arms**
Abbey Terrace, Winchcombe, nr Cheltenham,

Glos GL54 5HH
Tel: 01242 602358    **£ - P - 5 rooms**
Email: plaisterers.arms@btinternet.com
Olde Worlde Inn located in the centre of Winchcombe

**The White Hart Inn**
See main entry above

# ISLES OF SCILLY

### SAINT AGNES
**Turks Head**
Saint Agnes, Isles of Scilly TR22 0PL
Tel: 01720 422434    **££ - 1 room**
Special island Pub

### TRESCO
**The New Inn**
New Grimsby, Tresco,
Isles of Scilly TR24 0QQ
Tel: 01720 422844    **£££ - 14 rooms**
Definitely worth the journey to this remote island Pub

# SOMERSET

## ALLER, LANGPORT
**The Old Pound Inn**
See main entry opposite

## BECKINGTON
**Woolpack Inn**
Beckington, Somerset BA3 6SP
Tel: 01373 831244      **££ - P - 11 rooms**
Country Inn

## BISHOPS LYDEARD, TAUNTON
**The Leth Bridge Arms**
Gore Square, Bishops Lydeard, Taunton,
Somerset
Tel: 01823 432234      **£ - P - 8 rooms**
Email: phutchings@tinyworld.co.uk
16thC village Inn ideal for families 6 miles
from Taunton

## BISHOPSTON, MONTACUTE
**Kings Arms Inn**
Bishopston, Montacute, Somerset TA15 6UU
Tel: 01935 822513      **££ - P - 15 rooms**
Village Inn 3.5 miles from Yeovil

## BRIDGWATER
**Bower Green**
Bower Lane, Bridgwater, Somerset TA6 4TY
Tel: 01278 422926      **£ - P - 3 rooms**
Country Inn 1 mile from Bridgwater

**Cobblestones Inn**
71 Eastover, Bridgwater, Somerset TA6 5AP
Tel: 01278 452628      **£ - 3 rooms**
200 yards from Bridgwater town centre

## BROADWEY, ILMINSTER
**Bell Inn**
Broadwey, Ilminster, Somerset TA19 9NG
Tel: 01460 52343      **£ - P - 1 room**
Traditional village Inn 2 miles from Ilminster

## BRUTON
**Royal Oak Inn**
Coombe Street, Bruton, Somerset BA10 0EN
Tel: 01749 812215      **£ - P - 3 rooms**
Located 5 minutes walk to the town centre

## BURNHAM-ON-SEA
**Dunstan House Inn**
Love Lane, Burnham-on-Sea,
Somerset TA8 1EU
Tel: 01278 784343      P - 6 rooms
Country Inn on the edge of town

## BURTLE, NR BRIDGWATER
**The Tom Mogg Inn**
See main entry opposite

## CANNINGTON, BRIDGWATER
**The Friendly Spirit**
Brook Street, Cannington, Bridgwater,
Somerset TA5 2HP
Tel: 01278 652215      **£ - P - 8 rooms**
Village Inn with resident ghost

**The Kings Head Inn**
12–14 High Street, Cannington, Bridgewater,
Somerset TA5 2HE
Tel: 01278 652293      **£ - P - 6 rooms**
17thC village Inn 3 miles from Bridgwater

## CASTLE CARY
**The George Hotel**
See main entry on page 172

**The Horse Pond Inn**
The Triangle, Castle Cary, Somerset BA7 7BD
Tel: 01963 350318      **££ - P - 4 rooms**
Email: horsepondinn@aol.com
Village Pub with Motel

# The Old Pound Inn

*Aller, Langport, Somerset TA10 0RA*

**£ - P - R - BM - BG - C - 6 rooms**

Tel / Fax: 01458 250469

Built in 1571, The Old pound Inn is situated on the A372 Langport to Bridgwater road, and was voted as the, coveted JPC National Award, "Pub of the Year" 1999 and 2000. It is ideal for bird watching, walking and fishing. The Fleet Air Arm Museum and the Hains Motor Museum are nearby.

Bar food is provided, and the a-la-carte restaurant caters for 50 (flambé a speciality). There is also a function room which can seat 100, or 200 for a buffet. The six beautifully appointed en-suite rooms have tea / coffee facilities and colour television. In the well stocked bar there is a wide variety of beers and over 70 malt whiskies for your delectation

# The Tom Mogg Inn

*Station Road, Burtle, nr Bridgwater, Somerset TA7 8NU*

**£ - P - R - BM - BG - C - 6 rooms**

Tel: 01278 722399
Email: tommogg@telinco.co.uk
Web: www.tommogg.co.uk

Come and visit The Tom Mogg Inn, in Burtle, where you will be assured of a warm welcome by Janet and Steve Gillbert, who have recently celebrated their third successful year of ownership - and their thirty third Wedding Anniversary!

All the food served at The Tom Mogg Inn is freshly prepared from local ingredients. Each month, patrons of the Carvery eat their way through more than a tonne of the best of British meat.

The bar in the Tom Mogg is a free-house and very well stocked, with four real ales always on tap, a spacious skittle alley, a large beer garden and a friendly atmosphere. There are six comfortable *en suite* bedrooms; three are family rooms. Single: £25.00 - Twin: £20.00 pp.

Family rooms / Weekly rates and a two bedroomed well furnished cottage to let by negotiation The Tom Mogg Inn is proud to host interesting local events, and has been featured in the press for their "Murder Mystery" evenings.

CHURCHINGFORD
**The York Inn**
Honiton Road, Churchingford,
Somerset TA3 7RF
Tel: 01823 601333   **£ - P - 3 rooms**
Email: wdattheyorkinn@aol.com
Web: www.the-york-inn.freeserve.co.uk

Local village pub situated 5 miles from Taunton

CLEVEDON
**Campbells Landing**
22 The Beach, Clevedon,
Somerset BS21 7QT

# The George Hotel

*Market Place, Castle Cary, Somerset BA7 7AH*

**££ - P - R - BM - PW - C - 14 rooms**

Tel: 01963 350761     Fax: 01963 350035
Email: sarslou@aol.com
Web: www.georgehotel-castlecary.co.uk/

The George Hotel is a friendly, family run, thatched 15th century Country Town Hotel, situated in the centre of the historic town of Castle Cary, nestling in the beautiful undulating hills of South Somerset. All the seventeen *en suite* guest rooms have been individually designed (some traditionally, others with a modern appeal) and offer all the home comforts including colour TV, radio, direct dial telephone and tea / coffee making facilities.

A traditional A La Carte menu, alongside the chef's daily specials, can be enjoyed in either of the two contrasting bars at The George Hotel, or, for more intimate dining the lovely beamed and wood panelled restaurant is available.

Tel: 01275 872094     **£ - 8 rooms**
Next to the pier 5 minutes walk from the town centre

## COMBE HAY, BATH
**The Wheatsheaf**
Combe Hay, Bath, Somerset BA2 7EG
Tel: 01225 833504     **££ - P - 3 rooms**
Email: www.the-wheatsheaf.freeserve.co.uk
Village Inn 4.5 miles from Bath

## COXLEY, WELLS
**The Pound Inn**
Burcott Lane, Coxley, Wells, Somerset BA5 1QZ
Tel: 01749 672785     £ - P - 2 rooms
Email: poundinnwells@aol.com
17th century Inn 2 miles from Wells

## CREWKERNE
**Antelope Inn**
North Street, Crewkerne, Somerset TA18 7AJ
Tel: 01460 73553     **£ - P - 3 rooms**
Local town Pub

**The George Hotel**
Market Square, Crewkerne, Somerset TA18 7LP
Tel: 01460 73650     **££ - 13 rooms**
Email: eddie@thegeorgehotel.sagehost.co.uk
Web: www.thegeorgehotel.saganet.co.uk
17thC Inn near the centre of this market town

**The Manor Arms**
North Perrott, Crewkerne, Somerset TA18 7SG
Tel: 01460 72901     **£ - P - 9 rooms**
Email: info@manorarmshotel.co.uk
Web: www.manorarmshotel.co.uk
Village Inn 3 miles from Crewkerne

## DITCHEAT
**The Manor House Inn**
Ditcheat, Somerset BA4 6RB
Tel: 01749 860276     **££ - P - 3 rooms**
Village Inn 7 miles from Wells

## DOULTING, nr SHEPTON MALLETT
**Abbey Barn Inn**
Doulting, nr Shepton Mallett, Somerset BA4 4QD
Tel: 01749 880321     **££ - P - 3 rooms**
Village Inn 2 miles from Shepton Mallet

## DULVERTON
**Anchor Inn**
Exbridge, Dulverton, Somerset TA22 9AZ
Tel: 01398 323433     **££ - P - 6 rooms**
Country Inn 12 miles from Tiverton

## DUNBALL
**Admiral's Table Inn**
Bristol Road, Dunball, Somerset TA6 4TM
Tel: 01278 685671     **£ - P - 14 rooms**
Inn with restaurant

# The Rest and Be Thankful Inn

*Wheddon Cross, Exmoor, Somerset TA24 7DR*

**££ - P - 5 rooms**

Tel: 01643 841222    Fax: 01643 841813
Email: enquiries@restandbethankful.co.uk
website: www.restandbethankful.co.uk

The Rest and be Thankful Inn, once an old coaching house, offers you a warm welcome and is situated in the highest village on Exmoor. Great care has been taken in creating the five, 1 twin, 3 doubles and 1 single, *en suite* (showers) luxurious bedrooms.

All rooms have colour TV, direct dial telephone, fully stocked refrigerated "mini bar", tea / coffee making facilities, clock / radio, hair dryer, trouser press and are centrally heated, sound proofed and double glazed. Some enjoy views to Dunkery Beacon – the highest point in Somerset.

## DUNKERTON HILL, nr BATH
**The Prince of Wales**
Dunkerton Hill, nr Bath, Somerset BA2 8PH
Tel: 01761 434262    **££ - P - 5 rooms**
Country Inn 6 miles from Bath

## EAST COKER, YEOVIL
**The Halyar Arms**
Moor Lane, East Coker, Yeovil,
Somerset BA22 9JR
Tel: 01935 862332    **££ - P - 6 rooms**
Country Inn 3 miles south of Yeovil

## EVERCREECH, SHEPTON MALLETT
**The Bell Inn**
Bruton Road, Evercreech, Shepton Mallet,
Somerset BA4 6HY
Tel: 01749 830287    **£ - P - 3 rooms**
Village Inn 4 miles from Shepton Mallet

**Pecking Mill Inn**
Evercreech, Shepton Mallet, Somerset BA4 6PG
Tel: 01749 830336    **££ - P - Rooms**
16thC Inn near the Bath & West showground

## EXMOOR
**The Rest and be Thankful Inn**
See main entry above

## FROME
**The Sun Inn**
6 Catherine St, Frome, Somerset BA11 1DA

Tel: 01373 471913    **£ - 6 rooms**
Busy Pub in Frome town centre

## GLASTONBURY
**The Who'd a Thought It Inn**
17 Northload Street, Glastonbury,
Somerset BA6 9JJ
Tel: 01458 834460    **££ - P - 6 rooms**
Email: reservations@whodathoughtit.co.uk
Web: www.reservations.whdathoughtit.co.uk
Village Inn very near to the centre of
Glastonbury

**The Greylake Inn**
Greinton, Bridgwater, Somerset TA7 9BP
Tel: 01458 210383    **£ - P - 4 rooms**
Email: scottstavely@freeuk.com
Village Inn 3 miles from Street

## TAUNTON
**The New Inn**
Halse, Taunton, Somerset TA4 3AF
Tel: 01823 432352    **£ - P - 5 rooms**
Village Inn 7 miles from Taunton

## HENSTRIDGE, TEMPLECOMBE
**The Fountain Inn**
High Street, Henstridge, Templecombe,
Somerset
Tel: 01963 362722    **£ - P - 6 rooms**
Web: www.fountaininn.fsnet.co.uk
Village Inn 7 miles from Sherbourne

## HOLCOMBE, BATH
**The Ring 'O' Roses**
Stratton Road, Holcombe, Bath, Somerset,
BA3 5EB
Tel: 01761 232478    **££ - P - 8 rooms**
Email: ringofrosesholcombe@tesco.net
Country Inn with an excellent restaurant, 6
miles from Shepton Mallet

## HORSINGTON
**Half Moon Inn**
Horsington, Somerset BA8 0EF
Tel: 01963 370140    **£ - P - 4 rooms**
Village Inn 3 miles from Wincanton

## ILCHESTER
**Ilchester Arms**
The Square, Ilchester, Somerset BA22 8LN
Tel: 01935 840220    **£££ - P - 8 rooms**
Country hotel 5 miles from Yeovil

## KELSTON, BATH
**Old Crown**
Kelston, Bath, Somerset BA1 9AQ
Tel: 01225 423032
Pub owned by Butcombe Brewery

## KILVE
**The Hood Arms**
Kilve, Somerset TA5 1EA
Tel: 01278 741210    **££ - P - 6 rooms**
Country Inn 12 miles from Yeovil

## LANGPORT
**White Lion**
North Street, Langport, Somerset
Tel: 01458 250319    **£ - P - 2 rooms**
Small town Pub in Langport

## LYDFORD, nr SOMERTON
**Cross Keys Inn**
Lydford, nr Somerton, Somerset TA11 7HA
Tel: 01963 240473    **£ - P - 3 rooms**
Village Inn with camping / caravans / rooms

## MARTOCK
**The Nags Head**
East Street, Martock, Somerset TA12 6NF
Tel: 01935 823432    **P - 1 Flat**
Email: thenagschef@aol.com
Village Inn 7 miles from Yeovil

**The White Hart Hotel**
East Street, Martock, Somerset TA12 6JQ
Tel: 01935 822005    **££ - P - 11 rooms**
Near the centre of this large village

## MELLS, FROME
**The Talbot Inn**
High St, Mells, Frome, Somerset BA11 3PN
Tel: 01373 812254    **££ - P - 8 rooms**
15thC village coaching Inn 12 miles from Bath

## MIDSOMER NORTON, RADSTOCK
**Greyhound**
High Street, Midsomer Norton, Radstock,
Somerset BA3 2LE
Tel: 01761 412974    **£ - P - 4 rooms**
Located near the centre of town

## MINEHEAD
**Britannia Inn**
1 Manor Road, Minehead, Somerset TA24 6EH
Tel: 01643 702384    **£ - 4 rooms**
Village Inn in the suburbs of Minehead

**The Old Ship Aground**
Quay Street, Minehead, Somerset TA24 5UL
Tel: 01643 702087    **£ - P - 13 rooms**
Email: enquiries@oldshipaground.co.uk
Web: www.oldshipaground.co.uk
Town Pub 10 minutes walk from the centre

## MONTACUTE
**The Phelips Arms**
The Borough, Montacute, Somerset TA15 6XB
Tel: 01935 822557    **££ - P - 3 rooms**
Email: thephelipsarms@aol.com
Village Inn 4 miles from Yeovil

## NETHER STOWEY
**Rose and Crown**
St Mary Street, Nether Stowey,
Somerset TA5 1LJ
Tel: 01278 732265    **£ - P - 4 rooms**
Village Inn 9 miles from Taunton

## NORTH CADBURY, YEOVIL
**The Catash Inn**
North Cadbury, Yeovil, Somerset BA22 7DH
Tel: 01963 440248    **£ - P - 3 rooms**
Email: clivesandrs@catash.com
Web: www.catash.com
17thC Inn at the centre of North Cadbury

NORTON ST PHILIPS
**George Inn**
High St, Norton St Philip, Somerset BA3 6LH
Tel: 01373 834224    **££ - P - 8 rooms**
Country Inn 8 miles from Bath

PORLOCK
**The Ship Inn**
High Street, Porlock, Somerset TA24 8QT
Tel: 01643 862507    **£ - P - PW - 10 rooms**
Village Inn 5 miles from Minehead

PRIDDY
**New Inn**
Priddy Green, Priddy, Somerset BA5 3BB
Tel: 01749 676465    **£ - 6 rooms**
Country house 3 miles from Wells

QUEEN CAMEL
**Mildmay Arms**
High St, Queen Camel, Somerset BA22 7NJ
Tel: 01935 850456    **£ - P - 6 rooms**
Email: mike@mildmayarms.greatxscape.net
Web: www.mildmayarms.greatxscape.net
Village Inn 6 miles from Yeovil

RADSTOCK, nr BATH
**The Fromeway**
Fome Road, Radstock, nr Bath,
Somerset BA3 3LG
Tel: 01761 432116    £ - P - 3 rooms
Family Pub 8 miles from Bath, 11 from Wells

RUDGE, FROME
**The Full Moon at Rudge**
Rudge, Frome, Somerset BA11 2QF
Tel: 01373 830936    **££ - 6 rooms**
Email: fullmoon@lineone.net
Web: www.thefullmoon
Country Inn and restaurant 10 miles from Bath

SHEPTON MONTAGUE
**The Montague Inn**
Shepton Montague, Somerset BA9 8JW
Tel: 01749 813213    **££ - P - 3 rooms**
Village Pub & restaurant 15 miles from Yeovil

SHIPHAM
**The Miners Arms**
The Square, Shipham, Somerset BS25 1TW
Tel: 01934 842146    £ - P - 3 Rooms
Village Inn 15 miles from Weston Super Mare

SPARKFORD
**The Sparkford Inn**
High Street, Sparkford, Somerset BA22 7JN
Tel: 01963 440218    **£ - 10 rooms**
Village Inn 7 miles from Yeovil

STOKE ST GREGORY
**Rose and Crown**
Woodhill, Stoke St Gregory, Somerset TA3 6EW
Tel: 01823 490296    **£ - 4 rooms**
Country Pub 9 miles from Taunton

STRATTON-ON-THE-FOSSE,
RADSTOCK
**The Kings Arms**
Stratton-on-the-Fosse, Radstock,
Somerset BA3 4RA
Tel: 01761 232346    **£ - P - 2 rooms**
Country Pub located 2 miles from Midsomer
Norton

TAUNTON
**Lowtrow Cross Inn**
Upton, Taunton, Somerset TA4 2DB
Tel: 01398 371220    **£ - P - 3 rooms**
Email: lowtrowcross@aol.com
Traditional rural Inn 20 miles from Taunton

**Masons Arms**
Magdalene St, Taunton, Somerset TA1 1SG
Tel: 01823 288916
Town Pub with rooms

TRULL, TAUNTON
**The Winchester Arms**
Church Rd, Trull, Taunton, Somerset TA3 7LG
Tel: 01823 284723    **£ - P - 6 rooms**
Village Inn 1 mile from Taunton

WAMBROOK
**The Cotley Inn**
Wambrook, Somerset TA20 3EN
Tel: 01460 62348    £ - P - 2 rooms
Country Inn situated just one-and-a-half miles
from Chard

WATERROW
**The Rock Inn**
Waterrow, Somerset TA4 2AX
Tel: 01984 623293    **£ - 8 rooms**
Village Inn with local real ales

WELLINGTON
**Green Dragon Inn**
South Street, Wellington, Somerset TA21 8NR
Tel: 01823 662281     **£ - P - 3 rooms**
Traditional town Pub near the centre

WELLS
**Mermaid Inn**
Tucker Street, Wells, Somerset,BA5 2DZ
Tel: 01749 672343     **£ - P - 4 rooms**
E-mail: pjasomerset@aol.com
Traditional Inn 5 minutes from town centre

WEMDON
**Cottage Inn**
Wemdon Hill, Wemdon, Somerset TA6 7PZ
Tel: 01278 423259     **£ - P - 3 rooms**
Country Inn 2 miles from Bridgwater

WEST HUNTSPILL
**Crossways Inn**
West Huntspill, Somerset TA9 3RA
Tel: 01278 783756     **£ - P - 4 rooms**
Country Inn 4 miles from Bridgewater

WESTHAY, nr GLASTONBURY
**Bird In Hand**
Main Rd, Westhay, nr Glastonbury, Somerset
Tel: 01458 860229     **£ - P - 1 room**
Typical village Inn 4 miles from Glastonbury

WILLITON
**Foresters Arms**
55 Long Street, Williton, Somerset TA4 4QY
Tel: 01984 632508     **£ - P - 8 rooms**
Village Inn 15 miles from Taunton

WILLITON
**Windmill Inn**
West Quantockhead, Williton, Somerset
Tel: 01984 633004
Country Inn with rooms

WINSCOMBE
**The Royal Oak Inn**
See main entry below

**Woodborough Inn**
Sandford Rd, Winscombe, Somerset BS25 1HD
Tel: 01934 844167     **££ - P - 5 rooms**
15 minutes from Weston Super Mare

WITHYPOOL
**Royal Oak Inn**
Withypool, Somerset TA24 7QP
Tel: 01643 831506     **£££ - P - 8 rooms**
Country Inn 25 miles from Taunton

WIVELISCOMBE, TAUNTON
**White Hart**
The Square, Wiveliscombe, Taunton, Somerset
Tel: 01984 623344     **££ - P - 10 rooms**
Web: www.wiveliscombe/whitetharthotel.com
Inn located in the centre of this small town

WOOKEY HOLE, WELLS
**Wookey Hole Inn**
Wookey Hole, Wells, Somerset, BA5 1PB
Tel: 01749 676677     **££ - P - 5 rooms**
Email: toadhall@lineone.net
Web: www.wookeyholeinn.com
Village Inn 3 miles from Wells

---

# The Royal Oak Inn

Winsford, Somerset TA24 7JE

**P - Rooms**

Tel: 01643 851455     Fax: 01643 851009
Email: enquires@royaloak-somerset.co.uk
Web: www.royaloak-somerset.co.uk

On the edge of Exmoor National Park in the centre of an ancient riverside village you will find a very charming place. Dating from the 12th Century and looking immaculate beneath a toupee of thatch, the attractive Royal Oak Inn and Hotel has been lovingly decorated and furnished, subtly combining open fireplace and oak beams with modern facilities.

YEOVIL
**White Horse Inn**
10 St Michaels Avenue, Yeovil,
Somerset BA21 4LB
Tel: 01935 476471 **£ - P - 3 rooms**
Popular local Inn within walking distance to
the town centre

# WILTSHIRE

BROAD CHALK, SALISBURY
**The Queens Head Inn**
1 North Street, Broad Chalke, Salisbury,
Wiltshire
Tel: 01722 780344 **££ - P - 4 rooms**
Village Inn 8 miles from Salisbury

CASTLE COMBE
**The Castle Inn**
Castle Combe, Wiltshire SN14 7HN
Tel: 01249 783030 **££ - P - 11 rooms**
Lovingly preserved 12th century Inn in the
lovely village of Castle Combe

CHISELDON, SWINDON
**Patriots Arms**
6 New Road, Chiseldon, Swindon,
Wiltshire SN4 0LU
Tel: 01793 740331 **£ - P rooms**
Village Inn 4 miles from Swindon

BOX, nr CORSHAM
**Queens Head**
High Street, Box, nr Corsham,
Wiltshire SN13 8NH
Tel: 01225 742340 **£ - Rooms**
Village Pub on the A4, 5 miles from Bath

COLLINGBOURNE DUCIS
**The Shears Inn**
The Cadley Road, Collingbourne Ducis,
Wiltshire SN8 3ED
Tel: 01264 850304 **££ - P - 6 rooms**
Rural country Inn located 12 miles from
Marlborough

BOX
**The Quarrymans Arms**
Boxhill, Box, Wiltshire SN13 8HN
Tel: 01225 743569 **£ - P - 2 rooms**
Inn and restaurant 2 miles from Corsham

BRADFORD-ON-AVON
**Plough Inn**
Bradford Liegh, Bradford-on-Avon, Wiltshire
Tel: 01225 862037 **£ - Rooms**
Country Inn 2 miles from Bradford-on-Avon

COMPTON BASSETT, CALNE
**White Horse Inn**
Compton Bassett, Calne, Wiltshire SN11 8RG
Tel: 01249 813118 **££ - P - 7 rooms**
Village Inn 15 miles from Marlborough

# The White Hart Hotel

*High Street, Cricklade, Wiltshire SN6 6AA*

**££ - P - R - BM - BG - C - 2 star - 15 rooms**

Tel: 01793 750206        Fax: 01793 750650
Email: bill@whitehart-cricklade.com
Web: www.whitehart-cricklade.com

Elizabeth I was Queen of England when The White Hart first opened its doors, it was then rebuilt in 1890. Even today, it still oozes late Victorian comfort whether you are staying overnight or just visiting the large, plush lounge.

All of our hotel rooms are clean, comfortable and equipped with a TV, telephone, hairdryer and tea and coffee making facilities. The White Hart boasts a fully licensed restaurant with a menu freshly prepared by our resident chef. Food is served either in the bar or restaurant between 12 pm until 2 pm and then in the evenings from 6:30 pm until 10 pm.
Single Room - £45.00 (Includes breakfast). Twin or Double - £60.00 or £45.00 single occupancy

CORTON, nr WARMINSTER
**Dove Inn**
Corton, nr Warminster, Wiltshire BA12 0SZ
Tel: 01985 850109        **££ - P - 4 rooms**
Email: info@thedove.co.uk
Web: www.thedove.co.uk
Village Pub in the heart of the Wylye Valley

CRICKLADE
**The White Hart Hotel**
See main entry above

CRICKLADE, SWINDON
**The White Lion**
50 High Street, Cricklade, Swindon,
Wiltshire SN6 6DA
Tel: 01793 750443        **££ - P - 5 rooms**
Email: info@whitelion-inn.com
Web: www.whitelion-inn.com
17th century village Inn

DINTON, SALISBURY
**The Penruddocke Arms**
Hindon Rd, Dinton, Salisbury, Wiltshire SP3 5EL
Tel: 01722 716253        **£ - P - 6 rooms**
Village Inn 6 miles from Salisbury

DOWNTON, nr SALISBURY
**The Bull Inn**
Downton, nr Salisbury, Wiltshire SP5 3HL

Tel: 01725 510374        **££ - P - Rooms**
Owned by local brewer Hopback. Local ales

FONTHILL, GIFFORD
**Beckford Arms**
Fonthill, Gifford, Wiltshire SP3 6PX
Tel: 01747 870385        **££ - P - 8 rooms**
Country Inn 12 miles from Salisbury

FOVANT, SALISBURY
**Penbroke Arms**
Fovant, Salisbury, Wiltshire SP3 5JH
Tel: 01722 714201        **£ - P - Rooms**
Email: mwillo@aol.com
Traditional Pub 10 miles from Salisbury

GREAT BEDWYN, MARLBOROUGH
**The Cross Keys Inn**
High Street, Great Bedwyn, Marlborough,
Wiltshire SN8 3NU
Tel: 01672 870678        **£ - P - 2 rooms**
Village Inn 5 miles from Marlborough

GREAT WISHFORD, NR SALISBURY
**The Royal Oak**
See main entry opposite

GRITTLETON, CHIPPENHAM
**Neeld Arms**
The Street, Grittleton, Chippenham,

# The Royal Oak

*Langford Road, Great Wishford, nr Salisbury, Wiltshire*

**£ - P - Rooms**

Tel: 01722 790079     Email: s.deschamps@btinternet.com

A beautiful ivy covered free house pub in a picturesque village and lovely part of the country The Inn has gorgeous rooms, character bar and a large restaurant. It is situated just 5 miles outside the historic city of Salisbury. Tariff single £25 ~ Double £50.

Wiltshire SN14 6AP
Tel: 01249 782470     **£ - P - 6 rooms**
Email: neeldarms@genie.co.uk
Web: www.neeldarms.co.uk
Village Inn 8 miles from Chippenham

## HAM, MARLBOROUGH
**Crown and Anchor**
Ham, Marlborough, Wiltshire SN8 3RB
Tel: 01488 668242     **£ - P - 2 rooms**
Village Inn 4 miles from Hungerford

## HEYTESBURY
**The Angel Inn**
High Street, Heytesbury, Wiltshire BA12 0ED
Tel: 01985 840330     **££ - P - 8 rooms**
Email: angelheytesbury@aol.com
Village coaching Inn 4 miles from Warminster

**The Red Lion Hotel**
42a High Street, Heytesbury, Warminster,
Wiltshire
Tel: 01985 840315     **£ - P - 3 rooms**
Village Inn set in beautiful countryside

## HIGHWORTH, SWINDON
**Fishes Inn**
10 Swindon Street, Highworth, Swindon,
Wiltshire SN6 7AH
Tel: 01793 763098     **£ - 3 rooms**
Four miles from Swindon

## HINDON
**The Angel Inn**
Hindon, Wiltshire SP3 6DJ
Tel: 01747 820696     **££ - P - 7 rooms**
Email: eat@theangel-inn.co.uk
Village Inn with restaurant

## KILMINGTON
**The Red Lion Inn**
Kilmington, Wiltshire BA12 6RP
Tel: 01985 844263     **£ - P - 2 rooms**
Village Inn 9 miles from Frome

## LACOCK
**Red Lion Inn**
1 High Street, Lacock, Wiltshire SN15 2LQ
Tel: 01249 730456     **££ - P - 6 rooms**
Tourist village Inn 5 miles from Chippenham

## LONGBRIDGE DEVERILL, WARMINSTER
**The George Inn**
Longbridge Deverill, Warminster,
Wiltshire BA12 7DG
Tel: 01985 840396     **££ - P - 10 rooms**
Web: www.thegeorgeinnlongbridgedeverill.co.uk
Busy village Inn 3 miles from Warminster

## LOWER CHICKSGROVE
**Compasses Inn**
Lower Chicksgrove, Wiltshire SP3 6NB
Tel: 01722 714318     **££ - P - 4 rooms**
Thatched Pub 10 miles from Salisbury

## MALMSBURY
**The Kings Arms Hotel**
High Street, Malmesbury, Wiltshire SN16 9AA
Tel: 01666 823383     **££ - 8 rooms**
Historic 16th century town centre hotel / Pub

## MALBOROUGH
**Horseshoe Inn**
Mildenhall, Marlborough, Wiltshire SN8 2LR
Tel: 01672 514725     **££ - P - 3 rooms**
Traditional Inn 2 miles from Marlborough

**The Lamb Inn**
The Parade, Marlborough, Wiltshire SN8 1NE
Tel: 01672 512668    **£ - 6 rooms**
Located 200 yards from the town centre

MELKSHAM
**Parsons Nose**
30 High Street, Melksham, Wiltshire SN12 6LA
Tel: 01225 702947    **£ - P - Rooms**
Town centre local

MELKSHAM
**Kings Arms Hotel**
Market Place, Melksham, Wiltshire SN12 6EX
Tel: 01225 707272    **££ - P - 10 rooms**
In the market place near the centre of town

MERE
**Butt of Sherry**
Castle Street, Mere, Wiltshire BA12 6JE
Tel: 01747 860352    **£ - P - 2 rooms**
Village local Pub 20 miles from Yeovil

**Old Ship Inn**
Castle Street, Mere, Wiltshire BA12 6JE
Tel: 01747 860258    **££ - P - 19 rooms**
Email: oldshiphotel@hotmail.com
16thC coaching Inn in the centre of Mere

MIDDLE WINTERLOW, SALISBURY
**Pheasant Hotel**
London Road, Middle Winterlow, Salisbury,
Wiltshire SP5 1BN
Tel: 01980 862374    **P - Rooms**
Large roadside Inn with restaurant

NORTH NEWNTON
**The Woodbridge Inn**
North Newnton, Wiltshire SN9 6JZ
Tel: 01980 630266    **£ - P - 4 rooms**
Email: thewoodbridge@btconnect.com
Country Pub 10 miles from Devizes

OGBOURNE ST ANDREW
**Wheatsheaf Inn**
Ogbourne St Andrew, Marlborough,
Wiltshire SN8 1RZ
Tel: 01672 841229    **£ - P - 3 rooms**
Village Inn 2 miles from Marlborough

OGBOURNE ST GEORGE,
MARLBOROUGH
**The Old Crown**
See main entry below

ORCHESTON, SALISBURY
**The Crown Inn**
Stonehenge Park, Orcheston, Salisbury,
Wiltshire SP3 4SH
Tel: 01980 620304    **£ - P - 2 rooms**
Email: stp@orcheston.freeserve.co.uk
Village Inn 12 miles from Salisbury

SALISBURY
**The Devizes Inn**
53 Devises Road, Salisbury, Wiltshire SP2 7LQ
Tel: 01722 327842    **£ - 4 rooms**
Situated 5 minutes walk from the town centre

**The White Horse Inn**
38 Castle Street, Salisbury, Wiltshire SP1 1BN

---

# The Old Crown

*Ogbourne St George, Marlborough, Wiltshire SN8 1SQ*

**P - 5 rooms**

Tel: 01672 841445    Fax: 01672 841056
Email: theinnwiththewell@compuserve.com
Web: www.theinnwiththewell.com

Set in the midst of the Ridgeway Path, Europe's oldest Highway, The Old Crown has been the Village Local for over 300 years as well as a Coaching Inn during the 17th Century. Our luxurious accommodation comprises of 4 purpose built Twin Rooms and 1 Double Room, all *en suite*, Colour TV, Hair dryer and Hospitality Tray.

Tel: 01722 327844    **£ - P - 10 rooms**
Quiet town Pub 5 minutes walk to the town
centre

## SALISBURY
**The Avon Brewery Inn**
75 Castle Street, Salisbury, Wiltshire SP1 3SP
Tel: 01722 416184    £ - 2 rooms
Friendly Pub 5 minutes walk to the centre

**Barford Inn**
Salisbury, Wiltshire SP3 4AB
Tel: 01722 742242    **££ - P - 4 rooms**
Email: ido@barfordinn.co.uk
Web: www.barfordinn.co.uk
Village Inn 6 miles from Salisbury

## SOUTHWICK, TROWBRIDGE
**Farmhouse Inn**
Frome Road, Southwick, Trowbridge, Wiltshire
BA14 9QD
Tel: 01225 764366    **£ - P - 3 rooms**
Village Inn with restaurant 1 mile from
Troubridge

## STAPLEFORD
**The Pelican Inn**
Warminster Rd, Stapleford, Wiltshire SP3 4LT
Tel: 01722 790241    **£ - P - 5 rooms**
Roadside village Pub located 8 miles from
Salisbury

## STEEPLE ASHTON, TROWBRIDGE
**Longs Arms Inn**
High Street, Steeple Ashton, Trowbridge,
Wiltshire BA14 6EU
Tel: 01380 870245    **£ - P - 2 rooms**
Web: www.stayatthepub.freeserve.co.uk
Village Inn 5 miles from Trowbridge

## STOURHEAD
**Spread Eagle Inn**
Stourhead, Wiltshire BA12 6QE
Tel: 01747 840587    **££ - P - 5 rooms**
Country Inn 10 minute walk to Stourhead

## TILSHEAD, SALISBURY
**The Black Horse Inn**
High St, Tilshead, Salisbury, Wiltshire SP3 4RY
Tel: 01980 620104    **£ - P - 4 rooms**
Rural village Inn 9 miles from Devizes

## UPTON LOVAL, WARMINSTER
**Prince Leopold**
Upton Lovell, Warminster, Wiltshire BA12 0JP
Tel: 01985 850460    **£ - P - 6 rooms**
Email: princeleopold@lineone.net
Web: www.princeleopoldinn.co.uk
Quiet riverside Inn just 5 miles from
Warminster

## WARMINSTER
**The Old Bell Inn**
42 Market Place, Warminster,
Wiltshire BA12 9AN
Tel: 01985 216611    **£ - P - 14 rooms**
Town centre Inn

## WINTERBOURNE MONKTON, SWINDON
**The New Inn**
Winterbourne Monkton, Swindon,
Wiltshire SN4 9NW
Tel: 01672 539240    **£ - P - 5 rooms**
Traditional Inn situated just 8 miles from
Swindon

## WROUGHTON, SWINDON
**Fox and Hounds**
1 Markham Road, Wroughton, Swindon,
Wiltshire SN4 9JT
Tel: 01793 812217    **££ - P - 8 rooms**
Inn at the edge of this large village

# Northern Ireland

## CO ANTRIM, ARMAGH, DOWN, FERMANAGH

## CO ANTRIM

### CARNLOUGH, BALLYMENA
**Bridge Inn (McAuleys)**
2 Bridge Street, Carnlough, Ballymena,
Co Antrim BT44 0ET
Tel: (028) 288 85669   **£ - 5 rooms**
Village Inn 15 miles from Ballymena and 12
miles from Larne

### CARRYDUFF, BELFAST
**Ivanhoe Inn**
Carryduff, Belfast, Co Antrim BT8 8EU
Tel: (028) 908 12240   **£££ - P - 23 rooms**
Email: info@ivanhoehotel.freeserve.co.uk
Inn / hotel with a public bar, 20minute drive to
Belfast centre

### CARNLOUGH
**Londonderry Arms Hotel**
20 Harbour Road, Carnlough, Co Antrim
Tel: (028) 2888 5255   **££ - P - 35 rooms**
Ivy clad Inn once owned by Winston Churchill.
Next to the Harbour

## CO ARMAGH

### LURGAN
**The Ashburn Hotel**
81 William St, Lurgan,
Co Armagh BT66 6JB
Tel: (028) 383 25711   **£ - P - 13 rooms**
Town centre hotel with a public bar

## CO DOWN

### BANBRIDGE
**Downshire Arms Hotel**
95 Newry Street, Banbridge,
Co Down BT32 3EF
Tel: (028) 406 62638   **££ - P - 9 rooms**
Web: www.downshirearms.com
Located in the town centre, lively bar

CASTLEWELLAN
**Chestnut Inn**
28–34 Lower Square, Castlewellan, Co Down
Tel: (028) 437 78247 **£ - P - 7 rooms**
Large Pub in the centre of town

CASTLE ESPIE
**Old School House Inn**
Castle Espie, 100 Ballydrain Comber,
Newtownards, Co Down BT23 6EA
Tel: (028) 975 41182 **££ - P - 12 rooms**
Web: www.theoldschoolhouse.com
Country Inn 10 miles from Belfast

CRAWFORDSBURN
**The Old Inn**
Crawfordsburn, Co Down
Tel: (028) 9185 3255 **££ - P - 32 rooms**
16th century Inn with open log fires, 5 miles
from Belfast

KILKEEL
**The Kilmorey Arms Hotel**
41 Greencastle Street, Kilkeel, Co Down
Tel: (028) 4176 2220 £ - P - 30 rooms
An Inn / hotel with "The Smugglers" public bar.
12 miles from Newry

PORTAFERRY
**Portaferry Hotel**
The Strand, Portaferry, Co Down
Tel: (028) 4272 8231 **££ - P - 14 rooms**
Waterside Inn on the Ards peninsula with an
award winning restaurant

**CO FERMANAGH**

ENNISKILLEN
**The Three Way Inn**
247 Ashwoods Flito, Enniskillen,
Co Fermanagh
Tel: 02866 327414 **££ - P - 4 rooms**
Country Pub 2 miles from Enniskillen

# Scotland

## BORDERS

DUNS
**White Swan Hotel**
31 Market Street, Duns, Borders
Tel: 01361 883338     **£ - P - 6 rooms**
In the centre of the small town of Duns

EARLSTON
**White Swan Hotel**
High Street, Earlston, Borders TD4 6DE
Tel: 01896 848249     **£ - P - 6 rooms**
Village Inn 12 miles from Galashiels, Ideal golf
/ fishing / hunting

EDDLESTON, nr PEEBLES
**Horse Shoe Inn**
Eddleston, nr Peebles, Borders EH45 8QP
Tel: 01721 730225     **££ - P - 7 rooms**
On the A703 20 miles south of Edinburgh

BONCHESTER BRIDGE, HAWICK
**Horse and Hound Inn**
Bonchester Bridge, Hawick, Borders TD9 8JN
Tel: 01450 860645     **££ - P - 10 rooms**
Email: rebecca.hope@themail.co.uk
300 year old coaching Inn 6 miles from
Hawick

BOSWELLS
**Buccleuch Arms Hotel**
The Green Street, Boswells, Borders TD6 0EW
Tel: 01835 822243     **£ - P - 19 rooms**
Email: bucchotel@aol.com
Web: www.buccleucharmshotel.co.uk
An old coaching Inn just 10 miles from
Galashiels

CARLOPS, nr PENICUIK
**Allan Ramsay Hotel**
Carlops, nr Penicuik, Borders,EH26 9NF
Tel: 01968 660258     **P - 6 rooms**
Country Inn 13 miles from Edinburgh

DENHOLM
**Fox and Hounds Inn**
Main Street, Denholm, Borders,TD8 8NU
Tel: 01450 870247     **£ - P - 3 rooms**
Country Inn on the A698, 5 miles from Hawick

GALASHIELS
**Abbotsford Arms**
63 Stirling Street, Galashiels, Borders TD1 1BY
Tel: 01896 752517     **££ - P - 14 rooms**
Email: abb2517@aol.com
Web: www.abbotsfordarms.co.uk
Family run Inn 32 miles south of Edinburgh

INNERLEITHEN
**Traquair Arms Hotel**
Traquair Road, Innerleithen, Borders EH44 6PD
Tel: 01896 830229     **££ - P - 15 rooms**
Email: traquairarms@scottishborders.com
Web: www.traquair-arms-hotel.co.uk
Hotel / Inn in a small country town 6 miles
from Peebles

LAUDER
**Lauderdale Hotel**
1 Edinburgh Road, Lauder, Borders TD2 6TW
Tel: 01578 722231     **££ - P - 10 rooms**
Email: enquiries@lauderdale-hotel.co.uk
Web: www.lauderdale-hotel.co.uk
Town Pub 25 miles from Edinburgh

SELKIRK
**Gordon Arms**
Selkirk, Borders TD7 5LE
Tel: 01750 82232      **£ - P - 6 rooms**
Email: thwgordonarms@aol.com
Very rural Inn 11 miles from Selkirk

ST MARY'S LOCH
**Tibbie Shiels Inn**
St Mary's Loch, Borders TD7 5LH
Tel: 01750 42231      **P - Rooms**
Web: www.tibbieshiels.co.uk
Old Loch side Inn

SWINTON
**Wheatsheaf Hotel**
Main Street, Swinton, Borders TD11 3JJ

Tel: 01890 860257      **££ - P - 7 rooms**
An award winning Inn that boasts excellent
food

TUSHIELAW
**Tushielaw Inn**
Tushielaw, Borders TD7 5HT
Tel: 01750 62205      **£ - 3 rooms**
A village Inn located about15 miles from
Selkirk

TWEEDSMUIR
**The Crook Inn**
Tweedsmuir, Borders ML12 6QN
Tel: 01899 880272      **££ - P - Rooms**
This is reputed to be the oldest Inn in
Scotland

# CENTRAL SCOTLAND

KIPPEN
**Cross Keys**
Main Street, Kippen, Central Scotland FK8 3DN
Tel: 01786 870293      **£ - P - 2 rooms**
Email: crosskeys@kitten70.fsnet.co.uk
Village Pub 10 miles from Stirling

**Crown Hotel**
Fore Road, Kippen, nr Stirling, Central
Scotland FK8 3DT
Tel: 01786 870216      **£ - P - 4 rooms**
A local village Inn situated about 10 miles
from Stirling

UDDERSTON, GLASGOW
**Ashley House**
720 Old Edinburgh View Park, Uddingston,
Glasgow, Central Scotland G71 6LE
Tel: 01698 815651      **£ - P - 9 rooms**
A busy local Pub located on the main road

# www.stayinapub.com

# DUMFRIES AND GALLOWAY

Village Inn with restaurant 15 miles from
Castle Douglas

## ISLE OF WHITHORN
**The Steam Packet Inn**
Harbour Row, Isle of Whithorn,
Dumfries and Galloway DG8 8LL
Tel: 01988 500334    **Rooms**
Email: steampacketinn@stcassect.com
Harbour-side Inn with accommodation

## CASTLE DOUGLAS
**Old Smugglers Inn**
Auchencairn, Castle Douglas, Dumfries and
Galloway DT7 1QU
Tel: 01556 640331    **£ - P - 3 rooms**
Inn with restaurant 8 miles from Castle Douglas

## CANOBIE
**Riverside Inn**
Canonbie, Dumfries and Galloway DG14 0UX
Tel: 01387 371512    **££ - P - 7 rooms**
Email: riverside@langholm.org
Traditional village Inn 12 miles from Carlisle

## CREE TOWN, NEWTON STEWART
**Barholm Arms**
St Johns Street, Cree Town, Newton Stewart,
Dumfries and Galloway DG8 5HP
Tel: 01671 820553    **£ - P - 5 rooms**
Coaching Inn 30 miles from Stranraer

## DALBEATTIE
**Pheasant Hotel**
1 Maxwell Street, Dalbeattie,
Dumfries and Galloway DG5 4AH
Tel: 01556 610345    **£ - Rooms**
Town centre Inn with restaurant

## DALRY, nr CASTLE DOUGLAS
**Clachan Inn**
10 Main Street, Dalry, nr Castle Douglas,
Dumfries and Galloway DG7 3UW
Tel: 01644 430241    **£ - P - 6 rooms**
Web: www.clachaninn.com

## KIRKCOWAN
**Craighlaw Arms Hotel**
23 Main Street, Kirkcowan, Dumfries and
Galloway DG8 0HQ
Tel: 01671 830283    **£ - P - 2 rooms**
Village Inn 7 miles from Newton Stewart

## LOCKERBIE
**Douglas House Courtyard**
See main entry opposite

## MOFFAT
**Allanton Hotel**
High Street, Moffat, Dumfrieshire DG10 9HL
Tel: 01683 220343    **£ - P - 7 rooms**
Town Inn and Pub

**Black Bull Inn**
Churchgate, Moffat, Dumfries and Galloway
DG10 9EG
Tel: 01683 220206    **£ - 12 rooms**
Village Inn close to the centre of Moffat

## PORTPATRICK
**Downshire Arms Hotel**
Main Street, Portpatrick, Dumfries and
Galloway DG9 8JJ
Tel: 01776 810300    **££ - 19 - rooms**
Situated by the quay in this fishing village

## PORT WILLIAM
**Monreith Arms Hotel**
3 The Square, Port William, Dumfries and
Galloway DG8 9SD

# Douglas House Courtyard

*Eaglesfield, Lockerbie, Dumfries and Galloway DG11 3PQ*

**£ - P - R - BM - BG - PW (kennels) - C 3 chalets**

Tel: 01461 500215

Email: mike@douglashouse.free-online.co.uk

Douglas House Courtyard

The Douglas House bar and restaurant is located just half a mile from M74 at J 20, 6 miles north of Gretna, and is the Ideal location for the one night stop off on your way to the Highlands or a base for the South of Scotland, Borders and the North of England.

All chalet rooms are complete with *en suite* showers, TV, kettle. There are also facilities for the disabled.

Average room price, Single £23.00 / Double £36.00 / Family room £40.00

Tel: 01988 700232    **Rooms**
Town Pub

### STRACHUR
**Creggans Inn**
Strachur, Dumfries and Galloway PA27 8BX
Tel: 01369 860279    **£££ - P - 14 rooms**
Country Inn 18 miles from Dunoon

### STRANRAER
**Arkhouse Inn**
17–21 Church Street, Stranraer,

Dumfries and Galloway DG9 7JG
Tel: 01776 703161    **£ - Rooms**
Town Pub

### WIGTOWN, NEWTON STEWART
**Bladnoch Inn**
Bladnoch Village, Wigtown,
Newton Stewart, Dumfries and
Galloway DG8 9AB
Tel: 01988 402200    **£ - P - 4 rooms**
Email: peter@bladnoch.freeserve.co.uk
Rural village Inn 1 mile from Wigtown

# FIFE

### CRAIL
**Croma Hotel**
33–35 Nethergate, Crail, Fife KY10 3TU
Tel: 01333 450239    **£ - P - 6 rooms**
Web: www.cromahotel.co.uk
In a small fishing village near to the harbour

### CUPAR
**Pitscottie Inn**
2 Ceres Road, Cupar, Fife KY15 5TD
Tel: 01334 828244    **£ - P - Rooms**
Country Pub / restaurant excellent for golfers

DOLLAR
**Castle Campbell Hotel**
11 Bridge Street, Dollar, Fife SK14 7DE
Tel: 01259 742519    **££ - P - 8 rooms**
Hotel / Pub on the main street

ELIE
**The Ship Inn**
The Toft, Elie, Fife KY9 1DT
Tel: 01333 330246    **£ - 6 rooms**
Email: info@shipelie.com
Village Inn that is a 20 minute drive to St
Andrews

INVERKEITHING
**Hat and Ribbon**
67–71 High Stt, Inverkeithing, Fife KY11 1NW
Tel: 01383 417616    **£ - P - 5 rooms**
Modern wine bar in the centre of town

LOWER LARGO
**Crusoe Hotel**
2 Main Street, Lower Largo, Fife KY8 6BT
Tel: 01333 320759    **££ - P - rooms**

Home of the real life Robinson Crusoe,
Alexander Selkirk

MARKINCH
**Town House Hotel**
1 High Street, Markinch, Fife KY7 6DQ
Tel: 01592 758459    **££ - 4 rooms**
Email: townhouse@aol.com
Inn with a restaurant and accommodation

NORTH QUEENSFERRY
**Ferrybridge Hotel**
1 Main St, North Queensferry, Fife KY11 1JO
Tel: 01383 416292    **££ - P - 6 rooms**
Village Pub located just 4 miles from
Dunfermline

SAINT ANDREWS
**Links Hotel**
Golf Place, Saint Andrews, Fife KY16 9JA
Tel: 01334 472059    **£££ - 6 rooms**
Web: www.golfplace.com
Local village Inn 5 minutes from the golf
course

# GRAMPIAN

ABERDEEN
**Dutch Mill Hotel**
7 Queen Street, Aberdeen, Grampian
Tel: 01224 322555    **££ - P - 9 rooms**
Town centre Inn with a public bar

**Ferryhill House Hotel**
169 Bonaccord Street, Aberdeen, Grampian
Tel: 01224 590867    **££ - P - 9 rooms**
5 miles from the city centre

ABOYNE
**Boat Inn**
Charlestown Road, Aboyne, Grampian
Tel: 01339 886137    **£ - P - self catering flat**
Email: boatinnltd@aol.com
Village Inn located about 30 miles from
Aberdeen

ABERCHIRDER
**Fife Arms Hotel**
The Square, Aberchirder,
Grampian AB54 5TA
Tel: 01466 780461    **£ - P - 3 rooms**
Villge Pub 8 miles fron Banff

BIELDSIDE
**Bieldside Inn**
37 North Deeside Road, Bieldside, Grampian
Tel: 01224 867891    **£ - P - 7 rooms**
Village Inn 5 miles from Aberdeen

ELLEN
**Ythan View Hotel**
Ellen, Grampian AB41 7DT
Tel: 01651 806235    **£ - P - 4 rooms**
Village Inn 8 miles from Ellen

FOCHABERS
**Gordon Arms Hotel**
80 High Street, Fochabers, Grampian IV32 7DH
Tel: 01343 820508    **££ - P - 14 rooms**
Former coaching Inn on the A96

JOHNSON
**Bird In Hand Hotel**
Beith Road, Johnson, Grampian
Tel: 01505 329222    **£ - P - 5 rooms**
Town hotel / Pub, 10 minutes from the centre

KEITH
**Grampian Hotel**
Regent Square, Keith, Grampian AB55 5DX
Tel: 01542 887342    **£ - 7 rooms**
Hotel and Pub on the outskirts of town

KILDRUMMY, ALFORD
**Kildrummy Inn**
Kildrummy, Alford, Grampian AB33 8QS
Tel: 01975 571227    **£ - P - 4 rooms**
Country Inn 10 miles from Alford

KINCARDINE
**Gordon Arms Hotel**
North Deeside Road, Kincardine, Grampian
Tel: 01339 884236    **££ - P - 6 rooms**
Village Inn 4 miles from Aboyne

LAURENCEKIRK
**Royal Hotel**
Laurencekirk, Grampian AB30 1AB
Tel: 01561 377487    **P - 4 rooms**
Village Inn 30 miles from Aberdeen

LOSSIEMOUTH
**Clifton Bar**
5 Clifton Rd, Lossiemouth, Grampian IV31 6DJ

Tel: 01343 812100    **£ - P - 5 rooms**
Water's edge Pub overlooking Moray Firth

MARYCULTER
**Old Mill Inn**
South Deeside Road, Maryculter, Grampian
Tel: 01224 733212    **£ - P - 7 rooms**
Old traditional Inn 7 miles from the centre of
Aberdeen

MARYKIRK, LAURENCEKIRK
**Marykirk Hotel**
Marykirk, Laurencekirk, Grampian AB30 1UT
Tel: 01674 840239    **Rooms**
Village Inn

MINTLAW
**Country Park Inn**
Station Road, Mintlaw, Grampian AB42 5ED
Tel: 01771 622622    **£ - P - 5 rooms**
Family friendly Pub in the village centre

PETERHEAD
**Palace Hotel**
Prince Street, Peterhead, Grampian AB42 1PL
Tel: 01779 474821    **££ - P - rooms**
Town centre Pub

ROTHES
**East Bank Hotel**
Rothes, Grampian AB38 7AU
Tel: 01340 831564    **P - 8 rooms**
Family village hotel and Pub

STRICHEN
**White Horse Hotel**
65 High Street, Strichen, Grampian AB43 6SQ
Tel: 01771 637218    **£ - P - 6 rooms**
Email: info@whhr.co.uk
Web: www.whhr.co.uk
Village Inn 7 miles from Fraserburgh

STRATHDON
**Allargue Arms**
Corgarff, Strathdon, Grampian AB36 8YP
Tel: 01975 651410    **P - 7 rooms**
Country Inn 32 miles from Alford

TURIFF
**Commercial Hotel**
Cuminestown, Turiff, Grampian AB53 5WJ

Tel: 01888 544205    **£ - P - 3 rooms**
Village Inn 30 miles from Aberdeen

TARLAND
**Aberdeen Arms Hotel**
The Square, Tarland, Grampian AB34 4TX
Tel: 01339 881225    **£ - P - 5 rooms**

Country Inn 32 miles from Aberdeen

TARVES
**Aberdeen Arms Hotel**
The Square, Tarves, Grampian AB41 0JX
Tel: 01651 851214    **£ - P - 2 rooms**
Country Pub 7 miles from Ellon

# HIGHLANDS

APPLECROSS
**Applecross Inn**
Shore Street, Applecross, Highlands IV54 8LR
Tel: 01520 744262    **£ - P - 5 rooms**
Ideal for climbers, walkers and bird watchers

AULDEARNS, NAIRN
**Covenanters Inn**
Auldearn, Nairn, Highlands IV12 5TG
Tel: 01667 452456    **£ - P - 14 rooms**
Country Inn 2 miles from Nairn

AULTBEA
**Aultbea Hotel**
Aultbea, Highlands IV22 2HX
Tel: 01445 731201    **££ - P - 8 rooms**
Village Inn deep in the country

AVIEMORE
**The Old Bridge Inn**
Dalfaber Rd, Aviemore, Highlands PH22 1PU
Tel: 01479 811137    **£ - P - Bunkhouse**

Email: nigel@highlandcateringresourses.co.uk
Country Inn just outside Aviemore

BALINTORE
**Balintore Hotel**
East Street. Balintore, Highlands IV20 1UA
Tel: 01862 832219    **£ - P - 4 rooms**
Village hotel 7 miles from Tain

BRORA
**Bayview Hotel**
Golf Road, Brora, Highlands
Tel: 01408 621206    **£ - P - 4 rooms**
Country hotel 30miles from Inverness

CONTIN, nr STRATHPEFFER
**Achilty Hotel**
Contin, nr, Strathpeffer, Highlands IV14 9EG
Tel: 01747 421355    **£ - P - 12 rooms**
300 year old coaching Inn, family run

EDDERTON, TAIN
**Ardmore Lodge Hotel**
Edderton, Tain, Highlands IV19 1LB
Tel: 01862 821266    **£ - P - 5 rooms**
Country Inn in Tain

EVANTON, ROSSHIRE
**Novar Arms Hotel**
Evanton, Rosshire, Highlands IV16 9UN
Tel: 01349 830210    **££ - P - Rooms**
Country Pub 17 miles north of Inverness

GAIRLOCH
**The Old Inn**
Gairloch, Highlands IV21 2BD

# Heathmount Hotel

*Kingsmill Road, Inverness, Highlands IV2 3JU*

**££ - P - Rooms**

Tel: +44 01463 235877    Fax: +44 01463 715749
Email: heathmount@cali.co.uk

The Heathmount Hotel is a friendly Highland Inn, dating back to 1868, situated in a residential area five minutes walk from the town centre, bus and train stations, Inverness Castle and the river Ness. Each room contains an *en suite* with a bath and shower, colour television, tea / coffee facilities and a fresh fruit basket provided daily. Private car parking available.
Single: £45.00 per night - Double / Twin: £32.50 per person per night

Tel: 01445 712006    **££ - P - 14 rooms**
Olde coaching Inn 76 miles from Inverness

## GLENELG
**Glenelg Inn**
Glenelg, Highlands IV40 8JR
Tel: 01599 522273    **££ - P - 7 rooms**
Web: www.glenelg.com
Cosy highland Inn on the coast

## HELMSDALE, SUTHERLAND
**Belgrave Arms Hotel**
Helmsdale, Sutherland, Highlands KW8 6JX
Tel: 01431 821242    **£ - P - 9 rooms**
Village Inn / hotel

## INVERNESS
**Heathmount Hotel**
See main entry above

## ISLE OF SKYE
**Ardvasar Hotel**
Ardvasar, Isle of Skye, Highlands IV45 8RS
Tel: 01471 844223    **££ - P - 10 rooms**
Remotely situated in "The Wild Garden of Skye" – breathtaking

**Caledonian Hotel**
Wentworth Street, Portree, Isle of Skye,
Highlands IV51 9EJ
Tel: 01478 612641    **£ - P - 8 rooms**
Central village hotel with a lively public bar

**Old Inn**
Carbost, Isle of Skye, Highlands IV47 8SR

Tel: 01478 640205    **£ - P - 6 rooms**
Village Inn with rooms and 24 bed bunkhouse

**Portree House**
Home Road, Portree, Isle of Skye,
Highlands IV51 9LX
Tel: 01478 613713    **£ - Rooms**
5 minutes walk to Portree square

## LOCHAILORT
**Lochailort Inn**
Lochailort, Highlands PH38 4LZ
Tel: 01687 470208    **££ - P - 10 rooms**
Email: annekeenan@lochailort.fsnet.uk
Very rural Inn 25 miles from Fort William

## NAIRN
**Albert Inn**
1 Albert Street, Nairn, Highlands 1VL 4HP
Tel: 01667 454474    **P - 8 rooms**
Village Inn 12 miles from Inverness

## NEWTONMORE, INVERCLYDE
**Braeriach Hotel**
Main Street, Newtonmore, Inverclyde,
Highlands PH20 1DA
Tel: 01540 673279    **£ - P - 12 rooms**
Located in this small town

## ONICH
**Loch Leven Hotel**
Old Ferry Road, Onich, Highlands PH33 6SA
Tel: 01855 821236    **£ - P - 10 rooms**
Near the Ballachulish Bridge on the north shore of Loch Leven

PLOCKTON
**The Plonkton Hotel**
Harbour Street, Plockton, Highlands IV52 8TN
Tel: 01599 544274     **££ - P - 14 rooms**
Beautiful views across Loch Carron

**Plockton Inn**
Innes Street, Plockton, Highlands IV52 8TW
Tel: 01599 544222     **£ - P - 9 rooms**
Email: info@stayatplocktoninn.co.uk
Village Inn

POOLEWE
**Poolewe Hotel**
Poolewe, Highlands IV22 2JX
Tel: 01445 781241     **£ - P - Rooms**
Centre of Poolewe village

ROY BRIDGE
**Roy Bridge Hotel**
Roy Bridge, Highlands PH31 4AN
Tel: 01397 712236     **£ - P – Bunkhouse**
Email: ianmac9551@aol.com
Rural hotel / bar / restaurant 14 miles from
Fort William, ideal for outdoor pursuits

THE CLUANIE
**Cluanie Inn**
The Cluanie, Highlands IV3 6YW
Tel: 01320 340228     **££ - P - 12 rooms**
Near Loch Claunie on the A87 miles from any-
where

TONGUE
**Ben Loyal Hotel**
Tongue, Highlands IV27 4XE

Tel: 01847 611216     **££ - P - 10 rooms**
Country Inn by the sea just 40 miles from
Thurso

TORE
**Kilcoy Arms**
Tore, Highlands IV6 7RZ
Tel: 01463 811285     **£ - P - 3 rooms**
Country Inn near Inverness, mountains and
sea

ULLAPOOL
**Ferry Boat Inn**
Shore Street, Ullapool, Highlands,IV26 2UJ
Tel: 01854 612366     **££ - 9 rooms**
Village Inn in the centre of Ullapool

ULLAPOOL
**Altnaharrie Inn**
Ullapool, Highlands IV26 2SS
Tel: 01854 633230     **8 rooms**
Park in Ullapool and take the ferry across Loch
Broom.  Fantastic

**Arch Inn**
10–11 West Shore Street, Ullapool,
Highlands IV26 2UR
Tel: 01854 612454     **£ - P - 10 rooms**
Village Inn 60 miles from Inverness

WHITEBRIDGE, INVERNESS
**Whitebridge Hotel**
Whitebridge, Inverness, Highlands
Tel: 01456 486226     **£ - P - 12 rooms**
Web: www.whitebridgehotel.co.uk
Remote country Inn 25 miles from Inverness

# LOTHIAN

CHAMPANY, LINLITHGOW
**Champany Inn**
Champany, Linlithgow, Lothian EH49 7LU
Tel: 01506 834532     **£££ - P - 16 rooms**
Email: reception@champany.com
Located on the outskirts of Linlithgow

COLINTON, EDINBURGH
**Colinton Inn**
12 Bridge Street, Colinton, Edinburgh, Lothian
Tel: 01314 413218 **£ - 1 Flat**
5 minutes from Edinburgh town centre

DIRLTON, nr BERWICK
**Castle Inn**
Dirleton, nr North Berwick, Lothian EH39 5EP
Tel: 01620 850221 **££ - P - 8 rooms**
Village Inn ideal for golfers 3 miles from North Berwick

EAST LINTON
**Bridgend Hotel**
3 Bridgend, East Linton, Lothian ES40 3AF
Tel: 01620 860202 **£ - 6 rooms**
Country hotel / Inn 6 miles from North Berwick

EDINBURGH
**Ardmillan Hotel**
Ardmillan Terrace, Edinburgh,
Lothian EH11 2JW

Tel: 01313 379588 **££ - P - 10 rooms**
City centre Pub

LIVINGSTON
**Livingston Inn**
Charlesfield Lane, Livingston,
Lothian EH54 7AJ
Tel: 01506 413054 **££ - P - 12 rooms**
Town centre Inn

SOUTH QUEENSFERRY
**Hawes Inn**
Newmalls Road, South Queensferry,
Lothian EH30 9TA
Tel: 01313 311990 **£ - P - 14 rooms**
Village Inn on the Forth shore 9 miles from Edinburgh

UPHALL
**Oatridge Hotel**
2–4 East Main St, Uphall, Lothian AH52 5DA
Tel: 01506 856465 **£ - P - Rooms**
Village hotel and bar just 2 miles from Livingstone

# ORKNEY, SHETLAND AND WESTERN ISLANDS

**ORKNEY ISLANDS**

DOUNBY
**Smithfield Hotel**
Dounby, Orkney Islands KW17 2HT
Tel: 01856 771215 **££ - P - 7 rooms**
Web: www.orkneyhotels.co.uk
Village / country Inn 9 miles from Stromness

SANDAY ISLAND
**Kettletoft Hotel**
Sanday Island, Orkney Islands KW17 2BJ
Tel: 01857 600217 **£ - P - 6 rooms**
Email: tim@kettletofthotel.freeserve.co.uk
Web: www.kettletofthotel.co.uk
Located in the village on this small island

SAINT MARGARETS HOPE
**Belle Vue Hotel**
Saint Margarets Hope, Orkney Islands KW17 2SL
Tel: 01856 831383 **£ - 5 rooms**
Located 15 miles from Kirkwall

**Murray Arms Hotel**
Back Road, Saint Margarets Hope, Orkney Islands KW17 2SP
Tel: 01856 831205 **5 rooms**
Island village Inn

**STROMNESS**
**Ferry Inn Hotel**
John St, Stromness, Orkney Islands KW16 1DN
Tel: 01856 850280      **££ - P - 12 rooms**
Harbourside Inn

**VIRSAY**
**Barony Hotel**
Virsay, Orkney Islands KW17 2LS
Tel: 01856 721327      **£ - 10 rooms**
Island country Pub and hotel

Shetlands

Lerwick

**SHETLAND ISLANDS**

**HASWICK**
**Barclay Arms Hotel**
Haswick, Shetland Islands ZE2 9HL
Tel: 01950 431226      **£ - 6 rooms**
Island village Pub

Stornaway

Rodel
Lochmaddy

Lochboisdale

Castlebay

**WESTERN ISLANDS**

**POLOCHAR, LOCHBOISDALE**
**Polochar Inn**
Polochar, Lochboisdale, Western Islands
Tel: 01878 700215      **££ - P - 11 rooms**
Country Inn 15 miles from Lochboisdale

# STRATHCLYDE, AYRSHIRE, ARGYLE AND BUTE

Oban  • Dalmally

Lochgilphead

Rothesay

Port Ellen

Whiting
Bay

Campbeltown

**ARDFERN**
**The Galley of Lorne Inn**
See main entry opposite

**CLACHAN-SEIL**
**Tigh and Truish Inn**
Clachan-Seil, Strathclyde PA34 4QZ
Tel: 01852 300242      **£ - P - 2 rooms**
Rural country Pub 12 miles from Oban

**CROSS HOWE**
**Portland Arms**
24 Kilmarnock Road, Cross Howe, Strathclyde
Tel: 01563 522337      **£ - Rooms**
Village Inn 4 miles from Kilmarnock

# Galley of Lorne

*Ardfern, Nr Lochgilphead, Argyll PA31 8QN*

**££ - P - 7 rooms**

Tel: 01852 500 284
Email: galleyoflorne@aol.com

Originally an 18th Century Droving Inn, the Galley has maintained its character and atmosphere while benefiting from modern comforts and facilities. There are seven warm, comfortable *en suite* bedrooms, most with stunning views of the Loch. All public rooms, and bed rooms, are located on the ground floor.

The renowned restaurant offers meals prepared with fresh, local produce coupled with friendly, efficient service. Come and sample some cask malts and real ales alongside local characters and visiting yachtsmen from the nearby marina and you're bound to hear a legend or two!

# The Royal Hotel

*Girvan, South Ayrshire, Strathclyde KA26 9HE*

**£ - P - BR - BG - PW - C - 2 star STB - 7 rooms**

Tel: +44 (0)1465 714203
Email: info@royalhotelgirvan.com
Web: www.royalhotelgirvan.com/

The royal hotel is located on the West Coast of Scotland in an area of outstanding and largely unspoiled natural beauty. A five-minute walk from our door will bring you to the charming and picturesque Girvan harbour and miles of clean, sandy shore.

Ayrshire is the birthplace of the Open Championship, with courses at Troon, Turnberry, and the site of the first British Open at Prestwick. Five of our seven bedrooms have en suite facilities, and most have views over the town to the Firth of Clyde and Ailsa Crag.

DALRYMPLE
**The Kirkton Inn**
1 Main St, Dalrymple, Strathclyde KA6 6DF
Tel: 01292 560241      **££ - P - 11 rooms**
Email: captainn@btclick.com
Web: www.thekirktoninn.co.uk
Close to the centre of Dalrymple

GATEHEAD, nr KILMARNOCH, AYRSHIRE
**Old Rome Farmhouse**
Gatehead, nr Kilmarnock, Ayrshire, Strathclyde
Tel: 01563 850265      **£ - P Rooms**
Country Pub 3 miles from Kilmarnock

GIRVAN
**Ailsa Craig Hotel**
29 Old Street, Girvan, Ayrshire,
Strathclyde KA26 9HG
Tel: 01465 713754      **£ - P - 10 rooms**
Town hotel with bar and restaurant

**The Royal Hotel**
See main entry above

GLASGOW
**Cathedral House Hotel**
28 - 32 Cathedral Square, Glasgow,
Strathclyde G4 0XA

Tel: 01415 523519 **££ - P - 8 rooms**
Small hotel and bar with a restaurant 10 minutes walk from the town centre

**IRVINE**
**Eglinton Arms Hotel**
112–114 High Street, Irvine, Ayrshire,
Strathclyde KA12 8AH
Tel: 01294 278553 **P - 4 rooms**
Town centre Pub

**ISLE OF ARRAN**
**The Breadalbane Hotel**
See main entry below

**ISLE OF ISLAY**
**Harbour Inn**
The Square, Bowmore, Isle of Islay,
Strathclyde PA43 7JR
Tel: 01496 810330 **££ - P - 7 rooms**
Located in Bowmore, the main island village

**ISLE OF MULL**
**Bellachroy Hotel**
Dervaig, nr Tobermory, Isle of Mull,
Strathclyde PA75 6QW
Tel: 01688 400314 **£ - P - 7 rooms**
Lochside village Inn 1 mile from Tobermory

**KILBERRY, BY TARBERT**
**The Kilberry**
See main entry opposite

**LESMAHAGOW**
**Craignethan Hotel**
69 Abbey Green, Lesmahagow,
Strathclyde ML11 0EF
Tel: 01555 892333 **£ - P - 3 rooms**
Village Inn 15 miles from Hamilton

**LOCH LONG, ARDENTINNY**
**Ardentinny Hotel**
Loch Long, Ardentinny, Strathclyde PA23 8TR
Tel: 01369 810209 **££ - P - 9 rooms**
Country Inn 12 miles from Dunoon

**MAIDENS CULZEAN, AYRSHIRE**
**Ardlochan Hotel**
Maidens Culzean, Ayrshire,
Strathclyde KA19 8LA
Tel: 01655 760254 **£ - P - 5 rooms**
Country Pub with a caravan site

**MAUCHLINE, AYRSHIRE**
**Poosie Nansies Inn**
21 Londoun, Mauchline, Ayrshire, Strathclyde
Tel: 01290 550316 **Rooms**
Country Inn 6 miles from Ayr and Kilmarnock

**MILTON, DUMBARTON**
**Milton Inn**
Milton, Dumbarton, Strathclyde G82 2TD
Tel: 01389 761401 **£ - P - 14 rooms**
Email: hfilshie@aol.com
Village Inn 3 miles from Dumbarton

# The Breadalbane Hotel

*Kildonan, Isle of Arran KA27 8SE*

**£ - P - 5 rooms + 4 flats**

Tel / Fax: 01770 820284
Email: yvonne@breadalbanehotel.co.uk
Web: www.breadalbanehotel.co.uk

The Breadalbane Hotel is a warm and friendly coastal Inn with superb views of the Islands of Pladda and Ailsa Craig. In the quiet, picturesque, coastal village of Kildonan the Breadalbane attracts both locals and visitors alike to enjoy real ales and fine whiskies as well as excellent home cooked meals using fresh local ingredients.

All the rooms are finished to a high standard with *en suite*, colour TV, hair dryer, tea / coffee making facilities and little extras to make your stay more comfortable.

# Kilberry Inn

*Kilberry, by Tarbert, Argyll PA29 6YD*

**P - 3 rooms**

Tel: 01880 770223
Email: relax@kilberryinn.com
Web: www.kilberryinn.com

The Kilberry Inn, an original 'but n ben' cottage, was renovated some 17 years ago and trans-
formed into a quality hostelry with restaurant and letting bedrooms, exuding charm and character with some of the best home cooking in Argyll. It is a place of Award Winning food (winners
of "The Macallan Taste of Scotland Award for Best Bar Meal 2002"), friendly service, a warm
Scottish welcome and simple pleasures, a place to satisfy the most discerning guests and din-
ers, a place where above all you can relax and feel at home.

The Kilberry Inn offers cosy *en suite* bedrooms (two double and one twin) with the full range of
modern facilities, colour TV and coffee and tea making facilities, and is an ideal base for exploring the natural beauties of Kintyre and mid-Argyll.

NEWARTHILL, by MOTHERWELL
**Silverburn Hotel**
2 Loadhead Road, Newarthill, by Motherwell,
Strathclyde
Tel: 01698 732503     **£ - P - 6 rooms**
Village Pub 15 minute drive to Glasgow

PORT APPIN
**Macdonald Arms Hotel**
Port Appin, Strathclyde PA38 4BP
Tel: 01631 740219     **£ - P - Rooms**
Email: enquiries@mcdonaldarms.com
Also has a chalet £40.00 per night

# TAYSIDE AND PERTHSHIRE

ABERNETHY
**Crees Inn**
Main Street, Abernethy, Tayside PH2 91A
Tel: 01738 850714     **£ - P - 3 rooms**
Village Inn 9 miles from Perth

AMULREE, by DUNKELD
**Amulree Hotel**
Amulree, by Dunkeld, Tayside PH8 0EF
Tel: 01350 725218     **P - 12 rooms**
Country Inn 10 miles from Dunkeld

AUCHTERARDER
**Craigrossie Hotel**
1 High Street, Auchterarder, Tayside PH3 1DF
Tel: 01764 662458     **£ - P - 4 rooms**
Village Inn 14 miles from Perth

BALQUHIDDER, LOCHEARN HEAD
**Monachyle Mhor Hotel**
Balquhidder, Lochearn Head, Tayside FK19 8PQ

Tel: 01877 384622    **Rooms**
Countryside Inn

### BIRNHAM, DUNKELD
**Oak Inn and Birnam House Hotel**
Perth Rd, Birnam, Dunkeld, Tayside PH8 0BQ
Tel: 01350 727699    **££ - P - 6 rooms**
Hotel and Pub next door to each other, 12
miles from Perth

### BRIDGE OF EARN
**Cyprus Inn**
Back Street, Bridge of Earn, Tayside PH2 9AB
Tel: 01738 812313    **£ - P - 4 rooms**
17th century village coaching Inn

### BRIDGEND, CALLANDER
**Bridgend House Hotel**
Bridgend, Callander, Tayside FK17 8AH
Tel: 01877 330130    **£ - P - 5 rooms**
Small town Pub 400 yards from the centre

### BURRELTON
**The Burrelton Park Inn**
High Street, Burrelton, Tayside PH13 9NX
Tel: 01828 670206    **£ - P - 5 rooms**
Country village Pub 10 miles from Perth

### DUNDEE
**Downfield Inn**
530 Strathnarthine Road, Dundee, Tayside
Tel: 01382 826633    **P - Rooms**
Local traditional Pub

### FORFAR
**Plough Inn**
48 Market Street, Forfar, Tayside, DD8 3EW
Tel: 01307 462006    **£ - Rooms**
Inn on the outskirts of Forfar

**Queens Hotel**
12–14 The Cross, Forfar, Tayside DD8 1BX
Tel: 01307 462533    **Rooms**
Family run town hotel with public bar

### FORTINGALL
**Fortinghall Hotel**
Fortingall, Tayside
Tel: 01887 830367    **£ - P - 10 rooms**
Country hotel with a public bar 8 miles from
Aberfeldy

### GLEN, by TAYSIDE
**Foulford Inn**
Glen, by Tayside PH7 3LN
Tel: 01764 652407    **£ - P - 9 rooms**
Country Inn with a golf course 5 miles from
Criess

### GLENDEVON
**The Tormaukin**
See main entry opposite

### GLENFARG
**The Bein Inn**
Glenfarg, Tayside PH2 9PY
Tel: 01577 830216    **£ - P - 11 rooms**
Email: inquiries@beininn.com
Set in a wooded glen 10 minute drive into
Perth

### INVERKELLER, nr ARBROTH
**Chance Inn**
Main Street, Inverkeller, nr Arbroath, Tayside
Tel: 01241 830308    **£ - P - 4 rooms**
An Inn with a restaurant 8 miles from Arbroath

### KINROSS
**The Muirs Inn Kinross**
See main entry opposite

### JOHNSHAVEN
**Anghor Hotel**
New Road, Johnshaven, by Montrose,
Tayside DT10 0HD
Tel: 01561 362288    **£ - 2 rooms**
Fishing village 7 miles from Montrose

### LAWERS, ABERFELBY
**Ben Lawers Hotel**
Lawers, Aberfelby, Tayside PH15 2PA
Tel: 01567 820436    **£ - P - 4 rooms**
Small village hotel and bar

### MEIKLEOUR
**Meikleour Hotel**
Meikleour, Tayside PH2 6EB
Tel: 01250 883206    **Rooms**
Village Inn

### MONIFIETH
**Monifieth House Hotel**
8 Albert Street, Monifieth, Tayside DD5 4JS

# The Tormaukin Hotel

*Glendevon, Perthshire FK14 7JY*

**P - Rooms**

Tel: 01259 781252
Email: enquiries@tormaukin.co.uk
Web: www.tormaukin.co.uk

All the Olde Worlde charm with all the modern comforts.

This Idyllic 18th Century Hostelry offers a very warm welcome, comfortable accommodation, varied menus using the finest Scottish local produce, fine wines and real ales, all in a relaxed pub atmosphere.

Ideal base for golfing, fishing and other country pursuits – see web site for details.

---

# The Muirs Inn

*49 Muirs Kinross, Perth and Kinross, Tayside KY13 8AS*

**P - 5 rooms**

Tel: 01577 862270
Email: themuirsinn@aol.com

Situated in the historical market town of Kinross in the heart of the Golf and Whiskey region of this wonderful part of Scotland.

The Muir Inn Kinross has an award winning Malting Restaurant with Scottish culinary cuisine, Mash Tun Bar and five unique character filled *en suite* bedrooms to make your stay friendly and welcoming.

---

Tel: 01382 532630  **Rooms**
Town bar

MOULIN
**The Moulin Hotel**
See main entry on page 200

MUTHILL
**Commercial Hotel**
11 Grumond Street, Muthill, Tayside PH5 2AN
Tel: 01764 681263  **£ - P - 3 rooms**
Traditional village coaching Inn

PERTH
**Cherrybank Inn**
210 Glascow Road, Perth, Tayside PH2 0NA

Tel: 01738 624349  **£ - P - 7 rooms**
City centre Pub

PITLOCHRY
**Ballinluig Inn**
Pitlochry, Tayside PH9 0LG
Tel: 01796 482242  **£ - P - 8 rooms**
A local village Inn situated just 4 miles from Pitlochry

WEEM
**Ailean Chraggan**
Weem, Tayside PH15 2LD
Tel: 01887 820346  **££ - P - 5 rooms**
Overlooking the Tay, the bar boasts many fine malt whiskies

# The Moulin Hotel

*11–13 Kirkmichael Road, Moulin, Pitlochry,
Tayside PH16 5EW*

**£ - P - R - BM - BG - C - 3 star STB - 15 rooms**

Tel: 01796 472196      Fax: 01796 477098
Email: enquiries@moulinhotel.co.uk
Web: www.pitlochryhotels.co.uk/moulinhotel

The hotel boasts 15 very comfortable *en suite* rooms, with TV and beverage tray, at the incredibly reasonable price of £25.00 per person per night – special breaks start at £15.00 pppn. The Moulin Hotel, with its own brewery, is perfectly sited in the village square of Moulin; the hotel is just three quarters of a mile from the bustling town of Pitlochry. It is possible to travel quickly to both east and west coasts and the Cairngorms, Speyside, Fife and Edinburgh are all within easy reach.

The Moulin Hotel Brewery was established by hotelier Chris Tomlinson, in the summer of 1995, "Brewing our own beer was a way of enhancing the heritage of the hotel," says Chris. The average output of Moulin is around 500 barrels per year.

The food is sensibly priced and available between 11 am–9.30 pm. The Garden restaurant is open for all the family and overlooks the pretty grounds and burn.

# Wales
## CLWYD

Tel: 01691 718896    **£ - P - 9 rooms**
Village Inn 6 miles from Chirk

## HAWARDEN, DEESIDE
**Glynne Arms**
Glynne Way, Hawarden, Deeside,
Clwyd CH5 3NS
Tel: 01244 520323    **£ - P - 4 rooms**
Village Inn 3 miles from Queensferry, ideal
rooms for contractors

## ABERGELE
**Bull Hotel**
Chapel Street, Abergele, Clwyd
Tel: 01745 832115    **£ - P - 5 rooms**
Town Pub 10 miles from Llandudno

## BABELL
**Black Lion Inn**
Babell, Clwyd CH8 8PZ
Tel: 01352 720239    **££ - P - 2 rooms**
Village Inn 4 miles from Carney

## BRETTON
**Glynne Arms**
Chester Road, Bretton, Clwyd CH4 0DH
Tel: 01244 660277    **£ - P - 5 rooms**
Village Inn 2 miles from Chester

## CYNWYD, CORWEN
**Blue Lion Hotel**
Cynwyd, Corwen, Clwyd LL21 0LE
Tel: 01490 412106    **£ - P - 1 room**
Located in the centre of Cynwed

## DENBIGH
**The Bull Hotel**
See main entry on page 202

## GLYN CEIRIOG, LLANGOLLEN
**Glyn Valley Hotel**
Glyn Ceiriog, Llangollen, Clwyd LL20 7EU

## LLANARMON DYFRYN, CEIRIOG
**West Arms**
Llanarmon Dyfryn, Ceiriog, Clwyd LL20 7LD
Tel: 01691 600665    **£££ - P - 17 rooms**
Email: bookings@thewestarms.co.uk
Traditional village Inn / restaurant 13 miles
from Oswestry

## LLANBEDR DUFFRYN, RUTHIN
**Griffin Inn**
Llanbedr Duffryn, Ruthin, Clwyd LL15 1UP
Tel: 01824 702792    **£ - P - 3 rooms**
Country Inn 2 miles from Ruthin

## LLANDDULAS
**Dulas Arms Hotel**
Abergele Road, Llanddulas, Clwyd LL22 8HP
Tel: 01492 515747    **P - 5 rooms**
Village Inn 4 miles from Colwyn Bay

## LLANDUDNO
**Alexandra Hotel**
Clonmel Street, Llandudno, Clwyd  LL30 2LG
Tel: 01492 876670    **£ - P - 9 rooms**
Local town Pub with restaurant

## LLANFERRES, MOLD
**The Druid Inn**
Ruthin Rd, Llanferres, Mold, Clwyd CH7 5SN
Tel: 01352 810225    **££ - P - 4 rooms**
**+ 1 apartment**
Local village Inn 8 miles from Mold

**LLANFWROG, RUTHIN**
**Ye Olde Cross Keys**
Llanfwrog, Ruthin, Clwyd LL15 2AD
Tel: 01824 705281     **£ - P - 3 rooms**
Village Inn 1 mile from Ruthin

**HORSHOE PASS, LLANGOLLEN**
**The Famous Britannia Inn**
Horseshoe Pass, Llangollen, Clwyd LL20 8DW
Tel: 01978 860144     **££ - P - 7 rooms**
Village Inn 2 miles from LLangollen

**LLANGOLLEN**
**Smithfield Hotel**
Berwyn Street, Llangollen, Clwyd
Tel: 01978 860107     **Rooms**
Good food and fine ales

**Wynstay Arms Hotel**
Bridge Street, Llangollen, Clwyd LL20 8PF
Tel: 01978 860710     **Rooms**
Email: bill@wynstayllan.demon.co.uk
Traditional Pub with good food and ales

**LLANNEFYDD, nr DENBIGH**
**The Hawk and Buckle Inn**
LLannefydd, nr Denbigh, Clwyd LL16 5ED
Tel: 01745 540249     **££ - P - 10 rooms**
17th century coaching Inn set between
Denbigh and Abergele

MARFORD
**Trevor Arms Hotel**
Marford, Clwyd LL12 8TA

Tel: 01244 570436     **£ - P - 29 rooms**
19th century coaching Inn, scene of public
hangings

**MILWR, HOLYWELL**
**Glan Yr Afon**
Milwr, Holywell, Clwyd CH8 8HE
Tel: 01352 710052     **£ - P - 7 rooms**
Situated in a Hamlet just 1 mile from Holywell

**PENTREFOELAS**
**Foelas Arms Hotel**
Pentrefoelas, Clwyd LL24 0HW
Tel: 01690 770213     **£ - P - 9 rooms**
Village Inn / hotel 6 miles from Betws-y-Coed

**RHYDLYDAN, BETWS-Y-COED**
**Giler Arms Hotel**
Rhydlydan, Betws-y-Coed, Clwyd LL24 0LL
Tel: 01690 770612     **£ - P - 7 rooms**
Located between Conwy and Porthmadog

**RHYL**
**Windsor Vaults**
41 Kinmel Street, Rhyl, Clwyd LL18 1AJ
Tel: 01745 353117     **£ - P - 8 rooms**
Small local Pub near the town centre

**ROSSET, WREXHAM**
**Golden Lion Hotel**
Chester Road, Rosset, Wrexham,
Clwyd LL12 0HN
Tel: 01244 571020     **£ - P - 4 rooms**
Village Pub 6 miles from Chester

# DYFED

## BONCATH
**Ffynone Arms**
New Chapel, Boncath, Dyfed SA37 0EH
Tel: 01239 841800    **£ - P - 4 rooms**
Village Inn with restaurant 5 miles from
Cardigan

## BRECHFA
**Forest Arms**
Brechfa, Dyfed
Tel: 01267 202339    **£ - P - 4 rooms**
Village Inn 12 miles from Carmarthen

## CAIO, LLANWRDA
**Brunant Arms**
Caio, Llanwrda, Dyfed SA19 8RB
Tel: 01558 650483    **£ - P - 4 rooms**
Village 12 miles from Carmarthen

## CARMARTHEN
**Castle Hotel**
Priory Street, Carmarthen, Dyfed SA31 1LR
Tel: 01267 233735    **£ - P - 3 rooms**
Town centre Pub

**Drovers Arms**
103 Lammas Street, Carmarthen,
Dyfed SA31 8SA
Tel: 01267 237646    **£ - P - 11 rooms**
Town centre Pub

**Rose and Crown Hotel**
115–116 Lammas Street, Carmarthen, Dyfed
Tel: 01267 237712    **£ - 6 rooms**
Located in the centre of town

## CWMDUAD, CARMARTHEN
**Yr Afon Duad Inn**
See main entry on page 204

## HUNDLETON
**Highgate Inn Hotel**
See main entry on page 204

## LLANARTHNEY
**Golden Grove Arms**
Llanarthney, Dyfed SA32 8JU
Tel: 01558 668551    **£ - P - 6 rooms**
Village Inn 8 miles from Carmarthen

## LLANDDEWI-BREFI, TREGARON
**New Inn**
Llanddewi - Brefi, Tregaron, Dyfed SY25 6RS
Tel: 01974 298452    **£ - P - 4 rooms**
Country Inn located about 3 miles from
Tregaron

## LLANDEILO
**White Hart Inn**
34 Carmarthen Road, Llandeilo,
Dyfed SA19 6RS
Tel: 01558 823419    **£ - P - 11 rooms**
Located just outside of Llandeilo 15 miles
from Carmarthen

## LLANFYNYDD, CARMARTHEN
**Farmers Arms**
Llanfynydd, Carmarthen, Dyfed SA32 7TG
Tel: 01558 668291    **£ - P - 2 rooms**
Country Inn 14 miles from Carmarthen

## LLANGRARNOG, LLADDYSUL
**Pentre Arms Hotel**
Llangrarnog, Lladdysul, Dyfed SA44 6SW
Tel: 01239 654345    **£ - P - rooms**
Seaside Pub almost on the beach

# A Fon-Duad Inn

*Cwmduad, Carmarthen, Carmarthenshire SA33 6XJ*

**£ - P - Rooms**

Tel / Fax: +44(0)1267 281357
Email: info@afonduad.com          Web: www.afonduad.com

Yr Afon Duad Inn is a friendly Inn in the small village of Cwmduad which is about 8 miles north west of Carmarthen on the A484, the main road from Carmarthen to Cardigan. Cwmduad is in the heart of the beautiful Teify Valley.

Gareth and Bet pride themselves on the superb range of top quality local, organic food served in the restaurant, and on the comfort of the accommodation which is available throughout the year at extremely competitive rates, either at the Inn itself or in an adjoining property, Dolau Cottage. The cottage will accommodate up to 6 guests, making it attractive to large families and groups, or those guests desiring a little more privacy. Contact us for tariff.

# Highgate Inn Hotel

*Hundleton, Pembroke SA17 5RD*

**££ - P - 5 rooms**

Tel: 01646 685904          Fax: 01646 681888
Email: windy.gail@virgin.net

The Highgate Inn Hotel is nestled in the quaint village of Hundleton, just two miles from the historic Norman town of Pembroke. The Hotel offers five newly refurbished, high quality, non-smoking ensuite double bedrooms complete with TV, tea / coffee making facilities.

LLECHRYD, CARDIGAN
**Carpenters Arms**
Llechryd, Cardigan, Dyfed SA43 2NT
Tel: 01239 682692     **P - 3 rooms**
Village Pub 3 miles from Cardigan

LLSTANDWELL
**Ferry House Inn**
Hazle Beach, Llstandwell, Dyfed SA3 1ET
Tel: 01646 600270     **£ - P - 6 rooms**
Village Inn 6 miles from Haverford West

MARLOES, HAVERFORD WEST
**Lobster Pot Inn**
Marloes, Haverford West, Dyfed SA62 3AZ
Tel: 01646 636233     **£ - P - 3 rooms**
Large country Inn with restaurant 8 miles from Milford Haven

NARBERTH
**Ivy Bush Inn**
5 High Street, Narberth, Dyfed SA67 7AR
Tel: 01834 860679     **£ - P - 3 rooms**
Located near the town centre

NEVERN
**Trewern Arms**
Nevern, Dyfed SA42 0NB
Tel: 01239 820395     **£ - P - 10 rooms**
Village Inn on the banks of the river 3 miles from Newport

NEWPORT
**Castle Hotel**
Bridge Street, Newport, Dyfed SA42 0TB
Tel: 01239 820742     **£ - P - 3 rooms**
Local town centre Pub

**Golden Lion Inn**
East Street, Newport, Dyfed SA42 0SY
Tel: 01239 820321 **£ - P - 15 rooms**
Email: goldenlionpems@aol.com
Village Inn 15 miles from Cardigan

PEMBROKE
**Old Cross Saws Inn**
109 Main Street, Pembroke, Dyfed SA71 4DB
Tel: 01646 682475 **£ - P - rooms**
Family run town centre Pub catering for
families

PEMBROKE DOCK
**Dolphin Hotel**
13 Pembroke Street, Pembroke Dock,
Dyfed SA72 6XH
Tel: 01646 685581 **£ - P - 9 rooms**
Quiet Pub near the docks

PENTRE, FENN, LLANDEILO
**Cottage Inn**
Pentre Fenn, Llandeilo, Dyfed, SA19 6SD
Tel: 01558 822890 ££ - P - 5 rooms
Rural Pub on the A40 3 miles from Llandeilo

PONT HENRI, nr LLANELLI
**Baltic Inn**
Pont Henri, nr Llanelli, Dyfed SA15 5RE
Tel: 01269 861409 **£ - 7 rooms**
Email: balticponthenri@hotmail.com
Edge of the village 7 miles from Llanelli

POPPIT SANDS, CARDIGAN
**Webley Hotel**
Poppit Sands, Cardigan, Dyfed SA43 3LN
Tel: 01239 612085 **Rooms**
Country seaside Inn

RHANDIRMWYN, LLANDOVERY
**The Royal Oak Inn**
Rhandirmwyn, Llandovery, Dyfed SA20 0NY
Tel: 01550 760201 **P - 5 rooms**
An old hunting lodge set in the Cambrian
Mountains

RHOS
**Lamb of Rhos**
Rhos, Dyfed SA44 5EE
Tel: 01559 370055 **£ - P - 5 rooms**
Village Inn 6 miles from Newcastle Emlyn

RHYDON OWEN, LLANDYSUL
**Alltyrodyn Arms**
Rhydon Owen, Llandysul, Dyfed SA44 4QB
Tel: 01545 590319 **P - 2 rooms**
Village Inn that is about 20 miles from
Carmarthen

SAINT DAVIDS
**City Inn**
New Street, Saint Davids, Dyfed SA62 6SU
Tel: 01437 720829 **£ - P - 6 rooms**
Local Inn in the centre of the village (This is
the smallest city in Britain)

SAINT FLORENCE, nr TENBY
**Parsonage Farm Inn**
Saint Florence, nr Temby, Dyfed SA70 8LR
Tel: 01834 871436 **£ - P - rooms**
Country Inn 3 miles from Tenby and the coast

nr SAUNDERSFOOT
**Wisemans Bridge Inn**
nr Saundersfoot, Dyfed SA69 9AU
Tel: 01834 813236 **£ - P - 3 rooms**
Sea front Inn 3 miles from Saundersfoot

TAL-Y-BONT, nr ABERYSTWYTH
**White Lion Hotel**
Tal-y-Bont, nr Aberystwyth, Dyfed SY24 5ER
Tel: 01970 832245 **£ - P - 5 rooms**
Village Inn on the main road, with beer garden
7 miles from Aberystwyth

TRIMSARAN, KIDWELLY
**Bryn Forest Inn**
Trimsaran, Kidwelly, Dyfed SA17 4LB
Tel: 01554 810056 **£ - P - 3 rooms**
Country Pub 4 miles from Llanelli and the
coast

UPPER CWM-TWRCH
**Y Stickle**
33 Heolgwys, Upper Cwm-twrch, Dyfed
Tel: 01639 831100 **£ - P - 4 rooms**
Village Inn 12 miles from Swansea

WOLF'S CASTLE
**The Wolfe Inn**
Wolf's Castle, Dyfed SA62 5LS
Tel: 01437 741662 ££ - P - 3 rooms
Country Pub 6 miles from Haverford West

# GWENT AND MONMOUTHSHIRE

Tel: 01495 792477    **£ - P - 3 rooms**
Small town Pub 8 miles from Newport

**BRYNMAWR, EBBW VALE**
**Hobby Horse**
30 Greenland Road, Brynmawr, Ebbw Vale,
Gwent NP3 4DT
Tel: 01495 310996    **£ - P - 2 rooms**
Located just at the edge of the village

**CALDICOT**
**Olde Tippling Philosopher Inn**
108 Chepstow Road, Caldicot, Gwent NP6 4JA
Tel: 01291 420337    **£ - P - 3 rooms**
Country Inn on the outskirts of Caldicot

**CLYTHA, ABERGAVENNY**
**Clytha Arms**
Clytha, Abergavenny, Gwent NP7 9BW
Tel: 01873 840206    **££ - P - 4 rooms**
Email: onebev@lineone.net
Pub / restaurant 6 miles from Abergavenny

**ABERGAVENNY**
**Abergavenny Hotel**
21 Monmouth Road, Abergavenny,
Gwent NP7 5HF
Tel: 01873 858183    **£ - P - 9 rooms**
Rural Inn near Abergavenny

**Black Lion**
Lion Street, Abergavenny, Gwent MP7 5PE
Tel: 01873 853993    **£ - P - 7 rooms**
Town centre Pub

**Kings Head**
60 Cross Street, Abergavenny,
Gwent NP7 5EU
Tel: 01873 853575    **£ - 5 rooms**
Email: kingsheadhotel@hotmail.com
16th century town coaching Inn

**ABERTILLERY**
**Mountain Pleasant Inn**
Alma Street, Abertillery, Gwent,NP3 1QD
Tel: 01495 216987    **Rooms**
Village Inn

**BLAENAVON**
**Castle Hotel**
94 Broad Street, Blaenavon, Gwent NP4 9ND

**EBBW VALE**
**Park Hotel**
Waunlwyd, Ebbw Vale, Blaina, Gwent NP3 6TN
Tel: 01495 371431    **££ - P - 9 rooms**
Village Pub with restaurant

**GROSMONT, nr ABERGAVENNY**
**Angel Inn**
Grosmont, nr Abergavenny, Gwent NP7 8EP
Tel: 01981 240646    **£ - 3 rooms**
Village Inn 12 miles from Abergavenny

**HENLLYS, CWMBRAN**
**Cwrt Henllys**
Henllys Village Road, Henllys, Cwmbran, Gwent
Tel: 01633 484697    **4 rooms**
Country Inn with restaurant

**LLANTHONY**
**Half Moon Hotel**
Llanthony, Abergavenny, Gwent NP7 7NN
Tel: 01873 890611    **£ - P - 9 rooms**

# The Hunters Moon Inn

*Llangattock, Lingoed, Abergavenny, Monmouthshire NP7 8RR*

**P - Rooms**

Tel: 01873 821499     Email: helene@hunters-moon-inn.co.uk     Web: www.hunters-moon-inn.co.uk

A warm welcome always awaits you at Hunter's Moon, a 13th century Inn on Off'a's Dyke national footpath. We serve real ales, draught cider and fine wines and our Taste of Wales restaurant offers traditional home made food using the best local ingredients. Accommodation is in comfortable *en suite* bedrooms, all with TV. We have special facilities for walkers. See web site for further details.

# The Bush Inn

*Penallt, Monmouth, Monmouthshire NP25 4SE*

**£ - P - 6 rooms**

Tel: 01600 772765
Email: reserve@bushinn.freeserve.co.uk
Web: www.welcomingyou.co.uk/thebushinn

Just 4.5 miles out of Monmouth, The Bush Inn is a fabulous 17thC stone building overlooking the beautiful Wye Valley and Forest of Dean. Our large ing bar area invites you to enjoy a wide range of reasonably priced bar meals, which includes a large selection of vegetarian and children's meals. We have smoking or non-smoking tables.

All rooms offer *en suite* bathrooms, colour television and tea / coffee making facilities. A family room is available, double and two single beds, with option of third bed or cot.

Email: halfmoonhotel@talk21.com
Country Inn 10 miles from Abergavenny

**LLANTRISANT**
**Greyhound Inn**
Llantrisant, Gwent NP5 1LE
Tel: 01291 672505     **££ - P - 10 rooms**
Country Inn 12 miles from Newport

**LLANVIHANGEL, CRUCORNEY**
**Skirrid Mountain Inn**
Llanvihangel, Crucorney, Gwent NP7 8DH
Tel: 01873 890258     **Rooms**
Wales oldest Inn. Unique, historic, charming

**LINGOED, ABERGAVENNY**
**The Hunters Moon Inn**
See main entry above

**NANTYGLO**
**The Golden Lion**
Queens Street, Nantyglo, Gwent NP3 4LW
Tel: 01495 291522     **Rooms**
Village Inn

**PANDY, ABERGAVENNY**
**Lancaster Arms**
Pandy, Abergavenny, Gwent NP7 8DW
Tel: 01873 890699     **£ - P - 2 rooms**
Village Inn 6 miles from Abergavenny

**PENALLT, MONMOUTH**
**The Bush Inn**
See main entry above

**SHIRENEWTON**
**Tredegar Arms**
The Square, Shirenewton, Gwent NP6 6RQ

Tel: 01291 641274    **£ - P - 2 rooms**
Village Inn 4 miles from Chepstow

**SHIRENEWTON, CHEPSTOW**
**Huntsman Hotel**
Shirenewton, Chepstow, Gwent NP16 6BU
Tel: 01291 641521    **£ - P - 9 rooms**
Country Inn 4 miles from Chepstow

**TINTERN, nr CHEPSTOW**
**Wye Valley Hotel**
Tintern, nr Chepstow, Gwent NP6 6SQ
Tel: 01291 689441    **££ - P - 9 rooms**
Village Inn 5 miles from Chepstow

**TREDEGAR**
**Coach and Horses**
Charles Street, Tredeger, Gwent NP2 4AE
Tel: 01495 722414    **£ - P - 5 rooms**
Local village Inn that's located just outside
Tredegar

**Ye Olde Red Lion**
97 Queen Victoria Street, Tredegar,
Gwent NP2 3PX
Tel: 01495 724449    **£ - P - 10 rooms**
Local town Pub

# GWYNNED

**ABERDOVEY**
**Penhelig Arms Hotel**
Aberdovey, Gwynedd LL35 0LT
Tel: 01654 767215    **£ - P - 14 rooms**
Email: penheligarms@saqnet.co.uk
Web: www.penheligarms.com
Located on the edge of the village overlooking
the sea, 4 miles from Tywyn

**BALA**
**Plas Coch Hotel**
High Street, Bala, Gwynedd LL23 7AB
Tel: 01678 520309    **££ - P - Rooms**
Small market town Pub

**BANGOR**
**Albion Hotel**
High Street, Bangor, Gwynedd LL57 1DQ
Tel: 01248 370577    **P - 10 rooms**
Town Pub popular with students

**BEDDGELERT**
**Prince Llewelyn Hotel**
Beddgelert, Gwynedd LL55 4UY
Tel: 01766 890242    **£ - Rooms**
Country Inn at the foot of Mount Snowdon

**BRYNCRUG, TYWYN**
**Peniarth Arms Hotel**
Bryncrug, Tywyn, Gwynedd LL36 9PH
Tel: 01654 711505    **£ - P - Rooms**
Rural Pub 2 miles from Tywyn

**CAERNARFON**
**Black Boy Inn**
North Gate St, Caernarfon, Gwynedd LL55 1RW

Tel: 01286 673604   **£ - P - 12 rooms**
15thC Inn within Caernarfon Castle Walls

## CAERNARFON
**Anglesey Arms**
The Quay, Caernarfon, Gwynedd LL55 1SG
Tel: 01286 672158   **£ - P - 3 rooms**
Quayside Inn with nice views

## CONWY
**George and Dragon**
21 Castle Street, Conwy, Gwynedd LL32 8AY
Tel: 01492 592305   **£ - 3 rooms**
Peaceful village Inn

## DYFFRYN, ARDUDWY
**Cadwgan Hotel**
Dyffryn, Ardudwy, Gwynedd LL44 2HA
Tel: 01341 247240   **£ - P - 4 rooms**
**+ 2 Flats**
Family village Inn 5 miles from Barmouth

## LLANDWROG
**Harp Inn**
Llandwrog, Gwynedd LL54 5SY
Tel: 01286 831071   **£ - P - 4 rooms**
Village Inn 6 miles from Caernarfon

## FFESTINIOG
**Abbey Arms Hotel**
The Square, Ffestiniog, Gwynedd LL41 4LS
Tel: 01766 762444   **£ - P - 6 rooms**
Village Inn 5 miles from Port Merrion

## MAENTWROG
**Grapes Hotel**
Maentwrog, Gwynedd LL41 4HN
Tel: 01766 590208   **££ - P - 6 rooms**

Email: grapeshotel@aol.com
Olde Worlde village Inn 10 minute drive to
Porthmadog

## NEFYN
**Nawhoron Arms Hotel**
St Davids Road, Nefyn, Gwynned, LL53 6EA
Tel: 01758 720203   20 rooms
Village Inn

## PENMAENPOOL, DOLGELLAU
**George III Hotel**
Penmaenpool, Dolgellau, Gwynedd LL40 1YD
Tel: 01341 422525   **£££ - P - 11 rooms**
Village country Inn 3 miles from Dolgellau

## RUTHIN
**Ye Olde Anchor**
Rhos Street, Ruthin, Gwynedd LL15 1DX
Tel: 01824 702813   **£ - P - 26 rooms**
Email: hotel@anchorinn.co.uk
Web: www.anchorinn.co.uk
Located in the town a short walk from the
centre

## TUDWEILIOG
**Lion Hotel**
Tudweiliog, Gwynedd LL53 8ND
Tel: 01758 770244   **£ - P - 4 rooms**
Village Inn located on the Lleyn Peninsula 12
miles from Pwllheli

## TY'N-Y-GROES
**Groes Hotel**
Ty'n-y-Groes, Gwynedd LL32 8TN
Tel: 01492 650545   **££ - P - 14 rooms**
Traditional country Inn just 3 miles from
Conwy

# www.stayinapub.com

# ISLE OF ANGLESEY

**AMLWCH**
**Kings Head**
Penrhyd, Amlwch, Anglesey,
Isle of Anglesey LL68 9TP
Tel: 01407 831887     **£ - P - 4 rooms**
Located in the town centre

**BEAUMARIS**
**The Liverpool Arms**
Castle Street, Beaumaris,
Isle of Anglesey LL58 8BA
Tel: 01248 810362     **££ - P - 14 rooms**
Email: inquiries@liverpoolarms.co.uk
Located in the centre of Beaumaris

**White Lion Hotel**
Castle Square, Beaumaris, Isle Of Anglesey
Tel: 01248 810589     **£ - 10 rooms**
Centre of town opposite Beaumaris Castle

**BENLLECH**
**Breeze Hill Hotel**
Benllech, Isle of Anglesey LL74 8TN
Tel: 01248 852308     **££ - P - 4 rooms**
Village Inn near Red Wharf Bay

**BRYNSIENCYN, LLANFAIR PG**
**The Groeslon**
See main entry below

**GAERWEN**
**Holland Arms Hotel**
Pentre Berw, Gaerwen, Anglesey, Isle of
Anglesey LL60 6HY
Tel: 01248 421651     **£ - P - 5 rooms**
Village Inn 8 miles from Gaerwen

**HOLYHEAD**
**Bull Hotel**
London Road, Valley, Holyhead, Isle of
Anglesey LL65 3DT
Tel: 01407 740351     **£ - P - 14 rooms**
A local village Inn situated 4 miles from
Holyhead

**Foresters Arms**
Old Post Road, Holyhead,
Isle of Anglesey LL65 2RL
Tel: 01407 760782     **£ - P - 3 rooms**
Traditional country Inn at the edge of
Holyhead

---

# The Groeslon

*Brynsiencyn, Llanfair PG, Anglesey LL61 6TU*

**P - Rooms**

Tel: 01248 430506
Email: groeslonhotel@ukonline.co.uk

The Groeslon is a charming village pub with outstanding views over the Menai Straits and
Snowdonia. The ideal base for walking, fishing, golfing and is close to The National Trust house
"Plas Newydd". Enjoy Traditional Home Cooked bar snacks in a friendly, welcoming atmosphere
with entertainment most weekends.

# MID, SOUTH AND WEST GLAMORGAN

## MID GLAMORGAN

### ABERDARE
**New Market Tavern**
Market Street, Aberdare,
Mid Glamorgan CF44 7DY
Tel: 01685 884414    **£ - P - 5 rooms**
Town Pub with restaurant

### BARGOED, CAERPHILLY
**Capel Hotel**
Park Place, Gilsach, Bargoed, Caerphilly,
Mid Glamorgan
Tel: 01443 830272    **£ - P - 2 rooms**
Small local Pub 12 miles from Caerphilly

### LIANTRISANT
**New Inn**
Swan Stt, Liantrisant, Mid Glamorgan CF2 8EY
Tel: 01443 222232    **£ - P - 3 rooms**
A local Pub in the old town

### PONTYCYMER
**Royal Hotel**
Bridgend Road, Pontycymer, Mid Glamorgan
Tel: 01656 870018    **£ - P - 2 rooms**
Village Inn 7 miles from Bridgend

### PONTYPRIDD
**Market Tavern Hotel**
Pontypridd, Mid Glamorgan
Tel: 01443 485331    **£ - P - 11 rooms**

Email: bookings@markettavernhotel.
    fsbusiness.co.uk
Web: www.markettavernhotel.fsbusiness.co.uk
Town centre hotel catering for all ages

### PORTHCAWL
**Lorelei Hotel**
Esplanade Avenue, Porthcawl,
Mid Glamorgan CF36 3YU
Tel: 01656 788342    **£ - 10 rooms**
Email: andy-lorelei@msn.com
Quiet local Pub not far from the sea front

### RHONDDA, CYNON TAFF
**Royal Hotel**
61 Briphweunydd Road, Trealaw, Rhondda,
Cynon Taff, Mid Glamorgan CF40 2UD
Tel: 01443 435293    **£ - P - 6 rooms**
Short drive to Porth, 5 miles from Pontypridd

### TREHERBERT, RHONDDA
**Baglan Hotel**
30 Baglan Street, Treherbert, Rhondda,
Mid Glamorgan CF42 5AW
Tel: 01443 776140    **P - rooms**
Email: baglanhotel@aol.com
Web: www.baglanhotel.homestead.com
Easy reach Cardiff, Swansea, Brecon Beacons

## SOUTH GLAMORGAN

### CARDIFF
**Quarry House**
St Fagans Rise, Cardiff,
South Glamorgan CF5 3EZ
Tel: 02920 565577    **£ - rooms**
Local community Pub 2 miles from Cardiff

COWBRIDGE
**Ye Olde Masons Arms**
66 High Street, Cowbridge,
South Glamorgan CF7 7AH
Tel: 01446 772633    **£ - P - 5 rooms**
In the centre of this small market town

LLANDALE, BARRY
**Green Dragon Inn**
Llandale, Barry, South Glamorgan CF62 3AQ
Tel: 01446 750913    **£ - P - 6 rooms**
15th century Inn 1 miles from Cardiff airport

LLANTWIT MAJOR
**Carpenters Arms**
Eglwis Brewis Road, Llantwit Major, South
Glamorgan CF61 2XR
Tel: 01446 792063    **£ - P - 3 rooms**
Village Inn 5 miles from Llantwit

PENARTH
**Manor House Inn**
Sully Road, Penarth, Cardiff,
South Glamorgan CF64 2TQ
Tel: 02920 709309    **£ - P - 6 rooms**
Country Inn 10 minute drive to Penarth

PONTARDAWE
**Pink Geranium Village Hotel**
Herbert Street, Pontardawe, Swansea,
South Glamorgan SA8 4EB
Tel: 01792 862255    **£ - Rooms**
Village Pub / hotel 8 miles from Swansea

REYNOLDSTON
**King Arther Hotel**
Higher Green, Reynoldston,
South Glamorgan SA3 1AD
Tel: 01792 390775    **£ - P - 7 rooms**
Email: info@kingartherhotel.co.uk
Web: www.kingartherhotel.co.uk
Country Inn 14 miles from Swansea on the
Gower Peninsula

SAINT GEORGES-SUPER-ELY,
CARDIFF
**Greendown Inn**
Drope Road, Saint Georges-Super-Ely, Cardiff,
South Glamorgan CF5 6EP
Tel: 01446 760310    **££ - P - 15 rooms**
Rural country Inn 4 miles from Cardiff

SWANSEA
**Salsa Salsa**
233 High Street, Swansea,
South Glamorgan SA1 1NZ
Tel: 01792 458080    **Rooms**
One of the "Pubs n Bars" group of Pubs

**WEST GLAMORGAN**

PONTARDDULAIS
**Fountain Inn**
111 Bolgoed Road, Pontarddulais,
West Glamorgan SA4 1JP
Tel: 01792 882501    **£ - P - 9 rooms**
Traditional Inn 7 miles from Swansea

PONTARDAWE
**Pen-Yr-Allt Hotel / Inn**
Alltwen Hill, Alltwen, Pontardawe,
West Glamorgan SA8 3BP
Tel: 01792 863320    **£ - Rooms**
Family run country Inn 9 miles from Swansea

# POWYS

Tel: 01982 553171    **£ - P - 5 rooms**
Located in the centre of town

## CAERHOWEL, MONTGOMERY
**Lion Hotel**
Caerhowel, Montgomery, Powys SY15 6HF
Tel: 01686 668096    **Rooms**
Village Inn

## CARNO
**Aleppo Merchant Inn**
Carno, Powys SY17 5LL
Tel: 01686 420210    **P - 6 rooms**
Located between Snowdonia and Brecon
National Parks

## CRICKHOWELL
**The Bear**
Brecon Road, Crickhowell, Powys NP8 1BW
Tel: 01873 810408    **££ - P - 35 rooms**
Email: bearhotel@aol.com
Village Inn In the centre of this small town

**Brittania Inn**
20 High Street, Crickhowell, Powys NP8 1BD
Tel: 01873 810553    **£ - 20 beds**
Village Inn 6 miles from Abergavenny

## BERRLEW
**Lion Hotel**
Berrlew, Powys SY21 8PQ
Tel: 01686 640452    **££ - P - 7 rooms**
Country village Inn 5 miles from Welshpool

## BRECON
**Bulls Head Inn**
86 The Street, Brecon, Powys LD3 7LS
Tel: 01874 622044    **£ - 2 rooms**
Town centre Pub located near the Cathedral

**Market Tavern Hotel**
Free Street, Brecon, Powys LD3 7BN
Tel: 01874 623595    **£ - P - 10 rooms**
Town Pub 4 minutes walk to the town centre

## BUILTH WELLS
**Llanelwedd Arms Hotel**
Llanelwedd, Builth Wells, Powys LD2 3SR
Tel: 01982 553282    **£ - P - 6 rooms**
Email: malcolmgrainger@lycos.com
Country Pub just outside Builth Wells close to
the Royal Welsh Show Ground

**White Horse Hotel**
High Street, Builth Wells, Powys LD2 3DN

## CWMDU
**The Farmers Arms**
See main entry on page 214

## DINAS MAWDDWY
**Y Llew Coch / The Red Lion**
See main entry on page 214

## ELAN VILLAGE
**Elan Valley Hotel**
Elan Village, Powys LD6 5HN
Tel: 01597 810448    **££ - P - 11 rooms**
Hotel with public bar 2 miles from Rhayader

## FELINFACH, BRECON
**Griffin Inn**
Felinfach, Brecon, Powys LD3 0YB

# The Farmer's Arms

*Cwmdu, Powys NP8 1RU*

**P - Rooms**

Tel: 01874 730464      Email: cwmdu@aol.com      Web: www.thefarmersarms.com

At the foot of the Black Mountains and with outstanding views of the Brecon Beacons from the well-appointed beer garden, The Farmers Arms is the ideal base for exploring the surrounding countryside. On offer is superb food, real ales, fine wines and comfortable *en suite* accommodation, recommended by the AA, Which and other leading guides.

# Y Llew Coch / The Red Lion

*Dinas Mawddwy, Powys, Wales*

**£ - P - Rooms**

Tel: 01650 531247      Email: rob@llewcoch.co.uk      Web: www.llewcoch.co.uk

Reasonably priced accommodation is available with some rooms having *en suite* facilities. All rooms are centrally heated, have colour TV and tea / coffee making facilities. There are 15 bedspaces in total and there is a private car park with secure cycle storage. Meals available range from sandwiches to steaks and daily specials, where possible using quality local produce. There is an extensive range of drinks and the inn is listed in the C.A.M.R.A. good beer guide.

The Red Lion is a centuries old traditional village Inn renowned for its good value home-cooked meals and accommodation all year round. It is set amidst the scenic beauty of southern Snowdonia, in the charming village of Dinas Mawddwy, which is featured in the AA book of British villages and many other publications.

---

Tel: 01874 620111    **££ - P - 7 rooms**
Email: enquiries@eatdrinksleep.ltd.uk
Country Inn located about 4 miles from
Brecon

**FELINFACH, nr BRECON**
**Plough and Harrow**
Felinfach, nr Brecon, Powys LD3 0UB
Tel: 01874 622709    **£ - Rooms**
Country Inn 4 miles from Brecon

**GWYSTRE, LLANDRINDOD-WELLS**
**Gwystre Inn**
Gwystre, Llandrindod-Wells, Powys LD1 6RN
Tel: 01597 851650    **£ - P - 3 rooms**
Country Pub situated 4 miles from Llandrindod
Wells

**HAY-ON-WYE**
**Kilverts Inn**
The Bullring, Hay-on-Wye, Powys HR3 5AG
Tel: 01497 821042    **£££ - P - 11 rooms**
Town centre Inn

**Old Black Lion**
26 Lion Street, Hay-on-Wye, Powys HR3 5AD
Tel: 01497 820841    **££ - P - 10 rooms**
Web: www.oldblacklion.co.uk
Village Inn majoring on good food

**HOEL TAWE, ABERCRAVE**
**Copper Beech Inn**
Hoel Tawe, Abercrave, Powys SA9 1XF
Tel: 01639 730269    **£ - P - 4 rooms**
Village local 8 miles from Abercraf

HOWEY, LLANDRINDOD WELLS
**The Drovers Arms**
See main entry below

LLANDINAM
**The Lion Hotel**
Llandinam, Abercrave, Powys SY17 5BY
Tel: 01686 688233    **£ - P - 4 rooms**
Village Inn 6 miles from Newtown

LLANDRINDOD-WELLS
**The Builders Arms**
Cross Gate, Llandrindod-Wells, Powys LD1 6RB
Tel: 01597 851235    **£ - P - 3 rooms**
Email: pub836@aol.com
Village Inn 3 miles from Llandrindod Wells

**Hundred House Inn**
Llandrindod-Wells, Powys LD1 5RY
Tel: 01982 570231    **£ - P - 5 rooms**
Country Inn 7 miles from Llandrindod Wells

LLANFIHANGEL-NANT-MELAN
**The Forest Inn**
See main entry on page 216

**Red Lion Inn**
Llanfihangel-Nant-Melan, New Radnor,
Powys LD8 2TN
Tel: 01544 350220    **£ - P - 7 rooms**
Country Inn 20 miles from Builth Wells

LLANFYLLIN
**Cain Valley Hotel**

High Street, Llanfyllin, Powys SY22 5AQ
Tel: 01691 648366    **££ - P - 13 rooms**
17th century  village Inn 15 minutes drive to
Welshpool

LLANGURIG
**Bluebell Inn**
Llangurig, Powys SY18 6SG
Tel: 01686 440254    **£ - P - 8 rooms**
Village Inn 20 miles from Aberystwyth

LLANYMYNECH
**The Horseshoe Inn**
See main entry on page 216

**Lion Hotel**
Llanymynech, Powys SY22 6EJ
Tel: 01691 830234    **Rooms**
Village Inn

LLANWRTYD-WELLS
**Belle Vue Hotel**
Llanwrtyd-Wells, Powys LD5 4RD
Tel: 01591 610237    **£ - P - 14 rooms**
Village Inn in the middle of nowhere, walkers
paradise

LLANYMYNECH
**Golden Lion**
Llanymynech, Powys SY22 6RB
Tel: 01691 830295    **£ - P - 5 rooms**
Email: goldenlion@themail.co.uk
Web: www.goldenlionhotel.4crosses.co.uk
Village Inn 8 miles from Oswestry

---

# Drovers Arms Inn

*Howey, Llandrindod Wells, Powys LD1 5PT*

**£ - P - 3 rooms**

Tel: 01597 822508    Email: info@drovers-arms.co.uk    Web: www.drovers-arms.co.uk

The Drovers Arms, a cosy village Inn set in beautiful Mid Wales, is a classic red brick Victorian building with lots of character, a high standard of décor and comfortable lounge bar featuring a log fire. The personal service, real ales, quality home cooked food and *en suite* rooms give The Drovers It's homely atmosphere. There are many attractions and places to visit in one of the most underestimated tourist locations in the UK.

The Drovers was named after the route taken by cattle drovers who used the route to take their cattle, sheep, pigs and geese to market, originally in Norman times.

# The Forest Inn

*Llanfihangel-Nant-Melan, Powys LD8 2TN*

**£ - P - 4 rooms**

Tel: 01544 350246   Email: forest.inn@btinternet.com     Web: www.mid-wales-accommodation

All rooms at The Forest Inn are on-suite, have tea / coffee making facilities, television and are central heated during the colder months. Rooms can be made up as twin or double-bedded. Cots can be added for small children.

The dining room at The Forest Inn is large enough to seat 50 + in comfort, during the quieter times curtains divide the room into smaller units. There is a large room available for functions or conferences for up to 60 + persons.

# The Horseshore Inn

*Arddleen, Llanymynech, Powys SY22 6PU*

Tel: 01938 590318     Email: thehorseshoe@hotmail.com

The Horseshoe Inn is a 17th century coaching inn situated in rural countryside on the Powys / Shropshire border alongside the A483. Ours is a welcoming freehouse with a friendly, warm bar, children's licence, two dining areas and a lounge bar (one no smoking). There are three cosy letting bedrooms available, 2 being e-suite, and the price includes full English breakfast and TVs in rooms.

The food is good, wholesome, home cooked fare using fresh, local produce. The house speciality is a "Traditional Sunday Lunch" served with a smile.

LLANYRE
**The Bell Country Inn**
See main entry opposite

LLYSWEN
**The Griffin Inn**
Llyswen, Powys LD3 0UR
Tel: 01874 754241      **££ - 5 rooms**
Busy village Inn located just 9 miles from Brecon

MONTGOMERY
**Checkers Hotel**
Broad Street, Montgomery,
Powys SY15 6PN
Tel: 01686 668355      **£ - P - 4 rooms**
Busy Pub in the centre of the village

MONGOMERYSHIRE
**Kings Head Hotel**
Meifod, Montgomeryshire, Powys SY22 6BY
Tel: 01938 500788      **£ - P - 4 rooms**
Pub with caravan site 10 miles from Welshpool

PAINSCASTLE
**Roast Ox**
Ithon View, Painscastle, Powys LD2 6JP
Tel: 07071 225853      **£ - P - 9 rooms**
Email: bopa@outdoor;sport.v:net.com
Village Inn 15 miles from Hereford.  Great for outdoor activities

PENYBONT, LLANDRINDOD-WELLS
**Severn Arms Hotel**
Penybont, Llandrindod-Wells, Powys LD1 5UA

# The Bell Country Inn

*Llanyre, Llandrindod Wells, Powys LD1 6DY*

**P - 9 rooms**

Tel: 01597 823959
Email: dgj.jones@virgin.net

Situated outside Llandrindod Wells. The Bell Country Inn offers access to the Elan Valley and the River Wye.

There are nine well appointed, comfortable, *en suite* bedrooms to make your stay relaxing and memorable. Built in 1890 recent extensions include a restaurant, with It's menu combining traditional and international dishes complemented by selected wines.

Tel: 01597 851224    **Rooms - PW**
Pets welcome

PONTROBERT, nr MEIFOD
**Royal Oak Inn**
Pontrobert, nr Meifod, Powys SY22 6HY
Tel: 01938 500243    **£ - P - 4 rooms**
Email: postmaster@royaloakinn.plus.com
Rural village Inn 10 miles from Welshpool

RADNOR
**Eagle Hotel**
Radnor, Powys LD8 2SN
Tel: 01544 350208    **P - 6 rooms**
Country Inn 6 miles from Kington

RHAYADER
**Crown Inn**
North Street, Rhayader, Powys LD6 5BT
Tel: 01597 811099    **£ - P - 3 rooms**
Town Inn 10 miles from Llandrindod Wells

**Lamb and Flag Inn**
North Street, Rhayader, Powys LD6 5BU
Tel: 01597 810819    **£ - P - 5 rooms**
Town centre Pub

TALGARTH, nr BRECON
**New Inn**
Bronllys Road, Talgarth, nr Brecon,

Powys LD3 0HH
Tel: 01874 711581    **£ - P - Rooms**
Village Pub 9 miles from Brecon

TALYBONT-ON-USK
**Star Inn**
Talybont-on-Usk, Powys LD3 7WX
Tel: 01874 676635    **£ - 2 rooms**
Village Inn 6 miles from Brecon

**Usk Inn**
Station Road, Talybont-on-Usk, Brecon,
Powys LD3 7JE
Tel: 01874 676251    **££ - P - 11 rooms**
Welsh Tourist Board 4 star Inn, 11 en suite
rooms

TRECASTLE
**Castle Coaching Inn**
Trecastle, Powys LD3 8UH
Tel: 01874 636354    **££ - P - 10 rooms**
17th century coaching Inn on the A40 west of
Brecon

LLANBRYNMAIR
**Wynnstay Arms Hotel**
Llanbrynmair, Powys SY19 7AA
Tel: 01650 521431    **£ - P - 6 rooms**
Village Inn situated about 11 miles from
Machynlleth

# UK Breweries
## ENGLAND

## AVON

**Bath Ales**
Hare on the Hill, Dove Street, Kingsdown, Bristol
Tel: 0117 907 1797

**Butcombe Brewery Ltd**
Butcombe, Bristol, Avon
Tel: 01275 472240

**Hardington Brewery**
Albany Buildings, Dean Lane, Bedminster
Tel: 0117 963 6194

**Lundy Company**
Marisco Tavern Brewery, Lundy Island, Bristol Channel
Tel: 01237 431831

**Pencaster Ltd**
9 Kent Road, Bishopston, Bristol
Tel: 0117 9241694

**Smiles Brewing Co Ltd**
Colston Yard, Colston Street, Bristol
Tel: 0117 929 7350, web: www.smiles.co.uk

## BEDFORDSHIRE

**Charles Wells Ltd**
The Eagle Brewery, Bedford
Tel: 01234 272766, web: www.charleswells.co.uk

**Nix Wincott Brewery**
Three Fyshes Inn, Bridge Street, Turvey
Tel: 01234 881264

**Whitbread Beer Company**
Porter Tun House, Capability Green, Luton
Tel: 01582 391166

**B and T Brewery Ltd**
The Brewery, Shefford, Bedfordshire
Tel: 01462 815080

**Potton Brewing Company**
10 Shannon Place, Potton, Sandy
Tel: 01767 261042, web: www.potton-brewery.co.uk

## BERKSHIRE

**Butts Brewery Ltd**
Northfield Farm, Great Shefford, Hungerford
Tel: 01488 648133

**Reading Lion Brewery**
The Hop Leaf, 163–165 Southampton Street, Reading,
Berkshire
Tel: 0118 931 4700

**West Berkshire Brewery Co**
Pot Kiln Lane, Frilsham, Yattendon, Berkshire
Tel: 01635 202638

## BUCKINGHAMSHIRE

**Chiltern Brewery**
Nash Lee Road, Terrick, Aylesbury, Buckinghamshire
Tel: 01296 613647

**Rebellion Beer Co**
Bencombe Farm, Marlow Bottom Road, Marlow
Tel: 01628 476594, web: www.rebellionbeer.co.uk

**Sam Trueman's Brewery**
School Lane, Medmenham
Tel: 01491 576100, web: www.crownandanchor.co.uk

**Vale Brewery Co**
4 Thame Road, Haddenham,
Tel: 01844 290008, Email: valebrewery@yahoo.co.uk

## CAMBRIDGESHIRE

**City of Cambridge Brewery Ltd**
19 Cheddars Lane, Cambridge
Tel: 01223 353939

**Elgood and Sons Ltd**
North Brink Brewery, Wisbech
Tel: 01945 583160, web: www.elgoods-brewery.co.uk

**Fenland Brewery**
Unit 4 Prospect Way, Chatteris,
Tel: 01354 696776, Email: fenland@users.breworld.net

**Milton Brewery**
Cambridge Ltd, Unit 111 Norman Industrial Estate,
Cambridge Road, Milton
Tel: 01223 226198

**Oak Brewery Spirit Vaults**
Leverington Road, Wisbech
Tel: 01945 583200

**Oakham Ales**
80 Westgate, Peterborough, Cambridgeshire
Tel: 01733 358300

**Payn Brewery**
Unit 1 Eco Site, St Marys Road, Ramsey,
Tel: 01487 710800, web: www.payn.co.uk

## CHANNEL ISLANDS

**Guernsey Brewery Co (1920)**
South Esplanade, St Peter Port, Guernsey
Tel: 01481 720143

**RW Randall Ltd**
Vauxlaurens Brewery, St Julians Avenue, St Peter
Port, Guernsey
Tel: 01481 720134

**Tipsy Toad Brewery**
St Peters Village, St Peter, Jersey
Tel: 01534 485556

## CHESHIRE

**Altrincham Brewing Company**
The Old Market Tavern, Old Market Place, Altrincham
Tel: 0161 927 7062

**Beartown Brewery**
Eaton Bank Industrial Estate, Varey Road, Congleton
Tel: 01260 299964

**Burtonwood Brewery Plc**
Bold Lane, Burtonwood, Warrington, WA5 4PJ
Tel: 01925 225131, web: www.burtonwood.co.uk

**Coach House Brewing Company Ltd**
Wharf Street, Howley, Warrington
Tel: 01925 232800

**Frederick Robinson Ltd**
Unicorn Brewery, Lower Hillgate, Stockport, Cheshire
Tel: 0161 480 6571

**Paradise Brewing Company**
Unit 2 The Old Creamery, Wrenbury Road, Wrenbury,
Nantwich
Tel: 01270 780916

**Sarah's Hophouse**
The Railway Inn, 131 High Street, Golbourne
Tel: 01942 728202

**Storm Brewing Company**
Cheshire Bakeries, Hulley Road, Macclesfield
Tel: 01625 432856

**Weetwood Ales Ltd**
Weetwood Grange, Weetwood, Tarporley
Tel: 01829 752377

## CLEVELAND

**Camerons Brewery Company**
Lion Brewery, Hartlepool, Cleveland TS24 7QS
Tel: 01429 266666

## CORNWALL

**Bird in Hand**
Wheat Ale Brewery, Paradise Park, Hayle
Tel: 01736 753974

**Blue Anchor**
50 Coinagehall Street, Helston, Cornwall
Tel: 01326 562821

**Driftwood Brewery**
Driftwood Spars Hotel, Quay Road, St Agnes
Tel: 01872 552428

**Keltek Brewing Company**
Highgate, Lower Allens, Tregony
Tel: 01872 530814

**Organic Brewhouse**
Unit 1 Higher Bochym, Curry Cross Lane, Mullion
Tel: 01326 241555

**Redruth Brewery**
The Brewery, Redruth, Cornwall
Tel: 01209 212244

**Sharp's Brewery**
Pityme Industrial Estate, Rock, Wadebridge
Tel: 01208 862121

**Skinner's Fine Cornish Ales**
Riverside View, Newham, Truro
Tel: 01872 271885

**St Austell Brewery Co Ltd**
St Austell
Tel: 01726 74444, web: www.staustellrewery.co.uk

**Ventonwyn Brewing Company Ltd**
Unit 2B, Grampound Road, Truro
Tel: 01726 884367

## CUMBRIA

**Barngates Brewery at the Drunken Duck Inn**
Barngates, Ambleside
Tel: 01539 436347

**Bitter End Brewing Company**
15 Kirkgate, Cockermouth,
Tel: 01900 828993

**Coniston Brewing Co**
Coppermines Road, Coniston, Cumbria,
Tel: 01539 441133, Email: i.s.bradley@btinternet.com

**Dent Brewery**
PO Box 10, Cumbria
Tel: 01539 625148
web: www.madeincumbria.co.uk/fooddir/dent.htm

**Derwent Brewery**
Unit 1B Derwent Mills, Cockermouth
Tel: 01900 826626

**Foxfield Brewery**
Prince of Wales, Foxfield, Broughton-in-Furness
Tel: 01229 716238

**Hesket Newmarket Brewery**
Hesket Newmarket
Tel: 016974 78066
Web: www.bdksol.demon.co.uk/hesket

**Jennings Brothers Plc**
The Castle Brewery, Cockermouth
Tel: 01900 823214, web: www.jenningsbrewery.co.uk

**Lakeland Brewing Company**
1 Sepulchre Lane, Kendal
Tel: 01539 734528

**Old Cottage Beer Co**
Unit 3, Hall House Industrial Estate, Kendal
Tel: 01539 724444

**Tirril Brewery**
The Queen's Head Inn, Tirril, Penrith
Tel: 01768 863219, web: www.queensheadinn.co.uk

**Yates Brewery**
Ghyll Farm, Aspatria, Cumbria
Tel: 016973 21081
Email: graeme@yatesbrewery.freeserve.co.uk

## DERBYSHIRE

**Whim Ales**
Whim Farm, Hartington, Buxton, Derbyshire
Tel: 01298 84991

**Brunswick Inn Ltd**
1 Railway Terrace, Derby, Derbyshire
Tel: 01332 290677

**Falstaff Brewing Company**
24 Society Place, Derby
Tel: 01332 299914, web: www.thefalstaff.co.uk

**John Thompson Brewery**
Ingleby, Derbyshire
Tel: 01332 862469

**Leatherbritches Brewery**
Bently Brook Inn, Fenny Bentley, Ashbourne
Tel: 01335 350278

**Lloyds Country Beers**
John Thompson Brewery, Ingleby
Tel: 01332 863426

**Museum Brewing Company**
Bass Brewery, PO Box 220, Burton-on-Trent
Tel: 01283 511000, web: www.bass-museum.com

**Townes Brewery**
Bay 9 Suon Buildings, Chesterfield
Tel: 01246 277994

## DEVON

**ABC Drinks**
New Road, Exeter, Devon EX6 8QG
Tel: 01626 891818

**Barum Brewery**
c/o The Reform Inn, Pilton, Barnstaple, Devon
Tel: 01271 329994, web: www.barumbrewery.co.uk

**Beer Engine**
Sweetham, Newton St Cyres, Exeter, Devon
Tel: 01392 851282, Email: peterbrew@aol.com

**Blackawton Brewery**
Washbourne, Totnes, Devon
Tel / Fax: 01803 732151

**Blewitt's Brewery**
Ship and Plough Inn, The Promenade, Kingsbridge Tel:
01548 852485

**Branscombe Vale Brewery**
Great Seaside Farm, Branscombe, Seaton
Tel: 01297 680511

**Clearwater Brewery**
2 Devon Units, Hatchmoor Industrial Estate, Torrington
Tel: 01805 625242

**Combe Brewery**
Mullacott Industrial Estate, Ilfracombe, Devon
Tel: 01271 864020

**Country Life Brewery**
Pursehill, Westward Ho
Tel: 01237 477615
Web: www.Mlangmead.freeserve.co.uk/pig2.htm

**Edwin Tucker and Sons Ltd**
Brewery Meadow, Stonepark, Ashburton
Tel: 01364 52403

**Exe Valley Brewery**
Land Farm, Silverton, Devon
Tel: 01392 860406
Web: www.execamra.freeserve.co.uk

**Hop Shop**
22 Dale Road, Mutley, Plymouth, Devon PL4 6ES
Tel: 01752 660382

**Jollyboat Brewery**
4 Buttgarden Street, Bideford, Devon
Tel: 01237 424343

**Kings Head Brewery**
Kings Head Ale House, 21 Bretonside, Plymouth
Tel: 01752 665619

**Mill Brewery**
Unit 18C Hanbury Buildings, Bradbury Lane, Newton Abbot
Tel: 01626 63322

**Otter Brewery**
Mathayes, Luppitt, Honiton, Devon
Tel: 01404 891285

**Points West Brewery**
Plymouth College of Further Education, Kings Road, Devonport, Plymouth
Tel: 01752 305890

**Princetown Breweries Ltd**
The Prince of Wales, Tavistock Road, Princetown
Tel: 01822 890789

**Scattor Rock Brewery Ltd**
Unit 5 Gridleys Meadow, Exeter,
Tel: 01647 252120, web: www.scattorrockbrewery.com

**Summerskills Brewery**
Unit 15, Pomphlett Farm Industrial Estate, Plymouth
Tel: 01752 481283

**Sutton Brewing Company**
31 Commercial Road, Coxside, Plymouth
Tel: 01752 255335

**Tally Ho! Country Inn and Brewery**
14 Market Street, Hatherleigh
Tel: 01837 810306

**Teignworthy Brewery**
The Maltings, Teign Road, Newton Abbott
Tel: 01626 332066

**The Beer Engine**
Newton St Cyres, Exeter
Tel: 01392 851282, Email: peterbrew@aol.com

## DORSET

**Cranborne Brewery**
Sheaf of Arrows, 4 The Square, Cranborne
Tel: 01725 517456

**Eldridge Pope and Co**
Weymouth Avenue, Dorchester, Dorset
Tel: 01305 251251, web: www.eldridge-pope.co.uk

**Goldfinch Brewery**
47 High East Street, Dorchester, Dorset
Tel: 01305 264020

**Hall and Woodhouse Ltd**
The Brewery, Blandford St Mary, Dorset
Tel: 01258 452141, web: www.badgerbrewery.com

**Palmers, Old Brewery**
West Bay Road, Bridport, Dorset
Tel: 01308 422396, web: www.palmersbrewery.com

**Poole Brewery**
The Brewhouse Brewery, 68 High Street, Poole
Tel: 01202 682345

**Quay Brewery**
Lapin Noir Ltd, Hope Square, Weymouth
Tel: 01305 777515

**Thomas Hardy Brewery**
Weymouth Avenue, Dorchester
Tel: 01305 250255

## COUNTY DURHAM

**Butterknowle Brewery**
Old School House, Butterknowle, Bishop Auckland
Tel: 01388 710109

**Castle Eden Brewery Ltd**
Castle Eden, Hartlepool
Tel: 01429 826007

**Derwent Rose Brewery**
115 Sherburn Terrace, Consett,
Tel: 01207 502585, web: www.thegreyhorse.co.uk

**Durham Brewery**
Unit 5a, Bowburn North Industrial Estate
Tel: 0191 377 1991, web: www.durham-brewery.co.uk

**High Force Hotel Brewery**
Forest-in-Teesdale, Barnard Castle
Tel: 01833 622222

**Hodges Brewhouse**
Unit 5a, Castle Close, Crook
Tel: 01388 763200

**Trimdon Cask Ales**
Unit 2c, Trimdon Grange Industrial Estate, Trimdon Grange
Tel: 01429 880967

## EAST SUSSEX

**Cuckmere Haven Brewery**
Exceat Bridge, Cuckmere Haven, Seaford
Tel: 01323 892247, Email: galleon@mistral.co.uk

**Dark Star**
55–56 Surrey Street, Brighton, East Sussex
Tel: 01273 701758

**First In, Last Out**
14–15 High Street, Old Town, Hastings
Tel: 01424 425079

**Forge Brewery Ltd**
The Two Sawyers, Pett, Hastings
Tel: 0845 6061616, web: www.forgebrewery.co.uk

**Harvey and Son (Lewes) Ltd**
Bridge Wharf Brewery, Lewes
Tel: 01273 480209, web: www.harveys.org.uk

**Hedgehog and Hogshea**
Belchers Brewery, 100 Goldstone Villas, Hove
Tel: 01273 324660

**Kemptown Brewery Co Ltd**
33 Upper St James Street, Brighton
Tel: 01273 699595

**Old Forge Brewery**
c/o The Two Sawyers, Pett, Hastings
Tel: 01424 813030

**Rother Valley Brewing Co**
Station Road, Gate Court Farm, Northiam
Tel: 01797 253535

**White Brewing Company**
Pebsham Farm Industrial Estate, Bexhill
Tel: 01424 731066

## EAST YORKSHIRE

**Hull Brewery Co Ltd**
144–148 English Street, Hull,
Tel: 01482 586364, Email: ellwood@brewcrew.co.uk

**Old Mill Brewery Ltd**
Mill Street, Snaith, Goole
Tel: 01405 861813

**Wawne Brewery**
Tickton Arms, Main Street, Tickton, Beverley
Tel: 01482 679876

## ESSEX

**Anglo-German Breweries Ltd**
227–247 Gascoigne Road, Barking
Tel: 020 859 15621

**Crouch Vale Brewery Ltd**
South Woodham Ferrers, Chelmsford
Tel: 01245 322744, Email: cvb@cwcom.net

**Famous Railway Tavern Brewing Co**
58 Station Road, Brightlingsea
Tel: 01206 302581

**Mighty Oak Brewing Company**
9 Prospect Way, Brentwood
Tel: 01277 263007, Email: moakbrew@aol.com

**Ridleys, Hartford End Brewery**
Chelmsford,
Tel: 01371 820316, web: www.ridleys.co.uk

## GLOUCESTERSHIRE

**Donnington Brewery**
Stow-on-the-Wold, Gloucester
Tel: 01451 830603

Farmers Arms
Mayhem's Brewery, Lower Apperley
Tel: 01452 780172

**Freeminer Brewery Ltd**
The Laurels, Sling, Coleford
Tel: 01594 810408

**Goff's Brewery Ltd**
9 Isbourne Way, Winchcombe
Tel: 01242 603383

**Home County Brewers**
The Old Brewery, Station Road, Wickwar
Tel: 01454 294045

**Stanway Brewery**
Stanway, Cheltenham, Gloucestershire
Tel: 01386 584320

**Uley Brewery**
The Old Brewery, Uley, Dursley
Tel: 01453 860120

**Wickwar Brewing Co**
Arnolds Cooperage, Station Road, Wickwar
Tel: 01454 294168

## GREATER MANCHESTER

**Boddingtons**
Strangeways Brewery, PO Box 23, Strangeways
Tel: 0161 828 2000, web: www.boddingtons.com

**Hydes Brewery Ltd**
46 Moss Lane West, Manchester,
Tel: 0161 226 1317, web: www.hydesbrewery.co.uk

**Joseph Holt Plc**
Empire Street, Cheetham, Manchester
Tel: 0161 834 3285

**JW Lees and Co**
Greengate Brewery, Middleton Junction
Tel: 0161 643 2487, web: www.jwlees.co.uk

**Lass O'Gowrie Brewhouse**
36 Charles Street, Manchester
Tel: 0161 273 6932

**Marble Brewery**
73 Rochdale Road, Manchester
Tel: 0161 832 5914

**Millgate Brewery**
Ashton Road West, Failsworth, Manchester
Tel: 0161 688 4910

## HAMPSHIRE

**Ballards Brewery Ltd**
Nyewood, Petersfield
Tel: 01730 821301
Web: www.real-ale-guide.co.uk/ballards

**Beckett's Brewery Ltd**
8 Enterprise Court, Basingstoke
Tel: 01256 472986

**Belcher's Southampton**
163 University Road, Highfield, Southampton
Hampshire, SO17 1TS

**Cheriton Brewhouse**
Brandy Mount, Cheriton, Alresford
Tel: 01962 771166, Email: bestbeer@aol.com

**George Gale and Co Ltd**
The Hampshire Brewery, Horndean
Tel: 01705 571212, web: www.gales.co.uk

**Hampshire Brewery**
Greatbridge Road, Romsey
Tel: 01794 830000
Web: www.hampshire.brewery.co.uk

**Itchen Valley Brewery**
New Farm Road, Alresford
Tel: 01962 735111, web: www.itchenvalley.com

**Newale Brewing Co Ltd**
6 Viscount Court, South Way, Andover
Tel: 01264 336336

**Packhorse Brewing Co Ltd**
5 Somers Road, Southsea
Tel: 023 9275 0450

**Red Shoot Brewery**
Toms Lane, Linwood, Ringwood
Tel: 01425 474792

**Ringwood Brewery Ltd**
138 Christchurch Road, Ringwood
Tel: 01425 471177, web: www.ringwoodbrewery.co.uk

**Spikes Brewery**
The Wine Vaults, 43–47 Albert Road, Southsea
Tel: 023 9286 4712

**Triple fff Brewing Company**
Station Approach, Four Marks, Alton
Tel: 01420 561422, web: www.triplefff.co.uk

**Winfields Brewery**
The Raven, Bedford Street, Portsmouth
Tel: 01705 829079

## HERTFORDSHIRE

**Harpenden Brewery**
The Red Cow, 171 Westfield Road, Harpenden
Tel: 01582 460156

**Tring Brewery**
81–82 Akeman Street, Tring, Hertfordshire
Tel: 01442 890721

**Verulam Brewery**
134 London Road, St Albans, Hertfordshire
Tel: 01727 766702

**Dark Horse Brewing Co**
Adams Yard, off Maidenhead Street, Hertford
Tel: 01992 509800, web: www.darkhorsebrewery.co.uk

**Green Tye Brewery**
Prince of Wales, Green Tye, Much Hadham
Tel: 01279 841041, web: www.gtbrewery.co.uk

**McMullen and Sons Ltd**
The Hertford Brewery, 26 Old Cross, Hertford
Tel: 01992 584911

**Sawbridgeworth Brewery**
Gate Inn, 81 London Road, Sawbridgeworth
Tel: 01279 722313

## ISLE OF MAN

**Bushy's**
The Mount Murray Brewing Co, Castletown Road, Braddan
Tel: 01624 661244

**Heron and Brearley Ltd**
Kewaigue, Douglas, Isle of Man
Tel: 01624 661120

**Isle of Man Breweries Ltd**
Kewaigue, Douglas, Isle of Man
Tel: 01624 661120

**Mount Murray Brewing Co Ltd**
Mount Murray, Castletown Road, Braddan
Tel: 01624 661244, web: www.bushys.com

**Okell and Son Ltd**
Falcon Brewery, Kewaigue, Douglas, Isle of Man
Tel: 01624 661120
Email: okells@ heronandbrearley.com

**Old Laxey Brewing Co Ltd**
Old Laxey, Isle of Man
Tel: 01624 862451

## ISLE OF WIGHT

**Goddards Brewery**
Barnsley Farm, Bullen Road, Ryde
Tel: 01983 611011

**Ventnor Brewery Ltd**
119 High Street, Ventnor, Isle of Wight
Tel: 01983 856161, web: www.ventnorbrewery.co.uk

**Yates Brewery**
The Undercliffe Drive, St Lawrence, Ventnor
Tel: 01983 854689

## KENT

**Ales of Kent Brewery Ltd**
The Old Stables, Boxley, Maidstone
Tel: 01634 669296

**East West Ales**
Unit 1 Manor Farm, Willow Lane, Paddock Wood
Tel: 01892 834040

**English Hop Products Ltd**
Hop Pocket Lane, Tonbridge
Tel: 01892 836555

**Flagship Brewery**
Unit 2 Building No 64, The Historic Dockyard, Chatham
Tel: 01634 832828

**Goacher's Brewery**
The Bockingford Brewery, Tovil Green Business Park, Maidstone
Tel: 01622 682112

**Kent Garden Brewery**
Unit 13 Davington Mill, Bysingwood Road, Faversham
Tel: 01795 532211

**Larkins Brewery Ltd**
Chiddingstone, Edenbridge, Kent
Tel: 01892 870328

**Shepherd Neame Ltd**
17 Court Street, Faversham, Kent
Tel: 01795 532206, web: www.shepherd-neame.co.uk

**Swale Brewery Company**
Castle Road, Sittingbourne
Tel: 01795 426871, web: www.swale-brewery.co.uk

## LANCASHIRE

**Blackpool Brewing Company**
George Street, Blackpool
Tel: 01253 304999

**Daniel Thwaites Plc**
Star Brewery, Blackburn, Lancashire
Tel: 01254 686868, web: www.thwaites.co.uk

**Hart Brewery**
Cartford Hotel, Cartford Lane, Little Eccleston
Tel: 01995 671686

**Moorhouses Brewery Co Ltd**
4 Moorhouse Street, Burnley
Tel: 01282 422864

**Picks Brewery**
Red Lion Hotel, Willows Lane, Accrington
Tel: 01254 233194

**Porter Brewing Co**
Rossendale Brewery, The Griffin Inn, Haslingden
Tel: 01706 214021

**Three B's Brewery**
Blackburn, Lancashire
Tel: 01254 208154

**Bank Top Brewery**
Unit 1 Back Lane, Vernon Street, Bolton
Tel: 01204 528865

**Leyden Brewing Company**
Lord Raglan, Walmersley Old Road, Nangreaves, Bury
Tel: 0161 764 6680

**Phoenix Brewery Ltd**
Phoenix Brewery, Green Lane, Heywood, Lancashire
Tel: 01706 627009

**Pictish Brewery**
Unit 9 Canalside Industrial Estate, Woodbine Street East, Rochdale
Tel: 01706 522227

**Saddleworth Brewery**
Church Inn, Uppermill, Saddleworth, Lancashire
Tel: 01457 820902

**Thomas McGuinness Brewing Co**
Cask and Feather, 1 Oldham Road, Rochdale
Tel: 01706 711476

**West Coast Brewing Co Ltd**
Kings Arms Hotel, 4a Helmshore Walk, Chorleton
Tel: 0161 273 1053

## LEICESTERSHIRE

**Banfield Ales**
The Brewery, Burrough-on-the-Hill, Melton Mowbray
Tel: 07956 246215,

**Belvoir Brewery Ltd**
Woodhill, Nottingham Lane, Old Dalby, Leicestershire
Tel: 01664 823455

**Blencowe Brewing Company**
Exeter Arms, Main Street, Barrowden, Rutland
Tel: 01572 747247

**Brewsters Brewing Company Ltd**
Penn Lane, Stathern, Melton Mowbray
Tel: 01949 861868

**Davis's Brewing Company Ltd**
The Grainstore Brewery, Oakham, Rutland
Tel: 01572 770065

**Everards Brewery Ltd**
Castle Acres, Narborough, Leicestershire
Tel: 0116 2014100

**Featherstone Brewery**
Unit 3, King Street Buildings, Enderby, Leicestershire
Tel: 0116 275 0952

**Grainstore**
Davis'es Brewing Company Ltd, Station Approach,
Oakham, Rutland
Tel: 01572 770065

**Hoskins and Oldfield Brewery Ltd**
North Mills, Leicester
Tel: 0116 262 3330
Email: hob@neptunegroup.demon.co.uk

**John O'Gaunt Brewing Company**
Unit 4B Rural Industry Estate, Melton Mowbray
Tel: 01664 454777

**Langton Brewery**
The Bell Inn, Main Street, East Langton, Market
Harborough
Tel: 01858 545278

**Parish Brewery**
The Old Brewery Inn, High Street, Somerby,
Leicestershire
Tel: 01664 454781

**Ruddles Brewery Ltd**
Langham, Oakham, Rutland
Tel: 01572 756911

**Shardlow Brewery Ltd**
British Waterways Yard, Cavendish Bridge
Tel: 01332 799188, Email: brewery@fsbusiness.co.uk

**Wicked Hathern Brewery Ltd**
46 Derby Road, Hathern, Loughborough
Tel: 01509 842364, Email: brewery@hathern.com

## LINCOLNSHIRE

**Blue Cow Inn and Brewery**
29 High Street, South Witham, Grantham
Tel: 01572 768432

**DarkTribe Brewery**
25 Doncaster Road, Gunness, Scunthorpe
Tel: 01724 782324

**Highwood Brewery Ltd**
Melton High Wood, Barnetby,
Tel: 01652 680020, web: www.tom-wood.com

**Oldershaw Brewery**
12 Harrowby Hall Estate, Grantham
Tel: 01476 572135

**Willy's Brewery Ltd**
17 High Cliff Road, Cleethorpes, Lincolnshire
Tel: 01472 602145

**Deeping Ales**
12 Peacock Square, Blenheim Way, Market Deeping
Tel: 01778 348600

**George Bateman and Sons Ltd**
Mill Lane, Wainfleet, Skegness
Tel: 01754 880317, web: www.bateman.co.uk

**Melbourne Brothers**
All Saints Brewery, 21 All Saints Street, Stamford
Tel: 01780 752186

## LONDON

**Asahi Breweries Ltd**
Denham Court Drive, Denham, Uxbridge, Middlesex
Tel: 01895 834947

**Belcher's Islington**
259 Upper Street, Islington
Tel: 020 722 64627

**Bright Partnership**
307 The Chandlerly, 50 Westminster Bridge Road
Tel: 020 7721 7590

**Dear Brothers**
13a Heybridge Way, Leabridge Road, Leyton
Tel: 020 8558 7190

**Fuller Smith and Turner Plc**
Griffin Brewery, Chiswick
Tel: 020 8996 2000, web: www.fullers.co.uk

**Guinness GB Ltd**
Park Royal Brewery, London
Tel: 020 8965 7700, web: www.guinness.com

**Meantime Brewing Company**
2 Penhall Road, Greenwich
Tel: 020 8293 1111, web: www.mean-time.co.uk

**O'Hanlon's Brewing Company Ltd**
114 Randall Road, Vauxhall
Tel: 020 7793 0803

**Pacific Oriental**
1 Bishopsgate, London,
Tel: 020 7929 6868, Email: peter.f@orgplc.co.uk

**Pitfield Brewery**
The Beer Shop, 14 Pitfield Street
Tel: 020 7739 3701

**Stag Brewing Company**
The Stag Brewery, Lower Richmond Road, Mortlake
Tel: 020 8876 3434

**Sweet William Micro Brewery**
William IV 816 High Street, Leyton
Tel: 020 8556 2460

**Young and Co Brewery Plc**
The Ram Brewery, Wandsworth
Tel: 020 8875 7000, web: www.youngs.co.uk

## MERSEYSIDE

**Beecham's Bar and Brewery**
Westfield Street, St Helens
Tel: 01744 623420

**Black Horse and Rainbow**
The Liverpool Brewing Company, 21–23 Berry Street,
Liverpool
Tel: 0151 709 5055

**Cambrinus Craft Brewery**
Home Farm, Knowsley Park, Prescot
Tel: 0151 546 2226

**Liverpool Brewery**
21–23 Berry Street, Liverpool
Tel: 0151 709 5055

**Passageway Brewing Company**
Unit G8 Norfolk Street, Liverpool
Tel: 0151 708 0730

**Robert Cain and Co Ltd**
Stanhope Street, Liverpool
Tel: 0151 709 8734, web: www.breworld.com/cains

## NORFOLK

**Blanchfields Brewery**
The Bull, Bridge Street, Fakenham
Tel: 01328 862560
Web: www.blanchfields-brewery.co.uk

**Blue Moon Brewery**
Pearces Farm, Seamere, Hingham
Tel: 01953 851625

**Buffy's Brewery**
Rectory Road, Tivetshall St Marys, Norwich
Tel: 01379 676523, web: www.buffys.co.uk

**Chalk Hill Brewery**
Rosary Road, Thorpe Hamlet, Norwich
Tel: 01603 477078

**Humpty Dumpty Brewing Company**
Reedham
Tel: 01493 701818
Web: www.humptydumptybrewery.com

**Iceni Brewery**
3 Foulden Road, Ickburgh, Mundford
Tel: 01842 878922

**Old Chimneys Brewery**
The Street, Market Weston, Diss
Tel: 01359 221411

**Reepham Brewery**
Unit 1 Collers Way, Reepham, Norwich
Tel: 01603 871091

**Wolf Brewery Ltd**
10 Maurice Gaymer Road, Attleborough
Tel: 01953 457775, web: www.wolf-brewery.ltd.uk

**Woodforde's Norfolk Ale**
Broadland Brewery, Woodbastwick, Norwich
Tel: 01603 720353, web: www.woodfordes.co.uk

**York Brewing Company**
York Tavern, 1 Leicester Street, Norwich
Tel: 01603 620918

## NORTH YORKSHIRE

**North Yorkshire Brewing Co**
84 North Ormesby Road, Middlesborough
Tel: 01642 226224

**Swaled Ale**
West View, Gunnerside, Richmond
Tel: 01748 886441

**Beer Lines York**
Pocklington Industrial Estate, York
Tel: 01759 306750

**Black Dog Brewery**
St Hildas, The Ropery, Whitby
Tel: 01947 821467
Web: www.synthesys.co.uk/black-dog

**Black Sheep Brewery**
Wellgarth, Masham, Ripon
Tel: 01765 689227, web: www.blacksheep.co.uk

**Brown Cow Brewery**
Brown Cow Road, Barlow, Selby
Tel: 01757 618937, web: browncowbrewery.f9.co.uk

**Cropton Brewery Co**
Woolcroft, Cropton, Pickering
Tel: 01751 417330

**Daleside Brewery**
Camwal Road, Starbeck, Harrogate
Tel: 01423 880022, web: www.dalesidebrewery.co.uk

**Dave Smith Brewing Services**
8 Church Street, Copmanthorpe, York
Tel: 01904 706778

**Franklin's Brewery**
Bilton Lane, Bilton, Harrogate
Tel: 01423 322345

**Hambleton Ales**
The Brewery, Holme on Swayle, Thirsk
Tel: 01845 567460

**Lastingham Brewery Co Ltd**
Unit 5 Westgate Carr Road, Pickering
Tel: 01751 477628

**Malton Brewing Co**
Crown Hotel, Wheelgate, Malton
Tel: 01653 697580, Email: neil@suddabys.demon.co.uk

**Marston Moor Brewery**
Crown House, Kirk Hammerton, York
Tel: 01423 330341

**Roosters Brewery**
Claro Road, Harrogate
Tel: 01423 561861, web: www.roosters.co.uk

**Rudgate Brewery Ltd**
2 Centre Park, Marston Business Park, Rudgate
Tel: 01423 358382

**Samuel Smith Ltd**
The Old Brewery, High Street, Tadcaster
Tel: 01937 832225

**Selby (Middlebrough) Brewery**
131 Millgate, Selby
Tel: 01757 702826

**T and R Theakston Ltd**
Wellgarth, Masham, Ripon
Tel: 01765 680000

**York Brewery Co Ltd**
12 Toft Green, Micklegate, York
Tel: 01904 621162, web: www.yorkbrew.demon.co.uk

## NORTHAMPTONSHIRE

**Carlsberg-Tetley Brewing Ltd**
140 Bridge Street, Northampton
Tel: 01604 668866, web: carlsberg.co.uk

**Cock Tavern**
Harborough Road, Kingsthorpe
Tel: 01604 715221

**Frog Island Brewery**
St James Road, Northampton
Tel: 01604 587772
Email: beer@frogislandbrewery.co.uk

**Nene Valley Brewery**
Unit 1 Midland Business Centre, Higham Ferrers
Tel: 01933 412411

**Parker and Son Brewers Ltd**
The Cannon, Cannon Street, Wellingborough
Tel: 01933 279629

## NORTHUMBERLAND

**Border Brewery Co Ltd**
Brewery Lane, Berwick upon Tweed
Tel: 01289 303303
Email: border@rampart.freeserve.co.uk

**Hexhamshire Brewery**
Leafields, Ordley, Hexham
Tel: 01434 606577

**Northumberland Brewery**
Ashington
Tel: 01670 819139

**Wylam Brewery Ltd**
South Houghton, Heddon-on-the-Wall
Tel: 01661 853377, web: www.wylambrew.co.uk

## NOTTINGHAMSHIRE

**Alcazar Brewing Company**
The Brewhouse, 33 Church Street, Old Bashford
Tel: 0115 942 2002

**Beeston Malting Co**
Dovecote Lane, Beeston, Nottingham
Tel: 01602 677859

**Bramcote Brewing Company**
236 Derby Road, Bramcote
Tel: 0115 939 3930

**Broadstone Brewing Company**
Wharf Street, Retford
Tel: 01777 719797
Email: broadstone.brewery@virgin.net

**Castle Rock Brewery Ltd**
Queens Bridge Road, Nottingham
Tel: 0115 985 1615, Email: castlerock@tynemill.co.uk

**Caythorpe Brewery**
3 Gonalston Lane, Hoveringham
Tel: 0115 966 4376

**Fellows, Morton and Clayton**
54 Canal Street, Nottingham
Tel: 0115 950 6795

**Fiddlers Ales Ltd**
The Fox and Crown, Church Street, Old Bashford
Tel: 0115 942 2002

**Hardy and Hansons Plc**
Kimberley Brewery, Kimberley, Nottingham
Tel: 0115 938 3611

**Holland Brewery**
Brewery Street, Kimberley, Nottingham
Tel: 0115 938 2685

**Leadmill Brewing Company**
118 Nottingham Road, Selston
Tel: 01773 819280

**Mallard Brewery**
15 Hartington Avenue, Carlton, Nottingham
Tel: 0115 952 1289, Email: Philip.mallard@tesco.net

**Mansfield Brewery**
Littleworth, Mansfield
Tel: 01623 625691

**Maypole Brewery**
North Laithes Farm, Wellow Road, Newark
Tel: 01623 871690

**Murphy and Son Ltd**
Alpine Street, Old Bashford, Nottingham
Tel: 01159 785494

**Red Shed Brewery**
10 Flixton Road, Kimberley, Nottingham
Tel: 0115 938 5360

**Springhead Fine Ales Ltd**
Old Great North Road, Sutton-on-Trent
Tel: 01636 821000, web: www.springhead.co.uk

## OXFORDSHIRE

**Bodicote Brewery**
9 High Street, Bodicote, Banbury
Tel: 01295 262327

**Edgote, Merivales Ales**
3 Snobs Row, Banbury
Tel: 01295 660335

**Henry's Butcher's Yard Brewery**
25 High Street, Chipping Norton
Tel: 01608 645334

**Hook Norton Brewery Co Ltd**
Brewery Lane, Hook Norton,
Tel: 01608 737210
Web: www.hook-norton-brewery.co.uk

**Merivales Ales Ltd**
Warden Brewery, Manor Farm, Banbury
Tel: 01295 660090

**Wychwood Brewery Ltd**
The Eagle Maltings, The Crofts, Witney
Tel: 01993 702574, web: www.wychwood.co.uk

**Old Luxters Vineyard**
Winery and Brewery, Hambleden, Henley-on-Thames
Tel: 01491 638330

**WH Brakspear and Sons Plc**
New Street, Henley-on-Thames
Tel: 01491 570200, web: www.brakspear.co.uk

## SHROPSHIRE

**Corvedale Brewery**
Sun Inn, Corfton, Craven Arms
Tel: 01584 861503

**Crown Inn**
Munslow Brewhouse, The Crown Inn, Munslow
Tel: 01584 841205

**Davenports Arms**
Main Street, Worfield, Bridgnorth
Tel: 01746 716320

**Hanby Ales Ltd**
The New Brewery, Aston Park, Wem
Tel: 01939 232432, Email: handy@dial.pipex.com

**Munslow Brewhouse**
Crown Inn, Munslow, Craven Arms
Tel: 01584 841205

**Salopian Brewing Company Ltd**
The Brewery, 67 Mytton Oak Road, Shrewsbury
Tel: 01743 248414

**Six Bells Brewery**
Church Street, Bishop's Castle
Tel: 01588 638930

**Three Tuns Brewery**
Salop Street, Bishop's Castle
Tel: 01588 638797, web: www.thethreetunsinn.co.uk

**Wood Brewery**
Wistanstow, Craven Arms
Tel: 01588 672523

**Worfield Brewing Company**
Station Lane, Hollybush Road, Bridgnorth
Tel: 01746 769606

## SOMERSET

**Abbey Ales Ltd**
The Abbey Brewery, 2 Lansdown Road, Bath
Tel: 01225 444437, web: www.abbeyales.co.uk

**Ash Vine Brewery**
Robins Lane, Frome
Tel: 01373 300041, web: www.ashvine.co.uk

**Bath Ales**
Dove Street, Kingsdown, Bristol, Avon
Tel: 0117 907 1797

**Beer Seller**
Wincanton Business Park, Wincanton
Tel: 01963 34264, web: www.beerseller.co.uk

**Berrow Brewery**
Coast Road, Berrow, Burnham-on-Sea
Tel: 01278 751345

**Bridgwater Brewing Company**
Unit 1 Lovedere Farm, Bridgwater
Tel: 01278 663996

**Butcombe Brewery Ltd**
Butcombe, Bristol, Avon
Tel: 01275 472240

**Cotleigh Brewery**
Ford Road, Wiveliscombe
Tel: 01984 624086, Email: cotleigh@cloveruk.net

**Cottage Brewing Company**
Lovington, Castle Cray
Tel: 01963 240551

**Crewkerne Brewery**
Crown Inn, 34 South Street, Crewkerne
Tel: 01460 72464

**Exmoor Ales**
Golden Hill Brewery, Wiveliscombe
Tel: 01984 623798, web: www.exmoorales.co.uk

**Hardington Brewery**
Dean Lane, Bedminster, Avon
Tel: 0117 963 6194

**Henstridge Brewery**
Henstridge Trading Estate, Henstridge
Tel: 01963 363150

**Juwards Brewery**
c/o Fox Brothers and Co Ltd, Wellington
Tel: 01823 667909

**Lundy Company**
Marisco Tavern Brewery, Bristol Channel, Avon
Tel: 01237 431831

**Milk Street Brewery**
The Griffin, Milk Street, Frome
Tel: 01373 467766

**Moor Beer Company**
Whitley Farm, Ashcott,
Tel: 01458 210050, web: www.moorbeer.com

**Oakhill Brewery**
The Old Maltings, Oakhill, Bath
Tel: 01749 840134

**Pencaster Ltd**
9 Kent Road, Bishopston, Bristol, Avon
Tel: 0117 9241694

**RCH Brewery**
West Hewish, Weston-Super-Mare
Tel: 01934 834447

## SOUTH YORKSHIRE

**Abbeydale**
Unit 8 Aizlewood Road, Sheffield
Tel: 0114 281 2712

**Barnsley Brewing Company Ltd**
Wath Road, Elsecar, Barnsley
Tel: 01226 741010

**Concertina Brewery**
9a Dolcliffe Road, Mexborough
Tel: 01709 580841

**Drummonds Brewery**
Unit 1, 443 London Road, Sheffield
Tel: 0114 255 4024

**Frog and Parrot Brewhouse**
64 Division Street, Sheffield
Tel: 0114 272 1280

**Glentworth Brewery**
Glentworth House, Crossfield Lane, Skellow
Tel: 01302 725555

**Hallamshire Brewery Services**
Liverpool Street, Sheffield
Tel: 0114 2431721, web: www.hallamshire.co.uk

**Kelham Island Brewery**
23 Alma Street, Sheffield
Tel: 0114 249 4804

**Stocks Brewery**
The Hallcross, 3334 Hallgate, Doncaster
Tel: 01302 328213

**Wentworth Brewery Ltd**
Wentworth, Rotherham
Tel: 01226 747070

## STAFFORDSHIRE

**Dark Peak Brewery**
1 Westfield, Cauldon Lowe, Stoke-on-Trent
Tel: 01538 308369

**Eccleshall Brewery**
The George Hotel, Castle Street, Eccleshall
Tel: 01785 850300

**Lichfield Brewery**
3 Europa Way, Boley Park, Lichfield
Tel: 01543 419919

**Titanic Brewery**
Lingard Street Burslem, Stoke-on-Trent
Tel: 01782 823447

**Bass Brewers Ltd**
137 High Street, Burton-on-Trent
Tel: 01283 511000, web: www.bass-brewwers.com

**Burton Bridge Brewery**
24 Bridge Street, Burton-on-Trent
Tel: 01283 510573

**Marston, Thompson and Evershed**
Shobnall Road, Burton-on-Tren
Tel: 01283 531131

## SUFFOLK

**Adnams Plc**
Sole Bay Brewery, East Green, Southwold
Tel: 01502 727200, web: www.adnams.co.uk

**Bartrams Brewery**
8 Thurston Granary, Station Hill, Bury St Edmunds
Tel: 01359 233303

**Cox and Holbrook**
Hillcroft House, High Road, Great Finborough
Tel: 01449 770682

**Earl Soham Brewery**
Earl Soham, Woodbridge,
Tel: 01728 685934, Email: malc@walker173.freeserve.co.uk

**Green Dragon Free and Brew House**
29 Broad Street, Bungay
Tel: 01986 892681

**Green Jack Brewing Co**
Oulton Broad Brewery, Oulton Broad
Tel: 01502 587905

**Greene King Plc**
Westgate Brewery, Bury St Edmunds
Tel: 01284 763222, web: www.greenking.co.uk

**King's Head Pub and Brewery Company**
The Kings Head, 132 High Street, Bildeston
Tel: 01449 741434

**Lidstone's Brewery**
Wickhambrook, Newmarket
Tel: 01440 820232, Email: lidstone_brewery@talk21.com

**Mauldons Brewery**
7 Addison Road, Sudbury
Tel: 01787 311055, web: www.mauldons.co.uk

**Munton and Fison Plc**
Cedars Factory, Needham Road, Stowmarket
Tel: 01449 612400

**Nethergate Brewery Ltd**
11–13 High Street, Clare
Tel: 01787 277244

**St Peter's Brewery Co Ltd**
South Elmham, Bungay
Tel: 01986 782322, web: www.stpeterbrewery.co.uk

**Tollemache and Cobbold Brewery**
Cliff Road, Ipswich
Tel: 01473 231723, web: www.tollycobbold.co.uk

## SURREY

**Anheuser-Busch Europe Ltd**
1 Church Road, Richmond
Tel: 020 8332 2302, web: www.budweiser.co.uk

**Belcher's Sutton**
2 High Street, Sutton
Tel: 020 866 17525

**Boston Experience**
1–3 Church Path, Woking
Tel: 01483 598586, web: www.boston-experience.com

**Cyder House Inn**
The Shackleford Brewery Co, Peperharow Lane,
Shackleford
Tel: 01483 810360

**Flamingo**
The Kingston Brewery, 88 London Road, Kingston
upon Thames
Tel: 020 8541 3717

**Hale and Hearty Brewery**
104 Upper Hale Road, Upper Hale, Farnham
Tel: 01252 735278

**Hog and Stump Brew Pub**
88 London Road, Kingston-upon-Thames
Tel: 020 8541 3717

**Hogs Back Brewery**
Manor Farm, The Street, Tongham,
Tel: 01252 783000, web: www.hogsback.co.uk

**Dorking Beers Ltd**
Unit E Vincent Lane, Dorking
Tel: 01306 875457

**Leith Hill Brewery**
The Plough Inn, Coldharbour, Dorking
Tel: 01306 711793

**Pilgrim Ales**
The Old Brewery, West Street, Reigate
Tel: 01737 222651

## TYNE AND WEAR

**Big Lamp Brewers**
Big Lamp Brewery, Grange Road, Newcastle-upon-
Tyne
Tel: 0191 267 1687

**Darwin Brewery**
University of Sunderland, Chester Road, Sunderland
Tel: 0191 515 2535

**Federation Brewery Ltd**
Lancaster Road, Dunston
Tel: 0191 460 9023

**Four Rivers**
Unit 10 Hawick Industrial Estate, Newcastle-upon-
Tyne
Tel: 0191 276 5302

**Hadrian Brewery Ltd**
Unit 10, Hawick Crescent Industrial Estate,
Newcastle-upon-Tyne
Tel: 0191 276 5302

**Mordue Brewery**
West Chirton North , Shiremoor
Tel: 0191 296 1879, web: www.morduebrewery.com

**Riverside Brewery**
The Gatehouse, Pallion, Sunderland
Tel: 0191 514 3212

## WARWICKSHIRE

**Bull's Head Brewery**
The Three Tuns, 34 High Street, Alcester
Tel: 01789 766550

**Church End Brewery Ltd**
The Griffin Inn, Church Road, Shustoke
Tel: 01675 481567

**Cox's Yard, Bridgefoot**
Stratford-upon-Avon
Tel: 01789 404600, web: www.coxsyard.co.uk

**Frankton Bagby Brewery**
The Old Stables Brewery, Church Lawford, Rugby Tel:
024 7654 0770

**Warwickshire Beer Company Ltd**
Cubbington Brewery, Queen Street, Leamington Spa
Tel: 01926 450747

## WEST MIDLANDS

**Aston Manor Brewery**
173 Thimblemill Lane, Aston, Birmingham
Tel: 0121 328 4336, web: www.astonmanor.co.uk

**Beowulf Brewing Company**
14 Waterloo Road, Yardley, Birmingham
Tel: 0121 706 4116, web: www.beowulf.co.uk

**Daniel Batham and Son Ltd**
Delph Brewery, 10A Delph Road, Brierley Hill
Tel: 01384 77229

**Enville Ales**
Cox Green, Enville, Stourbridge
Tel: 01384 873728, web: www.envilleales.com

**Highgate and Walsall Brewing Co**
Sandymount Road, Walsall
Tel: 01922 644453, web: www.astonmanor.co.uk

**Holden's Brewery Ltd**
George Street, Woodsetton, Dudley
Tel: 01902 880051, web: www.holdensbrewery.co.uk

**Rainbow Inn and Brewery**
73 Birmingham Road, Allesley Village, Coventry
Tel: 02476 402888

**Sarah Hughes Brewery**
Beacon Hotel, 129 Bilston Street, Dudley
Tel: 01902 883380

**Wolverhampton and Dudley Breweries**
Park Brewery, Bath Road, Wolverhampton
Tel: 01902 711811, web: www.fullpint.co.uk

## WEST SUSSEX

**Gribble**
The Gribble Inn, Oving, Chichester
Tel: 01243 786893, Email: elderflower@msn.co.uk

**Bertie Belcher's**
Hedgehog and Hogshead, Station Approach, Hove
Tel: 01273 733660

**Rectory Ales Ltd**
Streat Hill Farm, Streat, Hassocks
Tel: 01273 890570

**The Brewery on Sea Ltd**
Chartwell Road, Lancing
Tel: 01903 851482

**Weltons North Downs Brewery**
Nightingale Road, Horsham
Tel: 01403 242901, web: www.weltons.co.uk

## WEST YORKSHIRE

**Barge and Barrel Brewing Company**
10–20 Park Road, Elland
Tel: 01422 375039

**Blackmoor Brewery**
28 Woodedge Avenue, Dalton, Huddersfield
Tel: 01422 429731

**Boat Brewery**
Boat Inn, Main Street, Allerton Bywater
Tel: 01977 667788

**Briscoe's Brewery**
16 Ash Grove, Otley
Tel: 01943 466515

**Commercial Brewing Co Ltd**
Worth Brewery, Worth Way, Keighley
Tel: 01535 611914

**Fawcett's Malts Ltd**
East Field Lane, Castleford
Tel: 01977 552460

**Fernandes Brewery**
The Old Malthouse, 5 Avison Yard, Kirkgate
Tel: 01924 291709

**Fox and Newt Brewhouse**
9 Burley Street, Leeds
Tel: 01132 432612

**Goose Eye Brewery**
Ingrow Bridge, South Street, Keighley
Tel: 01535 605807

**HB Clark and Co**
Westgate Brewery, Wakefield
Tel: 01924 373328

**Kitchen Brewery**
Unit J Shaw Park Industrial Complex, Huddersfield
Tel: 01484 300028

**Linfit Brewery**
Sair Inn, 139 Lane Top, Huddersfield
Tel: 01484 842370

**Old Bear Brewery**
6 Keighley Road, Cross Hills, Keighley
Tel: 01535 632115

**Old Court Brewhouse**
Queen Street, Huddersfield
Tel: 01484 454035

**Osset Brewing Company**
Brewer's Pride, Healey Road
Tel: 01924 261333, web: www.brewery-ossett.co.uk

**Rat and Ratchet Brewery**
40 Chapel Hill, Huddersfield
Tel: 01484 516734

**Riverhead Brewery Ltd**
2 Peel Street, Marsden, Huddersfield
Tel: 01484 841270

**Ryburn Brewery**
c/o Ram's Head, Wakefield Road, Sowerby Bridge Tel:
01422 835413

**Salamander Brewing Company**
Harry Street, Dudley Hill, Bradford
Tel: 01274 652323

**Tigertops Brewery**
22 Oakes Street, Flanshaw Lane, Flanshaw
Tel: 01924 378538

**Timothy Taylor and Co Ltd**
Knowle Spring Brewery, Keighley
Tel: 01535 603139, web: www.timothy-taylor.co.uk

**Turkey Inn**
Goose Eye, Oakworth, Keighley
Tel: 01535 681339

**West Yorkshire Brewery**
Victoria Buildings, Burnley Road, Luddenfoot, Halifax
Tel: 01422 885930

## WILTSHIRE

**Microcheck**
Unit 12 Edington Station Yard, Edington, Westbury
Tel: 01380 830517

**Wylye Valley Brewery**
Dove Inn, Corton, Warminster
Tel: 01985 50109

**Archers Ales**
Penzance Drive, Churchward, Swindon
Tel: 01793 879929, web: www.archers-brewery.co.uk

**Arkells Brewery Ltd**
Kingsdown, Swindon
Tel: 01793 823026, web: www.arkells.com

**Bunce's Brewery**
The Old Mill, Netheravon, Salisbury
Tel: 01980 670631

**Foxley Brewing Co Ltd**
Unit 3 Homefarm Workshops, Mildenhall,
Marlborough
Tel: 01672 515000

**Hop Back Brewery**
Unit 20–24 Batten Road Industrial Estate, Salisbury
Tel: 01725 510986, web: www.hopback.co.uk

**Moles Brewery (Cascade Drinks)**
5 Merlin Way, Melksham
Tel: 01225 704734, web: www.molesbrewery.com

**Stonehenge Ales**
Mill Road, Netheravon, Salisbury
Tel: 01980 670631
Web: www.stonehenge.sagenet.co.uk

**Tisbury Brewery Ltd**
Church Street, Tisbury
Tel: 01747 870986

**Wadworth and Co Ltd**
Northgate Brewery, Devizes
Tel: 01380 723361, web: www.wadworth.co.uk

## WORCESTER AND HEREFORD

**Brandy Cask Brewing Company**
c/o 25 Bridge Street, Pershore
Tel: 01386 555338

**Cannon Royal Brewery**
The Fruiterers Arms, Uphampton, Ombersley
Tel: 01905 621161

**Dunn Plowman Brewery**
Bridge Street, Kington
Tel: 01544 231993
Email: dunnplowman.brewery@tlak21.com

**Evesham Brewery**
17 Oat Street, Evesham
Tel: 01386 443462

**Fat God's Brewery**
The Queens Head, Iron Cross, Evesham
Tel: 01386 871012, web: www.fatgodsbrewery.co.uk

**Frome Valley Brewery**
Mayfields, Bishop's Frome
Tel: 01531 640321

**Fromes Hill Brewery**
Wheatsheaf Inn, Fromes Hill, Ledbury
Tel: 01531 640888

**Hobson's Brewery and Co**
New House Farm, Tenbury Road, Cleobury
Tel: 01299 270837

**Jolly Roger Brewing Company**
50 Lowesmoor, Worcester
Tel: 01905 21540

**Malvern Hills Brewery Ltd**
15 West Malvern Road, Malvern
Tel: 01684 560165
Web: www.malvernhillsbrewery.co.uk

**Marches Ales**
Unit 6 Western Close, Leominster
Tel: 01568 610063

**Royall Cannon Brewery**
Fruiterers Arms, Uphampton, Ombersley
Tel: 01905 621161

**Shoes Brewery**
Three Horse Shoes Inn, Norton Canon, Hereford
Tel: 01544 318375

**SP Sporting Ales Ltd**
Cantilever Lodge, Stoke Prior, Leominster
Tel: 01568 760226

**Spinning Dog Brewery**
The Victory, 88 St Owens Street, Hereford
Tel: 01432 342125, Email: jfkenyon@aol.com

**St George's Brewing Co Ltd**
The Old Bakehouse, Bush Lane, Callow End,

Worcester
Tel: 01905 831316

**Teme Valley Brewery**
The Talbot Inn, Knightwick
Tel: 01886 821235

**Weatheroak Brewery**
Coach and Horses Inn, Weatheroak Hill, Alvechurch
Tel: 077 9877 3894

**Woodhampton Brewing Co**
Woodhampton Farm, Aymestrey
Tel: 01568 770503

**Wye Valley Brewery**
69 St Owen Street, Hereford
Tel: 01432 342546, web: www.wyevalleybrewery.co.uk

**Wyre Piddle Brewery**
Unit 21 Craycombe Farm, Fladbury, Evesham
Tel: 01386 860473

# NORTHERN IRELAND

**Hilden Brewery**
Hilden House, Grand Street, Lisburn, County Antrim
Tel: +44 (028) 92663863

**Whitewater Brewing Co**
40 Tullyframe Road, Kilkeel, Newry, County Down,
Tel: +44 (028) 41769449

# SCOTLAND

**Aberdeenshire Ales**
Mains of Inverbrie, Ellon, Aberdeenshire AB41 8PX

**Aviemore Brewery Co Ltd**
Unit 12 Dalfaber Industrial Estate, Aviemore,
Highlands
Tel: 01479 812222

**Belhaven Brewery Co Ltd**
Spott Road, Dunbar, East Lothian
Tel: 01368 862734, web: www.belhavenbrewery.co.uk

**Black Isle Brewing Co Ltd**
Taeblair, Munlochy, Ross-Shire, Highlands
Tel: 01463 811871

**Bolmer H.P. Drinks Ltd**
2 Hope Street, Edinburgh, Lothian
Tel: 0131 226 6005

**Borve Brew House**
Ruthven, Huntly, Moray, Grampian
Tel: 01466 760343

**Bridge of Allen Brewery Company**
Queens Lane, Stirlingshir
Tel: 01786 834555

**Broughton Ales Ltd**
The Brewery, Broughton, Biggar, Borders
Tel: 01899 830345

**Burntisland Brewing Co**
High Street, Burntisland, Fife
Tel: 01592 873333

**Caledonian Brewing Company**
42 Slateford Road, Edinburgh, Lothian
Tel: 0131 337 1286

**Devon Ales**
Mansfield Arms, 7 Main Street, Alloa,
Tel: 01259 722020, Email: john.Gibson@btinternet.com

**Dial-a-Keg**
55–57 Bangor Road, Edinburgh, Lothian
Tel: 0131 553 3880

**Far North Brewery**
Melvich Hotel, Sutherland, Highlands
Tel: 01641 531206, Email: melvichtl@aol.com

**Fisherrow Brewery**
Duddingston Park South, Edinburgh, Lothian
Tel: 0131 621 5501, web: www.fisherrow.co.uk

**Forth Brewery Company**
Eglinton, Kelliebank, Alloa
Tel: 01259 725511

**Fyfe Brewing Company**
469 High Street, Kirkcaldy, Fife
Tel: 01592 646211

**Glaschu Brewery**
250 Woodlands Road, Glasgow, Strathclyde
Tel: 0141 332 2862

**Harviestoun Brewery Ltd**
Devon Road, Dollar
Tel: 01259 742141, Email: harviestoun@talk21.com

**Heather Ale Ltd**
736 Dumbarton Road, Glasgow, Strathclyde
Tel: 0141 337 6298

**Inveralmond Brewery**
1 Inveralmond Way, Inveralmond
Tel: 01738 449448
Web: www.inveralmond-brewery.co.uk

**Iris Rose Brewery**
The Royal Hotel, High Street, Kingussie, Highlands
Tel: 01540 661898

**Isle of Skye Brewing Co**
The Pier, Uig, Isle of Skye
Tel: 01470 542477, web: www.skybrewery.co.uk

**MacLachlan's Brew Bar**
57 West Regent Street, Glasgow, Strathclyde
Tel: 0141 443 0595

**Maclay Group Ltd**
Thistle Brewery, Alloa, Central Scotland
Tel: 01259 723387

**McCowan's Brewhouse**
Dundee Street, Edinburgh, Lothian
Tel: 0131 228 8198

**Miller's Thumb Brewing Company**
300 Bearsden Road, Anniesland, Glasgow,
Strathclyde
Tel: 0141 954 5333

**Moulin Hotel and Brewery**
Kirkmichael Road, Pitlochry, Tayside
Tel: 01796 472196

**Orkney Brewery**
The Orkney Brewery, Quoyloo, Orkney
Tel: 01856 841802, web: www.orkneybrewery.co.uk

**Restalrig Village Brewery Ltd**
58 Loaning Road, Edinburgh, Lothian
Tel: 0131 468 6969

**Scottish and Newcastle Retail**
111 Holyrood Road, Edinburgh, Lothian
Tel: 0131 5562591

**Sulwath Brewers Ltd**
King Street, Southerness, Kirkbean
Tel: 01387 255849

**The Clockwork Beer Co**
1153–1155 Cathcart Road, Glasgow, Strathclyde
Tel: 0141 649 0184

**Tomintoul Brewery Co**
Mill of Auchriachan, Tomintoul, Ballindalloch
Banffshire, Grampian
Tel: 01807 580333

**Traquair House Brewery**
Traquair Estate, Innerleithen, Borders
Tel: 01896 831370
Web: www.traquair.co.uk

**Valhalla Brewery**
New House, Baltasound, Unst, Shetland
Tel: 01957 711658
Web: www.valhallabrewery.co.uk

# WALES

**Aberystwyth Ales**
Tregynnan Brewery, Llanrhystyd, Ceredigion, Dyfed
Tel: 01974 202388

**Bragdy Ynys Mon**
Cae Cwta Mawr, Talwrn, Ynys Mons, Isle of Anglesey
Tel: 01248 723801

**Bryncelyn Brewery**
Wern Fawr Inn, 47 Wern Road, Ystalyfera, West
Glamorgan
Tel: 01639 843625

**Bullmastiff Brewery**
14 Bessemer Close, Hadfield Road, Leckwith,
South Glamorgan
Tel: 01222 665292

**Ceredigion Brewery**
2 Brynderwen, Llangrannog, Llandyssul,
Ceredigion, Dyfed
Tel: 01239 654099

**Coles Family Brewery**
White Hart Inn, Llanddarog, Carmarthenshire, Dyfed
Tel: 01267 275395

**Cottage Spring Brewery**
Gorse Cottage, Graig Road, Upper Cwmbran, Trofaen,
Gwent
Tel: 01237 477615

**Felinfoel Brewery Company**
Farmers Row, Felinfoel, Llanelli, Carmarthenshire,
Dyfed
Tel: 01554 773357

**Flannery's**
1 High Street, Aberystwyth, Ceredigion, Dyfed
Tel: 01970 612334

**Merlin's Brewery Ltd**
Trawsfford Road, Ystradgynlais, Swansea, West
Glamorgan
Tel: 01639 849888

**Nag's Head**
Abercych, Boncath, Pembrokeshire, Dyfed
Tel: 01239 841200

**Newport Brewhouse**
4–5 Market Street, Newport, Gwent
Tel: 01633 212188

**Pembroke Brewery Co**
Eaton House, 108 Main Street, Pembroke, Dyfed
Tel: 01646 682517

**Plassey Brewery Ltd**
Eyton, Wrexham, Clwyd
Tel: 01978 780922

**Red Lion**
Long Bridge Street, Llanidloes, Powys
Tel: 01686 412270

**SA Brain and Co Ltd**
49 St Mary Street, Cardiff, South Glamorgan
Tel: 029 2039 9022

**Snowdonia Parc Brewery**
Waunfawr, Caernarfon, Gwynedd
Tel: 01286 650409

**Solva Brewing Co Ltd**
Panteg, Solva, Haverfordwest, Dyfed
Tel: 01437 720350

**Swansea Brewing Company**
Joiners Arms, Bishopston, Swansea,
West Glamorgan
Tel: 01792 290197

**Tomos Watkin and Sons**
Phoenix Brewery, Valley Way, Swansea, West
Glamorgan
Tel: 01792 775333

**Travellers Inn**
Tremeirchion Road, Caerwys, Mold, Clwyd
Tel: 01352 720251

**Warcop Country Ales**
9 Nellive Park, St Brides, Wentloog, Gwent
Tel: 01633 680058

**White Hart Inn**
Machen, Mid Glamorgan
Tel: 01633 441005